Library of
Davidson College

VOID

Isle de France Creole

Isle de France Creole

Affinities and Origins

Philip Baker
Chris Corne

447.9
B168L

Copyright © 1982 by Karoma Publishers, Inc.
All Rights Reserved
83-673
ISBN 0-89720-048-9 (paper)/0-89720-049-7 (cloth)

Printed in the United States of America

CONTENTS

Preface, *Robert B. Le Page*   vii

INTRODUCTION, *Philip Baker and Chris Corne*   1

PART A: A Contrastive Analysis of Reunion and Isle de France Creole French: Two Typologically Diverse Languages, *Chris Corne*   7

Introduction to Part A   8
A1, The Verbal System in Reunion Creole   11
A2, The Predicate in Isle de France Creole   31
A3, Final Vowel Truncation in Indian Ocean Creole French   49
A4, Notes on Final Vowel Truncation in Creole French Languages   64
A5, Some Specific Structures   79
A6, Two Different Linguistic Traditions   102
A7, Conclusion   120

PART B: On the Origins of the First Mauritians and of the Creole Language of Their Descendants: A Refutation of Chaudenson's "Bourbonnais" Theory, *Philip Baker*   131

Nomenclature and Conventions Adopted   132
B1, Background   134
B2, The Contested Aspects of the Peopling of Mauritius to 1735   142
B3, Links between MC and Other French Creoles: Some Evidence from Early Texts   206
B4, Identifying the Origins of MC   241
B5, Summary and Conclusions   258

BIBLIOGRAPHY   261
CHRONOLOGICAL LIST OF CREOLE TEXTS CITED IN CHAPTER B3   273
NAME INDEX   275
SUBJECT INDEX   283

PREFACE
by Robert B. Le Page

The "origins" of pidgin and creole languages in general, and of particular languages, have been the subject of keen debate among philologists and linguists for the past century or more. Among the more recent manifestations we have had the monogenetic theories propounded by Keith Whinnom and others. Participants in the debate have drawn attention to the widespread distribution of certain particular features, as R. W. Thompson did in *Creole Language Studies,* vol. 2, in 1961. Rarely, however, has the debate been informed by both the kind of demographic and social history on the one hand and the kind of typological descriptive analysis on the other that the authors of this book have brought together with respect to Mauritius and the relationship of its Creole French to Creole French dialects of the Caribbean (in particular, of Haiti) and of other Indian Ocean communities— in particular, Reunion.

The question has been approached in two ways. Philip Baker, who presents the second part of the book, deals in great depth with the settlement history of the island before going on to study the distribution of specific features in various Caribbean and Indian Ocean varieties of Creole French. He first embarked on research into the historical aspects of Mauritian Creole while preparing his B Phil dissertation at the University of York in 1976. The evidence that he now sets out here on the origins of the first Mauritians is, I believe, of the greatest importance in assessing the validity of theories as to the origins of Mauritian Creole itself. He presents as detailed a statement as can be derived from surviving sources of the movements of people into and out of the island during its formative years as a French plantation colony. It is tempting to draw a parallel with respect to Barbados on the one hand and Jamaica on the other with what he says in his summing up:

> I then compared the peopling of Reunion, Mauritius, and Haiti during the first half century of French rule in each territory. I found that Reunion differed from the others in two significant respects: the proportion of first-language speakers of French was considerably higher in Reunion than in Mauritius or Haiti, while the latter two were populated at a much faster rate than Reunion. This explains, I believe, why MC and HC have verbal systems which are much further removed from French than is that of RC. (p. 259)

In *Jamaican Creole* (1960) I pointed out that one of the reasons that Bajan was much closer in its grammar and lexicon to Standard English than was Jamaican Creole was that the proportion of Whites to Blacks in Barbados was far higher in the crucial formative years than in Jamaica, where Blacks rapidly outnumbered Whites by 10 to 1. But the parallel might be dangerously misleading. Barbadians certainly played a part in the first English conquest of Jamaica. Was Mauritius similarly indebted to Reunion? The demographic evidence seems to be that it was not, to any significant extent. Baker continues:

> However, this does not in itself account for all the features shared by MC and HC but not found in RC. Three other potentially important factors were identified: (1) features common to all known African pidgins (Heine 1979) are retained in both MC and HC; (2) innate rules common to all children on which those brought up in a largely pidgin-speaking community draw in order to "expand" that pidgin if they are not obliged, or do not have the opportunity, to acquire a nonpidgin language (Bickerton 1977, 1979); (3) the influence of African languages taken to both Mauritius and Haiti (Fon, Wolof, and those of the Mande group, etc.). I do not claim that this list is complete. Nor do I rule out the possibility that a *small* number of identical innovations might have occurred altogether independently of one another in both Mauritius and Haiti (the preposed pronouns *mo* and *to* might be just such innovations).
>
> In this study I do not provide a simple solution to the problem of accounting for striking similarities between MC and HC because I do not believe there is just *one*. My hope is that I have nevertheless succeeded in identifying at least some of the factors involved. If so, the task ahead is to determine their relative importance. (p. 259)

This modest statement contains, it seems to me, attitudes toward and insights into historical linguistic processes and concomitant social processes of the utmost importance to general linguistics and to creole studies.

Chris Corne has approached the problem through a typological examination of the Creoles of Reunion and Mauritius. In recent years there has been a considerable resurgence in Francophone countries of work on varieties of Creole French, and Robert Chaudenson has been among the leaders in this resurgence. His views on the linguistic affiliations of the Indian Ocean Creoles as a group have had wide currency. Chris Corne's careful contrastive analysis of certain features of the two languages leads him to different conclusions, which tie in closely with those of Philip Baker.

I am not competent to say whether the conclusions reached by these authors are well-founded, beyond remarking that the evidence they bring forward and the way in which they interpret it at least seem to establish a very firm foundation for any future debate. It is rare for evidence from historical demography and descriptive and historical linguistics to be married in as much careful detail as they are in this book.

Robert B. Le Page   September 10, 1981
Department of Language
University of York

Introduction

INTRODUCTION
by Philip Baker and Chris Corne

The Creole French languages of Mauritius, and, respectively, its former and continuing dependencies of the Seychelles and Rodrigues, have so much in common that it is descriptively economical to adopt a cover name. We follow Papen (1978b: xl) in opting for *Isle de France* Creole (IdeFC) as an appropriate label,[1] Mauritius having been known by this name under French rule. IdeFC differs rather sharply from the language known as Reunion Creole (RC), as can be readily determined by consulting the various descriptions of these published within the past decade, and as is made explicit in Part A of this work.

IdeFC and RC had long been neglected by linguists at the time Goodman wrote his influential work, *A Comparative Study of Creole French Dialects* (1964), Baissac's 1880 grammar of Mauritian Creole (MC) being the only adequate source available. Thus Goodman noted: "Virtually all my information about this group is restricted to Mauritius, there being very little material on any of the others. It may even be a mistake to treat them as a single group" (1964:16, note 2).

Most of Goodman's study was devoted to a detailed comparison of 40 lexical and grammatical items, for the most part occurring in all the varieties of Creole French on which he possessed adequate data. Goodman came to the conclusion that "only a common origin can explain the extensive and specific similarities between all the Creole [French] dialects" (1964:129). In reaching this conclusion he attached particular importance to innovations common to Mauritius and Haiti (and other American varieties of Creole French). He then demonstrated that there had been at least some West African influence in Mauritius. This led him to a second conclusion, that "its place of origin can scarcely have been other than West Africa, from which it was transported to the various parts of the world where Creole [French] is now found" (1964:130).

Whereas it is possible to disagree with Goodman's conclusions (cf. chapter B4 below), there can be no doubting the general validity of the data on which they were based. We are thus of the opinion that a necessary prerequisite to challenging Goodman's theory with regard to the origin of any one of the varieties of Creole French for which he had access to adequate data (i.e., any but RC) is to provide an alternative explanation for innovations common to America and the Indian Ocean.

Whereas Goodman lacked adequate data on RC, he was nevertheless aware of important differences between this and Mauritian Creole (MC) and felt the need to provide a possible explanation:

Introduction 3

When Reunion was colonized in 1664 (fifty years earlier than Mauritius), probably neither the West African slave trade nor the French slavers' pidgin had reached its fullest development. The West African influence in the Creole of Reunion and its connection with American Creole therefore was doubtless considerably less than was that of Mauritius. . . . By the time Mauritius was settled (1715 [sic]),[2] however, the West African slave trade was probably so well organized that, even though the island was settled in part from Reunion and was close to Madagascar, large numbers of West African slaves were imported there, and their pidgin (by this time quite well established) became the dominant linguistic element and soon developed into Mauritian Creole. Reunion Creole was not without influence in Mauritius, however, and the two dialects share certain important features which set them apart from American Creole, notably the historical shift without exception of the phonemes $š$ and $ž$ to s and z respectively. This is perhaps a feature of Malagasy origin although it should be noted that it occurs at least sporadically in Louisiana as well. . . . Until a better and more thorough description of Reunion Creole becomes available and the relevant historical background is investigated, it will be difficult to clarify the problem further. (Goodman 1964:132)

A much better and more thorough description of RC was published ten years later: Chaudenson's *Le lexique du parler créole de la Réunion*. This also investigated the relevant historical background, at least so far as the peopling of Reunion is concerned. Chaudenson established that scarcely any West Africans reached Reunion during the first five decades of its settlement—the presence of ten West Africans is noted in a census of 1704, but their number had declined five years later to two (1974:456). So far as is known, no other West Africans reached Reunion until 1730 (cf. B2.3.2 below; Chaudenson 1974:454). Chaudenson also reproduced a short text in RC which he dated as "entre 1714 et 1723" (1974:444). This text suggests not merely that RC already existed by that period but, more significantly, that RC has changed very little since then. Chaudenson draws the rational conclusion that West Africans cannot have played a significant role in the formation or subsequent development of RC (1974:1108). However, there does not appear to be any major conflict between this and what Goodman wrote concerning RC (cf. 1964:132, quoted above). Insofar as there is a major conflict between Goodman's theory and Chaudenson's position, it stems not from what the latter has proved about RC but rather from what he has claimed about the relationship between RC and IdeFC, e.g., that Reunion, Mauritius, Rodrigues, and the Seychelles are "quatre îles (ou groupe d'îles) où se parlent quatre créoles *issus plus ou moins directement d'une souche unique le 'bourbonnais'* (parler créole de Bourbon [former name of Reunion] dans la première moitié du XVIIIe siècle)" (1974:447; italics added); and that "Dès 1725 [misprint for 1715(?)], le créole est constitué; le 'bourbonnais' parlé par les immigrants de Bourbon qui débarquent à l'île de France en 1721 est déjà celui que parleront en 1770 ceux qui s'embarqueront à leur tour pour les Seychelles" (1974:449).

Chaudenson's "Bourbonnais" theory is based on three main premises. It is our belief that two of these can be shown to be faulty:

The first premise is that RC existed in essentially its modern form by the time the French colonization of Mauritius began. This we accept. It is supported by the text from the period 1714-23 mentioned above. (The text consists of the response of Marie, a slave belonging to one M. Ferrère charged with the crime of *marronnage*. According to Ricquebourg, the first man with this surname reached Reunion in 1721 [1976:277]. We thus propose in what follows to refer to the date of this text as ca. 1722.)[3]

The second premise is implied more than it is explicitly stated but is nonetheless of crucial importance. It is that all the Creole French languages of the Indian Ocean are typologically similar and belong to the same linguistic tradition. This we find difficult to justify.

The third premise is that speakers of "Bourbonnais" provided the major input to the formation of Mauritian Creole in the early stages of its development. We believe that such was not the case.

This book focuses on these two faulty premises. It consists of two parts: A, written by Chris Corne, and B, written by Philip Baker. Part A is especially concerned with the second of the premises on which the "Bourbonnais" theory is based (and chapter B3 is relevant to this). Chapter B2 is wholly devoted to examining the relevant aspects of the peopling of Mauritius in the period 1721-35 and thus tests the third of Chaudenson's premises. Our joint conclusion is that the "Bourbonnais" theory is not supported by the essential facts.

We do not deny that speakers of RC may have contributed something to the constitution of MC, but we are certain that their role was in no way predominant, and we insist that there are no rational grounds for supposing that any slave who arrived in the period 1728-35 learned to speak "Bourbonnais." In our view, the facts set out in Parts A and B render the theory of a "Bourbonnais" origin for MC untenable.

In the matter of the degree of similarity between IdeFC and RC, we do not deny a large body of shared vocabulary or a considerable measure of phonological agreement. However, we do not yet know what proportion of these are exclusive to IdeFC and RC. This can only be determined by a major survey such as that currently being undertaken by A. Bollée for the preparation of a pan-Creole French etymological dictionary. For the moment we can say that both IdeFC and RC have lexical items of Indian and Malagasy origin which are predictably absent from American Creole French (though it has yet to be determined to what extent IdeFC and RC share the *same* such items) but that IdeFC differs from RC in other respects (e.g., in the morphology of their French-derived nouns). Similarly, if the systematic absence of /ʃ/ and /ʒ/ in IdeFC and basilectal RC contrasts with American Creole French (ACF), there are certainly features which set RC off from IdeFC (e.g., retention of schwa; /we/ as a reflex of French orthographic *oi*); and there are other features apparently common to all varieties of Creole French for reasons which have not yet been determined (e.g., /ɣ/ as the reflex of French orthographic *r* in the environment /C_V/). In the matter of the essential differences between IdeFC and RC, we concentrate on syntax and verb morphology. A purely synchronic statement, supported by (but not in the least dependent upon) historical and comparative elements, places modern RC squarely in one camp, and the other Indian Ocean Creole French languages in another. The organizational principles underlying each of these two groupings are quite dissimilar, or, put simply, RC "works" differently from the others. The contrary view, that all the Indian Ocean Creole French languages belong to the same semantactic tradition, results on the one hand from a Eurocentric analysis of the facts and on the other from a concept of language which appears to confuse etymology with function.

We recognize that the first seventeen years of the peopling of Mauritius (in B2 below) may not have been the only decisive years of settlement from the point of view of the emergence of Mauritian Creole, though we are certain that these were of crucial importance. We confine ourselves to these years for two reasons. First, they are the years which saw slaves from West Africa form a significant proportion of the total slave population, and indeed an absolute majority of that from mid-1730 to mid-1735; they are years which amply illustrate the heterogeneity of the linguistic situation; and they reveal a positive dearth of "Bourbonnais"-speaking settlers who might have taught their language to newly arrived slaves. These facts all appear to be significant, in different ways. Secondly, these years are the subject of a recent article by Chaudenson (1979a) which contains important inaccuracies and which is, in our opinion, regrettably polemic in tone. The essence of this article is included in Chaudenson's recent (and otherwise admirable) book, *Les créoles français* (1979b).

If the "Bourbonnais" theory is our principal concern, it is certainly not our only one. Aspects of the RC continuum are examined in A3.3 and A6.2. We show that Seychelles Creole has some features which reflect the Réunionnais part in the early peopling of that territory (A5.4, A6.4). However, we are particularly concerned with a variety of grammatical items and constructions which suggest a link between IdeFC and ACF (A4.2, A5.2, A5.4.2, and B3.2). Some of these are features to which Goodman attached great importance in setting out his West African origin theory. For the most part these features are examined in greater detail or with reference to a wider range of early texts than is the case in Goodman (1964). We have also been able to add to Goodman's list of innovations common to IdeFC and ACF. In assessing the significance of these innovations, we take a cautious line. We are satisfied that they cannot all have occurred independently of one another in two widely separated geographical areas. However, this does not lead us to embrace, except in the most tentative fashion, any one of the theories that have been advanced thus far to explain features common to IdeFC and ACF. These theories are examined in B4 (cf. also A6.1, A7), and all are found wanting in one or more respects. Instead, we identify a number of factors potentially responsible for some of these shared features and suggest that further research is required before the relative importance of these factors can be assessed. This lack of a simple, alternative theory may disappoint some of our readers, but we would argue that the rejection of the notion that there can be just *one* explanation for innovations common to IdeFC and ACF is in itself a positive achievement. More has probably been accomplished during the 1970s in providing a basic understanding of the Creole French languages of the Indian Ocean than in any previous decade, and a large part of the credit for that belongs to R. Chaudenson. This book is an earnest attempt to advance that understanding. That the facts we present force us to reject the "Bourbonnais" theory does not in any way diminish the value of, nor our respect for, the study out of which that theory grew.

We have made a start on what appears to us to be a preliminary sine qua non of any theory of creolization: a detailed investigation of the history and linguistics and, tangentially, of the sociology, of one geographical area in which Creole languages are spoken. We have thus begun to respond to the desideratum expressed recently by Alleyne (1979:96) in reconstructing the sociolinguistic situation prevailing during the period which saw the emergence of RC and of IdeFC, respectively, and in providing a linguistic data base which appears to be consonant with the sociohistorical facts. This provides a relatively fine-tooth comb through which to filter any general theory. We are of course aware of the need for further research to fill in the gaps in our knowledge of Indian Ocean Creole French. But we would hope that similar studies of the historical and linguistic facts behind the emergence of the Caribbean Creole French languages will be undertaken in the near future. This, in our view, is where the priorities lie for the 1980s.

Philip Baker
London, U.K.

September 30, 1981
Chris Corne
Ngatea, N.Z.

Notes

1. Papen in fact writes *Ile-de-France*. In order to avoid any possible confusion—among librarians if not Creole specialists—it seems to us preferable to write the former name of Mauritius in the orthography current at the time it was so called, i.e., without the hyphens and with an *s* rather than the circumflex.

2. Ceremonies claiming possession of Mauritius were conducted by the French in both 1715 and 1721. There was no French presence on the island in the years between these two dates, but the permanent inhabitation of the island followed the second ceremony.

3. Domingue Ferrère (presumably from Ferreira) was born "vers 1686 dans l'évêché de Guarda" (Portugal) and died "15/12/1762 à Ste. Marie" (Reunion). He reached Reunion in 1721 (Ricquebourg 1976:277). No male person of this surname is noted as having been in Reunion prior to 1721. Two other persons of this surname arrived from Portugal in 1745 and 1746, respectively (Ricquebourg 1976:278, 279). Taken together with Chaudenson's reasons for giving 1723 as the latest possible date, it would appear that the court hearing must have taken place in 1721-23, and it thus seems appropriate to date Marie's testimony as ca. 1722.

Part A

A Contrastive Analysis of Reunion and Isle de France Creole French

Two Typologically Diverse Languages

INTRODUCTION TO PART A

The most superficial survey of the literature pertaining to Reunion Creole French is sufficient to convince any reader familiar with other Creole French languages that Reunion Creole is "different." It is quite different from the other Creole French languages spoken in the Indian Ocean, and is not mutually intelligible to them—this in spite of a number of phonological features and lexical items shared exclusively with them, and in spite of a large number of lexical items shared with them and with French (and with other Creole French languages). This common heritage means that passive (at least) bilingualism can be attained more rapidly than between quite unrelated languages.

The other Creole French languages spoken in the Indian Ocean are those of Mauritius, Rodrigues, and Seychelles. Although there are minor lexical, phonological, and syntactic differences, mutual intelligibility is high among these three languages. There can be no doubt that all three derive directly from a variety of Creole which evolved in Mauritius (once known as the Isle de France) in the eighteenth century. Following Papen (1975), the label "Isle de France Creole" is used as a cover term for these three languages. The Creole French of the Chagos Archipelago (Diego Garcia), increasingly influenced by Mauritian Creole French today following the transfer of the population a decade ago to Mauritius, belongs/belonged to the Isle de France group of languages.

In this contribution to the study of Indian Ocean Creole French, I present first a brief description of the verbal system of Reunion Creole. My analysis is one that has been more or less implicit in previous descriptions of the language, but which is here made explicit. No systematic attempt is made to handle the variation which is so characteristic of the linguistic situation in Reunion, but the basics of the Reunion Creole predicate system are presented in a clear and straightforward manner. Nonetheless, in section A3.3 I show that one small aspect of variation in Reunion Creole does in fact define (part of) the continuum which has been posited for Reunion Creole. This definition is in morphosyntactic terms. It demonstrates a reality hitherto more asserted than shown, but raises pertinent questions as to the nature of that continuum. The demonstration is necessarily approximate since I have had to work solely from published material, but it is nonetheless valuable both intrinsically and as an encouragement for future work to be done on the spot with native-speaker consultants.

I present also, in chapter A2, an analysis of the predicate system of Isle de France Creole. This analysis is somewhat different from any other hitherto proposed for this language (group). It provides what I believe to be an accurate representation of how Isle de France Creole actually "works" as a language. It will come as no surprise to readers already familiar with the languages subsumed under the appellation of the "Atlantic Creoles."

These two descriptions—of Reunion Creole in A1 and of Isle de France Creole in A2—show two typologically different languages. In chapter A3, I show that these two languages share a morphosyntactic rule, one which has no obvious model in any known variety of French. The synchronic data clearly point to a shared rule which cannot be, by any stretch of the imagination, an independent innovation in each language. So chapter A4 examines historical and comparative data in an attempt to explain this near-identity of syntactic process. This takes us to the Americas, and a number of near-parallels are examined. Of necessity, no conclusion is reached, but it is suggested that the phenomenon under investigation does not have its origins in the Indian Ocean Creole French languages.

Up to this point, the discussion shows two different languages which share a rather complex morphosyntactic rule. The area discussed is central to language— the predicate system, with its basic dissimilarities and its marginal affinities. In chapter A5 we look at a number of syntactic processes and their semantic motivations. It is shown: (1) that Isle de France Creole displays an originality in this department which has no model or analogue in Reunion Creole; and (2) that some apparently non-French syntactic patterns shared by Reunion and Isle de France Creole have in fact a French origin. Where there are non-French, exclusively shared patterns, historical evidence supplies an explanation.

In the next chapter (A6), this evidence is reviewed. It is shown that there is an affinity at a "deep" structural level between Isle de France Creole and American Creole French. The sociohistorical conditions of the genesis of Reunion Creole are briefly reviewed, and some speculative comments concerning the Reunion Creole continuum are advanced. The theory of the "Bourbonnais" origin of Isle de France Creole is summarized, and rejected on linguistic grounds, while a privileged relation between Reunion Creole and Seychelles Creole is admitted. The historical evidence seems to support these conclusions, the sociohistorical conditions of the genesis of Isle de France Creole being quite different from those mediating the emergence of Reunion Creole.

The final chapter (A7) to some extent attempts to summarize the preceding material and discussions. It is postulated that the structural and semantic affinities of Isle de France Creole and American Creole French must be ascribed to a common origin of some kind, and a number of hypotheses are very briefly considered.

Throughout this work, I avoid the term "dialect." The only unobjectionable use of this term is the strictly diachronic one (Italian and French are dialects of Latin). To speak of "Creole French dialects" implies that these languages are dialects of French in the same way that French is a dialect of Latin. But it is not at all evident that this is the case. It seems to me that the concept of "linguistic tradition" is crucial. I use "linguistic tradition" in the sense that the speech community always has a sense of cultural (including linguistic) continuity, regardless of an observer's perception of, for example, widespread lexical borrowing. In this perspective, Reunion Creole may perhaps be seen as a dialect of French, as I suggest below. The "continuities" involved in the emergence of all other Creole French languages seem to be of quite another tradition. A second reason for avoiding the term "dialect" is that this word, particularly but not exclusively in any kind of French context, too often has connotations of linguistic inferiority (cf. Calvet 1974 on the subject of linguistic imperialism). Pejorative connotations regarding their languages are something that speakers of Creole languages have had quite enough of already.*

---

*This work is based on research supported by the Research Committee of the University of Auckland, to the members of which, past and present, I express my heartfelt thanks. Many people have contributed, directly or indirectly, to various aspects of this study: Jon Amastae, Derek Bickerton, Bruce Biggs, Annegret Bollée, Michel Carayol, Robert Chaudenson, Ross Clark, Ian Hancock, Jim Hollyman, John Holm, Alex Hull, George Huttar, Pete Lincoln, Tom Markey, Brian McKay, Juliette McKibbin, Truus Meyer, Pierre-M. Moorghen, Raleigh Morgan, Ingrid Neumann, Bob Papen, Peter Stein, Loreto Todd, and Jeffrey Waite. Philip Baker has, of course, commented extensively on the entire text, and many of his suggestions have been incorporated. None of these people necessarily agree with anything I have written herein, and all inadequacies are, as always, my work and no one else's. I wish also to thank François Hoareau, Gabrielle Jean, Robert and Flora Mondon, Guy and Marie-Thérèse Savy, all from Seychelles, and Edlay Hojird, Dev Mooten, and Vadivel Vencatachellum, from Mauritius, for their friendship and hospitality while acting as consultants on their native tongues. So many people gave unstintingly of their time in Mauritius, Reunion, and Seychelles that it would be impractical to name them all here, but my gratitude is nonetheless real. Finally, without the help of Daphne Wong Too, this work would not have been written.

A1
The Verbal System in Reunion Creole

As I have already noted in the preceding introductory comments, Reunion Creole French (RC) is rather different in its general "physiognomy" from any of the other languages generally referred to as "Creole French." This fact is hardly new, but the precise nature of the difference has not been, to my knowledge, made as clear as it might have been. On the contrary, it is my belief that statements to date concerning RC, and its verbal system in particular, misrepresent to a greater or lesser degree the true situation. It is a fact that RC shares a number of phonological features and lexical items with the other Creole French languages spoken in the Indian Ocean, as well as a rather odd and highly visible syntactic process (which is discussed in some detail in A3 below). There is also some measure of "cultural identity" in the Creole-speaking areas of the Indian Ocean: an obvious example is in the field of folktales (cf. Carayol and Chaudenson 1978a), and there are no doubt many other, more subtle identities as well. All these shared features have contributed, in various measure, to a widespread (but erroneous) perception on the part of creolists that RC is in some sense the "same" kind of language as Mauritian or Seychelles or Rodrigues Creole. But this is not the case, as I shall show. The sketch of the RC verbal system given here aims at presenting an analysis which, while undoubtedly still incomplete in its detail, will contribute to our understanding of the system's functioning.

Most of what I shall have to say about the RC verbal system is not "new" and has in fact been more or less implicit in previous descriptions of the language. I attempt here to present explicitly the way in which the system actually works. This is a necessary first step in setting the record straight. As will be seen in due course, there are cases where an RC sentence comes out, segmental phoneme for segmental phoneme, identical to a sentence of the same or very similar meaning in Mauritian or Seychellois or Rodriguan. Such cases of surface convergence have led to the erroneous view (which I admit to having once shared, cf. Corne 1974-75, 1977a) that RC is basically a variant of an early Indian Ocean Creole French, a sort of "proto-IOC," that has been subjected to an intensive ongoing influence of metropolitan varieties of French (in contradistinction to Isle de France Creole, which has not undergone similar influences to anywhere near the same degree). Let me cite as an example the view that the set of "aspectual particles" of Isle de France Creole comprises the "core system" of RC tense/aspect marking (Valdman 1978b:77). This idea, which I believe to be incorrect, is completely understandable in light of the theses advanced in the important work by R. Chaudenson (1974) on RC concerning the "genetic" relationship of the Indian Ocean languages, and I shall return to this matter in due course (A6, and cf. B3.2.5, Part B). Meanwhile, my aim in this chapter is to give a clear picture of the RC verbal system.

The term "Reunion Creole French" is merely a label which covers a highly complex set of facts. Several varieties, ranging from the "créole des Hauts" (the "français créolisé" of Carayol and Chaudenson 1973) to what appears to be a more basilectal variety known in Reunion as "créole des Bas," coexist in a rather special kind of continuum situation. The terms "Hauts" and "Bas" are geographical designations, not social ones; although they imply geographical localization, this is not entirely the case today. Other locally used names for basilectal varieties are *parler malbar, parler ti-cafre,* and *causement cafre.* The exact nature of this continuum remains to be determined (but cf. sections A3.3, A4.1.1, and A6.2).

In Reunion, there is also a "nonmarked" French which is essentially identical to Standard French and a regional French which is immediately intelligible with the latter but which displays a number of phonological, morphosyntactic, and lexical differences therefrom (for details, see Chaudenson 1979c).

Variations in usage in RC are particularly noticeable in the verbal system generally. The set of variables concerned may or may not be classifiable according to possible implicational relations obtaining among them. No attempt at such a classification is made here, but such an attempt should, in my view, be given the highest priority in future research.

It is beyond the scope of this study (and in any case impossible on the basis of the data available to me) to try to describe RC verb morphology fully, with details of all verbs, regular and irregular, in all tenses, in all varieties of the language. But it is feasible to give a picture complete enough for my purpose, which is to demonstrate the way in which the system functions. The statement given here is based on data drawn from a variety of sources: the folktales published (in printed form but also—partially—on magnetic tape) by Barat et al. (1977), and the descriptive statements of Chaudenson (1974), Corne (1974-75), Moorghen (1975), and Papen (1975, 1978b). These statements are all based on firsthand contact with the language, to varying degrees. My own fieldwork consisted of two rather brief visits to Reunion in 1974 and 1976; R. Papen's work is based on a somewhat lengthier sojourn; P.-M. J. Moorghen is a Mauritian who has lived in Reunion for many years; and R. Chaudenson is a Frenchman who also has had many years' residence on the island. The works of Moorghen and Papen are not, unfortunately, widely available, but the essential points of my own 1974-75 article, of rather limited circulation perhaps, have been largely reproduced in Corne (1977a) and Corne and Moorghen (1978); R. Chaudenson's study of the lexicon of RC, with its "Notes grammaticales" (pp. 329-81), is undoubtedly the primary source of RC data for most creolists. In any case, none of the data adduced here in support of my analysis are in any way incompatible with what published material written in RC is available (e.g., Barat et al. 1977; Fourcade [1930] 1976), nor with those of previous descriptions. The analysis given here of these data, however, represents a belated but very necessary *mise au point.*

The transcription of RC material used here is for convenience only. It is basically my Seychelles Creole orthography (Corne 1977a, 1977b) which I have transferred in toto to RC. This procedure distorts the reality no more than any of the other systems proposed so far for RC (e.g., Barat et al. 1977)—or than the various French-based orthographies used by, say, Focard (1884) or Fourcade (1976). But nor is it intended to make *any* claims about RC phonology, unlike the transcription system used by Barat et al. (1977) and Carayol and Chaudenson (1978a and b) that claims to represent basilectal variants (Barat et al. 1977:9). Readers wanting further details on the vexatious question of RC orthography can profitably consult Barat et al. (1977:9-11) and the detailed study of certain features by Carayol and Chaudenson (1977). For detailed statements on RC phonology, see the descriptions given by Papen (1978a and b).

The morphosyntax of RC derives, as will be readily apparent, from (mainly seventeenth-century varieties of) French. In the verbal system, distinctions of tense and aspect are handled in a number of ways, most of which are characteristic of all (or most) varieties of RC. In what follows, it must be emphasized that a mass of detail has been left aside, and that I am not claiming 100 percent accuracy for what data are adduced. I am claiming that the picture of RC which emerges from the salient points of the system that are given below is an accurate portrayal of the way in which the language "works."

A1.1 The Copula

In RC the verb *et(r)* 'be' functions as a copula. It does not function as an "auxiliary verb" in the French sense. Its forms vary for tense, although not for person or number. These forms are:

Present *le, la*   Past *lete, te*
Future *sra, sora*   Conditional *sre, sore*
Past participle *ete, te*   Infinitive *etr, et*

The *-a/-e* distinction of Future/Conditional *sora/sore* is not stable, and it seems (I stress "seems") that either form may occur in either sense. Further, the Conditional in RC and its relation with the Future and the Past requires further research. Note also the *le/la* variation in the Present (cf. A1.2 below).

The copula is used in sentences such as:

Copula + adjective:

li le prese 'he is in a hurry'
l diab la pa pov 'the devil is not poor'
muê (le)te malad 'I was ill'

Copula + noun/pronoun:

u sora ê fam 'you will be a woman'
lete pa muê 'it wasn't me'

Copula + adverb/prepositional phrase:

ut mâze le dan ut tât 'your food is in your bag'
tue le la, dô! 'you're there, then!'

As in French, the copula is used to carry marks of tense (and aspect) which other lexical items such as adjectives or nouns or adverbs cannot carry.[1]

A1.2 The Auxiliary Verb *a(v)uar*

RC has an auxiliary verb, *a(v)uar* 'have', which is used to form tenses analogous to the *temps composés* of French. Like its French etymon *avoir*, the RC verb *a(v)uar* has a "full" sense, 'possess'. Its forms are:

Present *la, na, a, nana, ana*	Past *lave, nave*
Future *lora, nora*	Conditional *lore, nore*
Past participle –	Infinitive *a(v)uar*

Again, the *-a/-e* is unstable. As a "full" verb meaning 'possess', the forms *nana* and *ana* tend to be used in the Present, while the Past is handled by *te i ana* and *ti ana* (see A1.6 for *te i* and *ti* and a discussion concerning the element *i*) in the more basilectal varieties. I have not observed either *(n)ana* or *t(e)i ana* used as auxiliaries. In other tenses, the tendency is to use the verb *gaŷe* in the "full" sense:

u ava gaŷ ê bezmâ 'you will get a punishment'
usa u la gaŷ sa? 'where did you get that?'

(The "missing" *-e* of *gaŷe* in these two examples illustrates a phenomenon which I have labeled Final Vowel Truncation (FVT); this is discussed in chapter A3.)

As an auxiliary verb, the forms of *a(v)uar* are followed by a Past Participle, as in French:

muê la vni 'I came, have come'	(Fr. *je suis venu*)
muê lave koni 'I had known'	(*j'avais connu*)
muê lore/nore ale 'I would go, would have gone'	(*je serais allé, j'irais*)
muê nora pa fe mô travay 'I wouldn't do my work'	

Again, the precise relation of the Future and Conditional forms and their respective meanings is not completely clear to me, so I shall restrict my attention to the Present and the Past auxiliaries, followed by the Past Participle, as illustrated by the first two examples in the above list. These compound tenses handle distinctions involving the notion of Completion, i.e., completed action with respect to a given time reference. They correspond semantically very closely to the French Perfect, Pluperfect, etc., and may usefully be referred to by these names. The Perfect is generally constructed with *la*, the variant *a* being used occasionally as the auxiliary in what I assume to be more acrolectal varieties of RC.

The auxiliary verb *a(v)uar* is also used to construct compound tenses of the verb *etr* 'be':

muê nora ete malad 'I shall/would have been ill'

The form *la* + the Past Participle *ete* produces *lete* or *late:*

muê lete/late malad 'I have been ill'

However, this *lete*, unlike the *lete* we have just seen in A1.1 as the Past tense form of *etr*, may not be reduced to *te*, as far as I am aware. Thus, *muê lete malad* is ambiguous as to its reading (Past or Perfect), while *muê te malad* can only be Past tense. To further muddy the waters, the form *la* is occasionally replaced by *le* as auxiliary (and not solely with verbs which in French are constructed with *être* as their auxiliary), but this occurs *much* less frequently than the use of *la* replacing the Present tense *le* as seen in A1.1.

A1.3 Past Participles

RC verbs have participial forms, including Present Participles in *-â* (Fr. *-ant*) which I shall ignore here. For the vast majority of RC verbs, the Infinitive and the Past Participle are identical in form, e.g., *mâze* 'eat, eaten'. A minor difference between them is that they are not equally affected by the Final Vowel Truncation rule, as will be seen in due course.

A second and fairly important class of verbs has the Infinitive in *-ir*. Phonetically, *-ir* tends to become indistinguishable from the Past Participle in *-i* that is characteristic of this class (e.g., *vnir, vni* 'come').

For "irregular" verbs, there is sometimes disagreement as to the "correct" form for a given tense or function. This is particularly so of Past Participles. Thus, in more basilectal varieties we find (the more acrolectal form being given in parentheses): *prâ (pri)* 'taken', *met (mi)* 'put', *konet (koni)* 'known', *fan (fâdi)* 'split'. Note that these more basilectal forms are, as a general rule, the same as the Infinitive forms; this suggests different parsing strategies at different points on the continuum. The same kind of variation occurs for other verb forms as well, for example in the Present *met (me)* 'put', *viv (vi)* 'live', where again we see the tendency toward an invariable base. The assumption that the tendency toward invariant bases is "more basilectal," is just that—an assumption and nothing more; we cannot be sure until the necessary, detailed descriptive work has been accomplished.

A1.4 Particles?

Various tenses and/or aspectual distinctions in RC are handled by what appear at first glance to be "particles" preposed to an invariant verbal base. These elements are largely identical in form (and, in some cases, meaning) to the preposed particles of Isle de France Creole (see A2), and they thus confer on RC a distinct "family resemblance," at least for the casual observer. However, as the discussion here and in A2 will make abundantly clear, the view (for example in Valdman 1978b:77) that the set of aspectual particles of Isle de France Creole comprises the "core system" of RC tense/aspect verb marking is erroneous (cf. also A6.5).

The first such "particle" is *a, ava,* which precedes verbs (but not, apparently, the verb *etr;* i.e., *a(va)* does not seem to occur in copulative sentences) and is used for an Indefinite Future. It is followed regularly by an infinitival form of the verb. Examples are:

m a konet 'I shall know'
u ava gaŷ ê bezmâ 'you will get a punishment'

Unlike the Definite Future "marker" *sa((v)a)* (see below, A1.7), and contrary to the Isle de France Creole analogous forms *a, va, ava,* it cannot occur in a Past + Future configuration, i.e., as a Conditional. Thus, we have Isle de France Creole *ti ava,* but no corresponding RC **te i a(va).* There is another Indefinite Future form, *va.* This form, but not *a(va),* may be preceded by *i* (see A1.5, A1.6). There are significant differences from Isle de France Creole usage. First, in the Mauritian Creole equivalent of:

(RC) *kâ(k) li va ale, nu va mâze* 'when he leaves, we shall eat'

only one occurrence of *va* is possible:

(MC) *ler li ale, nu va mâze* 'when he leaves, we shall eat'

And second, while RC *va* may co-occur with pronominal as well as nominal subjects, RC *a(va)* is restricted to pronominal subjects; whereas in Isle de France Creole, *a, va,* and *ava* are not restricted in this way.

The second particle-style element is *fin(i),* for the Perfect (i.e., the Completive with respect to Present time); its Pluperfect (the Completive with respect to Past time) derivative is *te fin(i):*

muê te fini vuar 'I had seen'
nu i fin(i) met 'we have put'
sô sulezô fin pase 'his drunkenness is over/has passed' (Papen 1978b:376)
bibas fin sese 'the loquats *(Eriobotria japonica)* are dry/have dried'
(Chaudenson 1974:340)

The Perfect constructed with *fin* alone is relatively marginal, at least in the data available to me. The usual form of the Perfect is that outlined above in A1.2, with *la* + Past Participle (I shall return to this in A3). The Pluperfect constructed with *te fin(i)* seems more current than the Perfect with *fin* alone, but *te fin(i)* competes with *te i fin* + Infinitive, as well as with *lave* + Past Participle and with a cumulation of *lave* + *fini:*

li lave fini mâze 'he had eaten, had finished eating'

As a general rule, the "particle" *fin(i)* co-occurs with verbs in the Infinitive; however, *fini* does co-occur with Past Participles:

li fini fatige 'he has become tired'
li la fini vieyi 'he has become aged'

It also occurs occasionally with adjectives:

li la fini vie 'he has become old'

These last three examples are potentially significant. They are rather unusual, I think, in RC. But they do parallel rather well the analogous Isle de France Creole construction, in which predicates of this kind require the presence of *((f)i)n* (see A2.3). Cf. also *bibas fin sese, sulezô fin pase,* above.

A1.5 Affixes

The forms of *a(v)uar* and *et(r)* that we have seen may be considered as the result of affixation rules and morphological rules which convert underlying strings into surface forms. Similar sorts of rules account for the Future Negative forms, where a suffix *-ra* is attached to a verb stem:

mi i sâtra pa 'I won't sing'
mi i dorra pa 'I won't sleep'
mi i konetra pa 'I won't know'
mi i viêra pa 'I won't come'
mi i (v)uara pa 'I won't see'

Again, there is variation. The suffix *-ra* also appears as *-re*. There is disagreement as to the form of the stem of "irregular" verbs. In some varieties, there are nonnegative forms such as Future *pura* 'will be able', Conditional *vudre* 'would like', etc. While these latter appear to be characteristic of upper-mesolectal varieties of RC, a detailed study would be necessary to establish whether the variations mentioned here do in fact constitute a continuum.

The synthetic Future Negative forms are not obligatory in all (in any?) varieties of RC. The Future Negative may also be constructed with *(i) va pa* + Infinitive:

li va pa vole 'he won't steal'

This raises the question of whether *va* should be considered as a variant form of the Indefinite Future *a(va)*, since its distribution is in fact rather different. With noun subjects, *a* and *ava* do not co-occur; they are not preceded by *i;* and they do not occur in negative sentences. I do not know to what extent *va* is semantically distinguished from the Indefinite Future *a(va)* or from the Definite Future *sa((v)a)* which is discussed in A1.7.

Clearly, a complete study of RC would need to list the details of Infinitival suffixes (and the verb stems to which they are affixed, of course), Participial suffixes (and stems), and so on. It would also need to list the stems which, in at least some varieties of RC, take the Past suffix *-e:*

m i dize 'I said'
i vule pa marie '(s)he didn't want to marry'
l pti frer i dorme 'the little brother slept'
li mâze sô kari 'he ate his curry'

I shall have more to say about this Past tense in the next section.

A1.6 The Present and the Past

In many of the examples given so far, there is an element *i*. I have argued elsewhere (Corne 1974-75) that this may arise from a procedure of embedding a verb into a matrix containing either the Present or the Past form of the Copula.

Historically, it may be supposed that the Present tense of most verbs in all varieties of RC was formed by embedding the Present tense form of the verb in a matrix containing the Present copula *le*. This *le* is obligatorily deleted and the subordinator *ki* obligatorily reduced to *i.* The derivation is thus something along the lines illustrated in Figure 1 (p. 19): from an underlying /muê le ki [muê mâz]/, we have *m i mâz* 'I eat'. This analysis has some fairly obvious objections, not the least of which are the apparently quite unmotivated, phonologically speaking, reduction of *ki* to *i;* the unexplained reduction of *muê* to *m* (but note that the first person singular pronoun is also *m* before *a*); and the total lack of any attestation

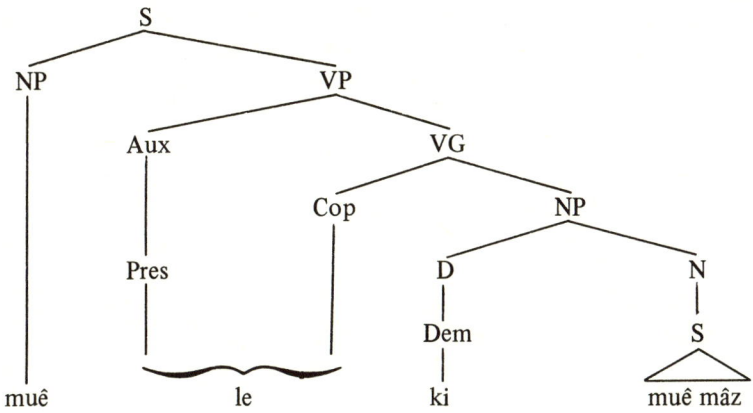

le deletion, *ki* reduction, Equi → *m i mâz*

Figure 1
Sample Present Tense Derivation in Reunion Creole

in any known RC text of *le ki.² However, in view of the Past tense formation (below), these objections cannot be held to carry much weight. Note in particular that I am not suggesting that this analysis represents any kind of psychological reality for present-day RC speakers. In fact, if *i* has any "meaning" in modern RC, it is presumably that of marking what follows as a verb, and I therefore propose to refer to it as a "verb marker" (cf. B3.2.2 in Part B).

Although there is no RC attestation of *le ki* to support this analysis, it is supported by comparative data from the French isolates of St. Barts and St. Thomas in the Caribbean (cf. Lefebvre 1976:138-39, 1979; Highfield 1979:94-100). In St. Thomas, there are sentences such as the following (in Highfield's orthography):

t'é ki vèy 'you are watching'
j'èté ki vèné 'I was coming (i.e., en route)'

which indicate the Present and the Imperfect Progressive, respectively, and also:

t'é ki va fer 'you are going to do'

which is referred to by Highfield (1979:99) as the Periphrastic Progressive Future or Near Future. If my underlying /le ki/ analysis is accepted, all three of these are paralleled in RC, in form if not precisely in function (although even here, the similarity is striking, as will be seen).

Two verbs are not, as a general rule, embedded under /le ki/. They are *a(v)uar* 'have' and *et(r)* 'be'. However, although the Future/Conditional of *avuar, nora/e* is not as a rule preceded by *i*, the Future/Conditional of *etr, s(o)ra/e* frequently co-occurs with *i*. Thus, we have the following paradigm:

muê le malad 'I am ill' *(*m i le malad)*
muê (le)te malad 'I was ill' *(*m i (le)te malad)*
muê s(o)ra/e malad 'I shall/would be ill'
m i s(o)ra/e malad 'I shall/would be ill'

I do not know the details of the distribution of *i* in the case of these two verbs. If *i* is seen as a verb marker, then sentences such as:

ki sa u i le? 'who are you?'
usa m i le? 'where am I?'
usa loto i le? 'where is the car?'

suggest that *etr* here is a "full" verb (State, Location/Existence/Equivalence/. . .), rather than simply a copula. But the presence of *i* does not appear to be obligatory, as shown by:

kel kote u lete ier? 'where were you yesterday?'

Chaudenson (1974:343) remarks that the use of *i* is frequent when the verb *etr* has the locative sense, but that it occurs sometimes also in nonlocative copulative sentences. Note also the use of *i* in *te i ana* mentioned above (A1.2), where *avuar* has its full sense of 'possess'.

We turn now to the Past tense, the formation of which is somewhat more complicated. It may be formed in a number of ways, some or all of which may coexist in the speech of the same speaker. That is, within successive clauses of the one sentence, the Past may be formed here in one way, here in another, with no apparent difference in meaning, although this last assertion manifestly needs to be carefully checked out. Some ways of forming the Past tend to be characteristic of some groups of speakers, although not, in all probability, exclusive to them; again, the lack of serious descriptive work on RC is painfully obvious.

We have already seen one procedure of Past tense formation. This is the suffixation of *-e* to a Past tense stem, and the embedding of the resultant verb under /le ki/. Thus, the Past tense stem of the verb *dir* 'say' is *diz-*. The stem + suffix produces *dize*. This form is then embedded in the way suggested above for the Present tense, and we arrive at:

m i dize 'I said'

Note that this suffix *-e* is not subject to the Final Vowel Truncation rule (A3).

Now the form *dize* may also be embedded in a matrix containing the Past tense of the copula, *(le)te*. Thus, we find, albeit relatively infrequently, sentences formed on the model of:

muê lete ki dize 'I said'

which happens to be a perfect parallel to the St. Thomas structure noted above, *j'èté ki vèné*. Here, as in the Present, *le* deletion and *ki* reduction apply, although they do so optionally and not obligatorily as they do in the Present. This produces a theoretical set of sentences:

muê lete ki dize
?*muê lete i dize
?*muê te ki dize
muê te i dize

'I said'

of which only the first and the last are attested in my files.

The *lete ki dize* model is, as stated above, relatively infrequently observed. More often, it is the Present tense form of the verb that is embedded under *lete ki*.

With the optional application of *le* deletion and *ki* reduction, the following forms of the Past tense are all attested:

muê lete ki mâz
muê lete i mâz
muê te ki mâz
muê te i mâz
} 'I ate'

The last of these, with *te i*, is the most frequent and the most widespread. Papen (1978b:377) claims it is the most basilectal form (cf. also Chaudenson 1979b:130).

Finally, there is a form *ti*, rather infrequent, which is presumably due to sandhi phenomena in rapid speech (*te i* → *ti*, cf. Chaudenson 1974:336).

Such forms as *lete ki ba* and *i bate* 'was beating, beat' can coexist in the usage of a given individual (Fourcade 1976:6, 18, passim).[3] The unreduced forms with *ki* may possibly be more frequent among older speakers. For R. Chaudenson (1974: 347, note 10) such forms as *te ki dize* represent a cumulation of two systems, a "Creole" *te i* Past marker and a "French" *-e* suffix, but as we have seen, the forms in *-e* are as much a part of RC as the *lete ki* structure is. In any case, what is of interest here is the multiplicity of usages rather than how they came about, and how (and if) the usages can be classified according to the implicational relations between them. That is, do they in fact fit into a continuum similar to the Guyanese model described by Bickerton (1975)? The multiple choices apparently facing the RC speaker are not all covered by the foregoing, however. In what I assume to be upper-mesolectal varieties, *ete i* has been observed. In Fourcade (1976:3), we note *late ki*, apparently for an ordinary Past (as opposed to Perfect) tense. On occasion, *lete* occurs without *(k)i*. There are no doubt other "anomalies" as well.

The treatment here implies that *i* (or *ki* in the Past) is in general obligatory before a verb, with the partial exceptions of *avuar, etr, a(va),* and *fin(i)*, as we have seen. In particular, forms of *etr* and *avuar* with an initial *l-* (or *n-*) generally do not occur preceded by *i*. This fact has an imperfect but nevertheless close parallel in relative clause embedding:

ê mun ki pas 'a person who passes by' *(ki)*
vuala en k la pa prese pur marie 'there's one who is in no hurry to get married'
(k + l-)
nana ê bug i viê 'there is a man who comes' *(i)*
nana ê bug le âmerdâ 'there is a man who is a nuisance' (∅ + *le*)
loto la koŷ ali lete ruz 'the car which hit him was red' (∅ + *la*)

Another roughly analogous case appears to be that the subject pronoun *(l)i* is frequently omitted before *le, la,* etc.:

le kui, la di 'it's cooked, (s)he said'

These phenomena are unlikely to be totally independent of each other (cf. B3.2.2), while at the same time the parallel with St. Thomas and St. Barts French is unlikely to be completely fortuitous either.

Let me here forestall some objections. I am aware of the possibility of *i* deriving from French *reprise du sujet* generalized from the third to the other persons. Valdman (1977:181-82) notes the use of embedded clauses introduced by *qui* in the speech of children and in colloquial varieties of French to express Progressive: the possibility that this use was generalized independently in St. Barts and in Reunion cannot be ruled out (Hull, personal communication). So, while I have noted elsewhere (Corne 1974-75:93) a somewhat apochryphal Old French model for *je suis qui* + Clause, and while I intend in subsequent chapters to refer to a variety of seventeenth-century French containing the *lete ki* structure, I am not wedded to the derivation suggested in Figure 1. Its realism or otherwise is not crucial; it is merely a suggestion as to a possible history of *i* in RC.

So much for the forms of the Present and the Past. For their semantics, it seems safe to say that these two tenses correspond rather closely to their French analogues. The Present expresses an action which takes place now; if the ongoing nature of the action (which is already inherent in this tense) is to be emphasized or disambiguated, then one of the periphrastic constructions to be described in A1.7 is used. For the purposes of the comparison of RC with Isle de France Creole, it is important to note that the progressive aspect in RC is inherent in the Present tense, and that a Progressive periphrastic expression *may* (not *must*) be used for emphasis or to avoid ambiguity. (Almost the exact reverse pertains in Isle de France Creole, A2.3.) The Present tense also expresses habitual or universal action: *m i bua d lo* 'I am a water drinker (not a rum drinker)'. The Past tense seems to correspond rather to the French Imperfect tense (as opposed to the Past Historic [Preterite]): ongoing action in the past, habitual action in the past. Again, the same situation as to the use of the Progressive expressions obtains as for the Present. A detailed study of the semantic dimensions and the uses of the Present and the Past remains to be done (although there are some useful comments in the 1975 article by Moorghen).

A1.7 Aspects

Other expressions of aspect are handled by means of periphrastic structures involving an Infinitive. Among these are *sa((v)a)* 'Definite Future':

m i sa sât ê româs 'I will sing a song'[4]
 (*m a sâte* 'I shall sing')
m i saa rod zerb 'I will look for grass'
m i sava tir mô lêz 'I will take off my clothes'

muê te i saa dir ali 'I would tell him' (+ an *if* clause)
li te i sa travay 'he would work' (+ an *if* clause)
m i sa fin mâze 'I will have eaten'

(sentences and glosses from Papen 1978b:374-76). Note that the verb *sava* has also a "full" sense of 'go, go away, leave':

m i sava 'I leave, go away'   (Chaudenson 1974:337)

Next, consider the Progressive. This is handled by means of a variety of periphrastic structures. The first is *etr apre:*

muê (le)te apre dormir 'I was sleeping'
li l(e) apre lir ê liv 'he is reading a book'

which competes with a "more standard" *etr âtren* (from *âtrê d*):

zot i s(o)ra âtren mâze 'they will be eating'
nu le pa âtren zue 'we are not playing'

and a noticeably "less standard" *po* (variant ?*apo to be confirmed):

nu le pa po zue 'we are not playing'
li (le)te po batay 'he was fighting'
zot i s(o)ra po mâze 'they will be eating'

(most sentences and glosses from Papen 1978b:375; for discussion on the form *(a)po,* see Papen 1978b:378-79).
There is an Imminent Future constructed with *etr pur* or *etr bô pur;* Papen (1978b:377) ascribes each form to different varieties of RC:

zot (le) pur batay 'they are about to fight'
muê lete bô pur ale 'I was about to leave'

The construction with *etr pur* is relatively rare, but it is attested from time to time, e.g., in Barat et al. (1977:16).
Finally, there is an Immediate Past ("to have just") which is constructed with either *sort* (from *sor d*) + Infinitive or with *vien* (from *viê d*) + Infinitive:

m i sort/vien mâze 'I have just eaten'
muê te i vien arive 'I had just arrived'

In the case of *etr apre/pur,* optional *le* deletion produces strings which resemble superficially certain structures in Isle de France Creole. Compare RC *te apre* in the example above with Isle de France Creole *ti (a)p(r)e.* In the case of *etr pur,* the semantics do not correspond at all (Isle de France Creole *pu* is a Definite Future), while in the case of *etr apre,* we may recall that its use is optional, to avoid ambiguity or to emphasize the ongoing nature of the action. In its Isle de France analogue, *(a)p(r)e* obligatorily marks on the surface underlying Progressive, i.e., the notion of Progressive is not inherent in the Isle de France Creole "Present" tense (see A2).

A1.8 Summary

The system as discussed so far is summarized in Table 1 on p. 26. The first person singular of the verb *mâze* 'eat' is used to illustrate the tense and aspect system with verbs. The first person singular of *etr malad* 'be ill' is similarly used to illustrate predicates containing the copula followed by adjectives, nouns, pronouns, prepositional phrases, or adverbs. In all cases, the sentences given are potentially complete, that is, they may be considered to be followed by a sentence boundary. It is, I hope, clear that the periphrastic constructions of, say, the Progressive, are made up of copula + a prepositional phrase, and are therefore represented by the *etr malad* illustrations.

As some of the examples given so far have clearly indicated, the placement of the negator *pa* is straightforward. It follows the first verb encountered in any given derivation, including *etr* and *avuar.* Some examples:

muê le pa malad 'I'm not ill'
m i mâz pa 'I don't eat'
m i mâze pa 'I didn't eat'
muê (le) p' apre mâze 'I'm not eating (right now)'
muê la pa fin(i) mâze 'I haven't finished eating'
muê la pa mâze 'I haven't eaten'

Consider now the following two sentences:

muê (le)te pa malad 'I was not ill'
muê (le)te i mâz pa 'I didn't eat'

The distribution of *pa* shows clearly that *(le)te* has a different status from *(le)te i:* the former is a verb; the latter is a marker of Past tense + the "verb marker" *i.*

From the foregoing, it can be seen that RC does not have a tense and aspect marking system based on "preposed particles." In this, it is quite unlike any other variety of Creole French anywhere, and quite unlike Isle de France Creole in particular, as we shall see. RC has relatively rigidly defined "parts of speech"

Table 1
Summary of Tense and Aspect in Reunion Creole

Present	*m i mâz*	*muê le malad (le/la)*
Past	*muê (le)te (k)i mâz(e)* *m i mâze*	*muê (le)te malad*
Future: Indef. Neg. Def.	*m a mâze (m ava; ?m i va)* *m i mâzra pa (m i va pa)* *m i sa((v)a) mâze (?m i va)*	*(m a tom malad)* *m i sra pa malad* *m i s(o)ra malad* *m i sa((v)a) et malad*
Fut.-in-Past, Conditional, Cond. Perf.	*muê te i sa mâze* *muê lore/nore mâze*	*m i s(o)re malad* *muê lora/nora ete malad* *muê lore/nore (e)te malad*
Completive (or Perfect)	*muê la mâze* *muê la fin(i) mâze* *m i fin(i) mâze* *mua fin mâze*	*muê lete malad (lete/late)* *muê la fini et malad* *muê la fini malad (?)*
Pluperfect	*muê (le)te (i) fin(i) mâze* *muê lave (fini) mâze*	*muê lave (e)te malad (?)* *muê te i fini et malad (?)*
Fut. Perf.	*m i sa fin mâze*	*m i sa fini et malad (?)*
Progressive: Present Past Future	*etr apre/âtren/po* *muê l' apre mâze* *muê (le)te apre mâze* *m i s(o)ra apre mâze*	* * * *
'have just' 'had just'	*m i sort/vien mâze* *muê te i sort/vien mâze*	*m i sort/vien et malad* *muê te i sort/vien et malad*
Imminent Fut.	*muê (le) pur mâze*	*muê (le) pur et malad (?)*

which play a crucial syntactic role. It has surface forms of a copula, *et(r)*; it has an auxiliary verb *a(v)uar*, the forms of which combine with Past Participles to form compound tenses; it has Infinitives; it has a relatively complex verbal morphology based on various verbal stems plus suffixes. It has the "verb marker" *i*, unknown in any other Creole French language (the *pa i* construction of Seychelles Creole may well derive from the RC "verb marker," but its role is quite different, see A5.4 and B3.2.2, and cf. Corne and Moorghen 1978:68-69).

The "particle"-style elements *a(va)* and *fin(i)* correspond in form at least, if not always precisely in distribution and meaning, to similar morphemes in Isle de France Creole; and the prepositions *apre* and *pur*, if *le* deletion has applied in negative or positive sentences in the Present or the Past tense, are reminiscent in form at least of the Isle de France Creole particles *(a)p(r)e* and *pu*. However, the structures underlying these similarities appear to be quite different in RC and in Isle de France Creole, although the precise set-up for all varieties in the RC continuum remains to be studied in detail.

RC verbs can be classified, at the very least, into morphological classes (or conjugations) according to the forms occurring as: (i) Present tense; (ii) Past tense, for those varieties which (putatively) do not form it solely by the *lete ki* + Present tense construction; (iii) Future Negative; (iv) Past Participle; (v) Infinitive. See Table 2 below.

Table 2
Verb "Conjugations" in Reunion Creole: A Few Examples

	'eat'	'serve'	'put'	'say'	'come'	'know'	'be'
(i)	mâz	serv	me(t)	di	viê	kone	le
(ii)	mâze	serve	mete	dize	vnc	konese	lete
(iii)	mâzra	servira	metra	dira	viê(n)ra	konetra	s(o)ra
(iv)	mâze	servi	met/mi	di	vni/mni	konet/koni	(e)te
(v)	mâze	servir	met(r)	dir	vnir	konet(r)	et(r)

Presumably, the smaller the number of different stems (for irregular verbs) in a given idiolect, or in other words the greater the tendency toward invariance, the closer that idiolect is to the basilect; but again, the need for a thorough investigation of the morphosyntactic variation in RC in order to establish definitively whether one is in fact justified in speaking of the RC continuum as though it were of the same kind as the Guyanese model must be insisted upon.

A1.9 The "Presentative Copula"

To complete this very brief overview of RC, let us now look at the form *se* and its companions. There is a Present tense form and a Past tense form of what Papen

(1978b:389) calls a Presentative Copula. Most of the following examples are from Papen's work. They illustrate first of all the Present tense form *se* and a prevocalic variant *set:*

se la pud mayok 'it is manioc powder'
se pa tu l mun ki kone tres kalime
    'it is not everyone who knows how to weave bamboo'[5]
se muê 'it's me'
se parsk la lin . . . 'it is because the moon . . .'
bulô, set ê bu d fer k nana ê zekru
    'a bolt is a piece of iron (steel) which has a nut'

The Past tense form is *sete:*

N, sete ê mo dâ la ger 'N was a word (used) in the war'

In the negative, there is often a Present tense form *ne* (and one would expect to find a Past **nete*, but I do not know if such a form exists):

ne pa tu l mun ki kone sa 'it's not everyone who knows that'

Other "presentative" elements are *le* (and its variant *la*) and *lete:*

le pa sa 'it's not that'
la pa d lo, sa! 'that's not water!'
lete mô fam 'it was my wife'

The *se* in the interrogative *ki se k?* 'who?' may perhaps in some sense be the "same" *se:*

ki se k na sa? 'who (is it that) has it?'

but I do not know whether ?**ki le k*, or ?**ki lete/sete k* are possible forms.

Focusing ("clefting") can be achieved without the use of any overt presentative element. In the Present, *se/le* may be deleted, and in the Past, *sete/lete* may be similarly deleted (it seems reasonable to suppose that such deletions are contingent on tense-marking in the following clauses, but I do not have confirmatory data at hand). For example:

dan basê, i fo met sa 'it is in the basin that it must be put'

But in the Past, *se* alone may not be deleted, i.e., **te* NP *(ki)* Clause.

These data suggest that *se, sete,* even if they do not retain their French structure of subject *ce* + *être* (a matter on which I prefer to make no judgment), are nonetheless specific contextually conditioned forms of the RC verb *et(r)*. As some of the above examples show, the negator *pa* follows. The forms themselves are identical to those of the copula apart from the initial consonant, and the copula itself may be used in lieu of the special forms.

A1.10 Conclusion

That the verbal system of Reunion Creole behaves in a manner which is clearly French cannot be doubted. It is based on an arrangement which requires a relatively rigid "parts-of-speech" categorization of lexical items. One can quite reasonably claim that the morphosyntax derives, in essence, directly from seventeenth-century regional varieties of French.

Nonetheless, the system is not devoid of "Creole" features. For example, the tendency in what I assume to be more "basilectal" varieties toward an invariable verb stem (A1.3) is one such feature. Such invariable stems occur, however, within the system as described here: thus, *m i met* 'I place', *muê la met* 'I placed' are basilectal, while *m i me* and *muê la mi* are less so. But these invariable stems do not modify the way in which the system actually functions. Another "Creole" feature is the use of *fin(i)* + Past Participle/Adjective. This seems semantically "non-French," and it is remarkably similar to the regular Isle de France Creole use of *fin,* as will be seen; further, this use of *fin(i)* to mark the Completive in stative predicates is a feature exclusively shared by the Indian Ocean representatives of the Creole French languages (although it is not attested in Reunion in this context in any early texts, cf. B3.2.5).

Apart from *fin(i),* all the other features of the RC verbal system can be shown to have "French" analogues.[6] Even the use of *a(va),* as in *m a(va) mâze* 'I shall eat', is paralleled elsewhere: compare the St. Thomas French structure *ma ki va fer* 'I am going to do' (Highfield 1979:67, 100). The surface configurations (in the Present) which are produced by optional *le* deletion with *etr pur* 'to be on the point of' and *etr apre* 'to be in the process of' (A1.7), and which are the same as surface structures in Isle de France Creole, do not correspond functionally and/or semantically with the latter. However, *le* deletion itself might be seen as a possible "Creole" feature: it occurs optionally but frequently with *lete (ki)*– and obligatorily, if my suggested derivation sketched in Figure 1 is accepted, in the Present tense of nonstative predicates–and with *apre* and *pur.*

Leaving morphosyntax aside, it may be noted that the semantics of the RC verbal system are also basically "French," in that the primary distinctions are temporal (Present, Past, Future), with aspectual/modal distinctions in a secondary role. A very clear example of this is the fact that progressive aspect does not have to be obligatorily marked by *etr apre* (etc.), since progressivity is inherent in the Present and the Past tenses.

I have explicitly stated that I am not attempting to deal here with the rampant variation in the RC verbal system, since to do so is at present impossible. What I have described is nonetheless the "core" system of RC, with "Creole" and "Frenchified" features duly noted. I have no direct evidence at all that the "Creole" features are (or are not) remnants of a now lost basilectal variety of RC, but there is evidence that the "core" system of RC has been in existence, relatively unchanged, since the beginning of the eighteenth century. I return to this in A6.2. In any case, there is no variety of RC today whose verbal system resembles, except superficially, the way in which the Isle de France Creole system operates (A2 below). The similarities are of form far more than of function or semantics.

As was pointed out at the beginning of this chapter, I am not claiming complete accuracy of detail in the data adduced in support of my assertion that Reunion Creole "works" in the way I have described. I am claiming that the picture, in its overall lines, is an accurate and not a misleading one, and that it is consistent with all the data currently available in published form in primary sources since at least 1884 (Focard).[7]

NOTES

1. *Sa* 'that' sometimes occurs as subject in sentences from which the Present tense copula *le* has been omitted:

sa ê bug fite 'that is one cunning fellow'
sa la sias, m i di au 'that is really bad luck (lit., 'diarrhea'), I tell you'

(sentences from Chaudenson 1974:360). I suspect that specific intonation patterns are used here to convey the emphasis of these sentences.
2. This analysis has another defect from the point of view of any theory of language which does not admit of unrecoverable deletions, since neither *le* nor *k* is recoverable here.
3. I am grateful to M. Carayol (personal communication) for confirmation regarding modern RC (Fourcade 1976 is a reprint of material originally published in 1930).
4. My inconsistent use of the forms 'will', 'shall', 'won't', 'shan't', 'would', and 'should' need not distract readers, whose own usage is quite likely to be different with respect to these items. The glosses given here are no more than guides, and the specification of the RC item being glossed (Definite future, in this case) allows an unambiguous reading of the RC sentence in each case.
5. *Kalime,* a type of bamboo indigenous to Reunion, see Chaudenson (1974:911).
6. By "French" analogues, I do not of course mean "Standard French." Cf. A6.5.
7. Sauzier (1904) gives 1885 rather than 1884 for Focard's work. According to Vintilă-Rădulescu (1976:179), Focard was also published separately in Saint-Denis in 1885, whence, no doubt, the date given by Sauzier (and repeated by other writers).

A2
The Predicate in Isle de France Creole

There have been a number of recent studies of Isle de France Creole (IdeFC) syntax. These include the works of Baker (1972) on Mauritian Creole (MC), Bollée (1977a) and Corne (1977a) on Seychelles Creole (SC), Corne and Stein (1979) on Rodrigues Creole (RoC), Papen (1978b) on all of these including Chagos Creole. There have also been a number of shorter studies on various specific areas of syntax (e.g., Corne 1977c, Moorghen 1975, Papen 1975). All these studies claim, implicitly or explicitly, that IdeFC has well-defined syntactic classes such as nouns, verbs, adjectives, and so on. This approach overlooks a crucial fact about IdeFC, which is the multifunctionality of lexical items.

The major result of this oversight is to make IdeFC grammar look much more like French than the facts actually warrant, and to hide its essential similarity with Creole languages of other lexical bases. As a corollary, of course, the essential *dis*similarity of Reunion Creole and IdeFC is also hidden. Minor, but serious, results are that the same lexical item has to be categorized in a number of different ways (e.g., as noun, adjective, and verb in the case of, say, *lager* 'fight, dispute; fighting; to fight; fought'), and a number of distributional and semantic facts are inadequately accounted for.

In IdeFC, it is the inherent meaning of lexical items that is basic, rather than the parts-of-speech categories typical of languages like French. The use of a given lexical item in multiple grammatical functions is a general phenomenon in Creole languages, as in many other languages, a relatively strict categorization into parts of speech being more an Indo-European phenomenon than a general one. The semantic features peculiar to a given lexical item may exclude it as a general rule from certain grammatical functions, but the fact remains that this item will not be excluded in principle from any other function appropriate to its meaning.[1]

A2.1 Predicates

The predicate head in IdeFC may consist of a single lexical item, or it may consist of an entire phrase. The predicate head may be preceded by a number of morphemes. These are of four types. In SC, but not in MC or RoC, there is the subject *reprise* marked by *i* (Corne 1974-75, 1977a:35-43; cf. also note 3 to A5 and Baker's remarks in B3.2.2). In IdeFC generally, the negator *pa* precedes particles which mark tense and aspect. These are:

ti 'Past/Anterior'   *pu, a, va, ava* 'Future/Irrealis'
fin, in, n 'Completive'   *ape, pe* 'Progressive'
fek 'Immediate Completion, to have just'

The particles occur either alone or in various combinations. They co-occur with the fourth type of preposed morphemes which consists of a small subset of adverbial elements (see A2.5 for details and discussion).

The following sentences illustrate a wide range of elements functioning as the head of the predicate (in each example, the head is boldface):

(SC) *i ti* **ran** *mua mô larzâ* 'he gave me back my money'
(SC) *zot ava* **al** *lekol* 'they will go to school'
(SC) *i ti* **pli ris** *ki mua* 'he was richer than I'
(SC) *i a n* **tro mir** *pur nu mâz li* 'it will be too ripe for us to eat'
(SC) *mô papa ti ê* **bô peser** 'my father was a good fisherman'
(SC) *i n* **ler** *pur nu ale* 'it is time for us to go'
(SC) *i ti* **lekol** 'he was at school'
(SC) *pa ti* **mua** *ki n fer sa* 'it was not I who did that'
(SC) *deme suar, mô pa pu* **la** 'tomorrow evening, I shan't be there'
(SC) *sa masin ti* **pur Msie Karl** 'the/that car used to be Mr. Carl's'

Predicates in IdeFC fall into at least three semantic categories. These are State, Process (or change of state), and Action. The subject of an active predicate is, in general, an Agent (or, if inanimate, an Instrument, but I shall use only the term Agent here). Process predicates imply a change in the state or condition of the subject, while state predicates establish an equational relation between the subject and themselves. State and process predicates have nonagentive subjects of several kinds (Beneficiaries, Experiencers, Patients, and so on). There are other possibilities as well. For example, in a sentence such as:

(SC) *labutik i ferm siz-er* 'the shop closes at six o'clock'

the sentence is active: something happens at six o'clock. In fact, as we shall see, the lexical item *ferm* 'close' is marked as active by the loss of its final vowel. And yet the lexical item *labutik* 'shop' cannot be said to be an Agent, anymore than it is in the following:

(SC) *labutik i ferme ozordi* 'the shop is closed today'

where the sentence is stative.

These semantic categories are not solely the result of semantic features pertaining to given lexical items (or phrases) appearing as the Head of the predicate. A given lexeme may be active in one predicate, processive in another, and stative in yet a third, interacting with the surface subject on the one hand, and with the particles and other material in the predicate on the other, to give rise to the meaning of the sentence.

Before I proceed to illustrate these concepts in action, so to speak, it will be helpful to digress briefly to examine the question of the Copula in IdeFC.

A2.2 The Notorious Underlying Copula

In several of the sentences cited in the preceding section, the English gloss contains a form, in the appropriate person and tense, of the verb 'to be':

(SC) *i ti lekol* 'he was at school'
(SC) *i a n tro mir pur nu mâz li* 'it will be too ripe for us to eat'

and the others. In these sentences, there is no trace of any item which corresponds functionally to the English copula.

In certain contexts, a form *ete* occurs, which at first flush seems to gloss as 'be'. In interrogative sentences:

(SC) *kot u liv (i ete)?* 'where is your book?'
(SC) *ki Zâ ti ete?* 'what was John (i.e., his job/status/etc. at that time)?'
(SC) *ki u (ete)?* 'who are you?'

including indirect interrogation:

(SC) *mô pa kone lekel (i ete)* 'I don't know which one it is'
(SC) *i môtre ki mayer Sesel pu ete ê zur*
'it shows what Seychelles will be like one day'
(SC) *râtre âkor dâ dife, koma u ti ete avâ*
'go back into the fire again, like you were before'[2]
(SC) *môtre mua koma serpâ ti ete dâ sa dife*
'show me how the snake was, (when it was) in the fire' (see note 2)

In sentences including the locative *(a)kot* 'where?, where':

(MC) *akot to pu ete?* 'where will you be?'
(MC) *akot li fin kapav ete?* 'where can he have been?'
(SC) *i n al kot lerua ti ete* 'he went where the king was'

And finally in Comparative sentences:

(SC) *i pli kuyô ki u (ete)* 'he is more stupid than you (are)'
(SC) *i ris mem degre ki nu (ete)* 'he is as rich as us (as we are)'
(SC) *i muês kuyô ki u (ete)* 'he is less stupid than you (are)'

Let me first dispose of possible sources of misunderstanding. The *i* preceding *ete* in two of the above examples is the subject *reprise* peculiar to modern SC (mentioned in A2.1), and is irrelevant to the present discussion. In some of the SC sentences given here, *ete* is noted as being optionally present or not: where there is a difference in meaning, this appears to be parallel to, if not the same as, the presence versus the absence of the verb 'to be' in the English glosses of those sentences. For practical purposes, I propose to ignore this difference. Note, however, the occurrence in MC of what may be called "truculent" questions:

(MC) *ki tua?* 'who the hell do you think you are?'
(MC) *ki tua pur to môtre mua sa?* 'who are *you* to show me that?'

but these are limited to the "universal present" and are manifestly a (stylistic) variant of the basic MC pattern. In the SC sentences given above, note that the optionality of *ete* is restricted to those cases where no preposed particle occurs.

A widespread line of reasoning concerning such sentences, and the question of the copula generally, goes something like this: these sentences (with *ete*) suggest that IdeFC has an underlying copula which has been exposed VP-finally (not prepausally, as shown by the two sentences from Neumann 1978, for example) as the result of the application of movement rules or, in the case of comparatives, by coreferential deletion rules. That is to say, one supposes an underlying structure such as:

/Zâ ti ETE lekol/ 'John Past Copula school'

(with the notion of Locative introduced in some manner or other). This string will then produce either:

(IdeFC) *Zâ ti lekol* 'John was at school'

or, by interrogation bearing on Location (Interrogative proform *(a)kot?*), it will be transformed into:

(IdeFC) *(a)kot Zâ ti ete?* 'where was John?'

This approach supposes that the nonappearance of *ete* is due to relatively low-level deletion rules. But note that there are at least two things wrong with this approach, which has been espoused for IdeFC by Bollée (1977a), Corne (1977a, etc.), and Papen (1978b), and for Creole French generally by Valdman (1973, 1978a). First, it supposes that the literally overwhelming majority of "copulative" sentences in IdeFC which do NOT contain any surface copula (type: *mo malad* 'I am ill') are in some way less basic than the minority of sentences which do contain *ete*. Second, the recoverability criterion for deletion rules is not met, in that there are no cases where *mo ete malad 'I am ill' is a conceivable IdeFC sentence. Valdman (1978a:235-36) argues that the American Creole French forms ye, se, and (if we may legitimately refer to nothing as being a "form") zero are contextually conditioned allomorphs of an underlying copula.[3] That is, Copula → ∅ in certain contexts. This notion and that of a low-level deletion of an underlying copula seem to be equivalent. It is the first of these two objections that seems to me to be the more important. The supposition that mo malad is less basic, because of the operation of an ete deletion rule of some sort, than the highly restricted set of contexts that do contain VP-final ete, seems to be indefensible.

One can advance a number of possible reasons for the adoption of a view which, as presented here, is clearly distorted. One is the more or less implicit assumption, which I now believe to be quite erroneous, that IdeFC is some kind of "French." This assumption has of course been bolstered and encouraged by the theory of Indian Ocean Creole "genesis" propounded by R. Chaudenson (1974), cf. A6.3. If IdeFC is assumed to be some special kind of French, then the item ete can be seen, in those contexts where it occurs, as the reflex of the naturally occurring French verb être in similar contexts, and the lack of ete in mo malad-type sentences must in consequence be seen as a deletion, i.e., a loss. A second reason, which in fact derives from the first, underlies the PS rules put forward by Corne (1977a) and Papen (1978b). If IdeFC is "French," then it ought to be describable in the same—or similar—terms; thus, the adoption of the framework used by Dubois and Dubois-Charlier (1970) for French gave rise to PS rules for IdeFC such as the following:

$$S \rightarrow NP + VP$$
$$VP \rightarrow Aux \mid VG$$
$$VG \rightarrow \left\{ \begin{array}{l} Copula + \left\{ \begin{array}{l} NP \\ AP \\ PP \end{array} \right\} \\ V + (NP) + (PP) \end{array} \right\}$$

This particular layout is from Corne (1977a:61), but is in essence if not in detail identical to the PS rules given by Papen. This approach is no doubt, as pointed out by Todd (1979a), an old-fashioned one, even within a transformational-generative framework. But any framework that forces a categorization into parts of speech will have a straitjacket effect: the parts of speech are but artifacts of the rules themselves, and are quite inappropriate to the language I am describing here.

The fact of the matter is that IdeFC does not have an underlying copula, and that no useful purpose is achieved by postulating one. I return to ete in A2.3 below.

A2.3 Illustrations of the IdeFC Predicate System

I shall illustrate the IdeFC system in operation by examining very briefly four different sets of data.

The particle *fin* (and its variants *in* and *n*) represents the notion of completion; it may be referred to as the Completive marker. If the subject of the sentence is an Agent, *fin* has a perfective sense, and the predicate (or, more precisely, the sentence itself) will be active:

(SC) *mô n mâz lavian* 'I have eaten the meat'
(SC) *mô ti n mâz lavian* 'I had eaten the meat'
(SC) *ler u ava n repar u loto* 'when you (will) have repaired your car'
(SC) *i ti a n bez mua* 'he would have hit me'

In these sentences, the lexemes *mâze* 'eat', *repare* 'repair', *beze* 'hit' have all lost their final vowel *-e*. This also marks these lexical items as being active, as we shall see in A3. Note, however, that *mâze* and *beze* are not *necessarily* used in this active, verbal manner, as the next illustrative sentence will show (as far as I am aware, *repare* is indeed restricted to "verbal" and "adjectival" uses); *mâze* is used in a "nominal" role, as the subject. Consider the following two sentences:

(SC) *nu mâze i n pare komela* 'our food/meal is ready now'
(SC) *i a n tro tar* 'it will be too late'

Here, the subject is nonagentive, and the presence of the completive gives an overall stative reading to the sentence. In both examples, and in all similar ones, the predicate head contains a lexeme whose conceptual definition includes the idea of possible modification over a given time span. In other terms, these lexical items may be said to be, by virtue of the semantic traits peculiar to them, inherently (or potentially) processive. Such lexemes in such sentences, used with *fin*, have a meaning close to that of 'to become' + their own meaning. Thus, in *nu mâze i n pare komela*, we have the idea of a meal which, not ready beforehand, has come to be so now; in *i a n tro tar*, we have the idea of a state which will come about, which will have become true, at some prospective future moment (marked by *a*). These sentences contain what I originally labeled as [-durative] statives (Corne 1977a: 61). Further examples are:

(SC)   *i n ler pur nu vini* 'it is time for us to come'
(RoC) *misie la in biê kôtâ* 'the gentleman is well satisfied'
(SC)   *loto i n kuver, koma u n dir mua*
       'the car is covered (now), as you ordered me'
(SC)   *sa tapaz ti n sitâ terib* . . . 'the noise was (= had become) so terrible . . .'
(SC)   *ler i n ase* 'when he has had enough'

These sentences, the predicate (head) of which we may consider to be processive without losing sight of their overall stative sense conferred by the use of *fin*, can now be compared to the following:

(SC) *lerua i bet* 'the king is stupid'
(SC) *tu le zur, nu mâze i pare dâ pti midi*
'every day, our meal is ready toward midday'
(MC) *normalmâ, tapisri kole lor miray ar lakol*
'usually, wallpaper is stuck to the wall with paste'

In these cases, *fin* does not occur. The subject is still nonagentive, and the sentences are still stative. The point here is that the state denoted by the predicate is a "permanent" one, and so *fin* is superfluous. These are the [+durative] statives of Corne (1977a:61). But in the "processive" predicates that we have seen above, the state is not a permanent one, and so *fin* must be used.

The second set of data concerns the Progressive marker *ape* (and its variant *pe*). This particle marks the noncompletive nature of an event, or the extended or ongoing duration of an event or a series of events: "l'action est envisagée dans son déroulement" (Moorghen 1975:19). This fact is not always immediately obvious from the English gloss. If the subject of the sentence is agentive, *ape* produces a clearly progressive, ongoing meaning;

(SC) *i pu pe mâz âkor* 'he will be eating again'
(SC) *zot ti ape fer bonavini* 'they were flirting'
(MC) *mo pe lasas zako* 'I am hunting monkeys'

In the following sentences, the subject is nonagentive, and the sentences are processive, as opposed to the active ones we have just seen. In some cases, a 'be . . .-ing' gloss is appropriate:

(MC) *mo pe deperi* 'I am losing weight'
(SC) *mô pe oblize fer sa* 'I am being obliged/forced to do it'
(SC) *dimun pe mor tu le zur* 'people are dying every day'

In others, the sense is better rendered by 'be getting' or by various paraphrases:

(SC) *mô pe dakor ek li* 'I am beginning/coming/getting to agree with him'
(RoC) *madam ape zalu* 'the lady is getting jealous'
(SC) *mô pe fatige tan sa tapaz* 'I am getting tired of hearing that noise'
(SC) *mô pe â-koler* 'I am getting angry'

and sometimes there appear to be language-specific differences of meaning:

(SC) *mô pe kôtâ li* 'I am coming/beginning/getting to love her'
(MC) *mo pe kôtâ li* 'I'm crazy about her (at this very moment)'
(SC) *mô ape lafê* 'I am getting hungry'
(MC) *mo pe fê* 'I'm starving, ravenously hungry'

But in all cases, *(a)pe* has its semantic value of Progressive. This point may perhaps be rephrased thus: there are no cases in IdeFC where underlying Progressive is not marked by *(a)pe* on the surface (in direct contrast to the Reunion Creole situation, see A1.6 above). This particle does not occur in stative sentences, the notions of Progressive and of an already achieved state being semantically incompatible.

The third set of data can be disposed of very rapidly. The prefix *re-* is one of a number of ways of expressing the notion of repetition, of doing something again (cf. Baker 1972:102, Papen 1978b:235). As might be expected, it occurs in active sentences:

(SC) *i a re-rul li avek u* 'he will roll it back to you again'
(MC) *li ti re-lav so lame* 'he washed his hands again'

and in processive ones:

(MC) *u pe re-malad âkor* 'you are falling ill yet again'

but not with stative ones.

The fourth set of data concerns the item *ete*, which was abandoned in A2.2. In that section of the discussion, I rejected the idea of an underlying copula in IdeFC, but did not assign any particular status to *ete*. As we have seen, *ete* occurs as the final element of the VP in Interrogatives, Comparatives, and Locative Relatives. We have also seen that in IdeFC generally, the aspect/tense particles precede the head of the predicate, and that this head may consist of almost any lexical item (or items) at all, or of an Adjective Phrase, a Prepositional Phrase, a Noun Phrase (see the examples in A2.1). The distribution of these particles depends on semantic criteria, including that of Stative (e.g., the nonoccurrence of *ape* in stative sentences; the use of *fin* to convert processives to statives). To account for *ete*, one need simply state that the notions of Location, Existence, or Equivalence are represented by the lexical item *ete* (which may be thought of as the stative pro-form par excellence) in just those cases where movement rules (WH-fronting, principally, but also coreferential deletion rules in the case of Comparatives) have shifted other lexical items capable of representing these notions. Let us take as an example the sentence:

(SC) *u liv i laba* 'your book is over there'

The lexeme *laba* represents, among other specific items such as 'that particular' position/place, the notions of Stative and Location. This may be crudely represented as:

Patient + non-Past + *i* + State + Location

wherein *laba* is a lexical item representing the last two semantic elements of State + Location. If we now wish to inquire as to the location of the Patient, the last notion, that of Location, is combined with a new element, that of Interrogation. This produces in IdeFC the lexical item *(a)kot?*, just as it produces *where?* in English. After fronting of this interrogative element (a perfectly usual interrogative procedure in IdeFC), we have:

(a)kot? + Patient + non-Past + *i* + State

To return to the SC example, this produces:

(SC) *kot u liv i ete?* 'where is your book?'

Now the non-Past is not overtly marked by any preposed particle. So in the context that we have here, [−Past] may be represented in the sentence or not, since the absence of *ti* already, by definition, "marks" the sentence as non-Past. The sentence *kot u liv i ete?* is clearly non-Past. SC, although not MC except as a stylistic variant, allows the optional omission of a surface representation of the semantic notion of State:

(SC) *kot u liv?* 'where is your book?'

(SC has a variant form of *kot*, *oli* 'where?'; *oli* cannot co-occur with any preposed particle, or with *ete*, see Corne 1977a:189). Since there is no preposed particle, and since this sentence is therefore not marked for Past, there is equally no need of any lexical item for the nonexistent non-Past "marker" to be preposed to. But if non-Past is to be overtly represented, *ete* is required, and pronouns must have the appropriate shape:

(SC) *i pli ris ki mua* 'he is richer than me'
(SC) *i pli ris ki mô ete* 'he is richer than I am'

I have already noted that MC appears to exploit this arrangement for stylistic purposes:

(MC) *ki to ete?* 'who are you?'

(MC) *ki tua?* 'who in hell are you? who do you think you are?'

but this may merely be an extension or a development of a preexisting distinction reflected in our two SC sentences *i pli ris ki mua/ki mô ete*. In direct contrast, where the context requires overt representation of Past, this is achieved with the particle *ti*. This is itself a preposed particle, and cannot carry stress. It requires a stressable lexical item before which to be preposed. *Ete* fills the stress requirement, and must obligatorily occur:

(SC) *kot u liv ti ete?* 'where was your book?'

but not **kot ti u liv?*, **kot u liv ti?*, or **ti kot u liv?* This is also the case when any other particle occurs.

The above four sets of data show the system in operation. The cases of *fin* and *ape* have been chosen as illustrations because their semantics are somewhat hard to deduce from the currently available descriptions of IdeFC, *re-* because its co-occurrence with *malad* is extremely instructive, and *ete* because the approach adopted here allows a coherent description of what *ete* is and what it does, without calling it a "copula." Together, all four sets show that the syntactic and semantic facts of IdeFC can be handled without any need to postulate an underlying copula in sentences of the *mo malad* 'I am ill' type.[4]

A2.4 The Form *se* in IdeFC

Let us now examine briefly the form *se* 'it is'. Focused ("cleft") sentences involve left dislocation of a constituent and embedding by relativization. Thus, from:

(SC) *divâ i n kas ban brâs* 'the wind has broken the branches'

by left dislocation of the subject (i.e., by focusing on *divâ*) we obtain:

(SC) *divâ, ki n kas ban brâs* 'it is the wind that broke/has broken the branches'

and of the object:

(SC) *ban brâs, ki divâ i n kase* 'it is the branches that the wind has broken'

The focused element is always the head of a stative predicate, marked for Past if appropriate:

(SC) *pa ti ê katiolo ki n disparet, ti ê kanot lapes*
  'it wasn't a dinghy that had disappeared, it was a fishing boat'

while the non-Past is unmarked:

(SC) *kot sô buldu mem, ki i dormi komela*
'it is at his girl's place that he sleeps nowadays'

The non-Past may however be optionally marked (in SC) by the subject pronoun *i* in affirmative "impersonal" sentences except with clock times (where *i* is obligatory). It is obligatorily unmarked with negatives:

(SC) *(i) êposib pur tuy mua* 'it is impossible to kill me'
(SC) *u kone i truaz-er e dmi?* 'do you realize it's three-thirty?'
(SC) *pa fasil pur koz ek Mari* 'it is not easy to talk to Mary'

The use of *se* appears to correspond to non-Past in affirmative sentences, since **se pa, *pa se, *se ti, *ti se* do not occur. The form *se* is well attested in IdeFC, although some speakers consider it to be "French" rather than Creole. The following sentences illustrate the patterns observed so far in SC:

(SC) *se ki mô ule fer u plezir* 'it is because I want to please you'
(SC) *larâzma(,) se larâzma* 'a deal is a deal'
(SC) *sa voyaz, se Lina ki n plere* 'this time, it is Lina who cried'
(SC) *u napa nariê pur dir âkor? nô, se tu*
'you have nothing further to say? No, that is all'

While *se* manifestly derives from French *c'est* 'it is', its distribution in IdeFC suggests that it is a surface representation of the semantic units [−Past] and [−Negative] in the context (principally although not exclusively) of focusing, rather than a surface form of a (nonexistent) copula. It is not inconceivable that the status of *se* is different from speaker to speaker. Let us suppose that it is indeed, as some speakers feel it to be, a French "influence." We have seen that the non-Past is generally unmarked, while the Past is marked by *ti*. The introduction of French *c'est*, IdeFC *se*, by French/Creole bilinguals, either now or at some time(s) in the past, does not distort the Creole system at all. There is a gap there, sometimes (in SC) filled by *i*, but usually unfilled. The form *se* can therefore be adopted by monolingual Creole speakers as an optional non-Past marker which will itself be stylistically marked as "prestigious." For bilinguals, meanwhile, it quite possibly retains its French structure of subject + copula. Note that since *ti* is an overt Past marker, the introduction of *c'était* 'it was' would clearly introduce a competing form. I have not yet observed the form **sete* either in the field or in written texts.

A2.5 Tense and Aspect in IdeFC

The predicate system of IdeFC is based on distinctions which are aspectual rather than temporal, these distinctions being handled by preposed particles.

The particle *ti* combines a temporal notion, Past, with an aspectual notion, Anterior. This latter notion accounts for two facts: first, the "meaning" of *ti* followed by the Future/Irrealis markers *pu* or *a*, see below; and second, in narrative material such as folktales, *ti* occurs with stative predicate heads, while nonstatives tend to occur with no particle (cf. Bickerton 1975:Chapter 2 for an explanation of why in systems which have the feature Anterior, past-reference nonstatives are unmarked, while past-reference statives receive Anterior marking). However, the tendency for past-reference nonstatives to be unmarked is, in IdeFC, no more than a tendency; an examination of published texts of various kinds rapidly reveals considerable variation, some speakers (or writers) marking all past-reference predicates. The nature of the material (e.g., didactic as opposed to narrative) may also turn out to be significant (see Waite, forthcoming). For convenience, I refer to *ti* as the marker of the Past, since that is what it does mark much of the time, but its Anterior marking role is important and must be kept in mind.

An unmarked predicate head, apart from the case just described, conveys the universal or habitual present:

(SC) *mô mâz lavian* 'I eat meat (i.e., I am not a vegetarian)'
(SC) *pa fiy ki deman mariaz ê garsô, me garsô ki deman mariaz fiy*
      'it is not the girl who asks a man to marry, but the man who asks the girl'

Future time is envisaged in two ways. There is an Indefinite Future (or Prospective) which is marked by *ava, va, a*. These markers may, for the purposes of this work, be considered as being free variants. In fact, there are minor distributional differences, and *va* tends not to be used in SC where it is now obsolescent. (Cf. Baker 1972:109, Bollée 1977a:57, Corne 1977a:103.) A co-occurrence restriction seems to be that these markers tend not to be used in negative sentences, although this is not true for all speakers (Corne 1977a:104-5). In negative sentences, the tendency is for the Definite Future marker *pu* to occur. The Definite and Indefinite Future are clearly and consistently distinguished in MC (Baker 1972:109-10). In SC, the contrast is at best vestigial, and it is *a* which is Definite and *pu* which is Indefinite (Bollée 1977a:57-58; Corne 1977a:103-5). Both forms express also the semantic notion of Irrealis, which includes futures, conditionals, and other modes which indicate that the event (or state) has not really happened (yet):

(SC) *mô ti kuar i pu al a-pie*
      'I thought he would come/was going to come on foot'
(SC) *i pa ti kone ki i pu fer*
      'he did not know what he would/was going to do'

In these two examples, *pu* occurs with no other particle in the subordinate clause, the main clause being marked for Past. But *ti* may combine with *pu, ava, va, a,* to express counterfactual conditions or the Future in the Past:

(SC) *si u ti aste lavian, i ti a mâze* 'if you bought meat, he would eat (it)'
(MC) *mo ti va ale, me lapli fin tôbe*
 'I would have gone/was going to go, but it rained'
(SC) *mô pa ti kuar si mô ti pu uar li*
 'I didn't think I would/was going to see him'

For the very limited data available at present concerning RoC, see Corne and Stein (1979:72-73); RoC does not appear to be significantly different from MC and SC in this respect.

As has been seen in A2.3 above, the notion of Completion plays an important role. It is marked by *fin, in, n.* These are, like *ava, va, a,* not quite in free variation, but they may be so considered here. The form *fin* is obsolescent in SC, being usually replaced by *in, n* (cf. Corne 1977a:113-15 for details). In MC, *fin* and *in* are essentially in free variation, while *n* is a contextually conditioned variant (Baker 1972:108). All three forms occur in RoC (Corne and Stein 1979:73). In IdeFC generally, the lexical item *fini* 'finish' may co-occur with the Completive markers:

(SC) *i n fini mâz sô banan* 'he has finished eating his banana'

The Progressive, i.e., the notion of ongoing action or progression, is marked by *ape* and *pe*. Both are used in SC, while in MC *ape* is becoming obsolescent. In RoC, the archaic form *apre* is still marginally extant, alongside *ape* and *pe*.

Immediate Completion, 'to have just', is marked by *fek*. The status of this marker appears to vary. Baker (1972:117, note 4) points out that some MC speakers allow *fek* to occur alone:

(MC) *Zan fek sorti* 'Jeanne just left'

while for others it occurs in an adverbial kind of role (cf. the "auxiliary adverbs" mentioned below):

(MC) *Zan in fek sorti* 'Jeanne has just left'

In SC, *fek* may be characterized somewhat differently, and there appears to be a distinction between *fek* and *n fek:*

(SC) *i fek al labutik, i pâkor returne*
 'he has just gone to the shop, he isn't back yet'

(SC) *i n fek al labutik, u âvi i al âkor?*
'he has just been to the shop (and has since returned), do you want him to go again'

(Corne 1977a:111)

Some MC speakers allow *fek fin* in lieu of the more usual MC/SC *(fi)n fek*. (Cf. also Bollée 1977a:59.)

As has been indicated, the preposed particles can combine. There has been some disagreement in the literature concerning which combinations may occur (see Waite 1981). Ignoring minor differences in the hierarchical categorization of the particles from language to language or from speaker to speaker (cf. *fek* above), it may be stated that some twenty-six combinations of up to four particles can occur. Two-particle combinations are quite usual. Three-particle combinations are relatively rare; there are occasional attestations in texts dating from 1880 to the present (cf. Table 15 in B3.2.5), and three-particle combinations do occur sometimes in spontaneous discourse (with *ti a n* being the most commonly occurring of these). Four-particle combinations are possible, and they produce acceptable, grammatical, and meaningful sentences (in MC and SC, to my personal knowledge, and I have no reason to believe that RoC would be any different). Such combinations of four particles are, however, extremely rare in actual usage, and seem to reflect not what people actually say, or even want to say, but rather what they *can* say when forced to do so by circumstances. I hesitate to suggest that the sole circumstances which produce such strings of particles are those engendered by a linguist grilling consultants. I suspect that such combinations would indeed occur if/when speakers found themselves under compulsion to express nuances in formal situations (such as the writing of serious literature, or the use of the language in a legal or legislative context); a body of usage would thus be constituted and subsequently perpetuated through the need to express more complex shades of meaning. Be this as it may, the three- and four-particle combinations elicited from consultants show clearly that the potential for such a development exists, and that when they do combine, the particles occur in a fixed order. This is *ti + ava/pu + fin + ape/fek*. Thus, any combination will select from this inventory, and the particles chosen will occur in the respective order. Examples are: *ti pe, ti pu, ti ava, ti n, ti fek, n fek, a n, ti a n*, etc.:

(SC) *mô ti a n marie, si mô pa ti mizer*
'I would have married, if I were not poor'

As the subordinate clause of this last example shows, the negator *pa* precedes all other particles:

(SC) *i pa ti âkor arive* 'he hadn't yet arrived'

(SC) *mô pa n uar person* 'I have seen no one'
(SC) *pa gaŷ atrape!* 'don't get caught'

There are two "exceptions" to this rule. First, a number of fixed expressions retain a reflex of the "French" word order (cf. B3.2.4):

(SC) *mô k(r)uar-pa* 'I don't think so'
(SC) *i ve-pa repon* 'he does not (wish to) reply'
(SC) *se-pa koma zot dir* '(I) don't know the word for it'
(RoC) *li zet si-pa en ti ros* 'he throws something like a pebble'
(RoC) *si-pa ki si-sa* '(I) don't know what it is'

Second, the element *anu* marks the first person plural imperative:

(SC) *anu plis koko* 'let's go and husk coconuts'

Although various writers have classed *anu* as a particle in the sense of *ti*, etc., above (cf. Corne 1970:14; Bollée 1977c:142), its status is clearly different, in that *pa* follows:

(SC) *anu pa desan â-vil* 'let's not go to town'[5]

Neither "exception" need retain our attention here. The basic fact about predicate negation in IdeFC is that the negator *pa* precedes the predicate head and also any other preposed predicate particles that may occur.

Certain "auxiliary adverbs" (Corne 1977a:118-21; = "preverbs," Baker 1972: 110) may occur in combination with the particles. These include: *nepli/napli* 'no longer', *âkor* 'always, still (and expected to terminate soon)', *tuzur, tultâ, tu letâ* 'still (and expected to continue) always, the whole time', *zame* 'never', *deza* 'already', *nek, zis, selma* 'only, always, merely', *mem* 'emphasizer', and perhaps also *sitâ* 'so well', *biê* 'well, really', *osi* 'also', *preski* 'almost'. The distribution and syntax of these elements requires further investigation, but the problem of analysis which they pose does not appear to be germane to the present discussion.

The foregoing is merely a thumbnail sketch of the system, and some detail has been omitted. Note that although I have alluded in passing to the variation that exists within IdeFC, such variation is minor compared to that which exists in Reunion. This is not to say that it can be ignored, and I shall have occasion to return briefly to this question in due course (A7). For the moment, the essential point to note is this: the IdeFC preposed particle system differs from that of other varieties of Creole French (ignoring RC) in two important respects. It contains the Completive marker *fin*, and this marker is fully integrated into the tense/aspect marking system. It also contains two Future markers, *pu* and *a(va)*, both of which have an Irrealis scope. As Bickerton (1981:Chapter 2) suggests, the inclusion of *fin* and *pu* into Aux has led to a complication and expansion of what is, or rather was, basically a "classic" Creole system: Anterior + Irrealis + non-Punctual (= Progressive in IdeFC).

A2.6 Summary and Conclusions

In summary then, IdeFC has a predicate system which is primarily aspectually oriented, with tense as a secondary concern. All distinctions of aspect and tense are handled by means of preposed particles. These may occur in a large number of different combinations of up to four particles, although two-particle combinations are the general rule, three-particle combinations less frequently occurring, and four-particle combinations somewhat suspect from the point of view of actual usage. These particles precede the head of the predicate. The interaction of the particles, the subject, the head, and other material in the predicate results in the interpretation of the sentence, in which the notions of State, Process, and Action are fundamental. There is no copula. In certain syntactic environments, a stative (and morphologically invariant) lexeme *ete* occurs. In "impersonal" sentences, an element *se* corresponds to a non-Past non-Negative predicate marker. Lexical items are (ignoring minor sandhi phenomena) morphologically invariant, apart from the operation of a rule of Final Vowel Truncation which will be examined in some detail in A3, but whose semantic dimension has already been alluded to.

As the examples given illustrate clearly, there is a certain correlation between the meaning of any given lexical item and the semantic categories of Action, Process, and State. A word such as *lapes* 'fish(ing)', whose conceptual definition includes that of an activity, may be grammaticalized as the head of the predicate in an active sentence:

(SC) *nu ti ava ape lapes si lapli pa ti tôbe*
'we would have been fishing if it had not rained'

whereas *peser* 'fisherman' is a lexeme which designates a person who performs the activity of fishing and in consequence can appear only in nominal types of environments, as in *ê bô peser* 'a good fisherman'. Such a noun phrase may of course occur as the head of the predicate, but usually only in a stative sentence:

(SC) *mô papa ti ê bô peser* 'my father was a good fisherman'

Similarly, a word such as *sagrê* 'regret':

(MC) *mo pu sagrê tua* 'I shall be sorry thinking of you'
(MC) *en grâ sagrê* 'a great chagrin, regret'

Not all lexical items have this kind of "syntactic liberty," however. For example, let us take the concept of 'guard(ing)'. In an active sentence, the lexeme *gard(e)* will be used:

(MC) *li pu gard mo zardê* 'he will guard my garden'

but in a stative one, the lexeme *gardiê* is called for:

(MC) *li pu gardiê mo zardê* 'he will be the guardian of my garden'

Compare now the following three uses of *bat(e)* 'beat':

(SC) *baba i n bat a-ter* 'the baby has fallen to the ground'
(SC) *i n gaŷ bate ek larul* 'he got beaten by the ocean swell'
(SC) *sa bate ki i n gaŷe ek larul* 'the/that beating he got from the ocean swell'

In the first of these, the sentence is active: the subject is agentive, and the final *-e* of *bate* has been deleted. In the second sentence, *bate* may be considered as processive: the subject is not an Agent, but rather an Experiencer, and the construction with *gaŷe* (which exists in all IdeFC languages, but which is most developed in SC and, on present information, least so in MC) is precisely a procedure for using in a processive sense lexical items which are more usually (as is indeed the case with *bate*) used in an active one (cf. A5.1); note that the sentence as a whole is stative as a result of the use of *(fi)n*. In the third sentence, *bate* occurs as the subject; its co-occurrence with *sa* 'the, this, that' shows that it is here being used nominally, and there is a fairly clear relation between nouns and states. To sum up, lexical items as predicate heads occur in an overlapping distribution among the semantic categories of Action, Process, and State (cf. Chafe 1970, Mourelatos 1978).

The multifunctionality of lexical items in IdeFC does not of course mean that lexical items do not belong to definable classes (cf. Voorhoeve 1980). There are, for example, form classes, such as those lexemes which are subject to the truncation of their final vowel (see A3). There are undoubtedly broad co-occurrence classes as well (e.g., lexemes co-occurring with *ape* and/or with *fin* and/or with *re-*), although the results (for French, but their application is far wider) reported recently by Gross (1979) suggest that the precise definition of such classes may be impossible. Nonetheless, the attempt needs to be made.

None of the facts adduced here are controversial. All are abundantly documented in the published literature from Baissac (1880) to the present day. Only the analysis of them offered here is "new."[6] Not only is it new, it also represents more accurately than any other analysis offered to date the way in which the IdeFC predicate system actually functions.

NOTES

1. Many striking examples of this phenomenon in Haitian Creole French (including proper nouns used as verbs) are given by Bentolila (1978). He refers to the phenomenon as "syntactic liberty." Cf. also the brief comparison of Cameroonian and SC in Todd (1979a).

2. Sentences from a Radio Seychelles story in Neumann (1978:152).

3. Note that while *ye* is the analogue of IdeFC *ete*, *se* is not the equivalent of IdeFC *se* 'it is', which is discussed below.

4. I am unconvinced that the underlying copula approach has any more validity for American Creole French than it has for IdeFC. Valdman (1978a:235-36) argues for an underlying copula in Haitian Creole, but ignores what seems to me to be an important paper by Saint Jacques Fauquenoy (1971).

5. Irrelevant to the description of IdeFC, but germane to the wider aim of contrasting and comparing IdeFC and RC, is the superficially similar RC imperative constructed with *anô/alô*:

(RC) *anô arturn uar* 'let's go back and see'

The placement of *pa* shows that *anô/alô* cannot be considered as a verb:

(RC) *anô asiz pa* 'let's not sit down'

The verb here is *asiz*. Contrast this with IdeFC *anu pa asize* 'id.', where the "verb" (the predicate head) is *asize*. In the RC sentence, *anô/alô* seems to be a particle of some kind.

6. "New" is written advisedly with quotation marks. This analysis was originally inspired by Christie's (1976) reanalysis of the predicate in Dominican Creole French. Until the end of 1978, I adhered to the underlying copula analysis, and saw in IdeFC the word classes of French (cf. the criticism leveled on just this matter by Todd 1979a). A study undertaken at the end of 1978 (McKibbin and Corne 1980) led to a reexamination of this analysis, and the rechecking of a lot of data with native speakers of SC and MC resident in New Zealand. A first attempt to describe the facts from a different point of view, but one which still retains parts-of-speech categories such as verb, adjective, etc., is embodied in Corne 1980 (written in early 1979). A shorter, French-language version of A1 and A2 (Corne 1981) represents my first attempt to present the current analysis.

A3
Final Vowel Truncation in Indian Ocean Creole French

Both Reunion Creole and Isle de France Creole share a curious phenomenon. In both, lexical items which in RC are all verbs and which, purely for convenience, I shall refer to as "verbs" in IdeFC as well, lose their final vowel in certain contexts. The phenomenon is commented on by Baissac (1880:41-42, 54-55, 119), and is mentioned more or less extensively in all recently published descriptions (Corne 1970:17-19, Baker 1972:98-99, for MC; Bollée 1977a:28-32, Corne 1977a:73-88, and 1977b, for SC; Chaudenson 1974:330-32 for RC; nothing significant available on RoC). An exhaustive study of the phenomenon in the MC used by Baissac (1880, 1888) is that of Juliette McKibbin (McKibbin and Corne 1980). The first attempt to deal with this subject on a pan-Indian Ocean Creole basis that I am aware of is the 1975 study by R. Papen (cf. also Papen 1978a, b). This relatively impressive outpouring of ink does not mean, however, that the matter is by any means clearly understood; the fact that the loss of the final vowel in IdeFC might have something to do with the semantic notion of Action is first mooted explicitly as recently as 1979 (Corne 1980), and a very significant fact about the phenomenon in RC–that it is one of the morphosyntactic dimensions of the RC continuum –is mentioned, very briefly, even more recently (Corne 1981). The statement given here is by no means exhaustive, but no important facts have been omitted.

A3.1 Final Vowel Truncation in Isle de France Creole
This area of IdeFC syntax illustrates clearly the role of the semantic categories of Action as opposed to Process and State. We have seen in A2 that some lexical items lose their final vowel. I shall refer to these lexemes as "verbs," but it must be emphasized that this is merely for convenience, as the same "verb" may also occur in quite non-"verbal" roles (cf. the example of *bate* 'beat(ing)' in A2).

A large subclass of "verbs" contains two forms. Stated very generally, such "verbs" have a long form with a final vowel *-e*, and a short form without this vowel. I shall refer to this phenomenon as Final Vowel Truncation (FVT). There are minor differences between MC and SC, and presumably RoC has a number of language-specific features as well, but these differences need not concern us here.

The subclass of "verbs" subject to FVT all end in *-e*, with the exception of *vini* '(be)come' and *sorti/surti* 'go out, leave, come from'. (One other exception may be noted: the "verb" *tiôbo/tiombo* 'seize', invariable in SC, for some MC speakers has a short form *tiom*.) The subclass is morphologically defined: FVT applies only to "verbs" which have at some point in their derivation the phonetic shape (X)VC*e*, i.e., vowel + consonant + vowel. The only consonant cluster which does not prevent FVT from applying is *r*C, but see below. Thus, *zue* 'play', *fie* 'trust', *kalme* 'calm', *promne* 'walk' are not subject to FVT, while *tire* 'pull', *large* 'release', and *tôbe* 'fall' are.

Five simultaneously applying rules account for all cases (cf. Koutsoudas, Sanders and Noll 1974, and Koutsoudas 1978). Rules 1, 3, 4, and on historical grounds Rule 5, are independently motivated. These rules are:

Rule 1: Lenition of syllable-final *r*

$$r \rightarrow : / V\_\_ \left\{ \begin{array}{c} \# \\ C \end{array} \right\}$$

(syllable-final *r* lengthens preceding vowel)

As stated, Rule 1 ignores the exact phonetic detail of diphthongization, and of vowel backing in MC (see Papen 1978a).

Rule 2: Final vowel truncation

$$\begin{array}{cc} V & \rightarrow \quad \emptyset/VC\_\_\#+X \\ [-back] & \quad] \text{Action} \end{array}$$

(a final non-back vowel, i.e., *-e* or *-i*, is deleted when the "verb" belongs to the appropriate class and where it is followed by specified items, symbolized here by X)

This rule requires some discussion. First, it claims that the long forms with *-e/-i* are basic and that the final vowel is deleted from them, rather than the reverse. This can be shown to be the case on distributional grounds, insofar as the long forms: (a) are the citation forms of the lexical items concerned; and (b) occur in a greater number of, and a wider variety of, environments than do the short forms. The "meaning" of Rule 2 is to signal the notion of Action (whence the ad hoc notation] Action). That is, it is as much a semantactic rule as a phonological one. Note that it is not necessary to specify in this rule the fact that only "verbs" are involved. I am using the term "verb" purely as a convenience; certain lexical items (which happen to derive etymologically from French verbs) are marked in the lexicon as being subject to Rule 2—this is signaled here, where relevant to the discussion, by the use of parentheses (*kon(e)* 'know', *don(e)* 'give'). Finally, the symbol X in Rule 2 is merely a shorthand notation for a relatively complex set of syntactic specifications. In spite of the fact that this area of IdeFC syntax has been fairly extensively studied, a few fuzzy areas remain in these specifications. However, it can be stated that Rule 2 applies when the element following the "verb" is a direct constituent of VP (object, dative, locative, another "verb," and various other elements, cf. McKibbin and Corne 1980). In other terms, Rule 2 applies when the following element X falls within the scope of the "verb":

(SC) *mô kon fer sa* 'I know how to do it' ("verb" *kon(e)*)
(SC) *i a don u sô kanot* 'he will give you his boat' (*don(e)*)
(SC) *nu n al lakaz* 'we went to the house' (*al(e)*)
(SC) *i komâs â-koler* 'he begins to get angry' (*komâs(e)*)
(SC) *zot kôtiŷ mâze* 'they continue to eat' (*kôtiŷ(e)*)
(SC) *u pa pu riy âkor ditu* 'you will never laugh again at all' (*riy(e)*)

When the following element is not within the scope of the "verb," or when a pause follows the "verb," Rule 2 does not apply:

(SC) *mô kone (ki) mô fer sa* 'I know that I do it' (*kon(e)*)
(SC) *zame mô ti pâse si ê zur nu pu fase*
  'I never thought that one day we should be annoyed (with each other)'
  (*pâs(e)* + *si*-clause)
(SC) *i sâte â desâdâ* 'he sings while on his way to town' (*sât(e)*)[1]
(SC) *laklos i sone pur dine* 'the bell rings for dinner' (*son(e)*)

Finally, the presence of a semantic unit [+Emphasis] seems to block the application of Rule 2, but since the exact details remain obscure, I shall ignore this here (but cf. A4.1.2 below).

Rule 3: Homorganic stop-nasal assimilation

$$\begin{bmatrix} +\text{cons} \\ +\text{voice} \\ +\text{stop} \end{bmatrix} \rightarrow \begin{bmatrix} +\text{cons} \\ +\text{nas} \end{bmatrix} \bigg/ \begin{bmatrix} -\text{cons} \\ +\text{nas} \end{bmatrix} \underline{} \#$$

(*b, d, g* become *m, n, ng* morpheme-finally after a nasal vowel)

Rule 4: Denasalization

$$\begin{bmatrix} -\text{cons} \\ +\text{nas} \end{bmatrix} \rightarrow \begin{bmatrix} -\text{cons} \\ -\text{nas} \end{bmatrix} \bigg/ \underline{} \begin{bmatrix} +\text{cons} \\ +\text{nas} \end{bmatrix}$$

(only phonemically oral vowels occur before nasal consonants)

This treatment of nasalization in IdeFC is fragmentary, but the details do not concern us here (cf. Corne 1977b, Papen 1978a). For a detailed justification for positing underlying nasal vowels, see Papen (1978b:148ff.). Examples of Rules 1-4 are:

```
l a r g e  (large 'release')      t ô b e  (tôbe 'fall')

    1 2                              4 3 2
    ↓ ↓                              ↓ ↓ ↓
l a : g ∅                         t o m ∅
```

In SC, but not in MC, many speakers do not apply Rules 3 and 4 when the following item is *u* 'you':

(SC) *mô demâd u* 'I ask you'

Rule 5 is of more restricted application. It is:

Rule 5: Consonant cluster simplification in FVT "verbs"

$$C_2 \rightarrow \emptyset / VC_1 \underline{\quad} \begin{bmatrix} V \\ -\text{back} \\ -\text{high} \end{bmatrix} \# \quad \text{Condition: } C_1 \text{ is not } r$$

In IdeFC, this rule affects only a few verbs, and even then not for all speakers: *res(te)* 'remain', *môt(re)* 'show', *sif(le)/suf(le)* 'whistle, blow', *trâble/tram* 'tremble'. In the MC recorded by Baissac (1880, 1888), Rule 5 affects a few other verbs: *ât(re)* 'enter', *rôf(le)* 'snore' (attested only in the reduplicated form *rôfrôfle*), *siv(re)* 'follow'. For details, see McKibbin and Corne (1980). An example of Rule 5:

```
t r â b l e  (trâble 'tremble')

    4 3 5 2
    ↓ ↓ ↓ ↓
t r a m ∅ ∅
```

As stated above, the application of Rule 2 signals action. This is without prejudice to the overall reading of the sentence, as the following examples show:

(SC) *i pe obliz mua vini* 'he is obliging me to come'
(SC) *zot pa kon koz frâse* 'they don't know how to speak French'
(SC) *i gaŷ li ê sok* 'he gets a shock'

(SC) *mô pu vin ris ê zur* 'I shall be(come) rich one day'
(SC) *sa kôpozer i apel Amed* 'that composer's name is Ahmed'
(SC) *ê lon i kut de rupi* 'one ell costs two rupees'
(MC) *so valiz pez vê liv* 'his suitcase weighs 20 pounds'
(SC) *labutik i ferm siz-er* 'the shop closes at six o'clock'

These sentences are variously active, processive, or stative, at least in their English glosses. In a sentence such as:

(SC) *labutik i ferm siz-er* 'the shop closes at six o'clock'

although the subject is not exactly an Agent, nor is it a Patient. The "verb" *ferm* expresses an action: something happens at six o'clock. Compare this with:

(SC) *labutik i ferme ozordi* 'the shop is closed today'

which is a stative sentence: the predicate merely describes *labutik*. This latter sentence may be compared in its turn with:

(SC) *labutik i n ferme komela* 'the shop is closed now'

where although the sentence as a whole is stative by virtue of the presence of *n*, the predicate is processive in the sense we have seen above (A2.4; the gloss is, more accurately, 'the shop has come to be, has become, shut now'). With the exercise of some ingenuity, one can find explanations for the application of Rule 2 in the apparently nonactive sentences included in the above list of examples. For example, since active sentences generally have Agents as their subjects, one could use agentivity to explain the application of the rule in the case of "infinitives" as in:

(SC) *i deman Zâ sât sa* 'he asks John to sing it'

where the underlying subject of the embedded clause is agentive, so that Rule 2 applies to *sât(e)*. Similarly in the case of *koz(e)* in *zot pa kon koz frâse* above. Agentivity can then explain the application of Rule 2 to *gaŷ(e)* in *i gaŷ li ê sok* above. In this example, which illustrates a structure largely peculiar to SC, there is coreference, or reflexivity, between the agentive subject *i* and the dative pronoun *li;* this explains the reading of this sentence, whereby we understand that the subject has some degree of responsibility for the shock he receives (cf. Corne 1977c:221). Note that *vin(i)* means not only 'become', but also 'come'. This is not a case of homonymy, and the lexeme does not have two meanings in IdeFC, but merely in the English (or French) glosses, and so again agentivity explains the application of Rule 2 in *mô pu vin ris* above. I think that the claim made here, that Rule 2 signals Action, is an accurate one. There is a problem with such items as *apel(e)* and *kon(e)*. Both items regularly receive Anterior marking in narrative material, as do past-reference statives generally. While *apel(e)* falls into the same general category (of "middle voice") as does *ferm(e)* in *labutik i ferm siz-er*, *kon(e)* does not, and I have no explanation for the application of Rule 2 in this instance. Whatever the explanation may turn out to be, I propose to consider all cases of the application of Rule 2 as marking *active* sentences.

A3.2 Final Vowel Truncation in RC

In RC, verbs may be classified as to whether or not they are subject to the FVT rule. More precisely, FVT applies only to the past participial and infinitival forms of verbs of the appropriate class. These verbs have past participles and infinitives which end in *-e* and *-i/-ir*. Most verbs in *-e* are subject to FVT, but the majority of those in *-i/-ir* are not. Examples are:

sât(e) 'sing'	*râtr(e)* 'enter'	*kur(i/ir)* 'run'
risk(e) 'risk'	*sort(i/ir)* 'go out'	*serv(i/ir)* 'serve'
asept(e) 'accept'	*sers(e)* 'look for'	*fin(i/ir)* 'finish'

The *-ir* ending is phonetically very close to the ending *-i*, by Rule 1. It is not clear whether they are phonologically distinct for all RC speakers, i.e., whether there are speakers for whom *sorti* would be both participle and infinitive (cf. Chaudenson 1974:330).

As in IdeFC, the subclass of verbs subject to FVT is morphologically defined: FVT applies only to verbs which have at some point in their derivation the phonetic shape $(X)VC_1(C_2)$ + suffix *-e/-i*. Rules 1, 3, and 4 apply as in IdeFC, but consider now the following sentences:

(RC) *nu la asepte* 'we accepted'
(RC) *nu la asep sô ed* 'we accepted his help'
(RC) *nu la asept ali* 'we accepted him'

(Papen 1975:9)

We note that in the last sentence, Rule 5 has not applied before a following object pronoun, and Papen (1978b:142) suggests that any following vowel may perhaps prevent Rule 5 from applying. This constraint needs to be included in the RC version of Rule 5. Of itself, this is a very minor difference between RC and IdeFC, and it may be ignored. But the fact that this constraint exists means that Rule 2 must also be modified for RC, since final vowel truncation operates following two consonants, and not just a single one as in IdeFC. Thus, we have something along the lines of Rule 2′:

Rule 2′: Final vowel truncation (Reunion)

V → ∅/C__# + X
[−back]   [past participle or infinitive]

(the specification of X in syntactic terms appears to be identical to the IdeFC specification, but see below). Thus:

a s e p t e   (*asepte* 'accept')   s o r t i r   (*sortir* 'go out')

       5 2′   1   2′ 1
       ↓ ↓   ↓   ↓ ↓
a s e p ∅ ∅   s o : t ∅ ∅

Note that in Rule 2′, the notation] Action is not present. In IdeFC, Rule 2 signals Action, but the RC Rule 2′ seems to be completely gratuitous. It applies to infinitives and past participles of the appropriate class of verbs, but it does not have any easily discernible function. This difference between RC and IdeFC presumably comes from the fact that the two languages are structured differently. The functioning of the predicate system of IdeFC is based on the concepts Action/Process/State. These are marked in various ways (co-occurrence restrictions with tense/aspect markers, for example, or with the *gaŷ* construction discussed in A5.1). The development of a "meaning" for FVT (cf. A4.1.2) is entirely in accordance with the way in which the language is structured. But RC is structured along quite different principles, and so while FVT has evolved almost identically in RC and IdeFC in morphosyntactic terms, RC has not needed to allocate a "meaning" to the rule — it applies to verbs, whatever their semantics happen to be. So I do not think that this difference, that FVT marks Action in IdeFC but not in RC, is particularly important from a comparative point of view, except insofar as it gives further demonstration of the fact that RC and IdeFC are typologically different. The real points of variance concern Rule 2/2′ and Rule 5, which together account for the wider application of FVT in RC (wider in the sense that a greater morphological variety of verbs is subject to FVT in RC than in IdeFC).

The syntactic contexts in which FVT is "required" to apply are essentially the same as in IdeFC. However, this statement is true only of the most basilectal varieties of RC. In general, the closer a given variety is to the acrolect, the greater the preference for long forms. Further, it appears to be the case that FVT does not necessarily apply equally to both infinitives and past participles within a given variety: in varieties close to the basilect, FVT tends to apply to both parts of speech to the same degree, while there is some evidence to suggest that in the more acrolectal varieties FVT applies with variable consistency to past participles and to infinitives. Unfortunately, the data available are somewhat scanty, but there can be no doubt that there is here the general outline of a continuum for FVT as a whole. For discussion and data, see A3.3. The status of past participles seems to be perceived as being different from that of infinitives, even in the absence of any morphological differentiation (as is the case, of course, for the very large class of verbs in -*e*). Infinitives, in some varieties at least, seem to be perceived differently according to the matrix in which they are embedded. In particular, the tendency is for only the short form to occur following Future *a*, while long forms may occasionally follow *sa((v)a)* and *va*.

The forms *fin* and *fini* also seem to be subject to different parsing strategies. They appear to be perceived as verbs (usually, but cf. Moorghen 1975:9) or as something akin to the preverbal particles of IdeFC. The Perfect, as we have seen, appears in various guises:

(1) *muê la mâze*
(2) *muê la fin mâze*
(3) *muê la fini mâze*
(4) *mua fin mâze*
(5) *m i fini mâze*
(6) *m a mâze*
(7) *m i fin mâze*

In its surface form, (6) is of course identical to the future constructed with *a;* since some speakers who use this form for the Perfect also use it for the Future, I assume that some other (contextual?) cues are used to avoid ambiguity. In the texts examined in Barat et al. (1977) (see A3.3 below for the list of these), (1) accounted for almost all occurrences of the Perfect.

Now *la* (and its variant *a*) is an auxiliary verb followed by a past participle, but the status of *fin(i)* is not always as clear. Generally, it is perceived as a verb. In (5) it is the Present of *finir* 'finish'. In (2), (3), (4), and (5), *mâze* is an infinitive (cf. *muê la fini konet* 'I knew, have come to know'). But in Barat et al. (1977:26) we find *li la fini vi* + NP 'he has seen NP'. Here, the occurrence of the past participle *vi* is explicable only if the string *la fini* is seen as an auxiliary on the same level as *la*. It may of course be simply an example of an analogical extension of the predominant pattern of *la* + Past Participle, but cf. the discussion concerning *fin(i)* in A1.4 above.

In (4), we have *mua* instead of *muê*[2] or *m i*. Now *mua* is not an uncommon variant of *muê* (M. Carayol, personal communication) in various contexts (*sa k mua la di* 'what I said', *li la di amua* 'he said to me'), but here only *mua* can occur. Moorghen (1975:9) analyzes *mua fin sâte* 'I have sung' as a reduced form of *muê la fin sâte*. The interesting point is that *mua fini + V does not seem to occur, and *mua fin* + V certainly looks "more Creole" than any of the other RC forms of the Perfect: *fin* looks more like a preposed particle than the past participle of a verb (and cf. also the Pluperfect *te fin* + V). It is perhaps this somewhat ambiguous status that is responsible for the obligatory application of FVT to the past participle (following Moorghen) *fini* in this context. Note that FVT applies optionally to *la fin(i)*, where the presence of *la* marks *fin(i)* unambiguously as a past participle. In (7), *i* marks *fin* as a verb, and the truncation of *-i* is perhaps due to analogy.

A3.3 Final Vowel Truncation and the RC Continuum

The FVT rule is highly variable from speaker to speaker, and in fact appears to be one of the features which defines the RC continuum. This interesting piece of information emerged from an examination of the RC folktales published in Barat et al. (1977).

These tales happen to illustrate different varieties of RC, as spoken by different speakers in various geographical locations. Before I look at the data drawn from these stories, a number of remarks need to be made about the source publication. *Kriké kraké* is noteworthy because it is (as far as I know) the only extensive collection of modern Reunion oral literature: twenty-five tales taped (1975-77) and transcribed in a carefully defined orthography (pp. 9-11). However, the tales have been slightly edited in the process of transcription, as may easily be determined by listening to the cassette tape, containing six of the stories as originally recorded, which is an optional extra sold separately from the volume. This editing is such that it removes a large measure of the value of the stories as examples of spontaneous narrative discourse (the representation of which is in any case clearly not the aim of the volume) while failing on the other hand to produce a text, for each speaker, that is truly representative of that speaker's phonological and grammatical system. Thus, in the first two pages of Conte 1 (13-14), I find five times the transcription *(la) fini* where the spoken text seems to have *(la) fin*. Another unhelpful procedure is the decision to "normaliser les principales variables [phonologiques] sur la variante ... basilectale" (p. 9) on the grounds that basilectal variants are predominant in Reunion and—irrelevantly—are the only ones in MC, SC, and RoC; thus, *sanb* 'bedroom' (Fr. *chambre*).[3] While this works more or less satisfactorily for varieties close to the basilect, elsewhere it produces misleading results (e.g., the transcription *ti pé demandé se ke ti vé, ti ora* for the spoken *tu peux d'mandé ce que tu veux, tu ôras,* p. 33 and on the cassette tape). A minor problem of parsing arises from the fact that melodic curves are not consistently marked by appropriate punctuation; since the FVT rule is sensitive to constituent structure, each clause must be parsed to find out whether it meets the syntactic specifications of the rule. Only then can it be determined whether the rule, if it has not applied, "should have" done so in that particular case. Lack of punctuation on occasion makes it difficult to decide whether *sa* is the direct object or a *reprise* of the subject, or whether *la* is a locative adverb (variant of *laba* 'there') or merely a tag of some kind.

Thus, an examination of the texts in Barat et al. is not an entirely straightforward matter, but nor is it impossible, and the criteria used are listed below.

No information is given in *Kriké kraké* about the speakers (age, socioeconomic status, etc.), nor even whether tales collected at the same location are told by the same or different speakers, but their geographical location is noted at the end of each tale. Using the map of population distribution given in Chaudenson (1974: xviii; also in Carayol and Chaudenson 1977:194) and the "Carte touristique et routière" produced by the French Institut géographique national (scale 1/100,000), I can at least indicate the environment of each tale. The stories examined were:

—Contes 1, 4, 10 from Sainte-Suzanne on the northeast coast, in an area of predominantly Indian ("Malabar") population; these tales were chosen at random from among the seventeen stories from the Ste.-Suzanne area included in the volume.
—Contes 5, 9, 15 from Grand-Ilet in the cirque de Salazie, an area of predominantly White ("Petit Blanc") population.
—Contes 8, 13 from Grand Coude, inland, north of St.-Joseph on the southern coast, also an area of predominantly Petit Blanc population.
—Contes 7, 19 from Etang Salé, on the southwest coast, in an area of predominantly Black and "mixed race" population.
—Conte 20, the only one in the collection from Dos-d'Ane, inland, southeast of the Le Port-La Possession plain on the northwest coast (the population map is unhelpful here, but Defos du Rau [1960:297] gives the population of the village of Dos-d'Ane as being White).

The criteria adopted for the study of the FVT phenomenon were as follows. Only three contexts which "require" FVT were used: +NP, +Infinitive, +Locative. Prepositions preceding infinitives, locatives, and dative NPs were ignored where they occurred. Any case where there was doubt as to parsing due to the transcription factors mentioned above was not counted. The forms *fin* and *fini* are not included in the figures for short and long forms, respectively. However, the verbal forms following *fin(i)* are included as infinitives, in spite of their somewhat ambiguous status (cf. A3.2 above). In the case of verbs in *-iye* (e.g., *kriye* 'call(ed)'), the forms transcribed with *-i* (e.g., *kri*, as past participle or as infinitive, not as present tense form) are included in the figures. Finally, the class of verbs which are subject to FVT in RC does not contain precisely the same members as the corresponding verb class in IdeFC (e.g., *ale* 'go' is subject to FVT in IdeFC but not in RC). Since the membership of the RC class is yet to be determined, I cannot be certain that all short forms included in the figures do in fact have a long form in basilectal RC. Some short forms have been excluded for the same reason (e.g., *travay* 'work') where they are known to be invariable in IdeFC.

Thus, the figures given in Table 3 (p. 59) will undoubtedly not correspond to those which another might derive from the same texts. But even if they are necessarily imprecise, they nonetheless indicate trends. Note that in most cases, the number of occurrences is too small to constitute a reliable statistical sample.

Figure 2 (p. 60) is an attempt to represent the situation revealed by the figures

Final Vowel Truncation in Indian Ocean Creole French 59

Table 3
Incidence of Short and Long Forms in Selected Contes from *Kriké kraké*

Region	Infinitives		Past Participles				Total Short	Approx. % Short
	Short	Long	Short		Long	Total		
Dos-d'Ane	62 100%	0	17	94.5%	1	80	79	99%
Ste.-Suzanne	104 85%	18	40	81.5%	9	171	144	84%
Grand Coude	24 68.5%	11	28	78%	8	71	52	73%
Etang Salé	18 64%	10	7	35%	13	48	25	52%
Grand-Ilet	10 33.5%	20	17	63%	10	57	27	47.5%

Note: all percentages are rounded to the nearest 0.5

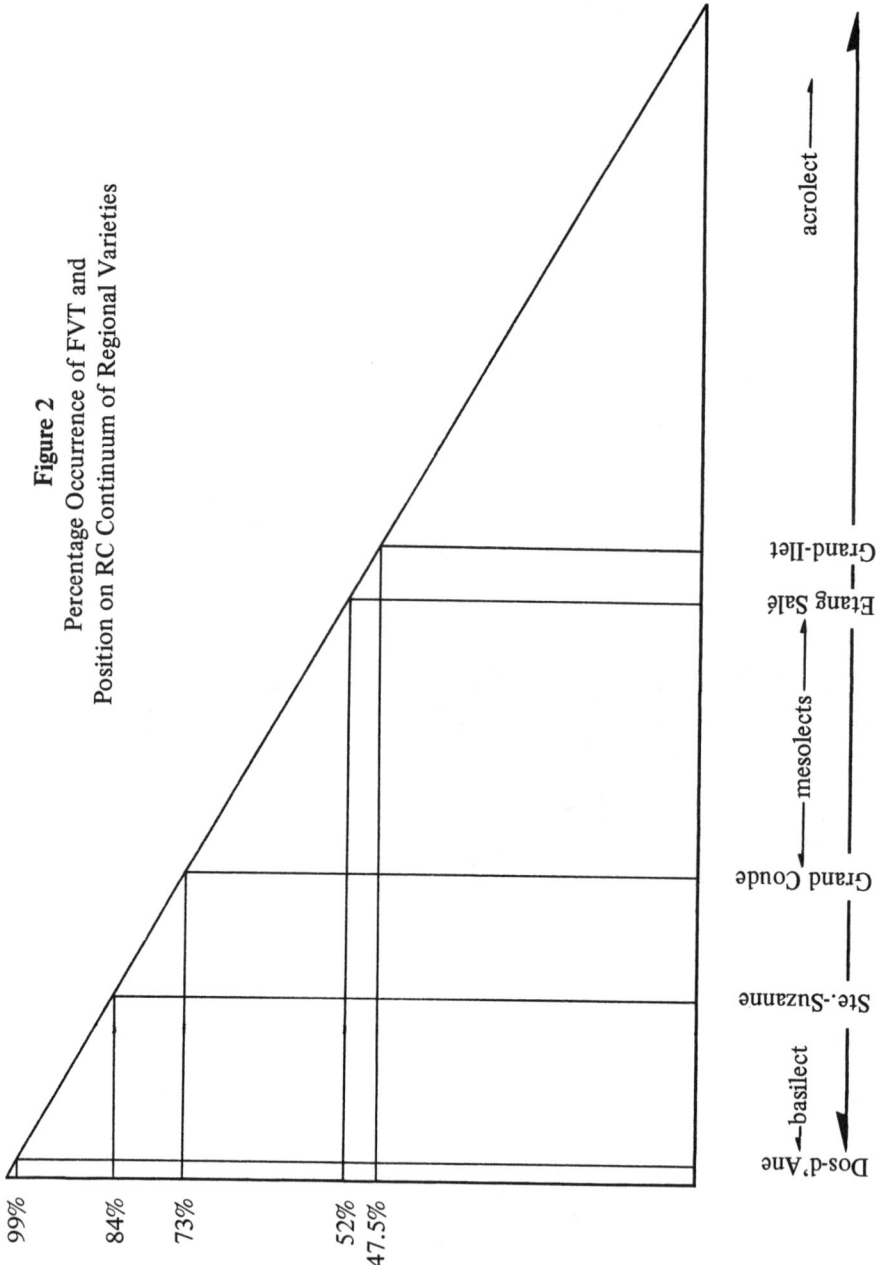

Figure 2
Percentage Occurrence of FVT and
Position on RC Continuum of Regional Varieties

in Table 3. In Figure 2, the percentage occurrence of short forms is plotted on the vertical axis, while the relative position of each lect is displayed on the horizontal axis. The whole represents in a linear manner the RC continuum for FVT. In the absence of any information as to the speaker or speakers in each case, it is not possible to say whether each variety is in fact "typical" of its region. Table 3 and Figure 2 are ordered according to the overall occurrence of FVT, but as Table 3 shows, the percentages for infinitives and past participles taken separately do not correspond perfectly to this ordering. In both cases, basilectal and near-basilectal usage is fairly constant, FVT applying rather consistently to both parts of speech. In less basilectal varieties, there are some interesting variations. In Grand-Ilet, as illustrated by the Contes at least, FVT tends not to apply to infinitives, whereas in the Etang Salé variety illustrated here it is past participles that tend to occur in the long form. The number of occurrences in both cases is rather small, but if a larger sample confirms these trends, it would seem to be the case that the status of past participles is perceived as being different from that of infinitives. If in fact this apparent differentiation between the two parts of speech is confirmed by further research, then my analysis of the RC verbal system, which in effect predicts that just such differences are involved, will be supported thereby, for these lects at least. In the case of Grand-Ilet, the percentage trend correlates well with the fact that these Contes show a large number of "French" features, including: prepositions *à, de;* possessives *ma, votre;* verb morphology *nous sommes, ils sont;* pronouns *elle, je;* future *je vais dire;* liaison *vous-z-avez;* interrogative inversion *avez-vous?;* word order *je vais vous donner.* So, while a larger data base would undoubtedly modify the detail of my results, it would be unlikely to disprove the essence of my conclusions.

Any conclusion drawn on the basis of these data must necessarily be fragile. However, I think that I am justified in claiming that the RC continuum has been shown to have a (morpho)syntactic dimension as well as a phonological one. This needs to be said, because while Carayol and Chaudenson (1977) have studied the phonological dimension, and while such a syntactic continuum has been either implicitly assumed or explicitly asserted to exist in numerous works (e.g., Chaudenson 1979b:129-30; Carayol and Chaudenson 1973), it has not heretofore been shown to exist. We can be fairly confident that a larger sampling will validate the general outline of this first and rather approximate demonstration.

The basis of the claim that the continuum is ordered as shown here, with Dos-d'Ane and Ste.-Suzanne at the basilectal end and Grand-Ilet toward the acrolectal end, rather than the reverse, is not based solely on the evidence of the 1977 data with respect to FVT and the supporting evidence of the occurrence of many "French" features in the Grand-Ilet lect. There is also evidence that FVT applied obligatorily one hundred years ago (see A4.1.1). I am probably on relatively safe ground in claiming that the consistent application of FVT is a feature of basilectal RC. Note, however, that I am *not* claiming that the Dos-d'Ane idiolect represented in Conte 20 is basilectal in *all* respects. Indeed, all that has been shown is that there is a continuum in RC with respect to one morphosyntactic feature. It has not yet been shown that the RC continuum is of the same kind as the Jamaican or Guyanese model. To show that there are parallels, we should examine other grammatical features, and determine whether there is any kind of implicational relation among them. For example, are the Grand-Ilet pronouns *elle* and *je* features which appear at a specific stage of decreolization? Or the synthetic past in *-e* as opposed to *lete ki* + V? Is "decreolization" even an appropriate term to use with reference to the Grand-Ilet variety of RC? The amount of unglamorous, nonprestigious drudgery of data collection and analysis still required before any real progress can be made is quite clear and should in my view be given top priority by workers in contact with native speakers.

A3.4 Summary

It can be seen from the foregoing that FVT applies in both RC and IdeFC in what is essentially the same phonological environment. The fact that it applies to past participles and infinitives in RC for no apparent semantic reason, as opposed to its clear semantic function of signaling the concept of Action in IdeFC, seems to be a function of the different structures of the two languages, and this fact may be considered marginal for the purposes of this work. The syntactic environment in which it occurs is for all intents and purposes identical in both cases. There is a discrepancy involving the optionality or otherwise of the rule within these environments: those which require it in IdeFC merely allow it in RC. In view of the data adduced in A3.3 (and see also A4.1.1), this may perhaps be seen as an effect of "decreolization."

The fact that Rule $2'$ does not apply to the "synthetic" Past in RC is worth a moment's pause. The rule does not apply for a very obvious reason. If it were to apply to *m i mâze* 'I ate', it would produce *m i mâz* 'I eat'. This obvious fact leads to a significant surface difference between RC and IdeFC. Compare the following:

(RC) *m i mâz la vian* 'I am eating the meat'
(RC) *m i mâze la vian* 'I ate the meat'
(SC) *mô mâz lavian* 'I am a meat-eater'
(SC) *mô ti mâz lavian* 'I ate meat'
(SC) *mô ti mâze lavian!* 'I really ate meat!' (heavy stress on *mâze*)

The presence or absence of the final vowel has quite different semantic consequences in the two languages, but it is only in IdeFC that the FVT rule is operating in these examples. Compare now the following complete sentences:

(RC) *m i mâz* 'I eat, am eating'
(SC) *mô mâze* 'I eat'

but never:

(SC) *mô mâz

Although the FVT rule operates essentially in an identical way in RC and IdeFC, its actual consequences in concrete terms are rather disparate. This surface dissimilarity needs to be stressed, because while there are cases of complete surface convergence, as in:

(RC, IdeFC) *nu a sort deor* 'we shall go outside'

these are the exception rather than the rule.

NOTES

1. There is a minor error of observation in Corne (1977a:78 (e)). I state there that the long form is used when a "gerundive" follows the "verb":

(SC) *i pe vini â sâtâ* 'he is coming, and singing while doing so'

This is indeed the most usual case, but some speakers seem to parse the constituents differently so that the short form also occurs, albeit infrequently:

(SC) *i pe vin â sâtâ*

2. The string *muê fin* in Corne and Moorghen (1978:65, Tableau I) is an error.
3. The irrelevancy is underscored by the fact that IdeFC has only *lasam* 'bedroom'.

A4
Notes on Final Vowel Truncation in Creole French Languages

A comparison of IdeFC and RC on a synchronic basis shows that their verbal systems are underlyingly quite different. In spite of this, the final vowel truncation rule (FVT) applies in both systems in a largely identical manner. The optionality of the rule in RC is perhaps due to decreolization, and in IdeFC the rule has a semantic dimension (Action) which it does not have in RC, this difference being a function of the different structural organizations of the two languages.

It is inconceivable that FVT should be an independent innovation in both RC and IdeFC. The problem is, where did the rule originate?

A4.1 Indian Ocean

The data available to me on early states of MC and RC are incomplete and they alone cannot provide an answer. Nevertheless, they provide some interesting information.

A4.1.1 Reunion

An examination of the early texts reproduced in Chaudenson (1974:1148-52) suggests that by 1856 the FVT rule was operating essentially as in modern RC. Prior to 1856 (texts pp. 1147-49), only long forms (eleven of them in all) occur in the three contexts +NP, +V, +LOC. These data are so scanty that no conclusions can be drawn. Furthermore, with the exception of the first text (p. 1147) dated by Chaudenson at ca. 1715—although more probably ca. 1722 (see note 3 in the Introduction to Part A above)—and containing a single RC sentence:

Moin la parti maron parcequ'Alexis l'homme de jardin l'était qui fait à moin trop l'amour[1]

all these texts contain structures which suggest either inaccurate reporting (e.g., "pour faire z'habits à moi," p. 1149; "moi ne connais plus al'y," p. 1148) or incomplete/handicapped second-language acquisition (the constant use of the long forms—French infinitives—adds to this impression). The 1856 text by Louis Héry (pp. 1150-51) contains a number of rather non-RC oddities, but offers sixteen examples of FVT for twenty verb occurrences (in the three contexts). Héry's work is criticized by Volcy Focard (1884:198-210, 228-30) on the grounds that Héry was a European, that he had learned RC as an adult, and that in any case his works in RC were for him but "un pur passe temps." Focard follows this criticism with a detailed illustration in support of his contention that these works do not represent "true" RC. While it is possible that it simply did not occur to Focard that RC

Notes on Final Vowel Truncation in Creole French Languages 65

might have changed in the intervening thirty or so years, I am inclined to trust his judgment. In every case where he explicitly claims to be representing "real" RC, his language is entirely consistent with modern basilectal usage (and with the ca. 1715/1722 fragment).[2] In turn, this suggests that RC, in at least one of its varieties (see below), has remained remarkably stable over a long period of time.

Focard is quite aware of the existence of different varieties of RC. He distinguishes a "patois de l'immigrant indien" (p. 222), which we may assume is a pidginized version of RC, and claims differing pronunciations for three population groups —"créoles des bois" or "petits créoles" (= Whites, créole des Hauts), "noirs indigènes" [sic] (= Blacks, créole des Bas), "cafres" and "malgaches" ("que l'esclavage et l'immigration ont naturalisés chez nous") (p. 182). He then gives an illustration of each of these varieties (pp. 183-84):

Ainsi, supposons une rencontre entre deux descendants de ces "bon blancs." Ils s'abordent:
—Ah! vla Dessaline, quouq y dit, mon crèôle (crai-ole).
—Ma foi, pas grand çose, mon brave Maillott, inque tantine Zézette que la perde son cien, l'attrapé *juin dujussion* de *mayoc bouyu*.
—Dis pas, don, le pauve Cascavelle l'a succombè (succombait).
—Voui, mon crèôle, c'été t'in famé cien, in bon çassère de tang.
Voulez-vous une pareille rencontre entre deux noirs indigènes?
—Ah! vla Zean-Baptiss, qué nouvelle?
—Nouvelle n'a point.
—Zautt la dit malhère l'arrive la case ton tantine, ma Phrasie.
—N'a pas rive malhère, inque le cien tantine l'a crévé.
—Tout de bon, son zoli ptit cien coton là?
—Voui, ça minme.
—Quoué ça que l'avé?
—L'avé dijission mayoc bouï.
Voulez-vous entendre deux cafres s'entretenir d'un même malheur: la mort d'un chien arrivé récemment?
—Bouzou: quou qui di à vous?
—Eh, eh, li là, ça va, ça va coume ça minme.
—Mai zou di là, vou y mace tout sel: aquoulé Lacouti? (Langouti).
—Ah! vou y conné pas? . . . Lacouti li mot.
—Li mot! qui malade li cien là la gagné?
—Mayoc la fé mot à li, l'attape douzousson. Li la fini là mainme.
Saisissez-vous, Messieurs, la différence, et remarquez-vous que plusieurs des mots restés français dans la bouche des petits créoles et des noirs indigènes ne se font plus entendre chez les cafres?

Focard makes it abundantly clear that for him the only "real" RC is that of the "noirs indigènes," not that of the "créoles des bois" (p. 189). In the examples he gives, I can find little to differentiate these two varieties syntactically. An examination with respect to FVT of all those sentences where Focard claims to be representing "real" RC yields fascinating results (the songs on pp. 231ff. were excluded). Using the same three contexts (+NP, +V, +LOC) and applying the same set of criteria noted in A3.3, we find for infinitives thirty short forms (excluding two cases of *travay* 'work') and only one long form (*ranzé*, p. 192), or approximately 97 percent application of FVT; for past participles, twenty-seven short forms (only one long form, *attrapé*, p. 183, occurs in the text cited above illustrating the "créole des bois," i.e., not "real" RC in Focard's terms)—that is, 100 percent application. Overall, FVT applies in 98 percent of cases—in other words, consistently and obligatorily. Although fifty-nine tokens is not really a sufficient statistical base, this conclusion is justified in two ways. On the one hand, this usage is consistent with what one would expect on the basis of the 1977 data from Dos-d'Ane and Ste.-Suzanne, given the general nature of Creole continua (cf. Bickerton 1975). On the other hand, Focard's usage in other respects does not appear to differ in any significant syntactic particular from that of modern basilectal RC.

The stories in Fourcade (1976), first published in 1930, are chronologically equidistant from both Focard and Barat et al. In the preface to the 1976 edition, R. Chaudenson sounds a warning: 'Il ne faut cependant pas voir [dans ce livre] un document authentique sur le créole de l'époque; il s'agit de l'oeuvre d'un lettré et ... il est illusoire d'y chercher une réproduction fidèle du parler populaire." In view of this, it is somewhat surprising to discover that Fourcade's usage with respect to FVT is completely in accord with both Focard and the modern RC of Dos-d'Ane and Ste.-Suzanne. I examined only pages 3-23. These yielded 162 tokens: infinitives, 83 short and 5 long (94.5 percent FVT); past participles, 71 short and 3 long (96 percent FVT). In other words, with an overall application rate of 95 percent for FVT, Fourcade's usage is more basilectal than that of modern Ste.-Suzanne, and is completely comparable to that of modern Dos-d'Ane and of Focard's "real" RC of 1884. A cultured man Fourcade may well have been, but he obviously knew his Creole.

To summarize this rather scanty historical material, one may note that by 1856 (Héry) the FVT rule is applying in RC at least three-quarters of the time. There is no trace of it before this date in the material currently available to me. By 1884 (Focard), the rule is applying consistently, as it does today in basilectal varieties of RC. The continuum with respect to FVT established in A3.3 is consistent with the historical evidence, but one question that remains unanswered is whether the mesolectal varieties of modern RC are *losing* the FVT rule or whether they are progressively *acquiring* it. Only an examination of other aspects of the RC continuum will enable a correct interpretation to be made.

Notes on Final Vowel Truncation in Creole French Languages 67

A4.1.2 Mauritius

In 1976, P. Baker examined the long and short forms of "verbs" that today have both forms (pp. 50-51). The criteria used (described on p. 47 and in note 17 of Baker 1976) are not entirely compatible with mine, as used for RC. I count all "verb" occurrences, including repetitions of the same "verb," in the three contexts of +NP, +V, +LOC (with the proviso that any locative counted must fall within the scope of the "verb," or, in other terms, that it be a direct constituent of VP). The results obtained are nonetheless compatible with Baker's.

Dialogue with a Mozambique Slave (Pitot 1805) is reproduced as Appendix I in Baker (1976:92-94). The two participants are the slave and a White questioner. For the slave, FVT applies twelve times, and does not apply eleven times, while for the White, the figures are four times and nine times, respectively. This may be compared with the MC catechism of Lambert (1828; reproduced in Laray 1888-92a), where again we have Questions and Replies. FVT does not apply at all in the Questions, but five (or possibly six) short forms appear in the Replies (for details, see Corne 1977a:91-92). Both of these texts suggest that there was considerable variation in the application of FVT in Mauritius at that time, and that the presence of short forms is in some way characteristic of "slave" usage, although not confined to it.[3]

Freycinet (1827:407), who visited Mauritius in 1818, states that the two texts he gives illustrate the two varieties of MC that are the most divergent from each other. The first purports to be the MC of a Malagasy slave. In the three contexts, FVT applies forty times and does not apply eight times. (It also applies twice prepausally and twice at a clause boundary. This indicates, I think, that the rule already has its semantic function of marking Action—the lexemes concerned are *mars* 'walk', *pâs* 'think', and *tâd/tan* 'hear'—but that contextual constraints are not yet stabilized.) This text, collected in Mauritius in 1818, predates Lambert's catechism by a decade.

The second text is a fable of La Fontaine translated into MC by F. Chrestien. I have included the figures derived from this fable, collected by Freycinet in 1818, in the totals derived from Chrestien's other two works (1831, 1838). Taking Chrestien's work as a single output, one finds that FVT applies only 74 times, as opposed to 238 cases where it has not applied, i.e., almost the exact opposite of the picture in Freycinet's Malagasy text. In other words, the variation in usage noted above seems to remain the rule, with "slave" usage rather distinct from "White" usage. In Chrestien, there are three cases of "verb" + *âkor* 'again', where the short form occurs, three cases of the short form + Manner/Time adverbials, and two cases of short forms (versus one long form) with a following prepositional phrase with *avek* 'with'.

"White" usage of long forms is also attested in the *Proclamation* of W. Nicolay (1835). Ignoring one case of *appele* which appears to be a typographical error (cf. three occurrences of *appelé* and one of *appellés*), only four short forms occur as opposed to thirty-nine long forms in the three contexts.

In 1855, we have the *Poésies créoles* of P. Lolliot. This relatively substantial body of data is somewhat difficult to evaluate. The author "adjusts" his Creole to meet the exigencies of (classical) French poetical meter. The style is also at times distinctly declamatory, which itself produces a problem of interpretation. In modern MC, as was alluded to in A3.1, the presence of the semantic notion of emphasis may prevent FVT from applying. An example of this is:

(MC) *to kone, mo n rode to zafer la* 'you know, I did look for your whatsit'
    (nonemphatic: *rod*)

(cf. also the brief discussion in Corne 1977d:38). These two problems combined render parsing of Lolliot's poetry as difficult as the decisions as to what should be counted and what omitted. As examples of these difficulties, we may note that both *môt* (p. 49) and *môtre* 'show' (p. 119) are attested, but also on p. 119 we have [*nu*] *montre li* 'we show him' with what appears to be, unless it is a mere typographical error, a French schwa, since the line concerned requires that the syllable spelled -*tre* be pronounced. As for parsing problems, consider the following two lines:

(MC, 1855) [*li*] *metté par terr' son çapeau*
    'he puts his hat on the ground' (p. 50)
(MC, 1855) *li tendé dans bois sourti gardien*
    'he hears the guard come out of the woods' (p. 61)

In modern MC, in both cases, the NP would follow the "verb," which would occur in the short form. In such cases, which are numerous in this text, I have classified the "verb" as being followed by NP. Finally, on p. 118, we find the following:

(MC, 1855) [*mo*] *fin' lèv' ensemb' zot* 'I was raised alongside them'

Here, although *lev(e)* is clearly occurring in a stative sentence, FVT has applied (been applied?) to produce the required six syllables. Given these problems, it would be foolish to pretend that the following figures are in any way definitive, but they do give a crude indication of the position (the same kinds of problems occur, albeit to a lesser degree, in the evaluation of Descroizilles [1867] below). Keeping this in mind, one finds in the three key contexts in Lolliot, 135 long forms and 155 short. With a following prepositional phrase with *avek/asam* 'with', there are three long forms and six short. In sentences containing *res(te)* 'remain' and *vin(i)* 'become', where the following element may be seen as an attribute of the subject, FVT applies twice, and does not apply seven times. There are four cases where FVT applies with a following adverbial or phrase of manner.

Some twelve years later, Descroizilles (1867) also provides a relatively large body of data. In the three key contexts, we find 133 long forms and 85 short forms. With *âkor*, there are six occurrences of short forms, and six of long forms. In sentences containing *turn(e)* 'become again', *vin(i)* 'become', *res(te)* 'remain', *apel(e)* 'be called', where the following element may be seen as an attribute of the subject, FVT applies seven times, and does not apply thirteen times. Further, FVT applies three times with a following manner adverbial or phrase, and four times in other contexts including the "idiom" *ki vu âbras?* 'what does it matter to you?' and *get* 'look' prepausally. Although long forms predominate, we can see here the pattern of modern MC, as is most clearly represented by the following:

(MC, 1867) *tout fine ramasse asamb*
    'all is gathered up together'   (Descroizilles 1867:iii)

Compare modern MC:

(MC) *latet torti fin ramas âba lakok*
'Tortoise's head is pulled up underneath (his) shell'
                                                                             (Corne 1970:50)

Assuming the author of this text to be a Franco-Mauritian, it is clear that the FVT rule is no longer the near-exclusive preserve of "slave" usage.

In any event, even if the modern MC pattern is clearly emerging in both Lolliot and Descroizilles, it is equally as clear that there is still a high degree of variation as to the obligatoriness of the FVT rule, at least in "White" usage. I cannot evaluate the significance, if any, of the following fact: in both authors, the "verb" *les(e)* 'leave, let' occurs (in the key contexts) exclusively in the short form, *les* (five times in Lolliot; eleven times in Descroizilles).

This variation in "White" usage may be contrasted with the evidence of the anonymous catechism of ca. 1860 (Anon. ca. 1860). Of twenty-eight forms in the appropriate contexts, all are short. A copy of this catechism in the reference division of The British Library (London) has with it a handwritten letter, written by the Reverend Adam Clarke-Smith, which reads in part: "I send ... as a present to the museum a copy of the only book, I *believe*, ever printed ... in Créole—the language that we used to speak in to the half-castes [and] Indians in Mauritius" (italics his). This does not suggest that the catechism was newly published at the time of writing (November 14, 1861). It may be assumed that the MC of this text reflects "non-White" usage of the 1850s, at least.

The MC poems in Pitot (1878) are of marginal interest with respect to FVT, in that the exigencies of syllabification frequently give rise to long forms where the short forms might, on the evidence of Baissac (below), have been expected. In the prose passages which intersperse the first poem (pp. 7-13), FVT applies consistently (twenty-six short, two long; both long forms occur as *vini* 'become' + an "adjectival" attribute of the subject). In Pitot's verse, there are fifty-seven short forms and twenty long.

This brings us to the 1880s, with the work of Baissac (1880, 1888) and the translation of St. Matthew by Anderson (1885). The question of FVT in Baissac's work has been the subject of an exhaustive study (McKibbin and Corne 1980), the results of which are summarized here. In the three key contexts, the FVT rule applies consistently (3,351 short forms to 68 long ones). It applies consistently with following *âkor* (49 short forms, no long ones), with a following manner adverbial or phrase (202 short, 9 long), with a following prepositional phrase with *av(ek)/asam* (109 short, 10 long). This is, in effect, the modern MC usage, although it is not completely stabilized. For example, short forms occasionally occur prepausally or at a clause boundary, including the "idioms" *ki mo âbras?* 'what does it matter to me?' (cf. Descroizilles above) and *Bôdie sulaz!* 'God help you', and the "verbs" *vin* 'come', *al* 'go', *tan* 'hear', *kriy* 'call', prepausally. The semantic concept of Action is clearly operative:

(MC, 1888) *Latête tourtie fine ramasse en bas lacoque*
'Tortoise's head is pulled up underneath (his) shell'
(Baissac 1888:9, cf. the examples from 1867 and 1970 given above)

Among the exceptions to the application of FVT, we may note that several fall within the domain of Rule 5 (consonant cluster simplification). As noted in A3.1, this rule affects only a few verbs (*res(te)* 'remain', for example) and even then not for all speakers. This variation appears, in light of the evidence from Baissac, to be of long standing. There is a clear indication of the linguistic variation current in Mauritius at this time in the story reported by Baissac (1880:105-8) as told by "un vieux Mozambique" wherein Baissac assures his readers that he has tried to preserve the original pronunciation and "physionomie." Of the eighteen "verbs" in the appropriate contexts, only one occurs in the short form (*kup*, p. 106).

The usage with respect to FVT attested by Baissac's work is largely confirmed by Anderson (1885). The application of FVT in this sizable body of data has been the subject of an exhaustive analysis (Meyer 1980). in the three key contexts, FVT applies consistently (1,359 short forms to 39 long forms). It applies consistently with following *âkor* (24 short, 2 long), but there is some degree of optionality with a following manner adverbial or phrase (61 short, 24 long); similarly, with a following prepositional phrase with *av(ek)* (24 short, 9 long). Two short forms occur prepausally (*tracasse* 'worry' and *çape* 'save, escape'), but these may be typographical errors. As in Baissac, the semantic concept of Action is operative. (See now Table 4, p. 71.)

I have noted the use in some of the above texts of short forms occurring prepausally. In this connection, it is perhaps indicative of earlier usage that in the

Table 4
Incidence of Short and Long Forms in Early MC Texts
(Contexts +NP, +V, +LOC)

Date	Author, Text, or Speaker	Short Forms	Long Forms	Approx. % Occurrence of FVT
1805	Mozambique slave	12	11	52%
	Questioner	4	9	30.8%
1818	Malagasy slave	40	8	83.3%
1828	Lambert	6	81	6.9%
1818-38	Chrestien	74	238	23.7%
1835	Proclamation	4	39	9.3%
1855	Lolliot	155	135	53.4%
1867	Descroizilles	85	133	39%
ca. 1860	Catechism	28	0	100%
1878	Pitot	83	22	79%
1885	Anderson	1,359	38	97%
1880-88	Baissac	3,351	68	98%

speech of a 93-year-old Rodrigan man, we find:

(RoC, ca. 1975) *get, u pa truv en pie?* 'look, can you not see a tree?'
(Corne and Stein 1979:71)

while in the speech of an 83-year-old woman in Seychelles we have:

(SC, ca. 1972) *mô zâfâ i dispite ek mua, i dispit, i dispit, i dispit*
'my children argue with me incessantly'
(SC, ca. 1972) *mô va gaŷe baba* 'I was going to have a baby'
(the context of this sentence is Past)   (Corne 1977a:90).

Here, we see both short forms prepausally and long forms + NP.

Although the evidence is not conclusive, there is a clear implication that the FVT rule appeared initially in "slave" Creole, while "master" Creole used long forms. This is obviously an oversimplified view, since Whites had at all times access to French morphology and syntax (e.g., the use of *ofr* for modern IdeFC *ofer* 'offer' by Descroizilles [1867:10]), while the exposure of non-Whites to French would have been highly variable. The picture then is that of a morphosyntactic rule being gradually adopted and gaining a semantic value quite absent from any variety of French.

It is tempting to suppose that the fact that FVT applies in the same way in modern MC, SC, and RoC indicates that the basic morphological alternation, with its modern semantic dimension and its modern syntactic constraints—at least in embryonic form—existed in (some variety of) MC by the end of the eighteenth century. However, the fact that Seychelles and Rodrigues were "Mauritian" colonies has meant continuing and relatively close contact throughout their history. Such contact has clear linguistic implications, and cannot be ignored. For example, the only form of the Progressive aspect marker attested in Baissac's work is *apre;* this form is still marginally extant in RoC (Corne and Stein 1979:74), but MC, SC, and RoC today all use *(a)pe* (cf. B3.2.5).

A4.1.3 Summary

The evidence provided by the work of Héry (1856) shows the presence of FVT in RC by that time. This is confirmed by the evidence derived from the work of Focard (1884), where FVT applies consistently. FVT also applies consistently in modern basilectal varieties of RC, but not enough data are currently available to determine whether the mesolectal varieties of modern RC are acquiring or losing the rule.

In Mauritius, the FVT rule existed in "slave" usage from at least 1805, and perhaps as early as ca. 1780, while the Malagasy text in Freycinet suggests strongly that by 1818 the rule had acquired its modern semantic dimension in "slave"

Creole. By the middle of the century, the rule was no longer typical of "slave" usage alone, and while the modern pattern was clearly emerging at this time, there was still a high degree of variability. However, the evidence of Baissac in 1880, where the modern system was operating, for all intents and purposes, suggests that the variation noted in 1867 (Descroizilles) was not perhaps typical of all sections of the Mauritian community at that time, Baissac's texts having been collected from elderly informants (Baissac 1888:iii). In fact, Baissac comments explicitly on the linguistic heterogeneity prevailing in Mauritius, but also states that there was at that time a "real" MC (Baissac 1880:vii-viii), and that that was what he intended to describe.

A4.2 American Creole French

Verb morphology in American Creole French (ACF) has some parallels with Indian Ocean Creole French (IOC) with respect to the final vowel truncation rule. Goodman (1964:60-61) briefly studies FVT operating on the verb *vin(i)* 'to (be)- come': "[In all Creole French languages], save in Louisiana, one finds a form without as well as a form with a final *i*. In Antillean Creole, where the former is rare and seems to be restricted to Guadeloupe, and in French Guiana where it is fairly common, it alternates freely with the latter. In Haiti and Mauritius, however, the two are contextual alternants; the latter occurs clause or sentence finally, the former, if followed by [a] complementary word or phrase. In Mauritius this identical pattern exists for almost all verbs with final *e* and a number of verbs with final *i*, while in Haiti it exists for a small number of both types." Goodman concludes: "the existence of this alternation pattern in both Haiti and Mauritius, and traces of it in other Creole dialects ... is strong evidence for the close historical connection between all of them." We have already seen the facts for the IOC languages: they are considerably more complex than Goodman, dependent largely on published material, could have known in 1964. Let us now examine the American side of the story.

A4.2.1 Louisiana Creole French (LC)

In LC most verbs in -*e* have a short form for the habitual non-Past, the long form elsewhere:

mo kup 'I cut' (habitual non-past)
mo kupe 'I (have) cut' (completive, *j'ai coupé*)
mo te kupe 'I cut' (habitual past); 'I had cut' (past completive)
m(o v)a kupe 'I shall cut'

(see Lane 1935:13-14 for further details of conditional, etc.). It is the first two of the above sentences which are of interest to us here. In both cases, there is no preposed predicate particle of aspect or tense, and the truncation of -*e* is the sole differentiating characteristic. Compare now the following two sentences:

šop-la frem a siz-er 'the shop closes at six o'clock'
šop-la freme žodi 'the shop is shut, has shut, today'

(These two sentences, as well as the following two, were provided by Ingrid Neumann, personal communication. The transcription and glosses are mine. Neumann stresses the incomplete and preliminary nature of her LC data as of November 1979.) The LC *frem/freme* contrast is not a perfect parallel of the *ferm/ferme* contrast of IdeFC (which also occurs as *frem/freme*), as in SC *labutik i ferm siz-er* 'the shop closes at six' and SC *labutik i ferme ozordi* 'the shop is closed today'. In IdeFC, the contrast is one of Active versus Stative. In LC, it appears to be one of habitual non-past versus completive, with perhaps a subsidiary active/stative dimension. Whether this should be seen as a tense distinction or as an aspectual one is not at present entirely clear, but the surface similarity of IdeFC and LC in this instance is striking. Further, LC has a rule similar to Rule 5, Consonant Cluster Simplification:

li sam biê malad 'he seems very ill'
li sâble malad ier 'he seemed ill yesterday'

Again we see the ∅/-e contrast, this time interacting with the LC version of Rule 5.

So we seem to have here a rule of FVT which shares at least some of the phonological attributes of the IdeFC rule, and perhaps some of the semantic ones as well, although the parallel is admittedly imperfect. There is also, however, an interesting albeit rather obvious parallel between LC and RC: the ∅/-e contrast of LC may well have a temporal dimension of non-Past versus Past (if Completive is seen as being Past in some sense). As far as I am aware, only RC, among Creole French languages, has a similar ∅/-e contrast in some varieties (RC *m i mâz* versus *m i mâze*, corresponding to Present versus Imperfect). However, unlike RC, LC does not have an auxiliary verb *avuar* for the Completive (or Perfective), using rather a zero "marker" in conformity with the general ACF pattern, and other tense and aspect distinctions are handled by means of preposed markers and combinations thereof. A. Hull (personal communication) has pointed out that the nineteenth-century LC texts do not show FVT (except with *don* 'give' in all contexts, present and past). He hypothesizes that FVT originated among bilingual (Creole/Cajun) speakers who felt the need to distinguish between present habitual and past punctual (and he notes that the postposition of *pa* in *mo kup pa* versus its anteposition in *mo pa kupe* also supports this view).

A4.2.2 Haitian Creole French (HC)

I have been unable to find a comprehensive statement concerning the FVT rule in HC in any of the sources consulted, but all mention the existence of short and long forms for a small number of "verbs" (Comhaire-Sylvain 1936, Faine 1937, Hall 1953, d'Ans 1968, Valdman 1970, 1978a:90-91). My transcriptions of HC make no phonological claims; in particular, I have assumed predictable nasalization of vowels contiguous to any nasal consonant.

The "verbs" involved (with approximate glosses) are: *al(e)* 'go', *kon(e)* 'habitual action or state', *fin(i)* 'have just; completive', *met(e)* 'place',[4] *pòt(e)* 'carry, bring', *ret(e)* 'remain, stay', *sòt(i)* 'have just', *vin(i)* 'come, become', *uet(e)* 'take off', *gad(e)* 'look at'. Also *geŷe/gaŷe* ~ *gê/gâ* 'have', presumably via *geŷ/*gaŷ. Some of these "verbs" have a "full" sense as well as a modal one (*kone* 'know', *sòti* 'leave'), but it is not clear whether in this full sense these occur with the short form as frequently (or at all?) as when they have the modal sense.

The alternation short/long appears to be free, except in clause-final position, where only the long form appears. Comhaire-Sylvain (1936:103) claims that the short form may be used with a following NP (not a pronoun, however) or PP, while d'Ans (1968:84) states that the alternation is completely free except clause-finally (he says "sentence-finally"; the assumption that clause-finally is what is meant is mine). It is clear from the examples given in all sources that a following "verb" also allows the short form.

Phonologically, d'Ans points out that in all cases, an apicoalveolar consonant is involved. With the exception of *geŷe/gaŷe*, the apicoalveolar consonant appears to be a real restriction on the deletion rule; I say "appears," because while Comhaire-Sylvain gives a closed list of "verbs" (those above, minus *gad(e)*; her list and Hall's [1953:30-31, with a reference to Comhaire-Sylvain] are identical), the lists given by both Faine (1937:145) and d'Ans (1968:84) are qualified by "among the most usual verbs having a short and a long form." In any case, even if this constraint turns out to be a real one, it could well be simply fortuitous. All the "verbs" are frequently occurring ones, and most have the status of semi-auxiliaries of various kinds.

Valdman (1970:218) notes that the modal auxiliaries *sòti, fini, vini* "usually" lose their final vowel. That this is so is presumably because these items are undergoing a "grammaticalization" (cf. the status of IdeFC *fin*, an aspect marker, and RC *fin(i)*, a modal verb and/or marker; similarly, *fek* 'have just' is a preposed predicate particle in MC, but is still a modal in SC [and in HC]; see Corne 1977a:96-102).

In the meantime, we have an optional rule of final vowel truncation:

Rule 2″: Final vowel truncation (Haiti)

$$V \rightarrow \emptyset / VC\_\_\# + X$$
$$[-back]$$

Rule 2″ applies to a very small subset of (highly recurrent) "verbs." C may be restricted largely to apicoalveolar. The syntactic environment X includes a following verb, noun (but not pronoun), or adverbial element (mainly Locative), or, if we accept d'Ans's statement, X may be anything except a clause boundary. The optionality of the rule is perhaps questionable in view of Valdman's claim above.

I think it is obvious that the limited statements in the available literature do not come close to exhausting the subject. Detailed study of HC will undoubtedly reveal information concerning synchronic regional/dialectal variation and diachronic development of the FVT rule. For example, a perusal of the "Conversations créoles" in Ducoeurjoly (1802:357-91) showed 102 cases of the "verbs" listed above in an appropriate context, all occurring in the long form. I am not as yet in a position to evaluate the significance (if any) of these data, but they do suggest the value that such detailed studies will have.

Meanwhile, we have Rule 2″ above, apparently optional, and restricted to a tiny handful of "verbs." Its nonapplication before a pronoun object (following Comhaire-Sylvain) is quite different from the similar restriction on Rule 5 in RC. Rule 2″ stands alone in HC; Rule 1 applies, but only in a diachronic sense, as does something similar to Rule 5, again diachronically. Finally, FVT in HC does not appear to have the semantic dimension that it has in IdeFC. These all seem to be important differences in the operation of FVT in HC and in IdeFC/RC.[5]

A4.2.3 Lesser Antillean and French Guiana Creole French

Among the Lesser Antillean languages, traces of FVT are few and far between. In Guadeloupe, Goodman (1964:60) notes *vin(i)* 'come', qualified as "rare." In Laurent and Césaire (1976), *vin* occurs a number of times, generally when followed by other constituents, but in one instance prepausally (p. 39). *Mete* and *met* 'put, place' both occur when followed by a direct object (e.g., on p. 219), and there is one instance of a short form *tin* of *tini* 'have, hold' (p. 207). In Dominica, Taylor (1977:219) reports a case of semantic differentiation involving an alternation of -e/∅: *mòde* 'bite' versus *mòd* 'take the bait' (cf. also *mete* 'put' and *met ba* 'give birth'). This alternation is presumably fossilized. For Saint Lucia, Valdman (1978a: 91) gives two examples: *al(e)* 'go' and *tòb(e)* 'fall', both followed by a locative prepositional phrase.

For French Guiana, Goodman notes *vin(i)* again, quoting Auguste Horth (*Le patois guyanais*, Cayenne, 1949:20, 72). I have not been able to consult this latter work. There is no mention of the phenomenon in Saint-Quentin (1872) nor in Saint Jacques Fauquenoy (1972).

These data are so sparse as to render any useful conclusions impracticable. Valdman's conclusion, to the effect that *all* Creole French languages have certain "verbs" which optionally undergo FVT in certain contexts (1978a:90), seems too broad a generalization. The most that can be said at present is that a very small number of "verbs" in Lesser Antillean and in Guyanais lose their final vowel under conditions which remain to be elucidated, and that this phenomenon is marginal.

A4.3 Discussion

French clearly provides plenty of appropriate models in a morphological sense (*sorti(r), sorte(nt); manger/é/ez/ai(en)t, mange(nt)*, etc.). Such models have semantactic reflexes in LC and in some varieties of RC. In both these languages, the alternance of zero and *-e* retains some of its "French" significance:

(RC) *m i mâz*
(Fr) *je mange* } 'I eat' versus *m i mâze*
je mangeais } 'I ate'

(LC) *mo kup*
(Fr) *je coupe* } 'I cut' versus *m ape kupe*
je suis après couper (dial.) } 'I am cutting'

In HC and IdeFC, and in RC for infinitives and past participles, the reflexes of the French models[6] have been integrated into completely new systems involving specific phonological and syntactic constraints. I leave open, perforce, the question as to the precise degree of resemblance between HC, IdeFC, RC, and LC with respect to their FVT rule(s), the point being that the phenomenon exists in both some American, and all Indian Ocean, Creole French languages.

The detail of the development of the FVT rule in any of the languages is unknown. But the very existence of the rule in both geographical areas and particularly in RC shows that Goodman's "close historical connection" is to be found in seventeenth-century colonial varieties of French rather than in a (West African) Pidgin French substratum. Unless, of course, we wish to accept for the Indian Ocean a Mauritian "slave" origin for the FVT rule, with a subsequent spread from Mauritius to Reunion. A priori, this is an unlikely sequence, but not an impossible one. The FVT phenomenon does show up earlier in MC texts than in RC ones, although this may be purely happenstance. The evidence of the MC texts, which suggests a slave origin for the FVT rule, cannot be regarded as conclusive in view of the RC facts.

These brief and fragmentary remarks barely scratch the surface of the problem, and the present "nonconclusion" is no doubt a temporary state of affairs. As more detailed data become available on, for example, early HC texts and the linguistic detail of regional variation in Haiti, and as (or if) more early MC and RC texts come to light, it may become possible to provide definitive answers to the question of where, when, and how the rule of final vowel truncation originated.

The point of this lengthy examination of the FVT rule in the Creole French languages has been to show that the origins of the rule are not to be found in the Indian Ocean. Thus, although the present-day near-identity of the rule in both RC and IdeFC can hardly be due to chance parallels of independent innovation, its existence cannot be used to "prove" a common "ancestor" for these languages apart from some variety or varieties of seventeenth-century French. At best, the FVT phenomenon in the Indian Ocean suggests convergence due to areal interaction, but we are not yet in a position to state categorically that IdeFC owes the rule to RC, or vice versa.

NOTES

1. In Chaudenson (1974:444) where this sentence is quoted, there are two minor spelling differences (both correct French): *marron* for *maron,* and *parce qu'Alexis* for *parcequ'Alexis.*

2. Focard (pp. 221-27) corrects the text of the first stanza of a song, *Nounoutte,* which had appeared in an earlier volume of *BSA.* This same song is reproduced in Laray (1888-92b: 146-47) in a different orthography and with some changes. These changes are generally in the direction of "more correct" RC grammar or lexicon, but by no means all of Focard's suggested emendations are adopted. I cannot evaluate the significance of this, but I suspect that the original text (the one criticized by Focard) was indeed aberrant from the point of view of any variety of RC, and that the (later) version of the song given by Laray had already been "Reunionized" by successive singers/transcribers.

3. The precise date on which the Mozambique slave text was first written down, and by whom, is not known. But the application of FVT in the Mozambique slave's usage is consistent in a broad sense with the Malagasy slave's usage, in Freycinet (1827) below.

4. As a modal auxiliary meaning 'may', only the short form *met* occurs.

5. Cf. the slightly misleading assertion in Corne and Moorghen (1978:72) to the effect that the FVT rule operates in IdeFC/RC under conditions unknown in any other variety of Creole French.

6. The development of such forms as IdeFC *al* 'go' from *ale* (Fr. *aller* but not, as far as I know, **alle*) can be seen as an analogical extension of the alternation patterns produced by the operation of FVT rule(s) (Goodman 1964:61).

A5
Some Specific Structures

In this chapter, data are adduced concerning a number of areas of syntactic structure. The "*get*-passive" of IdeFC is briefly described, and parallel constructions in other Creole languages are presented. Then, in A5.2, clefting (or "focusing") of "verbs" in IdeFC is examined. This feature of IdeFC has not heretofore been mentioned in the literature, and I label it, following Taylor, "double predication." Again, parallel structures in other Creole languages are briefly presented, and I discuss even more briefly the possible provenience of these structures. In A5.3, I present the structure I have elsewhere called "Indefinite Subject Deletion" and suggest a new analysis of it. These three areas of syntax in IdeFC have no known parallels in RC, but in A5.4.1 I turn to a discussion of the "mysterious *i*" of SC in one of its manifestations, and suggest a possible origin for the SC *pa i* structure. It is claimed that it derives ultimately from RC. In A5.4.2 another structure with *pa*, this time in sentence-initial position, is dealt with, and shown to have analogues in other Creole languages. Finally, in A5.5, two structures common to RC and IdeFC, the "sylleptic dual" and the *dâ*-"gerundive," are discussed and shown to derive from French.

A5.1 The *gaŷ* Construction

This structure of IdeFC has been described in some detail in a number of recent publications (chronologically, Corne 1977d, 1977c, 1977a; Corne and Moorghen 1978; Papen 1978b; Corne and Stein 1979; Corne 1980). What follows is a summary of the salient facts, and my analysis of them.

In SC, there is a structure consisting of the lexical item *gaŷe* 'get' (always truncated, *gaŷ*) which corresponds roughly in its semantics to the English "*get*-passive," so called (cf. Gee 1974). Some examples are:

(SC) *zot pu gaŷ peye par guvernma* 'they will be paid by the government'
(SC) *zot ava pe gaŷ peye* 'they will be getting paid'
(SC) *pâgar u a gaŷ tape* 'careful you don't get hit'
(SC) *i ti n gaŷ pardone* 'he was pardoned'
(SC) *i pe gaŷ servi par plizier serviter* 'he is being served by several servants'
(SC) *Pier i n gaŷ elekte minis* 'Peter was/got elected Minister'
(SC) *lisiê i gaŷ morde ek pis* 'dogs get bitten by fleas'
(SC) *i ti gaŷ âvoy Sesel par guvernma*
  'he was sent to Seychelles by the government'
(SC) *sez i n gaŷ repare* 'the chair got repaired'
(SC) *tu nu kalu i n gaŷ buar* 'all our toddy got drunk'

The subject of such sentences tends to be more often a person than an inanimate object, although both occur. The subject of the main clause is underlyingly an Agent (or an Instrument in the case of a subject with inanimate reference), the embedded clause following *gaŷ* is a stative. To some extent, the *gaŷ* construction often implies sympathy for, agency of, intentionality or responsibility on the part of, or some more or less direct involvement on the part of, the surface subject. However, for at least some speakers, there seems to be a tendency to use the *gaŷ* construction in lieu of "ordinary" stative sentences, so that there is a near-identity of meaning between, say:

(SC) *Pier i n elekte minis*
(SC) *Pier i n gaŷ elekte minis*   'Peter has been elected Minister'

In all the examples given above, the item following *gaŷ* may also occur as the predicate head in active sentences, for example:

(SC) *guvernma pu pey zot* 'the government will pay them'
(SC) *guvernma ti âvoy li Sesel* 'the government sent him to Seychelles'

But the construction is not limited to such "verbal" items, as the following show:

(SC) *zot gaŷ fre asuar* 'they get cold at night'
(SC) *Pol i n gaŷ prezidâ* 'Paul got to be president (has been elected)'

The *gaŷ* construction tends not to occur with certain "adjectival" kinds of items, such as *fatige* 'tired', *âraze* 'very angry', *oblize* 'obliged', *forse* 'forced', *sipoze* 'supposed', *okipe* 'busy', *â-koler* 'angry', *zalu* 'jealous', *zoli* 'pretty', but the reason for this is not entirely clear. A possible, albeit partial, explanation is as follows. As noted above, the embedded clause is a Stative, that is, it has a Patient as its (coreferential) subject, along the lines of:

lisiê i gaŷ $_{NP}$[*lisiê i morde ek pis*]

Lexemes, such as *kole* 'stick, stuck', which meet the phonological specifications of the FVT rule and which may occur as predicate head in Active clauses, occur also in Processive and Stative clauses. Whatever the ultimate reading of a sentence containing the *gaŷ* structure, a reading which will of course depend in part on the preposed predicate particles chosen, the net result of the embedding process is to render the embedded sentence processive. Note now that the FVT rule does not apply to the predicate head in either Processives or Statives, and that these two categories are not therefore clearly differentiated in surface structure. I suggest that the use of the *gaŷ* construction provides a marked procedure for just such a differentiation (and it is perhaps for this reason that some speakers tend to use it more than others), so that

i ti n pardone 'he was pardoned'

is a Stative, although the head *pardone* is in some sense representing Process, while in

i ti n gaŷ pardone 'he was pardoned'

the embedded head *pardone* is clearly marked as being Processive. Now in the case of the "adjectival" type of item listed above, it may be supposed that such items represent Process more transparently than does an item such as *kole* 'stuck'; *okipe* 'busy' seems a clear enough candidate in this respect, and note that *okip* means 'look after':

(SC) *i pe okip sô lakaz* 'she looks after his house'

While the rule of final vowel truncation does not normally apply to the lexical item following *gaŷ*, it may do so:

(SC) *u pu gaŷ kup u liku* 'you will get your head (neck) cut (off)'
(SC) *i n gaŷ met dâ prizô* 'he got put in prison'
(SC) *tu ban zil ki ti n gaŷ apel Trua-Frer*
      'all the islands which had been named Trois-Frères'

If my claim to the effect that the FVT rule marks Action is correct, then sentences such as these pose a problem of analysis, in that the embedded clause is a (subjectless) Active. I return to this matter in A5.3 below, where the procedure I have in the past labeled Indefinite Subject Deletion is discussed from a new perspective.

The *gaŷ* construction occurs currently in SC. In RoC, the facts are less well documented. In fact, I have precisely three attested cases of the construction:

(RoC) *kâ kan gaŷ gro, nu kup li* 'when the cane gets big, we cut it'
(RoC) *nu gaŷ buku so isi* 'we get very hot here'
(RoC) *mo fin gaŷ morde ek zâgiy* 'I have been bitten by a sea eel *(Muraena)*'

This last, from Chaudenson (1974:688), is completely compatible with the SC *lisiê i gaŷ morde ek pis* 'dogs get bitten by fleas' noted above (and is also acceptable to some, but not all, MC speakers; see Corne 1978:87, note 7; I return to the MC case below). While *gaŷ gro* does not appear to be acceptable for any of the MC or SC speakers I have been able to consult, it seems completely in line with the *gaŷ so* example following, and with the SC *gaŷ fre* sentence cited above. The most we can conclude from this is that RoC may have the *gaŷ* construction and use it similarly to SC, and that it definitely has a "rudimentary" form of the construction.

Since RoC is known to be, in some respects at least, an archaic version of MC, we must now look to the incidence of the construction in MC. In modern MC, some speakers allow the construction in at least some cases, as noted above. The MC speakers I have consulted on this point reject all the SC sentences with *gaŷ* listed above, although all claim that the meaning is transparent to them. The only widespread exception to this general rejection of the SC structure concerns a restricted number of lexemes: *gaŷ bate/beze* 'get beaten' (both very common), and, for some speakers, *gaŷ morde* 'get bitten', *gaŷ tuye* 'get killed', *gaŷ blese* 'get hurt', *gaŷ kraze* 'get crushed, run over':[1]

(MC) *li fin gaŷ beze ar Zâ* 'he was beaten (up) by John'
(MC) *zot fin gaŷ bate ar lekip lapolis* 'they were beaten by the police team'

My consultants unanimously claim that in such cases, *beze* and *bate* are being used as "nouns" (*en beze, en bate* 'a beating'). This claim may be treated with some caution, however. MC, along with the other two IdeFC languages, displays the use of multifunctional lexical items, such that even numerals may be used as the predicate head in active sentences. Compare the use of the numeral *vê-nef* (also *vêt-nef*) 'twenty-nine' in *koze sif* ('numerical slang', cf. Baker 1972:144-45) to mean 'urine, urinate':

(MC) *li pe vêt-nef* 'he is urinating'

Given such multifunctionality, it may be more justified to consider that MC, like RoC, has a rudimentary form of the *gaŷ* construction, the precise domain of which varies for different speakers, but which is in any case restricted. This is consonant with the scanty historical evidence. The earliest attestation that I have of the construction is in Chrestien (1831): *moi gagné batté* 'I get beaten' (p. 52; also in Chrestien 1838:10). In Descroizilles (1867:4) we find:

faire gagné grondé souvent '(to) get told off often'

and Baissac (1888:395, 420) has *gagne baté* and, on p. 180:

to va gagne lingué 'you will be beaten (up)'

All the MC cases of the *gaŷ* construction noted so far, in historical sources or in contemporary MC, involve the semantic field of assault (usually physical, but also verbal in Descroizilles).

In RC, there is no trace that I have been able to discover of a construction in any way similar to the SC (and the rudimentary MC and RoC) *gaŷ* construction. In common with IdeFC, RC uses the lexical item *gaŷ(e)* 'have, get' followed by a direct object:

(RC) *muê la gaŷ sa avek Zili* 'I got that from Julie'
(RoC) *mo fin gaŷ sa avek li* 'I got that from him'
(MC) *mo a gaŷ en baba* 'I shall have a baby'
(SC) *mô a gaŷ ê baba* 'I shall have a baby'

This usage occurs also in popular and dialectal varieties of metropolitan French, and in seventeenth-century popular French (Chaudenson 1974:768-70). It is clearly the ultimate surface source of the IdeFC construction, but IdeFC, and especially SC, has developed it in a novel (from the point of view of French) way. But not in a way utterly unknown among other Creole languages, as we shall see. RC does have, however, another construction using the verb *gaŷe*. The sense is somewhat different, however, in that the RC *gaŷ(e)* + Infinitive means 'to be able':

(RC) *m i gaŷ lir* 'I can (am physically able to) read'
(RC) *bonom osi gaŷ pi koze* 'the fellow also can no longer talk'

This construction seems to have a reflex in IdeFC:

(RoC) *sa madam la pa pu gaŷ kôprâ li ditu*
'this/that woman will be utterly unable to understand him'

I have been unable to elicit from my MC consultants any other similar constructions, and it is quite conceivable that this is a more or less fixed expression.

I conclude from these facts that SC has extended the potentialities of a pre-existing MC construction (reflected in RoC and perhaps more developed there than in MC) in a manner entirely consistent with the way in which the language functions. RC's contribution to this development is at best minimal, since the lexical item *gaŷe* has its source in French. The apparent semantic link between RC *gaŷe* 'be able' and the IdeFC fixed expression *pa gaŷ kôprâ* 'be utterly unable to understand' is too marginal to warrant consideration.

Whereas the *gaŷ* construction of SC stands out as an innovation in Indian Ocean Creole French (bearing in mind that a more detailed examination of RoC may reveal that the construction exists in a more fully fledged form than current data indicate—a fact which would not in any way allow one to conclude that the construction existed at an earlier date in RC, cf. B3.1), it is far from unique among Creole languages generally. For Creole French alone, I note the emergence in Haitian of a similar structure using not *gaŷe* but *truve* and/or *rete*:

(HC) *jeune homme la* **té-trouver blessé** *par ioun lautre*
'the young man was wounded by another'

(HC) *conduite li* **rêter** *critiqué de toutt moune*
'his conduct is criticized by everyone'

(Faine 1937:170; boldface his)

while in some urban varieties of St. Lucian Creole French, *twape* is used. Compare:

(SLC) *i ban* 'he was banned'
(SLC) *i twape ban* 'he got banned'

(These examples, and others, were reported to me by Philip Baker; they are from an unpublished thesis by Steve Jones, *Social Change and Language Change: The Development of an Urban Variety of St. Lucian Creole,* Cornell University, 1980.) In Papia Kristang, the Creole Portuguese of Malacca (cf. Hancock 1973), the verb *toká* 'incur, be affected by' is used in an analogous way:

(PK) *yo mudre* 'I bite'
(PK) *yo toká mudre* 'I am/get bitten'

(Ian Hancock, personal communication)

Get + "verb" occurs in Jamaican, Barbadian, and Trinidadian Creole English. In Jamaican, the *get*-passive occurs only with verbs of hitting and breaking, but there is no such constraint in the other two languages (Markey and Fodale 1980:18-19):

(JC) *Taam get biitop* 'Tom got beaten up'
(Trinidadian) *hi get bait* 'he was bitten'
(Barbadian) *di trii get kot* 'the tree was cut'

Markey and Fodale claim, I think correctly, that *get*-passives are distinctly mesolectal in Creole English continua (cf. also the St. Lucian data above), as opposed to basilectal "passives" such as:

(JC) *di graas kot* 'the grass was cut'

which are seen as passive/focus devices (cf. also Broadbridge 1980:11). Markey and Fodale also claim that *get*-passives represent a development initiated by co-occurrence with a restricted set of semantically related "verbs" (of assault); this claim is based on the Creole English data given above, and also on Indian Ocean Creole French data (derived from Corne 1977d). Indeed, the existence of the *gaŷ* construction in its most developed form in SC among the IdeFC languages supports this claim. However, while it is possible that further investigation will show that the *gaŷ* construction occurs more or less frequently in the usage of identifiable groups of speakers in Mauritius, Seychelles, and Rodrigues, on present information I cannot see in what sense it might be "mesolectal" in Indian Ocean Creole French. The contention that it is seems to depend on considering RC (no *gaŷ* construction), MC (limited use thereof), and SC (developed use thereof) as constituting a continuum similar to that postulated by Markey and Fodale for Caribbean Creole English languages.

A5.2 Double Predication: A Focusing Strategy

The term "double predication" is borrowed from Taylor (1977:183-84) to designate IdeFC sentences where the predicate head is copied in sentence-initial position. This is a focusing rule which copies without deletion, in contradistinction to all other focusing rules of IdeFC which *do* delete (cf. Corne 1977a:197-99). Some examples of "double predication" are:

(MC) *batté li capave batté* (Asgarally 1977:74)
 'he can beat her as much as he likes (it will be in vain)'
(MC) *rode Zâ ti ape rod so lisiê, me li pa fin truv li*
 'John was really *searching* for his dog, but he couldn't find it'
(MC) *debat li ti debat, me vag la ti resi zet li â-deor brizâ*
 'struggle as he would, the waves succeeded in throwing him beyond the reef'
(MC) *galupe li ti pe galupe, me zot ti resi trap li*
 'although he was running like hell, they were able to catch him'
(SC) *mâze i a kapab mâze, me zame i pu grosi*
 'eat as he might, he will never put on weight'
(SC) *taye i ape taye, me lapolis i ape vin derier li*
 'even though he is running as fast as he can, the policeman/men is/are coming up behind him'
(MC) *malad li ti ape malad, me dokter napa ti kapav soŷ li*
 'although he was falling gravely ill, the doctor could not treat him'

(The two SC examples were obtained from an elderly speaker resident in New Zealand. They were rejected by other speakers in Seychelles; from Bollée, personal communication. The structure therefore appears to be obsolete in SC.) In all such sentences that I have recorded to date, the basic meaning is invariably one of emphasis and concession ('although', 'in spite of', 'be in vain').

This structure has been consistently overlooked in all recent descriptive statements on IdeFC. However, a similar structure occurs in the RoC text presented by Baker (1972:195; commented on briefly by Corne and Stein 1979:78). The context is a conversation between a dog and a king:

(RoC) *zape mem, to pa kon zape?* 'don't you even know how to bark?'

Baker remarks (p. 207) that this sentence-initial use of a "verb" + *mem* is not acceptable in modern MC. But it is perfectly acceptable in SC:

(SC) *zape mem, u pa kon zape?*
(SC) *zape mem, u pa kone?*

(The first of these is not acceptable to all speakers, but the second seems uncontroversial.) The meaning here is simply emphasis of the "verb" so fronted.

Consider now the following historical data:

(MC, 1855) *filao là na pas tini qui li tini!*
 'the filao *(Casuarina equisetifolia)* holds really fast'

(Lolliot, p. 26)

(MC, 1880) *napas tini qui li tini* 'he/it holds fast'
 napas vané qui li vané 'he/she runs + emphasis'

(Baissac, p. 199)

These sentences differ from the modern IdeFC data cited above in two respects: the fronted predicate head is negated, and the subordinator *ki* occurs. Modern MC has exactly the same structure:

(MC) *napa rode ki zot ti rode, ler Zan ti perdi so lasen lor*
 'they really searched diligently when Jeanne lost her gold chain'
(MC) *napa bure ki voler la ti bure, me lapolis ti resi may li*
 'the thief ran as fast as he possibly could, but the policeman managed to catch him'

This negation of the fronted predicate head is used for greater emphasis, as I have tried to indicate in the glosses given. The subordinator *ki* is obligatory, whereas it cannot occur with the nonnegated structures given at the beginning of this section. Baissac (1880:199) gives a third sentence:

(MC, 1880) *napas apéle vané ça qui li vané* 'that's not called *running!*'

Baissac identifies *napas vané qui li vané* as an "ellipsis" of this sentence, but this does not seem to be a necessary conclusion; the example with *apéle* looks more like an *expansion* of a basic Creole structure.

Double predication is a feature of many of the Atlantic Creoles (cf. Alleyne 1980a:103-4). The fronted predicate head in these languages is often preceded by an element corresponding to 'it is'. The meaning may be simply emphatic, but it is more often explanatory (see Taylor 1977:183-84 for a short discussion; the data given below are from Taylor unless otherwise indicated):

(Lesser Antillean) *(se) kuri mwê te ka kuri*
 'I was *running;* it is because I was running'
(Lesser Antillean) *(se) las u las* '(it is because) you are tired'
(Haitian) *lò m a rive, se kusie m a kusie* 'when I arrive, I shall go straight to bed'
(Sranan) *(a) lon mi wani lon gowe* 'what I want to do is run away'
(Jamaican) *a kom yu waan kom* 'it is just that you want to come'
(Djuka) *na kii mi dda kii tu pakila*
 'my father killed two peccaries' (Huttar 1975:15)
(Cameroonian) *na ròn i bin ròn, bòt di jandam bin dei fò i baksai* 'even though he ran as fast as he could, the policeman was catching up with him'
(Todd, personal communication; cf. Todd 1979a)

In this Cameroonian example, there is the same meaning of concession and emphasis as in IdeFC. Taylor (1977:184) notes a similar case in Lesser Antillean and in Jamaican. Here, nominal determinants precede the fronted predicate head:

(Lesser Antillean) *tut kuri mwê kuri, mwê pa te sa jwên yo*
 'run as I might, I was unable to overtake them'

In Djuka and in Jamaican, and no doubt elsewhere, the fronted predicate head may be negated, using in Djuka the negative particle *ná* 'not, not be' and in Jamaican *a no* 'it-is not':

(Djuka) *ná kii mi dda kii tu pakila* 'my father did not *kill* two peccaries
 (he merely wounded them)' (Huttar 1975:16)
(Jamaican) *a no tiif Kofi tiif di manggo* 'Kofi did not *steal* the mango'
(Bailey 1966:95)

This is in sharp contrast to the superficially similar MC construction with *napa* + predicate head + *ki* + sentence (see examples above); but Jamaican has another structure, exactly parallel to the MC one and contrasting with the Jamaican sentence just given:

(Jamaican) *no tiif Kofi tiif di manggo* 'Kofi *did* steal the mango'
(Bailey 1966:95)

It appears then to be the case that in spite of minor local differences, there is nothing in IdeFC that is not paralleled by similar structures in other Creole languages.

I am unaware of any similar structure in any variety, ancient or modern, of RC. It is of course possible that more detailed investigation of RC will reveal similar structures, but if, as I believe is the case, RC is a leveled variety of French, then such structures will be absent. French fronts everything but the verb, in the frame *c'est___qui/que* (the blank being filled by NP, PP, Adverb, but not, significantly, by Verb or Adjective). This prediction is advanced somewhat tentatively, however. The very fact that a structure reported by Baissac in 1880 should have gone unnoticed by various investigators of IdeFC in recent times is itself proof enough of the caution that is necessary.

There is a Verb + *que* + Verb structure (or structures), widely attested in the Romance languages generally, whose semantics are similar (emphasis, repetition, progression, concession), but whose syntax is at best a very imperfect parallel to the "double predication" structure of the Atlantic Creole languages and IdeFC (see the detailed study of the Romance structures in Lombard 1938:112-20; and cf. Bollée 1978). While I believe that no convincing case could possibly be constructed to show that the Romance structures are the model for "double predication" in IdeFC or in the American Creole French languages, the fact that French has such constructions as *coûte que coûte* 'whatever it may cost' and *vaille que vaille* 'whatever its value' (cf. Lombard 1938:118, note 1; 119, note 1) might perhaps be seen as a possible (if highly unlikely) reinforcing factor in the development of "double predication." Indeed, this Romance structure is reflected in at least some varieties of IdeFC: in MC, I have noted *kut ke kut* 'at all costs' (note the use of *ke* in lieu of the usual MC subordinator *ki*), while Bollée (personal communication) reports for SC:

(SC) *mâz ki mâz, prezâ ki i ana mâze* 'he can eat however much he wants, there is still food' (Bollée's gloss)

Although I do not have any examples, it may be supposed that RC also has reflexes of this structure.[2]

On the evidence, then, it appears that we have a structure in "double predication" which has no (convincing) French model and no (known) RC analogue, and which is essentially identical both semantically and syntactically to structures reported for the Atlantic Creoles generally and the Caribbean Creole French languages in particular.

The structure does have a parallel in the West African "Kwa" group of languages. This parallel is discussed, with examples, by various authors writing on the Atlantic Creole (English) languages (Alleyne 1980a:171-72; Holm 1980; Huttar 1975). Could it then be the case that "double predication" has its origin in the "Kwa" languages?

In Part B of this book, Philip Baker shows convincingly that speakers of these languages were present in Mauritius in the period 1727-35 (B2.4) in significant numbers; the possibility of a specific substratal influence cannot therefore be ruled out. There are, however, two major difficulties with a "Kwa substratum" explanation. First, how is it that Kwa speakers bequeathed this highly marked syntactic structure to IdeFC, but no other clearly identifiable syntactic structure? Second, although there is an as yet undetermined number of lexical items in IdeFC with Ewe, Fon, or Yoruba etymologies (Baker, personal communication), none of these items belong in the area of core vocabulary (cf. Bollée 1981). The question arises, therefore, of how Kwa speakers managed to impose a syntactic structure, while having so little lexical influence.

Bickerton (1981) sketches a plausible scenario for the development of this structure in Creole languages. It is based on the hypothesis that most Creole languages do not have VP as a major category, but do have V as such a category. Given a fronting rule which moves all major constituents (including V but not VP in Creoles), problems would arise in Creole languages, and in any other languages which have V as a movable constituent, unless the fronted V were to be copied/remain undeleted at the extraction site: preposed particles would remain stranded (thus, MC *li pe galupe* → **galupe li pe*), and other interpretation difficulties would arise (see Bickerton 1981:Chapter 2 for a detailed discussion; I discuss his theory of creolization briefly in A7). The explanation then is that any language with movement rules that involve V only, rather than VP, must develop a copying/nondeletion rule, that is, "languages independently invent rules when these are demanded by the structure of the language plus functional requirements."

For my purposes here, it is sufficient to note that IdeFC has "double predication," while RC does not (nor, if my view of RC syntax is correct, could it have). IdeFC may have acquired this rule in one of two ways: a specific West African substratal influence, or an independently evolved rule "demanded by the structure of the language plus functional requirements" (Bickerton 1981). Alternatively, both factors may have reinforced each other. In any case, this rule places IdeFC squarely in a tradition from which RC is excluded, and that is the point I wish to establish here.

A5.3 "Indefinite Subject Deletion" in IdeFC: Another Focusing Strategy

In previous publications, I have used the term "Indefinite Subject Deletion" to label such sentences as:

(MC) *lôtâ, ti degrad karo kan ar pios* 'in the old days, they/one/people cleared cane fields with pick axes'

This sentence is Active, as may be seen from the fact that the FVT rule has applied to *degrad(e)* 'clear'. Compare:

(MC) *lôtâ, karo kan ti degrade ar pios* 'in the old days, cane fields were cleared with pick axes' which is a Stative. In the case of the active sentence, the indefinite or general semantic agent may be (optionally) deleted (*dimun* 'people', *u* 'you', *zot* 'you (pl.), they'). Or so it seems, since MC speakers unhesitatingly provide such subjects if called upon to do so. In SC, the situation is far less clear, in that there are as yet undiscovered constraints on this procedure. Given MC sentences such as:

(MC) *kuma dir sa â kreol?* 'how is that said in Creole?'
(MC) *kâ ti kui li ar divê, li ti biê bô* 'when it was cooked with wine, it was really good'

SC speakers invariably (in my experience) provide an expressed Agent:

(SC) *koma u dir sa â kreol?* 'how do you say that in Creole?'
(SC) *kâ u/dimun/zot ti kui li* 'when you/people/they cooked it'

However, in subordinate clauses, the phenomenon does occur, albeit rather infrequently:

(SC) *mô a met u dâ lasal ki pu don bal ladâ*
'I shall put you in the hall wherein the ball will be held'
(SC) *i lev sa tapi ki ti n kuver M. avek*
'he lifts the bedspread/tablecloth with which M. was covered'

(For further examples, see Corne 1977a:169.) In RoC, the procedure appears to be identical to the MC pattern (Corne and Stein 1979:75).

To consider these subjectless sentences as having undergone an optional rule of indefinite subject deletion means that one is making an implicit assumption about IdeFC, to wit, that all IdeFC sentences must have subjects. We have already seen that this is not so, with respect to "impersonal" sentences (A2.4 above).

As has been shown elsewhere (Corne 1977d), IdeFC does not have a passive except in a marginal sense (roughly, in French-influenced varieties). By a "passive" I mean the European model whereby the Agent is expressed in a prepositional phrase, while the Goal (Patient, etc.) is the subject of the sentence. Now, passivization is in essence a focusing device; the fronting of a lexical item has as its motivational basis a shift in focus. In the absence of an expressed Agent, IdeFC tends to front the appropriate lexical item:

(MC) *lôtâ, ban esklav ti degrad karo*
'in the old days, slaves used to clear the fields (of stones)'

Here, *ban esklav* is the Agent, and IdeFC normally places the Agent in subject position.

Some Specific Structures 91

(MC) *lôtâ, karo ti degrade ar pios* 'in the old days, fields were cleared with picks'

Here, with no Agent expressed, *karo* is fronted, and this stative sentence is telling us something about the fields.

(MC) *karo ti degrad ar pios* 'the fields were cleared with picks'

In this case, the sentence is active, although the Agent remains unexpressed. Something happened, but there is predominant interest in the *karo,* and the Agent is either self-evident from context or irrelevant. But, as we have seen, MC and RoC, and SC in subordinate clauses, may front the predicate head (and any preposed particles) in order to focus attention on the action:

(MC) *lôtâ, ti degrad karo ar pios*
'in the old days, (they) cleared fields with picks'

The Agent is irrelevant, and it is not desired to focus the listener's attention on the fields, but on their clearing.

This procedure of predicate fronting in order to focus attention on the action is further evidence of the primacy of the semantic notions of Action versus non-Action in IdeFC. Let us now return to the *gaŷ* construction where the FVT rule has applied to the element following *gaŷ:*

(SC) *u pu gaŷ kup u liku* 'you will get your head (neck) cut (off)'

FVT has applied to *kup(e),* so that the focus in the embedded clause is on the action. Compare:

(SC) *u liku pu gaŷ sote* 'your head will be/get cut off'

where we are talking about *u liku,* and the embedded clause is processive, and

(SC) *u pu gaŷ u liku sote* 'you will get your head cut off'

where the focus is on *u* in the main clause and on *u liku* in the embedded clause.

It appears to be the case that of active clauses, only predicate-fronted active clauses may be embedded with *gaŷ*. SC thus retains here the pattern of using predicate-fronted sentences only in subordinate clauses, in this case in a specifically SC structure.

Predicate-fronting as described here appears to be unknown in RC. In allegro styles, specific (as opposed to indefinite) subjects are frequently omitted where the context renders misunderstanding unlikely, and the impersonal subject pronoun *i* may similarly not appear, but the specific, semantically-based fronting of the predicate head observed in IdeFC seems to be a development unconnected with RC.

A5.4 Negative Emphatic (Rhetorical) Questions

A5.4.1 In the preceding three sections, I have briefly examined structures which do not, as far as is known at present, have any RC analogue. The SC phenomenon with which this section is concerned can, however, be shown (if somewhat tenuously) to have its roots in the putative RC **le ki* and the attested RC *lete ki* construction. It is important to note that the SC structure I shall be sketching here does not exist at all in the other two IdeFC languages, either now or in any early text yet consulted.

This structure may be represented schematically as follows:

Subject + *pa* + *i* + preposed marker(s) + Head + (X) + ? + !

This aspect of the "mysterious *i*" in SC has been discussed, with varying degrees of detail, in a number of publications (Corne 1974-75; Corne 1977a, Corne and Moorghen 1978; Papen 1978b; and briefly in Bollée 1977a:79).

Let us first see some examples of such sentences:

(SC) *u pa i ti ape mâze?!* 'weren't you (even, really) eating?'
(SC) *nu pa i ava uar li?!* 'won't we even see him?'
(SC) *i pa i pu mâze?!* 'won't he (really) eat?'
(SC) *i pa i ana (dimun) ki kon koz frâse dâ sa pei?!*
      'isn't there *anyone* who knows how to speak French in this country?'

In all cases, the answer "no" is expected, and the speaker is expressing incredulous surprise. The pattern occurs also in subordinate clauses:

(SC) *u a truve si mô pa i a gaŷ u* 'you'll see if I don't (won't) get you'

and in negative emphatic statements as well:

(SC) *u pa i kôprâ mizer!* 'you really don't understand poverty'

but I do not know to what extent these latter usages are typical nor the exact meaning other than what I assume to be emphasis of some kind. It has been shown elsewhere that the subject-*reprise* by *i* in SC derives, at least in part, from the RC **le ki* construction (Corne 1974-75, Corne and Moorghen 1978), and the matter is discussed also by Baker (B3.2.2).[3] The *pa i* construction also has its source in this structure.

In RC, as we have seen, the negator *pa* follows the verb (A1.8 above). A pair of sentences such as the following:

(RC) *muê (le)te pa malad* 'I was not ill'
(RC) *muê (le)te (k)i mâz pa* 'I didn't eat'

illustrates that *lete* in the first sentence is a verb, but that the *lete* of *lete ki* is not, in modern RC; it marks the Past tense, and *i* is the "verb marker." Similarly, the Present tense equivalents of the above two sentences are:

(RC) *muê le pa malad* 'I am not ill'
(RC) *m i mâz pa* 'I don't eat'

the latter deriving from something along the lines of **muê le ki mâz pa* (see A1.6 above); these sentences show the (copula) verb *le* in the first case, and the putative underlying nonverb /le/ + "verb marker" *i* in the second. And yet clearly, at some point in the formation of RC, the (underlying) /le ki/ and the (attested) *lete ki* contained forms of the copula. This view is supported by the St. Barts and St. Thomas French evidence adduced earlier. Therefore, a categorial change has taken place at some point in the development of RC, so that **le pa ki* and **lete pa ki* do not occur.

Now, it is historical fact that considerable numbers of people from Reunion were involved in the early settlement of Seychelles (cf. Bollée 1977a:4-5). We need only suppose a tendency, in the RC(?) spoken by these settlers, toward the generalization of the structure /le ki/ such that all tenses and aspects be relegated to the embedded verb. This may not be entirely far-fetched; compare the RC Future copula:

(RC) *m i sra malad* 'I shall be ill'

where we may suppose an underlying /muê le ki sra/ 'I am who shall be'. That is, the Future of *et(r)* 'be' is itself embedded in a matrix containing the Present *(le)* of *et(r)*. The minimal context of any such generalization would have been Negative Emphasis. Now if this generalization also retained the status of *le* as a verb, the result would be, in the Past, for example:

/u le pa ki (le)te mâz la vian/

with *pa* following /le/, and Past tense marked on the following verb *mâz*. With the usual deletion of /le/ and the reduction of *ki* to *i*, we now have the SC negative emphatic question:

(SC) *u pa i ti mâz lavian?!* 'do you really not eat meat?'

In a synchronic description of SC, this *i* stands, semantically and distributionally, quite alone, apart from an equally mysterious *ni:*

(SC) *u pa ni ti kone si Bob pu vini*
'you didn't even know if/that Bob would come'

But *ni* is not a perfect parallel with *i,* in that it may follow, rather than precede, the preposed markers:

(SC) *u pa ti ni kone si Bob pu vini*

Furthermore, while the *pa i* construction is specific to SC, *ni* pops up in RoC in yet another context:

(RoC) *ni en fey u pa nâdrua kase*
'you don't even have the right to pick a single (leaf)'

paralleled in SC:

(SC) *ni ê simiz zot pa mete* 'they don't even wear a *shirt*'

Although both *i* and *ni* are used in emphatic negative sentences in SC, it does not seem possible to ascribe a common origin to both forms. The use of *ni* + a fronted nominal element in both RoC and SC suggests the existence of a similar construction in early MC (it is not, apparently, used in modern MC). The use of *ni* in a similar (but not identical) way to *i* in SC may be an independent development, encouraged by the existence of the *pa i* pattern.

I am fully aware of how feeble the proposed origin of the SC *pa i* construction must seem. There are no historical attestations of anything approaching the supposed /muê le pa ki te mâz/ of the early Reunion settlers in Seychelles (or anywhere else, for that matter). I advance it for two reasons. First, there is no other immediately obvious explanation for the structure. Second, it is the major piece of evidence that I have been able to uncover so far of a possible syntactic influence of RC on SC, exclusive of MC and RoC. There is one historical point which may require clarification. The settlement of Reunion began in 1663, and the *lete ki* construction is attested there by ca. 1715/1722 (Chaudenson 1974:444, 1106, 1147) and following (for details see A6.2). St. Barts was settled by Frenchmen by 1650 (cf. Highfield 1979:2), and the same structure is extant there. We may deduce from this that the structure was extant or at least potentially available in some variety or varieties of metropolitan French at this time. No other Creole French language, apart from SC, has any obvious reflex of the structure (assuming that the origin of the SC *pa i* construction is indeed as sketched above). The evidence amassed by Baker (B2.2) concerning the lack of Reunion settlers in Mauritius in the crucial early years of settlement correlates with the lack of any reflex of the RC *lete ki* construction in MC. But the presence of settlers from Reunion in Seychelles correlates with the presence of the *pa i* construction in SC.

A5.4.2 The *pa i* construction is not the only way of forming rhetorical questions in SC. As noted above, the *pa i* construction expects the answer "no." Another pattern expects the answer "yes." It is constructed with sentence-initial *pa:*

(SC) *pa u ti ape mâze?* 'weren't you eating?'
   (I won't believe it if you tell me you weren't!)
(SC) *pa mô ti dir u sa?* 'didn't I tell you so?' (of course I did!)

(For further examples and brief comment, see Corne 1977a:177.) In such sentences, *pa* corresponds to 'is it not so that?'; I am unaware of any RC parallel, but there are similar constructions in other Creole languages. In Cameroonian,[4] the negator *no* (which, like IdeFC *pa,* is usually in predicate-initial position) may also appear sentence-initially:

(CA) *no–bi–yu–bin–di–chòp?* 'weren't you eating?'   (Todd 1979a:918)
   NEG–be–you–PAST–PROG–eat

In Jamaican, the form *duont* 'is it not so (that)?' may occur sentence-initially (as well as finally):

(JC) *duont a Jan duu it?* 'is it not John who did it?'   (Roberts 1977:106)

In Providence Island Creole, the form is *ent* 'is it not so (that)?':

(PI) *ent mi ponkin vain da gro?* 'my pumpkin vine is growing, right?'
                                          (Washabaugh 1979:132; gloss his)

The semantic and formal similarity to the SC *pa* + Sentence construction is striking. While it is perhaps premature to draw any conclusions on the basis of these limited data, they are nevertheless highly suggestive. If the SC *pa i* construction may be seen as an influence of RC on SC, the *pa* + Sentence construction may perhaps be considered as a possible candidate for evidence of a non-French influence. Even if the SC construction may be derivable from French *n'est-ce pas que* (with appropriate deletions leading to *pa* alone), no such argument can be adduced for the parallel Creole English sentences. We appear to have here yet another structure which is essentially identical and which is shared by Creole languages of different lexical traditions. Washabaugh (1979:132) offers two hypotheses to account for the Jamaican and Providence Island sentence-initial tag. The first suggests a West African survival, noting that sentence-initial tags of this kind are infrequent (i.e., highly marked) in the world's languages, and that Fante (Akan) (a "Kwa" language), and Mandinka, two important West African languages of the Niger-Congo family, have this feature (cf. also Washabaugh 1980:89-90). Of course this hypothesis encounters the same objections as those raised earlier (A5.2) concerning a "Kwa" origin for "double predication." The second suggests natural change; Roberts (1977) notes a higher frequency of *duont* among children, and Washabaugh reports sentence-initial tags in the speech of four-year-old American children ('Right mosquitoes can't eat up clothes?' is cited in 1979:132). Children being typically the purveyors of natural changes in languages, such data support the natural change hypothesis. I have not yet observed any case in MC, ancient or modern, parallel to the SC construction. If such evidence is found, it might go some way toward supporting the West African survival hypothesis. If none is forthcoming, then two possibilities remain: either the SC construction represents an earlier MC structure which has dropped out of usage and which just happens to have never been recorded, or it is a case of natural change specific to SC (possibly having its origins in French *n'est-ce pas que*).

A5.5 Two More Structures

The Indian Ocean Creole French languages do share a large number of syntactic features, of course. Such shared features seem to be, in general, of relatively trivial interest, since they can be traced to a common origin in French. An obvious example seems to be question formation. I say "seems" because no detailed comparative investigation has been undertaken yet. There are, however, two structures which immediately strike the (more or less Standard) French-speaking investigator as being eminently peculiar to RC and IdeFC, and which at first glance do not appear to have any French model.

The first of these does not occur, as far as I am aware, in any other Creole French language. It is the "sylleptic dual":

  (RC) *zot de Marian, i rât(r) dâ l pti panie*
       'he and Marianne get into the little basket'
  (SC) *nu de Gabriel, nu ava ale* 'Gabrielle and I shall go'
  (RoC) *zot de Zâ, (zot) pu môte* 'John and he will climb/go up'
  (MC) *zot de sô garsô zot turn vitmâ lakaz*
       'she and her son quickly return home'

(The MC example is from Baissac 1888:275; modern MC does not appear to have retained this structure.)

This construction does not occur in Standard French, but remains extant in regional varieties thereof. It is discussed in some detail by Tesnière (1951), from whom the term "sylleptic dual" is taken. The existence of this construction in RC and IdeFC cannot, then, be taken as evidence of anything other than the unremarkable fact that seventeenth- and eighteenth-century varieties of French used it.

The second structure is somewhat more problematical. It is what I have called the *dâ-*"gerundive" (Corne 1977a:147-48). In this structure, in IdeFC, is a prime example of the multifunctionality of lexical items. Examples are:

(SC) *Zosefin, dâ sô â-koler, i kriye:* ...
 'Josephine, being angry, in her anger, cries out . . .'
(SC) *Frâki, dâ sô lager, i dir* . . . 'Franky, while fighting, says . . .'
(SC) *suvâ, dâ mô pe desan Lapas, mô uar Berto ek sô saret bef*
 'often, while going down to La Passe, I see Bertaud with his ox-cart'
(SC) *dâ mô pa rekonet sa de dimun, mô ti dir ek zot* . . .
 'not recognizing the two people, I said to them . . .'
(MC, 1888) *So manman vini; dans soencolère [sic] li crīe:* . . .
 'his mother comes and cries out in her anger' (Baissac, p. 109)[5]

In modern MC, the structure is highly constrained; only *dâ buar* 'in drinking' and *dâ zue* 'in playing' have been noted (and *pa, pe* seem to be excluded). Furthermore, no possessive occurs, and the reading is causal (as opposed to the "attendant circumstance" reading of the other examples given above):

(MC) *tu mo larzâ fini dâ buur larak* 'I have drunk all my money'
(MC) *tu to larzâ pu fini dâ zue kart* 'cardplaying will take all your money'

I do not know to what extent the construction is used in RoC, but the limited data available (Corne and Stein 1979:75) suggest a situation similar to SC:

(RoC) *dâ ape marse, ape rode* 'while (he) was walking and searching'

The use in some of these examples of the preposed *predicate* particle *(a)pe* 'Progressive' suggests embedding of a clause, but given the ability of IdeFC lexical items to appear in surface structure when "needed," this does not seem to be a necessary interpretation. The *dâ* construction is, except in modern MC, a substitute for an adverbial clause of time (simultaneity). Only *(a)pe* and *pa* among the predicate precursors have been observed. The use of the possessive is usual, but not obligatory:

(SC) *lerua dâ sâ kone, i dir* . . .

'the king, in his ignorance, says . . .'

Against the notion of clause embedding, note the following:

(SC) *dâ tu mô meg, u a kone sa ki mô kapab fer!*
'even though I'm skinny, you'll find out what I can do!'

Now, none of the above seem particularly "French." However, the same, or a very similar construction, is found in RC:

(RC) *alor dâ sô â-vwa-d-famiy la, li lave en âvi*
'so, being pregnant, she got a (pregnant woman's) fancy'
(Barat et al. 1977:24)

in Louisiana Creole French, albeit marginally:

(LC) *dô tu so led, li gê le vayô môyer*
'although he is ugly, he has nice manners'
(Neumann, personal communication)

and again in Haitian Creole French:

(HC) **lans flatter** *moune, li fine par trapper quichoye*
'by flattering people, he finally got something'
(Faine 1937:144; boldface his; he gives two further examples)

Un-French though the construction may appear, its occurrence in similar guise in IdeFC, RC, LC, and HC inevitably suggests a metropolitan French origin. It is precisely the un-Frenchness of the structure that renders this conclusion problematical. We have already seen that the FVT rule, occurring in American Creole French in various guises, and in RC and IdeFC in an identical way (semantics excepted), does not allow any unqualified conclusions to be drawn. Mutual influence (RC on IdeFC or vice versa) cannot be ruled out. For the *dâ*-"gerundive" construction, the same may well apply. However, it seems more likely that seventeenth- and eighteenth-century varieties of French contained a structure which is reflected in its basic form in HC and RC, and that the IdeFC construction is a local development of this basic model.

A5.6 Summary

What we have seen in this chapter is manifestly sketchy and incomplete, and is a clear indication of the work yet to be undertaken. But nevertheless, certain facts stand out.

Some Specific Structures 99

The development of the *gaŷ* construction in SC is an extension of a preexisting MC pattern, initiated in all likelihood by co-occurrence with a restricted set of semantically related lexical items in MC, the major input in the early linguistic situation of the Seychelles. This SC development has proceeded far enough to include the active, predicate-fronted clauses of IdeFC, producing a configuration unique among Creole French languages. The very model of the construction is lacking in RC. However, this type of development of a "passive" is not unparalleled among Creole languages elsewhere, be they of French lexical provenience (Haitian, St. Lucian) or other (Papia Kristang, West Indian Creole English).

Taylor's "double predication" is reflected in IdeFC in various ways, with similar semantic consequences. This is significant for a number of reasons. The *get/gaŷ* passives are what we might see as a "natural" and later (or "decreolizing") development (cf. Markey and Fodale 1980:18-19) and thus likely to occur in typologically identical languages, but double predication is not. Yet it is common in the American Creole French languages, and occurs in Creole English languages as well as in IdeFC. Ignoring the various Romance and IdeFC reflexes of the Latin construction represented in French by *coûte que coûte* (cf. Lombard 1938:112-20), which cannot realistically be seen as models for double predication, it may be asserted that the latter construction is unknown in any reported variety of French, including RC. It is, however, a well-known feature of the West African languages known as the "Kwa" group.

Thus, so far in IdeFC we have two procedures which cannot be shown to be of French origin. The first, the *gaŷ* construction, has developed to fill a semantic and syntactic "gap" in a language which is typologically different from French (which does not have such a gap, since French speakers already have at their disposal fully functioning passives, as well as "symmetrical" verbs [cf. Lagane 1967], pronominal [reflexive] verbs, and the structure with the indefinite *on* 'one, they, people'). The second, "double predication," may represent a West African substratal influence, and/or it may be an independent and early innovation arising from the very nature of creolization in Mauritius (and its occurrence in other Creole languages would then be due to the same universal processes operating in similar circumstances, cf. Bickerton 1981). It is used to handle semantic concepts which are dealt with in a variety of different ways in French. Both structures occur in Creole English languages, for the same reasons: on the one hand, a "natural" development in typologically identical languages (the *gaŷ* construction); and on the other hand, a West African substratal influence and/or a reflex of universal processes operating in creolization situations.[6]

The subjectless sentences of IdeFC appear to be an independent development. Be they cases of "indefinite subject deletion," as I have previously analyzed them, or cases of "predicate-fronting," as suggested here, they nevertheless appear to be unique among Creole languages. The procedure, whatever its correct analysis turns out to be, is not demonstrably French, is not a feature of RC, and is integrated

100 CORNE

into an entirely novel construction with *gaŷ* in SC.

These three areas of syntax in IdeFC demonstrate, if further demonstration is needed, the semantico-syntactic lack of indebtedness of IdeFC vis-à-vis RC.

The *pa i* construction of SC, on the other hand, seems to be a case where more or less direct RC influence is discernible. Although the analysis presented here has undeniable weaknesses, let us admit that this construction in SC does indeed betray the direct influence of RC, in the form of the putative **lete pa ki* structure. The crucial point to note is that *only* SC, of the IdeFC languages, has the *pa i* construction. There is not the slightest trace of it in MC or RoC, and even in SC it appears to be a specific development, semantically, of the putative RC structure. The superficially similar *pa*-initial sentences of SC, however, may perhaps be further evidence linking Creole French languages with Creole languages of different lexical bases.

The "sylleptic dual" of Indian Ocean Creole French is known to be a "French" structure. The construction with *dâ* (*lâ* in Haitian Creole French) seems to reflect a non-Standard French procedure which has been developed in IdeFC (and subsequently restricted in MC). Both look "non-French" at first flush, but in fact fit into a pattern of inheritance from French without any need to invoke a privileged role for RC as far as IdeFC is concerned.

NOTES

1. Papen (1978b:439) notes also: MC *si mo kokê sa moto la, mo pu gaŷ trape ar lapolis* 'if I steal that motorcycle, I'll get caught by the police'.
2. Note a reflex of the Spanish Verb + *que* + Verb structure in Philippine Creole Spanish (Zamboangueño), mentioned briefly in Forman (1972:222). While Forman claims (p. 235) that in Zamboangueño this structure follows a pattern common in the languages of the Philippines, the Spanish model should not be too readily dismissed as a possible source.
3. A propos of the term *reprise* to designate the element *i* which occurs between the subject and the predicate in SC. Following the abolition of slavery in 1835, the Royal Navy "liberated" in Seychelles a considerable number of Africans, presumably from the eastern region of Africa, found on slaving vessels that had been arrested in the general vicinity (some 2,400 slaves between 1861 and 1872; cf. Bollée 1977a:5). Now in Bantu languages the first element in the predicate is normally a "concord" prefix which reflects the class of the subject NP (whether this subject is present on the surface or not). The following statement, made with regard to the Punu language (a Kikongo dialect), in fact applies to Bantu languages generally (cf. Werner 1919):

> *Le préfixe verbal*
> Le PV est présent, qu'il y ait un sujet lexical ou non. Quand il y a un sujet lexical qui précède le verbe, le PV est identique au préfixe nominal (PN) du substantif sujet, sauf pour la classe 1 (la classe des personnes) [and a few other exceptions, varying from one Bantu language to another–Corne]

(Fontaney 1980:68)

Some Specific Structures   101

There is at least a superficial resemblance between the concord in Bantu languages and the SC "*i*-reprise." Compare the following data from Macua (Makúwa), the principal language of northern Mozambique:

Macua	SC	English
ekhoropa enalya	kurpa i ape mâze	'the snail is eating'
enalya	i ape mâze	'it is eating'

(*e-* 'class 7 concord prefix'; *-khoropa* 'giant African land snail, *Achatina sp.*'; *-na-* 'progressive'; *-lya* 'eat'; I am grateful to Mateus Katupha, a native speaker of Macua, for these data and glosses). Similarly in Swahili:

Swahili	SC	English
mtoto anaimba	zâfâ i ape sâte	'the child is singing'
anaimba	i ape sâte	'he/she is singing'

(*a-* 'he/she, class 1 concord prefix'; *mtoto* 'child'; *-na-* 'progressive'; *-imba* 'sing'). It is not impossible that the very term "subject *reprise*" may reflect Eurocentric thinking, and that the three mutually reinforcing factors mentioned by Baker (B3.2.2) were further reinforced by the Bantu pattern. However, while the use of *i* as a "reprise" of the subject in SC bears some resemblance to the concord and "pronoun" system of Bantu languages, the constraints on the co-occurrence of *i* with certain preposed particles remain largely unexplained (cf. Corne 1977a: 35-39).

Perhaps more importantly, the behavior of *fin (in, n)* with processive predicate heads in IdeFC is also reminiscent of the Bantu languages:

Macua	IdeFC	English
ekhukulu ehophweya	sez fin kase	'the chair is broken'

(*khukulu* 'something to sit on'; *-ho-* 'completive'; *-phweya* 'broken'). This parallel is potentially significant. The tripartite contrast of action, process, and state has been shown to be central to the operation of the predicate system of IdeFC (A2) and of at least some Atlantic Creole languages (Christie 1976)—it is probably valid for most others as well. While Haitian Creole French does have an element *fin* (its precise status and usage are unclear to me, cf. Valdman 1978a:218 and also A4.2.2 above), in the Atlantic Creoles generally the completive is signaled by the unmarked form of the "verb" (i.e., by zero). The specific use of *fin* detailed in A2.4 is a highly visible and area-specific feature of IdeFC (and even RC has, albeit marginally, possible traces of it; see A1.4). This IdeFC use of *fin* does not seem to be in any sense (except etymologically) a natural development of any variety of French that I am aware of, and is quite conceivably an (East or Southeast) African substratal influence (cf. A7).

4. For the sociolinguistic status of Cameroonian, see Gilman (1979). Cf. also Todd 1979b.

5. In Chrestien (1831:48), *dans son rodé* occurs; in context, the gloss 'in his search' seems more appropriate than 'while searching', but the structure itself is identical to the SC and MC (1888) examples given. Also in Chrestien (p. 45): *dans son causé;* this "nominal" use of *koze* 'speech' parallels modern usage.

6. A slightly modified version of A5.2, favoring the universalist view, will appear in *Te Reo* 24 (1981) under the title "Verb Fronting in Isle de France Creole."

A6
Two Different Linguistic Traditions

The preceding chapters have been devoted to descriptive matters. In A1, the verbal system of RC is shown to be fundamentally "French" in its makeup, and to be based on a relatively rigid "parts-of-speech" categorization of lexical items. The morphological, syntactic, and semantic structures are all basically "French." "Creole" features, such as the use of *fin(i)* (A1.4), do exist, but are rather marginal. In A2, a "new" analysis, which claims to represent the way in which the IdeFC predicate system actually functions, depicts a language whose organization is fundamentally different from that of RC. This system is based on the multifunctionality of lexical items, which are generally morphologically invariant. The system is essentially an aspectually based one, using preposed particles. The notions of Action, Process, and State are fundamental to the operation of the IdeFC system, in clear contrast to their relative unimportance in RC. In A3, the rule of Final Vowel Truncation is shown to be shared by both IdeFC and RC. This rule has a clear semantic motivation in IdeFC, in that it marks Action, but it seems to apply in RC quite gratuitously as far as meaning is concerned. However, the rule does define a continuum in RC, even though the interpretation of this fact remains ambiguous in the absence of detailed study. It is so highly unlikely as to be almost impossible that this rule should be an independent innovation in RC and IdeFC, and A4 attempts to survey the historical and comparative evidence in order to elucidate the origin(s) of the rule. While the evidence is not conclusive, I suggest that the rule does not have its origins in the Indian Ocean, and its existence cannot be used to "prove" a common "ancestor" for these languages. So chapters A3 and A4, then, taken together, show that the major similarity between the RC and the IdeFC "verbal" systems, namely, the phenomenon of final vowel truncation, does not imply a commonality of structure and function; the two systems are irreconcilably different. In A5, the central system of predication is left aside, and a number of other structures are briefly examined. The *gaŷ* construction is shown to have no RC (and no French) model, but it has parallels in various Creole languages of different lexical stock. The Atlantic Creole structure of "double predication" is reflected in IdeFC in various ways, but again, no RC and no French model for it is known. Predicate-fronting (or "indefinite subject deletion") is not demonstrably either French or RC. So we have here three syntactic structures with specific semantic motivation, which have nothing whatsoever to do with RC. The *pa i* construction of SC does, however. But only SC has this structure, and this correlates with the known presence of settlers from Reunion in Seychelles in the early phase of settlement. The sylleptic dual and the *dâ* construction, common to RC and IdeFC, were chosen to illustrate a common heritage from French.

Two Different Linguistic Traditions   103

Any number of other structures could have been chosen in their stead, but these two are interesting because it is not immediately obvious that they are in fact of French origin.

This material demonstrates that RC and IdeFC are not only different in the way they "work" at the most basic levels of semantics and syntax, but also that IdeFC contains structures which are typically "Creole" (i.e., non-French and having parallels in other lexically diverse Creole languages; cf. also Todd 1971a: 918-19).

A6.1 IdeFC and American Creole French (ACF)

The prevailing view until very recently has been that IdeFC, in common with ACF, has an underlying copula which is deleted on the surface in most environments (e.g., Valdman 1978a:232).

In ACF, as in IdeFC, lexical items are multifunctional, and the predicate system as described here for IdeFC is fundamentally that of ACF as well. In particular, "nonverbal" elements occur as the predicate head, generally without any copulative element. The exception in ACF is the structure NP *se/sa* NP, where *se/sa* look suspiciously like copular forms. However, at least one writer (Saint Jacques Fauquenoy 1971) offers an alternative analysis of these forms, which have usually been seen as the copula (e.g., Valdman 1978a:232-41). I do not wish to argue here the question of the precise status of these items, since it is not directly relevant to the discussion. Suffice it to say that the facts show that ACF and IdeFC are fundamentally identical with respect to sentences with a "nonverbal" predicate head. In ACF, a stative lexeme *ye* occurs in the same (or very similar) contexts as does IdeFC *ete*. As we have seen, an adequate description of current IdeFC syntax is obtained without recourse to a putative underlying copula, *ete* being seen as a stative of location, existence, or equivalence, and IdeFC *se* as an optional and quite possibly prestigious and/or nonbasilectal non-Past marker in focused sentences.

This situation may be compared with that obtaining in RC, where the copula occurs regularly as in French, and is inflected for tense. Even if the RC copula were to be analyzed as an inserted (by a relatively late rule) element to carry tense/aspect distinctions which other lexical items such as adjectives or nouns cannot carry (cf. such pairs in English as: *Adjectives cannot/are unable to carry tense markers in English;* or *The committee met three times/There were three meetings of the committee*), it would nevertheless be the case that RC is clearly differentiated from IdeFC by such an insertion rule. Whether one adopts such an analysis or adheres to a simpler view, namely, that RC has a copula and IdeFC does not, the surface presence of the RC verb *et(r)* in its various shapes and functions shows that the organization of RC is very different from that of IdeFC.

The question of the copula aside, it is well known that the ACF languages share some or all of the characteristics of IdeFC described in A2. Louisiana Creole French is a partial exception to this statement; for example, the placement rules for the negator *pa* are not quite the same (Lane 1935; Morgan 1959, 1976; Hancock n.d.; Hull, personal communication; Neumann, personal communication). Like IdeFC, the ACF languages have aspectual rather than temporal systems, utilizing preposed particles. These may appear in combinations, although there are fewer combinational possibilities in ACF than in IdeFC. All the ACF languages, with the exception of Louisiana Creole French, share with IdeFC the combination Past/ Anterior + Future/Irrealis + non-Punctual/Progressive, in that order. These facts contrast very sharply with the RC system as described in A1, where not only are preposed "particles" the exception rather than the rule, but also the combination corresponding to Past + Future + Progressive, RC **te i sa et(r) apre* (+ Infinitive), does not occur at all (and *va, a* do not occur in combination with the Past tense). In Dominican Creole French at least, and undoubtedly in other ACF languages as well, the semantic notions of Action, Process, and State have linguistic consequences very similar to those we have seen for IdeFC (Christie 1976). Similar does not mean identical, of course. Taylor (1977:178ff.) has shown that the values of specific aspectual particles are not the same in Lesser Antillean Creole French as in Haitian Creole French (and that the former agrees with Sranan [Creole English] while the latter agrees with Jamaican Creole English). The absence of any particle in ACF generally indicates, approximately, non-Anterior, while in IdeFC it indicates non-Past. But these are matters of detail, not substance, and do not affect the basic point. This is that IdeFC and ACF function in a strikingly similar way in their systems of predication. As has been demonstrated, RC is quite different; its relatively rigid "parts-of-speech" categorization, its auxiliary verb, its tense system, indeed its whole organization—all show it to be a variety of French. It is, therefore, justifiable to group IdeFC, but not RC, with the ACF languages.

But these latter belong to the language group known as the Atlantic Creoles. These share, in broad terms, the characteristics noted above: the manner of forming negative sentences, aspectual preposed particles, combinations thereof, multifunctional lexical items; in short, the system of predication is in essence, if not in every detail, the same. They also share more specific structures, such as double predication (A5.2). The fact that there are some constructions in some Atlantic Creoles which do not appear to have any parallel in IdeFC is irrelevant. For example, the recent survey of verb serialization by Jansen et al. (1978)—a construction apparently absent from IdeFC[1]—shows that there is a wide range of uses among various Atlantic Creole languages. These too are matters of detail, not substance, and IdeFC must be seen, at the very least, as belonging to a linguistic tradition quite different from that of RC.

A6.2 The Origins of RC and the Reunion Linguistic Continuum

Very broadly, the history of Reunion may be divided into three periods. The first of these, from 1663 to around 1715, is the period of small-scale agriculture. The second, from 1715 to 1815, is the period of coffee production for export.

The third, from 1815 to the present, is the era of the sugar plantation. Within this third period, the *Départementalisation* of the island in 1947 heralds significant changes.

These three periods have demographic and linguistic correlates. In the first period, RC emerges in a recognizably modern form in a situation where French is both socially and numerically dominant. In the second, there is an influx of French settlers, an even greater influx of slaves, and the Petits Blancs emerge as a distinct group. In the third, this group develops, slavery is abolished, and there is in consequence a massive inflow of indentured laborers from India. Subsequent to 1947, there is an increasing metropolitan French presence and an increasing contact with Standard French through schooling and modern communications media. I shall deal briefly with each of these periods in turn.

The era of small-scale agriculture (Chaudenson 1974:452-65; Defos du Rau 1960:132-38; Rosset 1967) constitutes the first period. The continuous habitation of Bourbon (Reunion) dates from 1663, when two Frenchmen and ten Malagasies, including three women, landed from Fort Dauphin (Madagascar). In 1665, some twenty Frenchmen initiated the permanent colonization of the island. The picture which emerges over the next fifty years or so is characterized by a number of features.

The most striking feature is the number of mixed marriages between French men and Malagasy women (the first child of such a marriage was born in 1667 and is thus the first French "Creole"). From 1678 on, some fourteen or so young Indo-Portuguese women arrived, and rapidly contracted marriages with French colonists. A locally-born population of mixed ascendancy was thus rapidly established: some 92 individuals representing approximately 34.5 percent of the total population in 1686. Equally important is the size and origin of the slave population. Throughout this period, slaves were numerically fewer than colonists. Its composition was as follows: locally-born individuals of diverse parentage (33 percent in 1704, 38 percent in 1709), involuntary immigrants from Madagascar (35.5 percent in 1704, 24 percent in 1709), from India (14.5 and 24 percent), from East Africa (14.8 and 12.5 percent). Within a framework of French dominance, both social and linguistic, the essential features of this period are the importance of the Malagasy group (about half of all women present on the island in 1686 were of Malagasy origin) and the rapid establishment of a locally-born population of mixed Franco-Malagasy or Franco-Indo-Portuguese ascendancy.

The settlers of French origin in this period came from various parts of France. Mainly artisans, often illiterate, their "French" would certainly have been far removed from the Court usage of seventeenth-century France from which modern Standard French ultimately derives. The "official" language of the new colony was, as contemporary documents (governors' reports, the Petition of 1678 [see Rosset 1967:97-99], etc.) show, recognizably seventeenth-century "Court" French, and it may be assumed that at least some early colonists approximated this usage in speech. Nevertheless, while the dominant linguistic element was "French," this "French" must have rapidly become a more or less leveled variety or varieties, incorporating elements of the original regional dialects from France, plus perhaps something along the lines of Hull's ([1975] 1979) concept of Maritime French, cf. also Faine (1939:16). This mixing of linguistic subsystems, producing a leveling or a "common core" grammar (cf. Bailey 1973:33), and the "inherent tendency" of French toward the simplification of the inflectional system (Chaudenson 1974:1125; cf. also the lengthy discussion of the concept of "advanced French," pp. 1132-43), go some little way toward accounting in a general sense for RC as I have described it in A1.

But this is far from being the whole story. Chaudenson has shown, correctly in my opinion, that RC existed in essentially its modern form by ca. 1722. The by now much-quoted sentence:

(RC, ca. 1722)*Moin la parti maron parcequ'Alexis l'homme de jardin l'était qui fait à moin trop l'amour*
'I ran away because the gardener Alexis was making love to me (?—was courting me?) too much'
(Chaudenson 1974:444, 1106, 1147)

although very brief, displays three morphosyntactic features characteristic of modern RC. These are: (i) the variation in form of the first person pronoun, *muê* as subject, *amuê* as object; (ii) the perfect tense constructed with the auxiliary *la* and the past participle *parti;* (iii) the *lete ki* construction for the past tense. The speaker of this sentence is identified as a *bonne,* that is, a domestic servant. That she is a slave is deducible from the fact that she is charged with the crime of *marronnage* 'running away', a crime committable only by slaves. This does not necessarily mean, however, that the sentence quoted is typical of all slave usage, since at any given moment there would have been newly arrived slaves who found themselves in a situation of handicapped language learning (cf. the impression of "inadequate" RC conveyed by some of the early nineteenth-century texts given by Chaudenson 1974:1147-48), nor does it mean that only (some category of) slaves used this speech form. But it does show that *at least some* slaves, in 1722 or thereabout, were speaking a language remarkably similar if not identical to modern RC.

The very fact that this language of ca. 1722 is essentially that of modern times suggests that it was in widespread use, sufficiently widespread at least so that the massive immigration which characterized the second period of Reunion's history (see below) had a relatively minor impact upon it. It may be assumed, therefore, that by 1722 the language attested by the domestic servant's deposition was, while not the sole variety of "French" spoken on the island, at least the vehicular language, the vernacular, of Bourbon. While leveling pressures undoubtedly existed in the small community of seventeenth-century Bourbon, while in the absence of strong normative pressures the "inherent tendencies" of French may well have had a free rein, and while the language learning efforts of newly arrived slaves are all factors in the emergence of this vernacular, a major factor must have been the presence of the first generation(s) of locally-born children, and especially those of mixed ancestry, i.e., children of families where the parents did not share the same first language. (The possibility of both the Malagasy and the "Indo-Portuguese" women of the very early settlement period having at least some knowledge of French prior to their arrival in Reunion must be allowed for, of course.) Note that the emergence of a vernacular does not imply linguistic homogeneity on a community-wide basis. On the contrary, it seems safe to suppose that there were a multiplicity of usages, ranging from impaired second-language acquisition among new slaves through the vernacular to more or less "official" French, while the first languages of (some) slaves must have retained limited currency (with Malagasy being an obvious candidate).

In summary, at the end of the first period, RC had emerged in a situation of linguistic diversity wherein French, in various guises, was the dominant factor.

In the course of the eighteenth century, the population increased enormously. There was a sizable influx of settlers from France. In contrast to the colonists of the first period, these settlers were often the scions of bourgeois or aristocratic families. By 1740, the entire coastal zone of the island was settled. The slave population, necessitated by the extension of coffee planting, increased spectacularly. Whereas slaves constituted 42.4 percent of the total population in 1704, they formed by 1788 some 81 percent of a population of about 46,000. In order of numerical importance, there were East Africans, locally-born slaves, Malagasies, and small numbers of Indians and West Africans.

This is to say, then, that many individuals found themselves in a situation of handicapped second-language learning with respect to their target language. Throughout, the target may well have been slightly different from case to case. Some slaves, such as domestic servants, would have had a relatively close contact with their European or their locally-born masters, while others, such as field slaves on larger properties, would have been relatively isolated from such contact, except as mediated through more acculturated members (including locally-born ones) of the slave community. (This picture of extremely diverse patterns of contact may be contrasted with the more intimate contact of the first period, when properties were relatively small and slaves outnumbered by colonists.) It may be fairly safely assumed, however, that the target language in the majority of cases would have been the *lete ki* vernacular variety of French. Foreign-born slaves, in all likelihood, produced unstable, pidginized versions of this target. Their offspring were thus supplied with the nucleus of a grammatical code, lexicon, and phonology, while being at the same time exposed, to varying degrees, to the *lete ki* vernacular. Let us suppose that this process did take place along the broad lines indicated, and that the result was the forerunner of the créole des Bas. It is conceivable that such speech forms may have contained structures similar to those of IdeFC, along the lines of Bickerton's "natural semantax" creolization theory; the use of *a* and *fin* as particle-style elements are possible candidates as evidence of this (see the brief discussion in A7).

In spite of the relative prosperity enjoyed by the island in the eighteenth century, there was an ongoing pauperization of growing numbers of colonists, which led ultimately to the appearance of a new human group, the Petits Blancs (Defos du Rau 1960:144-47). As a group, they are at this stage distinguished by the fact of their poverty and their widespread lack of slave ownership. Their linguistic significance, however, does not appear until the third stage of the island's development, when sugar became the principal crop.

The third period is characterized by the cessation of slave importation and a high rate of manumission, by the system of indentured labor (from India) introduced in 1828, and by the development of the Petits Blancs group. This group consisted of impoverished colonists, often younger sons and often of mixed ancestry, established on the periphery of the sugar plantations, living from hunting, fishing, small-scale agriculture, and various expediencies (petty theft, begging, casual work). After the abolition of slavery, some 30,000 slaves abandoned the cane fields, and many established themselves in the Hauts, alongside the Petits Blancs. The twin pressures of a growing population and a growing acreage of cultivatable land given over to sugar cane plantations led to the implantation of Petits Blancs in the cirques (Salazie, then Cilaos, marginally in Mafate) and the high plains (Plaine des Cafres, Plaine des Palmistes) (cf. Defos du Rau 1960:147-56). The history of the colonization of the cirques and the high plains is in each case different, but I do not know to what extent or if this fact has contemporary linguistic consequences (but cf. the Grand-Ilet data given in A3.3 above). However, we may assume that the créole des Hauts emerged in this period. The presence of large numbers of indentured laborers, mainly from India and to a lesser degree from East Africa (Mozambique), and the formation of the ethnic group known as "Malabar" undoubtedly had linguistic consequences, in terms of pidginization (of *lete ki* French) and possible incipient creolization of this by the children of these immigrants.

The *Départementalisation* of Reunion in 1947 has led to an increase in the exposure of the population, in highly varying degrees, to the normative pressures of standard contemporary French, through the establishment of schools and the presence of relatively large numbers of Metropolitans. The position of French in Reunion has been described in some detail by Chaudenson (1979c:547-67, 598-611), and need not retain us here.

The linguistic situation in Reunion may now be considered in light of the foregoing brief remarks.

Taken as a whole, we could refer to the Reunion linguistic situation as constituting a "post-Creole" continuum (although in so doing, the fact that RC is typologically different from IdeFC and the Atlantic Creoles generally is ignored). Chaudenson (1979b:129-31) specifically refers to it as being, in the present state of knowledge, the only Creole French territory (again, the nature of RC is overlooked) which has a continuum analogous to that described for Guyana by Bickerton (1975). He gives six hypothetical sentences to illustrate the phonetic, lexical, and syntactic changes which occur as a basilectal RC moves through mesolectal varieties and finally becomes French. A 1977 study by Carayol and Chaudenson demonstrates the existence of such a continuum insofar as phonological changes are concerned. I have shown above (A3.3) that the rather scanty data available concerning the morphosyntactic rule of final vowel truncation suggest a possible (morphosyntactic) definition of a continuum. But I have also drawn attention to the fact that these data do not allow us to conclude that mesolectal varieties of RC are progressively *losing* this rule (as opposed to acquiring it). I am not so brash as to cast doubt upon the existence of a continuum in Reunion (cf. Gueunier 1980 for a discussion of variation within one small community in Reunion). I think we may accept without reservation that there is indeed a continuum in which RC is the basilect as against an acrolectal Standard (or possibly Reunion regional) French. I do, however, question whether the overall situation is parallel to the Guyanese one. In Guyana, historical and contemporary evidence shows a Creole English basilect, an acrolectal English which is distinctively Guyanese in suprasegmental, lexical, and phonological features but which is nonetheless undeniably English, and a movement by which the basilect is moving, chronologically speaking, ever closer to the acrolect, i.e., yesterday's mesolect is today's basilect (Bickerton 1975). The RC case seems to parallel this, if the only two poles considered are RC (basilect) and French (acrolect)—still ignoring of course the fundamentally different nature of the Guyanese basilect (a "true" Creole) and the Reunion basilect (not a "true" Creole), although this difference may well be quite irrelevant.

But what data I have lead me to suspect that there is a second, more or less independent "continuum." I am not sure if "continuum" is an appropriate term to use with respect to the relative status of créole des Bas and créole des Hauts, since it is not at all certain that the overt upward mobility motivation that underlies the Guyanese model is present in the contemporary Reunionese situation with respect to the Bas and Hauts varieties of RC. (In fact, given the wealth of pejorative names—*yab, yul, pat-zon*, etc.—applied by other Reunionese to the Petits Blancs, such motivation appears unlikely in the extreme.) However, it may be historically appropriate to apply the term to the relation between the créole des Bas and that of the Hauts. I shall refer to this "continuum" as the Reunion Creole continuum (as opposed to the Reunion post-Creole continuum above). The basilect would be the créole des Bas, which itself, historically, may be supposed to have emerged in the eighteenth century, as suggested above, as the result of slave pre-Creole with *lete ki* French as the target. The *lete ki* French, on its side, would be influenced by French in various guises throughout the eighteenth and nineteenth centuries and, at an early stage and perhaps subsequently, by slave pre-Creole and/or the créole des Bas. The end result of this interaction would then be the créole des Hauts. If this historical speculation has any foundation, the Reunion Creole continuum may be seen not so much as a function of the desire for and/or the possibility of upward social mobility, as a network of registers having their origins in geographical, social, and historical factors and serving various functions (group identity, perhaps?). In any case, both the créole des Bas and the créole des Hauts participate in an as yet unknown way in the Reunion Creole "continuum" today. Thus, from the point of view of French, both are more or less separate and more or less "basilectal" starting points in the Reunion post-Creole continuum.

Figure 3 (p. 111) is a crude attempt to represent this situation. The arrows are intended to represent the dynamics of a situation to which both the boxes and the necessarily overly abstract discussion above lend a falsely static air. Solid arrows represent major influences; broken arrows represent minor ones. My feeling is that the historical facts and what meager data there are go some way toward supporting this view of the contemporary linguistic situation in Reunion, but in the final analysis it must be admitted that Figure 3 remains highly speculative (albeit a lot more likely than my previous speculations on the subject, cf. Corne 1978:85, Corne and Moorghen 1978:73).

A6.3 The "Bourbonnais" Theory

In 1974, R. Chaudenson proposed a theory of the relation between RC and IdeFC. The basic elements of this theory are as follows:

1. By ca. 1715, the "primitive pidgin" of Bourbon (= Reunion) had become a Creole (1974:1106).
2. RC existed in essentially its modern form at that time (A6.2).
3. A comparison of RC, MC, SC, and RoC shows the "obvious analogy" of their lexical, phonological, and grammatical systems, which in turn implies a "common origin"; this origin would be "Bourbonnais," i.e., pre-1715 RC (1974:1106, 1115).
4. African slaves played a very minor role in the formation of "Bourbonnais" or early MC (1974:1107-9).
5. MC did not develop in the Isle de France (= Mauritius) but is a direct offshoot of "Bourbonnais," which was taken to Mauritius by the first settlers from Reunion; thus, slaves imported in large numbers after 1730 found themselves in a linguistically homogeneous situation since those masters and slaves already present spoke a single language, "Bourbonnais" (1974:446, passim).
6. Ca. 1800, MC and RC were less divergent than they are today, and it is the predominantly White population of Reunion and the constant use of, and the "extremely powerful influence" of, French which account for the fact

Two Different Linguistic Traditions   111

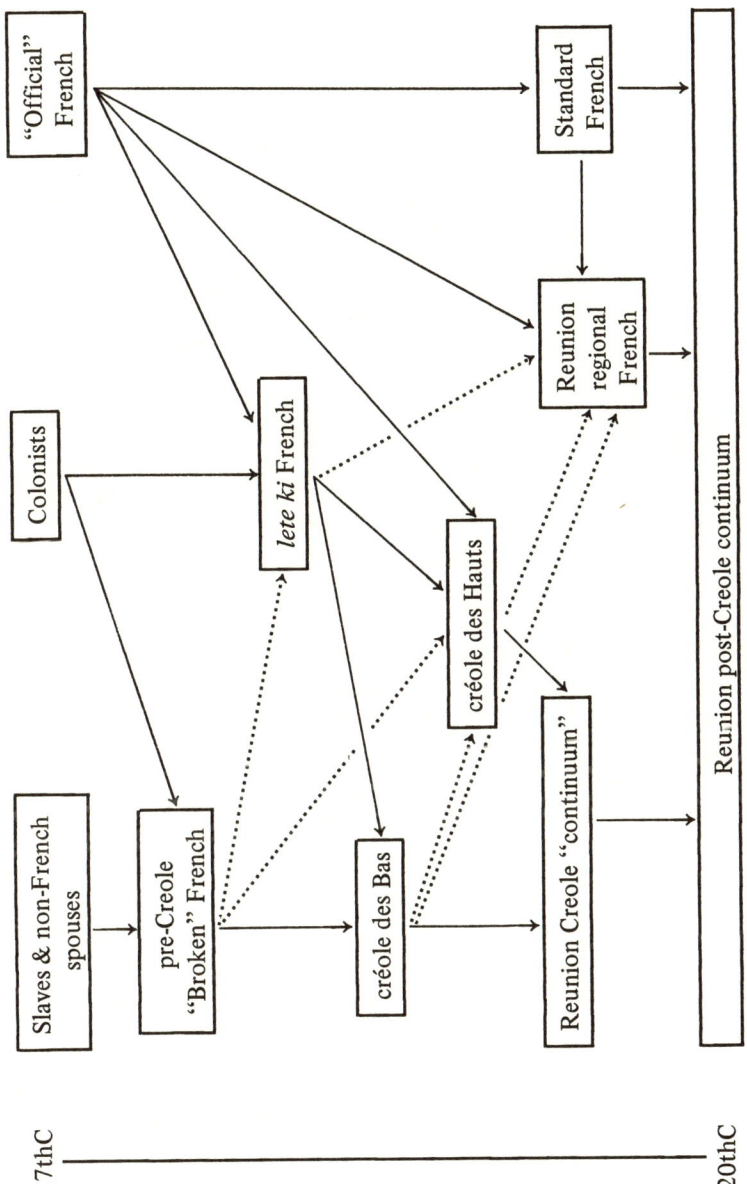

Figure 3
A Speculative View of the Reunion Language Situation and the Reunion Creole "Continuum"

that RC and MC are so different today (1974:447-49, 1117-18).

There are a number of flaws in this theory. With respect to (1), there is no documentary proof that such a primitive pidgin ever existed. If any such did exist, it could only have been in the forms of speech produced by adult second-language learners. In that RC existed by about 1715 (cf. the fragment of ca. 1722), (2) is correct. But RC, as I have shown, is typologically different from IdeFC and ACF. Thus, the "primitive pidgin" of (1) has not become a "Creole," it has become RC, that is, a leveled variety of French. As for (3), the "obvious analogy" between the grammatical systems of RC and IdeFC is anything but obvious, as I have shown in A1 and A2. The precise degree of similarity of the phonological and lexical systems remains to be established (cf. the difficulties encountered by Papen 1978b: Chapter 2, in attempting to establish a "common core" inventory of Indian Ocean Creole French phonemes), but I think it will be agreed that the predicate system is the central area where "obvious analogies" must be established. The only one I have been able to identify unambiguously is the RC use of *fini* + adjective, and even this appears to be rather marginal in RC (A1.4). The lack of such analogies in the predicate system implies not a common origin but the exact opposite. That African slaves (4) played a very minor, not to say insignificant, role in the formation of RC (or "Bourbonnais") is quite correct. The situation in Mauritius, however, is quite the reverse (Baker, B2.3). Point (5) need not be discussed now, since Chaudenson himself now rejects it (see below). The circularity of the argument in (6) is obvious. The ca. 1722 sentence is "almost exactly" what a present-day RC speaker would use to say the same thing (1974:444). But ca. 1800, MC and RC were less divergent than they are today, RC having been subject to constant pressure from French (1974:449, 1117-18). He cannot have it both ways. Either the ca. 1722 sentence represents a language fundamentally identical to modern RC, or it represents one fundamentally similar to MC and dissimilar to modern RC since this latter is supposed to have "evolved" away from MC. The evidence of other early texts of a reliable nature (e.g., Focard 1884) shows that to invoke continuing contact between French and RC to explain the difference between the latter and IdeFC is not a tenable approach. On the contrary, the evidence is that RC, in at least one of its manifestations, has remained remarkably stable for a long time. That there are indeed varieties of RC which are "decreolizing" due to contact with French is not at issue.

The central point is (3). If it is incorrect, as I believe it is, the implication that "Bourbonnais" is the common origin of RC and IdeFC is clearly wrong.

Five years later, this theory remains unchanged in its essentials and its conclusions: "la parenté des parlers de l'océan Indien est ... non seulement génétique mais structurelle" (Chaudenson 1979b:71). Moreover, this relationship, we are told (p. 46), is obvious "pour le témoin le moins averti"; I suggest rather that it is only the most casual observer who will conclude that there is any structural similarity between the predicate systems of RC and IdeFC. However, there are some differences between the 1974 version of the "Bourbonnais" theory and the 1979 version. First, "Bourbonnais" is redefined as the Creole spoken in Reunion before 1721: "cette distinction, *purement chronologique,* permet d'éviter toute confusion avec le réunionnais sans préjuger des rapports structurels entre ces deux états du même parler" (1979b:46, note; italics his). This is a rather different proposition from the syntactic similarity of "Bourbonnais" and IdeFC which is clearly a central feature in the 1974 presentation. Second, bolstering his case with the Mauritius settlement statistics of his 1979a article (which, by the way, show a highly heterogeneous linguistic situation rather than the homogeneity of the 1974 theory, cf. (5) above), he introduces a two- (or even three-) tier approach. The terminology appears to be an inappropriate adaptation from the history of the development of computers. It goes like this: the emergence of "Bourbonnais" gives a "first-generation" Creole; MC would be a "second-generation" Creole, having emerged from a linguistic situation which includes French, slave languages, and an imported (first-generation) Creole which serves as the local contact language and is "probably" learned by the first slaves introduced onto the island (i.e., "Bourbonnais" or RC is still in effect the predominant element); SC and RoC would be "third-generation," since they emerge from a situation containing RC and MC (1979b:46, 71).

This multi-tier idea appears to be a necessary addition to the theory to compensate for the redefinition of "Bourbonnais." But, except insofar as it lessens Chaudenson's dependency on "decreolization" to explain the differences between modern MC and modern RC (cf. point (6) above), this redefinition does not in fact alter in any significant respect that I can see his original 1974 statement of his theory, that early RC ("Bourbonnais") is the original element common to RC and IdeFC. The essential structural dissimilarity of RC and IdeFC is not accounted for. In order for the modified 1979 theory to be acceptable, it needs to be shown that there were sufficient numbers of RC speakers in Mauritius in the early years of settlement (a fact denied by Baker in B2.2 below) and that RC was sufficiently widespread in Mauritius for slaves to identify RC as their target language (this is similarly denied by Baker, cf. B4 below). It also needs to be shown that MC, quite apart from SC or RoC, reflects RC structures and "function words" in unmistakably central roles.

The system of predication surely meets the requirement of centrality. But, as I have shown, the only parallels are marginal, and RC and IdeFC are organized in quite different ways. Note also the absence from any past or present variety of RC of the "Immediate Completion" marker *fek* of IdeFC, or of any reflex of the *gaŷ* construction. In the case of *fek,* had RC had the central role ascribed to it by the "Bourbonnais" theory, one would have expected RC *vien* or *sort* to have been adopted rather than *fek.* (That the etymon of *fek* was a feature of "colonial" or Western varieties of French is shown by its existence in Haitian.) In the case of the gaỹ construction, the argument is slightly different. It may be argued that languages without "passives" develop them in various ways, of which *get*-passives are one (Markey and Fodale 1980). This has happened in IdeFC, but not in RC, because this latter has (always had) the French model to hand. I do not mean by this that RC displays frequent use of French-style passives, with the Agent introduced by *par*. But it does have past participles and a copula. In French, even in the literary language, full passives are relatively infrequent; in the spoken language, even more so. But the partial passive (i.e., with the Agent unexpressed) is frequent in both French and RC, and is clearly marked as such by the presence of the copula and a past participle, But IdeFC does not have this possibility; it has, instead, developed its own distinctive way of handling the situation. If "Bourbonnais" had had the central role hypothesized by Chaudenson, the necessity for IdeFC to have developed its own passivization method is not evident.

In the preceding chapters, I have endeavored to survey a number of semantic, morphosyntactic, and syntactic facts that seemed to me to be susceptible of casting light on the "Bourbonnais" theory. These facts force me to conclude that IdeFC does not reflect RC, but is an entirely different animal, and that therefore the "Bourbonnais" theory serves no useful purpose. The semantic-syntactic structures of RC and IdeFC are quite different, and some explanation of this difference must be sought.

A6.4 SC and RC—A Privileged Link

The reader will recall the SC *pa i* construction (A5.4.1). It was noted that settlers from Reunion were present in Seychelles in the early period of colonization, and I suggested that the *pa i* construction, although used in a novel way in SC, quite conceivably has its ultimate roots in the putative RC /le ki/ structure. There is not the slightest trace of any similar structure in RoC or MC.

There is other evidence of RC influence on SC, quite apart from a considerable number of shared patronyms, on the one hand, and the *pa i* construction on the other. For example, the concept of capability may be expressed in SC by the lexical item *nabu/nobu*. In RC, we have *abu/nabu* and *vnir abu (d):*

(SC) *mô nabu fer sa* 'I can do that'
(RC) *le ser, me i abu truve* 'it's expensive, but can be found'
(RC) *zot la esey reste, la pa vni abu* 'they tried to stay, but were unable to do so'
(Bollée 1977a:23; Chaudenson 1974:950-51)

MC and RoC have only *kapav* 'be able', SC has *kapab* in competition with *nabu/nobu*, and RC has *pe* 'be able, Present tense' and *et(r) kapab* 'be able', both clearly French structures. Another example is *komela* 'now'. This lexeme is attested in the Indian Ocean only in SC and RC. In RC, it occurs (occurred?) also as *kom le la* (e.g., Fourcade [1930] 1976:8). An anecdotal aside at this point: when I first came across this word in SC and asked what it meant, the gloss given by my consultant, in French, was *par le temps qui court,* which seems to correlate well with RC *kom le la* 'as it is now'. MC and RoC have only *aster(-la),* which is also used in RC (Chaudenson 1974:957-58).

These examples alone are sufficient to establish a privileged link between RC and SC that is not shared by MC and RoC. But such a link must be seen as a secondary, even minor matter. To illustrate IdeFC in A2, I used mainly SC examples, with a few from MC and RoC. These three languages constitute IdeFC, and the differences between them are no more important than, say, the differences between British, American, and Australian English. The level of intercomprehension between any variety of IdeFC and RC is low; IdeFC and RC are typologically different languages, and the existence of a privileged RC/SC link cannot be used as support for the "Bourbonnais" theory.

A6.5 Similarities and Identities between RC and IdeFC

Let me reiterate here briefly that there are many syntactic similarities between RC and IdeFC. These may be assumed to derive from the varieties of French that served as input to RC and MC. I am making here the following assumptions: (1) RC and MC are independent creations; (2) RoC is archaic MC in the formation of which RC has so marginal a role as to be negligible (cf. B3.1); (3) SC is basically (archaic) MC overlaid with secondary and minor influences from RC; (4) all have seventeenth/eighteenth-century varieties of French as the socially dominant linguistic input. We have seen (A5.5) the sylleptic dual and the *dâ-*"gerundive," both of which derive from the "French" input.

Other similarities, which at first glance appear to be exclusively shared by RC and IdeFC, turn out to be attested for other Creole French languages; this suggests derivation from the "French" input. Among such are the "loss" of the French connectives *à* and *de* (cf. Goodman 1964:53-54); a kind of "dual" which occurs with the names of parts of the body (RC *mô de zorey* 'my eyes', SC *mô de lizie* 'my eyes', French Guiana *so de wey* 'his eyes'; cf. Goodman 1964:26); reduplication of "adjectives" for attenuation (if post-posed) or intensification (if pre-posed; if the "adjective" concerned occurs as predicate head—or as the attribute of the subject, following *et(r)* in RC—intonation patterns distinguish these two contrasting meanings; similarly, in Haitian, cf. Comhaire-Sylvain 1936:42); and the use of *zot* for both second and third person plural (subject and possessive; see Comhaire-Sylvain 1936:61-62 for Haitian, and cf. Baker, B3.2.3 and Table 11 below; cf. also Goodman 1964:43-44).

Another case worthy of mention is the Future form in *a*. In RC we find *m a* 'I shall', while in allegro styles, in SC *mô a* becomes *m a.* This appears strictly non-French. But consider the following. In St. Barts French, the form *ma* occurs, as in *ma ki va* 'I shall' (Lefebvre 1976:139). In Martinique Creole French the usual form *mwê* may be replaced by *mâ* (Jourdain 1956:102, note). *Ma* + Infinitive is regular in most varieties of "basilectal" Canadian French, where it occurs as *ma*, but also as *mâ, mâva, mava;* it is a contracted version of *je m'en vas* + Infinitive (Hull, personal communication). I do not think there can be any doubt as to the source of all the Creole Future forms in *a, va,* and *ava,* although there has been in all Creole cases a reinterpretation from Future to Irrealis (with IdeFC a partial exception). In the case of IdeFC, a preexisting *mo* is competing with *ma,* and the step from *mava* to *mo va* seems logical. The point is that even such a typical feature as the Future/Irrealis particle *a* has a French origin, not only etymologically, but also structurally and functionally, and that its occurrence in RC as well as IdeFC is not, therefore, indicative of anything other than similar inputs.

The above similarities and identities, all traceable to "French," do not exhaust the subject, and I do not of course wish to deny that there are many shared items between RC and IdeFC, exclusive of French. As has been seen, both languages have the rule of Final Vowel Truncation, operating almost identically, but whose origin remains at best rather obscure. Another, perhaps equally striking, example is the use of the plural marker *ban* (discussed in some detail in B3.2.1). However, in neither case can it be shown that these features originated in RC. Perhaps more to the point is the use of *fin* to mark the Completive. RC, albeit marginally, uses *fin(i)* in stative predicates in a way identical to IdeFC (cf. the discussion in A1.10). In note 3 to A5, I have suggested a possible Bantu origin for this area-specific and visibly non-French feature of Indian Ocean Creole. This feature, as well as the tendency already noted in some varieties of RC toward an invariable verbal base, point to a common (and non-French) tradition. In the case of *fin,* we are in all likelihood looking at a specific substratal feature. The case of invariable verbal bases is in all probability a universal of pidginization/creolization. Fully developed in IdeFC, where creolization proceeded untrammeled within a classic sociohistorical and sociolinguistic situation, the tendency in RC, originating in the language-learning efforts of adult slaves and indentured workers in the second and third stages of Reunion's settlement, was restrained by the existence of an established island-wide vernacular, *lete ki* French. This vernacular would therefore have been the target language for the first-language-learning children of these immigrants. The very existence of *fin* and invariable verbal bases in some varieties of RC is proof that some creolization of the adult approximations to *lete ki* French must have occurred. That is to say, at least some of their children found themselves in a close approximation to a classic creolization situation, but one where the vernacular provided a major part of the input. It is perhaps here if anywhere that Chaudenson's concept of a "second-generation" Creole makes some sense, and the partial creolization of RC finds an explanation.

In any case, the exclusively shared syntactic features of the RC and the IdeFC predicate systems are relatively insignificant compared with: the features shared with other Creole French languages (and with various manifestations of "French"); and the basic differences underlying the two predicate systems and the semantactic operation of the two languages. The exclusively shared features have two possible origins: convergence due to areal interaction (FVT, *ban*), and creolization phenomena (*fin* from a specific substratum, invariable verbal bases). Creolization was partial in Reunion for historical reasons.

A6.6 The Origin of IdeFC

There is no difficulty in postulating a common origin for MC, SC, and RoC on linguistic grounds. Three languages so closely related as these clearly have a common source. Historically, this source is to be located in Mauritius.

The colonization of Mauritius began in 1721. The early period of settlement is characterized by a slave population comprising West Africans, East Africans, Indians, and Malagasies, who together outnumbered the French settlers. Chaudenson (1979a, 1979b:44-50) and Baker (1976 and here) disagree as to the relative proportions of the various human groups involved, and Baker denies any significant *settlement* originating from Reunion in the first fifteen years of settlement. The latter correlates well, it seems to me, with the linguistic evidence I have offered here. However, a crucial fact, on which both authors now agree, is that a highly heterogeneous linguistic situation obtained in Mauritius in the formative years of Mauritian Creole, which I place from 1721 to ca. 1750-70 (the first two or three generations of locally-born slaves; in fact, MC must have been emerging with the first generation of locally-born children, but the process would have been an ongoing one, cf. Le Page 1977:241-42). We can assume with some confidence that the basic social and linguistic conditions, including the presence of a large number of West Africans, prevailing in Mauritius were highly similar to those of other territories where Creole languages arose. That RC was one of the elements in the Mauritian pre-Creole situation, post-1735 (see B2) at least, seems likely (e.g., loss of the contrast in both RC and IdeFC between the alveolar and the palatal fricatives), but that it had anything like the preponderance Chaudenson ascribes to it seems most unlikely.

The Seychelles archipelago was colonized from 1770 (slightly erratically at first) from Mauritius, France, and Reunion. By this date, however, we may assume that an early form of MC was the established vehicular language in Mauritius, and that it became the vehicular language in Seychelles. Nevertheless, Reunion was the supplier of a large number of the new colonists, many of whom probably brought with them their Reunion-born slaves (Bollée 1977a:4-5). During the first decades of colonization, slaves (of all origins) represented approximately 85 percent of the total population. From 1810 to 1976, Seychelles was administered as a British colony. It was governed from Mauritius until 1903, when it became a separate colony. In spite of its distance from Mauritius, commercial and personal contacts existed (and exist today), and SC has followed to some extent the evolution of MC (e.g., nineteenth-century *apre* becomes modern *(a)pe*). The role of RC has been shown to be relatively minor in the development of SC.

In Rodrigues, the situation is different. What data are available show a mildly archaic variety of MC. The island appears to have been colonized, from Mauritius, ca. 1790. Baker (B3.1) shows a negligible RC influence, and this is congruent with the linguistic evidence.

All three IdeFC languages clearly have their origins, ultimately, in the MC that emerged sometime during the eighteenth century. RC cannot be shown to have a central position, either on historical or linguistic grounds, in the formation of any one of these. The actual modalities (or possible modalities) of the emergence of MC are discussed briefly by Baker (B4) and cf. the discussion in A7.

A6.7 Concluding Remarks

My conclusions, based on the linguistic evidence presented here, are that RC and IdeFC are two different and largely unrelated languages. The former derives directly from French, while showing some evidence of partial creolization. The latter is a new language, with an internal organization quite different from RC or French, which has emerged under sociohistorical conditions quite different from those under which RC evolved, but rather similar to those under which other Creole (French, English, etc.) languages came into being. The concept of "Bourbonnais" is a myth which lacks the necessary syntactic evidence to support it.

The structural relations between RC and IdeFC, contrary to Chaudenson's view (e.g., 1979b:71), are considerably less than obvious. It is not enough to say that the preposed predicate particles, in all varieties of Creole French (ignoring here Lesser Antillean *ke* 'Future' and *ka* 'Progressive'—approximate glosses only), derive from non-Standard or popular French periphrastic expressions of aspect (cf. Chaudenson 1974:1116, 1979b:80-83; Bollée 1977c:143, 1977b). The morphemes themselves clearly do derive in this way. For RC, one can reasonably claim that the morphosyntax derives directly from French. But to claim the same thing for IdeFC, solely on the basis of the etymology of its morphological units, would be, in light of the analysis given here, quite unjustified.

IdeFC has considerably greater affinities in the functioning of its predicate system with ACF than it has with RC, due to the sociohistorical conditions of its emergence and evolution. The verbal system of RC, although not devoid of "Creole" features, behaves (and appears always to have behaved) even in its most basilectal forms in a manner clearly reminiscent of French. The clearest affinity of the IdeFC and the RC "verbal" systems is in the operation, the mechanical operation not the semantic consequence/motivation, of the final vowel truncation rule, of whose history we are lamentably ignorant. This rule seems to indicate a structural relation that the operation of the rest of the "verbal" system appears to deny, but the evidence is at best ambiguous.

In conclusion, the surface and etymological similarity that is evident in the predicate systems of Reunion Creole and Isle de France Creole is potentially misleading. Fundamentally, each system deals with the reality to be expressed in completely different ways: the former is based on an arrangement that requires a relatively rigid parts-of-speech classification of lexical items that is absent in the latter.

It is especially in this respect that Reunion Creole, among Creole French languages, stands out as being qualitatively different from its "cousins," both in the Indian Ocean and in the Americas. There is no immediately obvious label which could usefully replace the term Reunion "Creole." This appellation is firmly anchored not only in Reunion itself but also in the literature. As long as it is clear that "Reunion Creole" refers to a specific phenomenon that is not identical with other "Creole" languages, either structurally or in the sociohistorical conditions of its genesis, the term can do no harm.[2]

NOTES

1. A possible parallel is the complementizer *pur-dir* in SC:

(SC) *i uar pur-dir i vre sa ê lisiê* 'he sees that it is true that it is a dog'

Reflexes of 'say' are similarly used as a complementizer in various Atlantic Creoles, e.g., Krio (Hancock 1976), Cameroonian (Todd 1979a), Sranan, Jamaican, Gullah (Jansen et al. 1978: 131). There may possibly be serial verb constructions in SC, but the only evidence I have is anecdotal in the extreme. On the island of La Digue, in 1974, I was walking along the road and had just passed a house when I heard a woman call out to someone:

(SC) *rod–divê–amene!* 'bring the wine, go get some wine' (?)
      look-for–wine–bring

As far as I could tell, this injunction was uttered with an unbroken imperative intonation contour. Unfortunately, this occurred on my second-to-last day on the island, and other commitments prevented my following it up there. While none of my SC consultants in New Zealand appear to use (or allow) such structures, verb serialization in SC (or in IdeFC generally) clearly needs to be further examined.

2. In fact, one could well envisage restricting the term "Creole" to Reunion, and labeling all other Creole French languages (following Alleyne 1980a) "Afro-French."

A7
Conclusion

The sociohistorical conditions prevailing in Reunion and in Mauritius and the different input languages explain the rather different languages which emerged in each territory.

In Reunion in the seventeenth century, the inputs were: (i) a more or less "standard" form of seventeenth-century French (written if not actually spoken by administrators, etc.); (ii) regional dialects of seventeenth-century French, some of which contained the *lete ki* structure; (iii) Malagasy and other various non-French languages spoken by slaves and others. This period is characterized by the constitution of a sizable group of locally-born children of mixed ancestry within a "French"-speaking and more or less "family" environment. Slaves were in a minority throughout this period. By the end of the seventeenth century, approximately, a version of the *lete ki* French had emerged as the vernacular language of the island.

In Mauritius, the inputs in the formative period are very different: (i) a more or less "standard" form of eighteenth-century French (written if not actually spoken by administrators, etc.); (ii) regional dialects of eighteenth-century French, apparently *not* containing the *lete ki* structure; (iii) various non-French languages spoken by slaves and others, including specifically West African languages (in contrast to seventeenth-century Reunion where African languages generally and West African ones in particular were for all practical purposes absent). Speakers of "French" were a small minority of the population. Baker suggests (B4) that by 1749, a mere twenty-eight years after the beginning of the settlement of the island, a foreign-born slave could identify MC as his target language and reach that target.

Chaudenson (1974) has argued that substrate languages are unlikely to have played a determining role in shaping RC: "... le créole résulte de l'évolution du français populaire et dialectal du XVIIe siècle et ... le rôle des langues vernaculaires [slave languages] est mineur si l'on considère les éléments 'positifs' qu'elles ont pu introduire dans le parler" (1974:1133). I think that he is essentially correct with respect to RC. However, as Valdman (1978b:89) points out, Chaudenson's position with respect to IdeFC is fundamentally the same. If it is admitted that the multifunctionality of lexical items and the way in which the system of predication, including the tense/aspect marking system, is organized, are "positive" elements, and if for "substrate languages" we understand "adult speakers of non-French languages and their Mauritian-born children," then Chaudenson's position with respect to IdeFC is erroneous.

IdeFC has a number of affinities with American Creole French generally. These cannot be due solely to chance parallels of independent evolution, nor do such features as lexeme multifunctionality, the predication system, or such syntactical

Conclusion 121

phenomena as double predication seem to be natural developments of French. Rather, a common origin of some kind, or a common kind of origin, is indicated.

A number of possibilities may be briefly considered.

1. The spoken varieties of French which were a common input to all Creole French languages would presumably have been relatively uniform from one colony to another, although it must be remembered that while the New World and Reunion were colonized in the seventeenth century, Mauritius was colonized in the eighteenth. Among the differences from the "standard" language as reflected in written French from the seventeenth century to the present day, the reduction of inflectional categories and the preponderance of analytic over synthetic constructions are obvious features (Valdman 1978b: 93). Some similarities among the individual Creole French languages obviously stem from the shared "French" input. These similarities seem to be predominantly lexical and phonological (segmental phonology; suprasegmentals remain to be studied), but some syntactic procedures are also included here, as has been seen.
2. A subcategory of the "French" input is the "parler des Isles" (Chaudenson 1974:591-96; cf. B4). Contacts among the plantation colonies in the form of population movement, such as sailors visiting both the Caribbean and the Indian Ocean, or colonists from the Caribbean settling in Mauritius in 1787-92 (see B4), must also be considered as a source of similarities among the Creole French languages.
3. Historical evidence does not, contrary to Valdman's statement (1978b:92), preclude the possibility of localizing a proto-Creole pidginized French in West Africa, since Baker demonstrates (B2.3) the presence of sizable numbers of West Africans in Mauritius in the early years. West Africans were also, as is well known, numerically the vastly predominant human group in most American plantation economies. However, there is no documentary evidence of such a speech form, and until such time as such evidence comes to light, this hypothesis may be excluded. This is not to deny that some individuals may have acquired some rudiments of French during transshipment aboard French vessels.

Similarities arising from these three more or less common inputs do not, at a basilectal level at least, imply the continuation of a *French* linguistic tradition, except in Reunion. A very general framework of language contact allows for degrees of contact with European culture and language: "the different positions of individuals in ethnosocial space give them differential exposure to the superstrate" (Bickerton 1975:199; cf. Alleyne 1971, 1979:105-6). The continuity of the French tradition in Reunion is accounted for, since there was, in the first period of settlement at least, close contact of slave and master (A6.2). At the same time, the noncontinuation of this tradition (except for a tiny, more or less elite minority) in Mauritius and in the Caribbean is also accounted for, at least in a general sense. In both places, there were a vast majority of field slaves and reduced contact with French, and languages with maximum deviancy from French emerged (cf. A6.6, but especially Part B).

Indeed, the functioning of the Creole French predicate system cannot be held to be a natural or plausible development from any kind of French (whereas that of RC, in contrast, can be so considered; the marginal "Creole" features of the RC system will be discussed below). If "French" input, in the three forms listed above, may be excluded as the source of Creole French semantactics, what other possibilities remain?

4. In a situation where large numbers of West Africans with a number of mother tongues but, like all humans, interacting or striving to interact with each other, are obliged to become second-language learners under unfavorable conditions, and where their children have their parents', or at least their mother's, language as well as the superstrate language both in its "pure" form and in the form of slaves' approximations to it as targets (the precise target for any given individual varying according to that individual's overall social circumstances), it may reasonably be assumed that at least some degree of West African "continuity" is maintained. Although the details of the tense/aspect marking system are different from one Creole language to another (cf. Taylor 1977:178ff.), and although there is not a point-for-point matching between any Creole tense/aspect system and any West African one (but cf. Bentolila 1971, cited by Valdman 1977:180), it is in the tense/aspect marking system that creolists have seen a West African substratal influence. The double predication structure (A5.2) could be seen as another case of such influence. Although I prefer the explanation for these facts that is offered by Bickerton's theory (Bickerton 1981), to which I return below, I do not think that a possible West African "specific" (in the sense of Givón 1979) substratal influence can be dismissed out of hand.

On the question of specific substratal influence, I have already noted the case of *fin* as a Completive marker in IdeFC. The use of *fin* appears to correspond directly to the use of the Completive in at least two East African languages (Swahili, Macua), and a specific substratum is entirely consonant with the presence of large numbers of slaves from that area of Africa. In this case, the substratal influence affects the central semantactic area of tense/aspect marking.

5. Givón (1979:21-30) hypothesizes a "universal substratum" to account for those features which appear to be explicable in terms of neither the substrate nor the superstrate language (such as the emergence of an apparently wholly new modality system in Krio). Bickerton (1981; and see also 1977,

1979) has put forward a comprehensive theory. Briefly, it claims that the predicate systems (among other features, including the double predication structure) of Creole languages of differing lexical derivation reflect the construction, by children confronted with a deficient input of the socially dominant language, of systems broadly representing an inherent universal grammar—that is, that Creole languages "reflect natural semantactic structures" (1977:64). The emergence in Hawaii of a variety of English within the context of a late nineteenth- or early twentieth-century indenture system, i.e., under sociohistorical conditions rather different from those mediating the emergence of IdeFC or ACF (seventeenth- and eighteenth-century plantation slavery), but evidencing many of those features of the "classical" Creole English languages which cannot be seen as English-derived, is a powerful inferential argument in support of the "natural semantax/universal substratum" hypothesis.

In the case of RC, this hypothesis may account for several facts. I have already allowed that those "Creole" features of RC that are suggestive of IdeFC (the particle-style elements *a*, *fin(i)*; the tendency toward invariable verbal bases) may be explicable in terms of creolization occurring in Reunion. Bickerton's claim is that the processes of creolization operate in the same way whenever language continuity is broken. We simply do not know at what stage in the evolution of the Reunion linguistic situation such "Creole" features may have emerged. It is only in the second and third periods of the settlement of Reunion (A6.2) that large numbers of involuntary and indentured immigrants found themselves in a situation of handicapped second-language learning (first-language in the case of locally-born children of such persons), when the vernacular (modified *lete ki* French) of the island had already appeared in clearly modern form as evidenced by the ca. 1722 fragment. It is not known to what extent the social conditions prevailing in the first stage of settlement (1663-ca. 1715) would have prompted recourse by children to innate language creation strategies. There is possibly an inferential argument, however. Pitcairn/Norfolk English is the product of a social situation whose broad outline is well known (see Harrison 1972; Ross and Moverly 1964). The early histories of Pitcairn and Reunion are curiously parallel: (a) speakers of a European language were culturally dominant and mainly male in the formative period of the vernacular language of each island; in the case of Pitcairn, English was kept alive in certain spheres such as religious instruction throughout that period; (b) both the Pitcairn and Reunion settlers remained in isolation (absolute in the case of Pitcairn, relative in Reunion) during this formative period; (c) females were predominantly (Reunion) or exclusively (Pitcairn) native speakers of non-European languages; (d) in both places, there was a rapid constitution of a locally-born infant population within a "family" setup. It remains to be shown whether "broad" Pitcairn/Norfolk English is typologically different from Creole English (including Hawaiian Creole

English)—it certainly has little enough in common with any variety of Pacific Pidgin English (Clark 1979)—and to what extent or whether it is typologically English in a way parallel (not necessarily identical) to the way in which RC is typologically French. If the results of a planned investigation into these matters to be undertaken in the near future show that Pitcairn/Norfolk English is typologically English rather than Creole, then the inference would clearly be that creolization did not take place in Reunion during the first stage of settlement. Meanwhile, we do not know. However, we do know that linguistic continuity was broken for large numbers of people in the second stage of settlement, and so we can infer that creolization began at that time and that the "Creole" features observable today arose then. Within the context of this creolization, the emergence of Completive marking by *fin(i)* may be seen, as in IdeFC, as an example of a specific Bantu substratal influence.

I have referred to the "Creole" features of RC as being marginal today. The term "marginal" is deliberately vague. I do not know whether they occur (predominantly or exclusively) in the speech of clearly identifiable groups or whether they occur in an apparently nonsystematic, occasional way in the speech of many such groups. In the absence of a definite answer to the question of whether there is any group of people not traceable to immigration from an IdeFC-speaking island that has a coherent grammar which contains (nonrestrictively) all or most of the IdeFC forms and uses them within a system as described fundamentally in A2, any assumption that such a group exists is just that: an assumption and nothing more. It seems more likely, on what evidence is available, that the presence of an established *lete ki* vernacular, as well as continuing immigration from France and the continued use of more or less "standard" varieties of French, combined to abort the incipient creolization process, resulting in what Bollée (1977b) has referred to as "partial creolization." Of these factors, I suspect that it was the established vernacular which was in fact the determining factor. It is well known that the massive immigration of Indians into Mauritius in the nineteenth century and that of Africans into the Seychelles between 1861 and 1872 caused no significant changes in the structure of MC or SC (as may be determined by comparing them with RoC, Rodrigues having remained untouched by such perturbations) (cf. Chaudenson 1974:446-48).

In the case of Mauritius, the conditions leading to creolization (creolization as envisaged by Bickerton's hypothesis) existed from the colony's inception. In this perspective, and given the composition of the population in the period 1721-35, then it is possible that the preposed particle system of tense/aspect that emerged was initially, or potentially, even more like that of ACF than it is today. The inclusion of the Completive (due to specific substratal influence) would have had, as a direct consequence, the erosion of the Anterior functions of *ti* (see Bickerton 1981:Chapter 2), thus helping give rise to the specificity of the IdeFC system as compared with the other Creole French languages. I mentioned in A2.5 that variation in IdeFC as to the combinability of preposed predicate particles should not be ignored. Published statements concerning combinability of particles are contradictory (see Waite 1981; and cf. Baker, note 21 to B3 below). It seems possible to advance two explanations for this. The first I have already mentioned in A2.5: the elicitation from consultants of combinations which no one ever has reason to use. The second is suggested by Bickerton (1981). At least some of the contradictions reflect the preservation synchronically in different groups of speakers or at different stylistic levels in the IdeFC population, of different stages in the modification of Aux due to the inclusion, in the "basic" Anterior + Irrealis + Progressive/non-Punctual system, of *fin* 'Completive', *pu* 'Definite Future', and *fek* 'Immediate Completion'. In this perspective, the earliest stages of the emergence of MC would have involved an Anterior-based system, while the inclusion of *fin* and a consequent tilting of the system toward a temporal one would have been a somewhat later development.

Whether this speculative view of the development of the IdeFC tense/aspect system is well-founded or not, it does not seem to me to be incompatible with specific substratal influences. Bickerton's theory does not at all depend on the precise details of human settlement in the Indian Ocean Creole-speaking islands (or anywhere else, for that matter); the fact that West Africans were a majority for a short period in Mauritius is therefore irrelevant for that theory, but it does leave open the possibility of substratal influence from West Africa. It is the opinion of some scholars (e.g., Alleyne 1980b:5) that any historical connection does not require large-scale quantitative migration from Africa or the New World to the Indian Ocean to have been significant linguistically. In any event, the particular properties shared by IdeFC and ACF, to the exclusion of RC, may not have a direct substratal origin, but their development has occurred exclusively in the substratum language(s) community. For Creole French languages, such development may be seen as taking place in essentially similar social situations (see B4): basically, the slavery of a polyglot majority of whom West Africans form sometimes the largest part but always, in the crucial early formative years, a substantial one (cf. Rens 1953 for the emergence of Sranan in a period of some forty years), and for whom access to the socially dominant language is variably restricted. Within this framework, differences would then be due to specific differences in the societies concerned. Other influences must be allowed for (East Africans, Malagasies, and Indians in the Indian Ocean, for example), as must later independent innovations (predicate-fronting in MC is perhaps a good example of this) and the effects of specific historical factors (the development of the SC *pa i* construction).

To sum up, I see the following factors as contributing to the emergence of two typologically different languages in Reunion and Mauritius (with the role played by the first generations of locally-born children being crucial, although producing different results in each case):

a. The "French" input is partially different (e.g., the *lete ki* structure appears to have been absent from the "French" taken to Mauritius).
b. The conditions for rapid creolization were absent from Reunion during the formative years of RC (1663-ca. 1715), while they were present in Mauritius from 1721-35 and beyond.
c. West Africans were present in Mauritius in significant numbers in the early years of settlement, while substrate languages are unlikely to have played a determining role in Reunion.

The affinities of IdeFC with ACF may be ascribed to a number of factors, rather than to any single one of them:

d. A relatively uniform "French" input, including the "parler des Isles."
e. A possible West African substratum.
f. The operation of universal processes of creolization within broadly similar communities, with children again in a crucial role.
g. Parallel independent evolution within typologically similar languages.

The specific features of IdeFC as opposed to ACF are due to:

h. Society-specific social conditions.
i. Minor differences in the "French" input.
j. Specific East African, Malagasy, and Indian substratal influences.
k. Independent innovations.

Indian Ocean Creole French is not so well known that no further work is necessary to elucidate details of language or of history.[1] But far more is known of these matters today than was the case a mere five or so years ago, and our lack of knowledge of the early settlement history of Haiti (for example) is thus the more obvious. Linguistically, a detailed comparison both synchronically and diachronically of IdeFC and Haitian Creole (i.e., one which goes beyond the work of Faine 1939 and Goodman 1964) may well throw more light on the shared features of these two languages. Ideally, of course, one could wish for detailed descriptions, with historical and sociological depth, of any number of the American Creole French languages. While the Indian Ocean Creole French languages, until a decade or so ago the most neglected of all Creole French languages, are now perhaps better known in a general sense than any American Creole French language other than Haitian, this fact should not obscure the need for detailed investigation, especially of language variation (of which, for the Indian Ocean Creole French languages, practically nothing is known at all.)[2]

Conclusion   127

What has been achieved by this study?

For the first time, Reunion Creole has been described in a way that reveals its basic mechanisms. These show that RC must be categorized as a variety of French. This does not mean that (more or less basilectal) RC speakers find access to Standard French particularly easy (the level of difficulty is roughly on a par with that of a speaker of English learning German or Dutch; cf. Cellier and Moorghen 1979, and the other articles in Cellier 1979), although it has yet to be shown to what extent a speaker from Grand-Ilet has easier access thereto than one from Dos-d'Ane or Ste.-Suzanne. I do not want to minimize the differences between RC and Standard French, except to point up the roughly equal differences between RC and IdeFC. Nevertheless, RC must be seen basically as a specific variety of French.

Isle de France Creole, on the other hand, has been shown to belong, if not to the mainstream, then at least to an important tributary of what might be called "Afro-French." The description of IdeFC is based on an approach which is "new" insofar as this language is concerned. The data advanced in my earlier study of SC (1977a; cf. Bollée 1977a, Papen 1978b) seem to be, with hindsight, basically accurate, in spite of some oversights (double predication, the *mâz ki mâz* reflex of the Romance construction, SC *to/tua/tô*, the co-occurrence of *ti* with past-reference statives and its nonoccurrence with past-reference nonstatives in narrative material, and no doubt other points which will turn up eventually). The same may be said of Baker's (1972; cf. Baissac 1880, Corne 1970) description of MC. But the approach adopted here in A2 shows these data in a rather different light, and one which points up their typological identity with the Atlantic Creoles and their fundamental dissimilarity to Reunion Creole. While a detailed reanalysis remains to be done for all areas of IdeFC syntax, no one with a knowledge of any Atlantic Creole can fail to be convinced that IdeFC belongs to the same tradition.

The rule of Final Vowel Truncation has been subjected to as close a scrutiny as the facts warrant, with somewhat disappointing results from a descriptive point of view, but with highly suggestive comparative inferences; the FVT rule cannot be seen as an exclusively shared and Indian Ocean-specific feature of RC and IdeFC. Moreover, the Reunion Creole (post-Creole?) continuum has been shown to have a morphosyntactic dimension, defined by the FVT rule, but this fact remains interpretable only ambiguously. It is not known, at this stage of research, just what the social (historical, regional) significance is (if any) of the presence versus the variable presence versus the absence of this rule in any given variety of RC. This interpretational problem notwithstanding, the discovery that the FVT rule defines (in some sense) a continuum in RC represents one of the more gratifying results to emerge from this study. Hitherto, that this morphosyntactic feature might delimit (one aspect of) the RC continuum had remained a totally unsuspected possibility. Future research on linguistic variation in Reunion, I suggest, should include detailed investigation of the social, regional, and "educational" distribution of this feature. From the perspective of this study, however, the distribution of the FVT rule is to some extent a side issue, significant though it may be in descriptive and Reunion-specific theoretical terms.

Syntactic data have been adduced concerning a number of specific structures. Isle de France Creole has been shown to have affinities with American Creole French, quite apart from its predicate system. Of these, two stand out. The development of the *gaŷ* construction is seen as a procedure which has evolved in typologically similar languages to compensate, as it were, for the lack of a marked passive; it is thus seen as a natural development, possibly connected with decreolization in some sense. The existence of the procedure of "double predication," until now overlooked by previous studies of Isle de France Creole (in retrospect, I blush for this too), has been shown to be parallel to similar or identical constructions in American Creole French (and in the Atlantic Creoles generally). It has close parallels in the "Kwa" languages. This may be an example of a specific West African substratal influence in Isle de France Creole, but it may also be ascribed to the very process of creolization itself. Other structures have been described, either to show a specific link between Reunion and Seychelles (a link which is supported by historical, patronymic, and lexical evidence), or to demonstrate a shared but not immediately obvious French connection between RC and IdeFC.

From a purely descriptive point of view, these are all positive gains. But they have a theoretical significance as well, in that the "Bourbonnais" theory, based largely if implicitly on the assumption that all Indian Ocean Creole languages are in some sense the "same," is badly weakened. I have sketched, in rather broad terms, the very different sociohistorical conditions in which IdeFC and RC emerged (Baker, in Part B, gives a very detailed account of the demographic history of Mauritius which mediated the emergence of Mauritian Creole; my brief sketch of the demography and sociology of Reunion in the period from 1663 to ca. 1715, while overly broad, at least points up the very basic differences between the two islands). It is my belief, on the evidence to date, that these very different sociohistorical conditions were responsible for the emergence of two very different languages on two neighboring islands settled a mere half-century apart in circumstances which, to a casual observer, might seem superficially rather similar.

Baker, in Part B, advances a detailed and, I believe, irrefutable body of historical demographic evidence. This is supplemented (in B3) by a careful diachronic comparison of a number of attested linguistic features in early texts. Neither the demographic nor the linguistic facts adduced by him support the contention that Reunion Creole had a great deal to do with the formation of Mauritian (and hence Isle de France) Creole.

My claims—that Reunion Creole is, and always has been, typologically different from Isle de France Creole, and that it evolved under conditions which were not conducive to creolization (in Bickerton's sense)—cannot be proven beyond doubt until the question of variation in Reunion Creole has been made the subject of detailed investigation. In essence if not in detail, I believe that Chaudenson is correct in claiming that Reunion Creole was constituted fundamentally in its modern form by around 1715, and that it has remained basically stable since (Chaudenson's contention [1974:449, 1117-18] that RC and MC were less divergent around 1800 than they are now is clearly an error of interpretation, cf. A6.3 above). By "Reunion Creole" I mean the language as I have described it in A1 above. The bulk of the variation in Reunion today is toward more "French" varieties (e.g., the language of Grand-Ilet, in A3.3), rather than toward those which are more "Creole" in the IdeFC sense.

In spite of this vulnerability (more apparent than real, I am sure), the linguistic evidence I have brought forward is completely in accord with the demographic and linguistic facts advanced by Baker. Reunion Creole and Isle de France Creole belong to two different linguistic traditions. Together, the historical and the linguistic facts render the "Bourbonnais" theory untenable, and a myth of the 1970s can be put to rest.

NOTES

1. For example, the use in SC of the personal pronouns *to* and *tua,* and the possessive *tô* (not mentioned in Bollée 1977a, Corne 1977a, or Papen 1978b) has just come to light. Baker (personal communication, 1981) reports the marginal use of these forms: in reprimanding a child, *tua* (not *u*) is the preferred form, and *to, tua, tô* also occur in children's rhymes.

2. The major target for such studies is obviously Reunion, where the continuum cries out for study and analysis. But no one as yet, as far as I know, has ever mentioned in print that some monolingual speakers of SC preserve traditional songs *(româs)* which are recognizably French in their semantactics and morphology, nor has any monograph been written on the linguistic correlates of the syncretism characteristic of the "medicine" practiced by the *bonom dibua* 'witchdoctor'. Further, the influence of RC is not yet dead in Seychelles: a well-known song, *Koste kot mua* 'Come close to me', contains two RC structures—*mô âbras a vu* 'I kiss you' (SC *mô âbras u*) and *vu le zoli* 'you are pretty' (SC *u zoli*). Both structures are explicitly identified as *burbone* "Reunionese" by my consultants.

Part b

On the Origins of the First Mauritians and of the Creole Language of their Descendants

A Refutation of Chaudenson's "Bourbonnais" Theory

NOMENCLATURE AND CONVENTIONS ADOPTED

Mauritius was so named by the Dutch who claimed possession of this previously uninhabited island in 1598. Dutch attempts to settle Mauritius were never very successful, and they abandoned the island in ca. 1710, moving to the Cape with all their slaves.[1] During the Dutch period, the French termed Mauritius "isle Maurice." On claiming possession in 1715 and again in 1721 when they occupied the island, they renamed it *isle de France*. However, this name did not immediately supersede that of *isle Maurice*, and both will be found in quotations below. In referring to this island at any time, I will write "Mauritius," its name in English since the Dutch period.

In the period from 1721-35, Reunion was known as *isle Mascarin* as well as by its official name of *isle (de) Bourbon*, and both these names will thus be found in quotations below. I will refer to this island in English as "Reunion," a name first introduced at the end of the eighteenth century and which has been the only official name since 1848.[2] I will also term people born on that island at any time *Réunionnais*, but, following Chaudenson (1974), I will occasionally use the term "Bourbonnais" to refer to a language spoken in Reunion in the early part of the eighteenth century.

In quoting from eighteenth-century documents, I have preserved the orthography of the original wherever possible.[3] However, I have consistently italicized the names of ships whether they are underlined or italicized in the original (as is frequently the case). The words "italics added," following a quotation, should thus generally be understood to apply to anything other than the names of vessels.

NOTES

1. The suggestion, made by De Rauville (1908) and quoted in Baker (1972:36, note 4), that the maroons who troubled the French in Mauritius in the period from 1722-25 were survivors from the Dutch period now appears to be without foundation. The maroons referred to in the De Nyon and De Hauville correspondence of 1722-23 (ANC C4 vl) are clearly identified as Malagasies who had arrived a few months earlier. Similarly, the Du Cros letter of 1725 (*Lettres édifiantes...*, 18:17) refers to all the maroons then present as Malagasies who had arrived since the French occupation of the island.

2. Bouet-Willaumez 1852:938.

3. I have occasionally introduced a space between two distinct words which were run together in the original, and have similarly written an apostrophe in certain cases where the quality of the original is such that I was unable to determine whether one had been written there or not. However, I have nowhere added, removed, or changed any letter or diacritic insofar as I was able to decipher the original correctly. The reader should thus be prepared for orthographic surprises such as *maitre* for *mettre* and *dont* for *donc*, particularly in extracts from ships' logs. In a few cases where I have not been able to consult the original, I have had to

quote from secondary sources. In that case, it should be noted that there is something of a tradition of "partially modernizing" old texts in Mauritius. Simply stated, this consists of systematic modernization of verb forms but only sporadic modernization of nouns (in particular) so that *tems* and *temps* or *isle* and *île* will sometimes be found in the same "modernized" text.

B1
Background[1]

It was probably Paul Meyer who, in 1872, first expressed the view that Mauritian Creole (MC) appeared to have more in common with a variety of American Creole French (ACF) than might reasonably be expected:

Q1 Il me semble même que le patois de l'île de France offre, dans la déformation du français, des analogies avec celui de Trinidad qui ne sont point expliquées suffisamment par la communauté du point de départ. (1872:156-57)[2]

The question of the relationship between MC, spoken in the Indian Ocean, and ACF, spoken in the Caribbean area, has for some time occupied a central place in the century-old debate about the relative contribution of the French and their slaves to the origin and elaboration of these languages. The Haitian Jules Faine became convinced, after reading Baissac (1880 and 1888), that MC and Haitian Creole (HC) shared a common origin. Believing that the slaves in these two territories had been brought from entirely different sources, he was unable to attribute any of the non-Standard French features found in both MC and HC to the influence of African languages. He thus deduced that the common source must have been the speech of French sailors, one group of people who certainly visited both Mauritius and Haiti. Faine supported his theory with a considerable body of material and remarked, on the final page of his book:

Q2 Dans l'étude comparée du Mauricien et de l'Haïtien, il ne s'agit plus de ces rencontres plus ou moins fortuites, mais de similitudes parfaites se répétant constamment et en nombre considérable. (1939:214)

Twenty-five years later, Goodman conducted a comparative survey of all the French Creoles for which adequate descriptions were available. In contrast to Faine, he found evidence to suggest that there had been at least some West African slaves in Mauritius, and this enabled him to envisage a common origin for all these Creoles and one in which Africans had played a more positive role:

Q3 Having established both the existence of West African influence in Mauritius and the close historical connection of all the French Creoles, one is able to formulate a much clearer idea of how Creole originated and developed. Only by positing a single origin for Creole can one account for this historical connection, and its place of origin can scarcely have been other than West Africa, from which it was transported to the various parts of the world where Creole is now found. It most likely developed out of a slavers' jargon of some sort, whose French element... may or may not have been the kind of dialectal mélange which Faine suggests, but which almost certainly incorporated a number of features of the slaves' native languages. (1964:130-31)

While Goodman lacked adequate data on Reunion Creole (RC), he was aware that it differed in important aspects from MC and sought to provide an explanation for this. The relevant passage was quoted in the Introduction to this volume, but it is repeated here for convenience:

Q4 When Reunion was colonized in 1664 (fifty years earlier than Mauritius), probably neither the West African slave trade nor the French slavers' pidgin had reached its fullest development. The West African influence in the Creole of Reunion and its connection with American Creole therefore was doubtless considerably less than was that of Mauritius though the pronoun *mwẽ* in Reunion, particularly the nasalization of the *e*, may indicate that such a connection was not entirely absent. By the time Mauritius was settled... however, the West African slave trade was probably so well organized that, even though the island was settled in part from Reunion and was close to Madagascar, large numbers of West African slaves were imported there, and their pidgin (by this time quite well established) became the dominant linguistic element and soon developed into Mauritian Creole. Reunion Creole was not without influence in Mauritius, however, and the two dialects share certain important features which set them apart from American Creole, notably the historical shift without exception of the phonemes *š* and *ž* to *s* and *z* respectively. (1964:132)

Chaudenson's *Le lexique du parler créole de la Réunion* (hereafter *Lexique*) was published ten years later in 1974. This work had been eagerly awaited as one which would clarify the position of RC vis-à-vis MC and other varieties of Creole French. While its author acknowledged that "Réunionnais et Mauriciens ne se comprennent pas! en créole du moins" (*Lexique*, p. 414), he nevertheless went on to claim, to the astonishment of at least this student of MC,[3] that RC, MC, Seychelles Creole (SC), and Rodrigues Creole (RoC) all originate from a single "stock" or "fount" *(d'une souche unique)*—what he termed "le créole 'bourbonnais' parlé à Bourbon au début du XVIIIe siècle" (*Lexique*, p. 446). In support of this he cited only Toussaint (1936:13) to the effect that the continuous habitation of Mauritius could be dated from the arrival of a small number of Réunionnais at the end of 1721. Chaudenson went on to claim, without referring to any supporting evidence, that Mauritius was peopled mainly from Reunion, and that new slaves introduced onto the island subsequently would have found themselves in a linguistically homogeneous situation in which both the slaves and slave owners already established there would have conversed with each other in "Bourbonnais" (*Lexique*, p. 446). Both of the latter claims are without foundation as will be shown below.

Being convinced that his view of the peopling of Mauritius was correct, Chaudenson felt that a detailed refutation of Goodman's hypothesis was unnecessary:

Q5 M. Goodman suggère que, comme tous les créoles français, le réunionnais pourrait être issu d'une "lingua franca" de l'Ouest africain. Quoique l'auteur fasse preuve de beaucoup de prudence et d'ingéniosité dans la formulation de son hypothèse, elle ne peut guère être accepté, du moins en ce qui concerne les parlers des Mascareignes et des Seychelles. Des rapprochements lexicaux et morphologiques rares et incertains, la présence d'esclaves guinéens aux Mascareignes ne peuvent suffire à la fonder. L'histoire du peuplement de ces îles prouve que si, comme nous l'avons nous-même signalé, un certain nombre d'esclaves furent amenés de la côte Occidentale d'Afrique, cette immigration, au demeurant réduite, eut lieu plus de trois quarts de siècle après le début de la colonisation [of Reunion], alors que le créole ["bourbonnais"] était déjà constitué. Ce n'est donc pas l'apport de quelques centaines d'Africains de l'Ouest aussitôt dispersées dans les "habitations" des deux îles qui a pu modifier le parler! (*Lexique*, pp. 1107-8)

However, as noted in the Introduction to this volume, these comments were not altogether justified. Goodman had suggested that the much earlier settlement of Reunion (than Mauritius) would explain both why there would be considerably less West African influence in RC than MC and why there should be major differences between these two Creoles. The real conflict with Goodman's theory stems directly from Chaudenson's claim that MC and the other Isle de France Creoles (IdeFC) are, in some sense, derivatives of RC. Chaudenson has thus far failed to come to terms with the evidence Goodman presented, in particular the innovations common to IdeFC and varieties of American Creole French.

In an unpublished B Phil dissertation written in 1976 and entitled "Towards a Social History of Mauritian Creole" (hereafter *Towards*), I devoted sixteen pages to such information as was then available to me on the peopling of Mauritius from December 1721 to June 1735.[4] On the basis of that incomplete evidence it seemed clear that:

1. Mauritius had not been settled from Reunion.
2. The numbers of West Africans who reached Mauritius from 1729 were sufficiently great for them to have formed a majority of the slaves from 1730 to 1735.

Since 1976, I have been conducting a far more detailed survey of the peopling of Mauritius and have had the opportunity of consulting most of the relevant documents concerning the period from 1721 to 1740 at first hand in the archives and libraries of both Mauritius and Paris. These documents include parish registers, correspondence, ships' logs, legal proceedings, etc. I have also been able to examine a number of publications to which I did not have access in 1976. I am thus now in a position to confirm in print that both (1) and (2) above are accurate. The details will be set out on later pages.

In a recent article and in a book, both of which are heavy on criticism but distinctly light on evidence, Chaudenson seeks to disprove my unpublished 1976 findings in *Towards*. I will refer to Chaudenson's article, "A propos de la genèse du créole mauricien: le peuplement de l'île de France de 1721 à 1735," and his book, *Les Créoles Français,* as *Genèse* and *Créoles,* respectively. Comment on *Towards* in *Créoles* begins:

Q6 La récente étude de Ph. Baker, "Toward [*sic*] a social history of Mauritian Creole" (Ph. D.

[*sic*] York, 1976), témoigne de façon exemplaire à la fois de l'évidente nécessité qu'il y a à fonder sur une étude historique précise toute hypothèse sur la genèse d'un parler, mais aussi le risque couru lorsque des données incertaines voire erronées, sont utilisées *en vue de démontrer, à toute force, une théorie préétablie.* Dans la première partie de cet ouvrage ... Ph. Baker s'est attaché à contester la théorie que nous avions présentée à propos de la genèse du mauricien. L'étude du peuplement conduit en effet à penser que la langue parlée à Bourbon avant 1721 ... a joué un rôle important dans la genèse du parler mauricien en raison du nombre et du rôle social des colons et des esclaves venus de l'île voisine et qui utilisaient ce "bourbonnais" ... Ph. Baker prend le contrepied de cette double assertion et soutient deux propositions opposées:

> a. Le rôle des créoles de Bourbon fut très faible puisque tous auraient, selon lui, quitté l'île de France à la fin de 1722 et qu'il n'y en aurait plus aucun entre 1722 et 1735.
> b. L'immigration ouest-africaine aurait été majoritaire; par conséquent, pourrait valablement être réintroduite une théorie monogénétique se fondant sur la présence à l'île de France d'un pidgin ouest-africain et conduisant à la fois à séparer sur les plans génétique et structurel le réunionnais des autres créoles de l'océan Indien et à rapprocher ces derniers des parlers de la zone caraïbe.

(*Créoles,* pp. 45-46; italics added)

Quotation 6 requires several comments:

1. The lack of foundation in the suggestion that I used doubtful and/or inaccurate information with the aim of showing, at all cost, that an earlier theory (Goodman's) was right, will be apparent to those with access to the dissertation concerned. Three possible origins of MC were considered briefly, adding a purely local origin to the theories of Goodman and Chaudenson, and it was made clear (*Towards,* pp. 54-55) that I took the view that further research was needed before definite conclusions could be drawn. The italicized part of the above quotation is thus both misleading and inappropriate. With regard to my inaccuracies, Chaudenson writes:

Q7 Les erreurs de Ph. Baker tiennent essentiellement à ce que la seule source à laquelle il se réfère est, inexplicablement, un ouvrage d'amateur, estimable certes, mais où les données fautives et les lacunes sont nombreuses. (*Créoles,* p. 46)

Chaudenson refrains from naming the author of this praiseworthy amateur work. As I referred to about 150 publications in *Towards,* quite a proportion of which might be described as the works of amateurs, it is not entirely clear which one Chaudenson regards as "la seule source." A likely candidate is perhaps Lagesse's *L'Ile de France avant La Bourdonnais* to which I referred a dozen times in the early pages of this dissertation. If so, the slur is unwarranted for this work includes the texts of a number of documents from the period 1721 to 1735 which have not been published elsewhere and is thus essential reading for anyone who has not had the opportunity to examine the originals. (Chaudenson's own references to Lagesse in both *Genèse* and *Créoles* bear witness to its usefulness.) While there are errors in this work, some of which I will refer to below, they are, for the most part, of only minor importance.

2. Chaudenson's information on the peopling of Mauritius is almost exclusively based on secondary sources, mainly works written or edited by Albert Lougnon. The most important of these is Lougnon (1958) which is concerned with shipping movements to and from the Mascarenes in the nine years to the end of 1735. This provides a lot of useful information relating to passenger arrivals and, less frequently, departures during that period, but it does not pretend to be a demographic study. Lougnon (1958) is the cited source for all but three of the details of arrivals given by Chaudenson for the period 1727 to 1735.

Chaudenson overlooks the works of Kuczynski (1948-49) and Bechet (1951-56). Kuczynski, a professional demographer, was perhaps the first to indicate that the Réunionnais contribution to the permanent settlement of Mauritius was rather small (1948-49:2.748, note 2; 753; 755, note 7). While Bechet was concerned only with the White population in the period from 1722 to 1767, a detailed examination of his work suggests that there were fewer than 20 White settlers from Reunion who arrived during that 46-year period, and that all but two of these reached Mauritius after 1735. In reviewing this work, Barassin wrote:

Q8 Et qu'il n'y a pas eu entre elles [Mauritius and Reunion] d'échange actif de population: les patronymes communs aux deux îles sont rares... et plusieurs contingents d'habitants sont passés de Bourbon à Maurice, mais, ils n'y sont pas demeurés ou ils n'y ont pas fait souche; le fond de [the White element in] la population mauricienne est, en quasi totalité, venu directement de France. (*RT,* nouv. sér. 2:236)

3. Chaudenson misrepresents my position somewhat in (a) on p. 137. The passage which most nearly corresponds to this in *Towards* runs: "I have not found any evidence to suggest that any other *settlers or slaves* from Réunion came to Mauritius until some time after 1735" (p. 14; italics added). I nowhere suggested that there were no temporary *visitors* from Reunion in the period from 1722 to 1735.

For the most part, the information on the peopling of Mauritius in *Créoles* is but an abbreviated version of that contained in *Genèse*. In the following pages I will therefore refer only to the latter except where *Créoles* differs in some important respect.

Genèse consists of two main parts. The first is a list of ships and their dates of arrival, together with brief details of the passengers they brought to Mauritius from 1721 to 1735. Chaudenson notes no arrivals between September 29, 1723 and January 2, 1727, and implies with the words "Les arrivés d'immigrants reprennent en 1727" (*Genèse*, p. 45) that there were none. In fact, in 1724 alone, there were at least five ships which brought additional soldiers to the island (see Table 1 in B2.1). There are many other omissions, errors regarding the dates of arrival of particular ships or concerning the origin and/or numbers of passengers they brought, and unsubstantiated assumptions on a variety of matters. All of these will be discussed below.

Chaudenson pays little attention to departures. The only ones he notes are those of some slaves and free Réunionnais who returned to their island in 1722-23, and those of 150 West Africans (Chaudenson's figure) who traveled on to Reunion in 1730. His use of the terms "immigrant" and "immigration" implies that everyone else who reached Mauritius remained there permanently. As will be shown below, this was certainly not the case. Most of the Swiss and French troops returned to Europe on completing their service, while quite a substantial proportion of those who had arrived with the intention of becoming permanent settlers in fact abandoned their concessions before mid-1735 and either moved to Reunion or returned to Europe (*CBI*, p. liv).[5]

Part Two of *Genèse* is subdivided into four sections. The first deals with the apparently conflicting censuses of 1735: 838 people according to La Bourdonnais' *Mémoire* (Lougnon and Toussaint 1937:9); 1,922 people according to a handwritten, undated note in the margin of a parish register (MA KA 2; the note is next to an entry for March 25, 1735, but is in a different hand). In *Towards* I had taken the former to be the more reliable of the two, and had speculated that the latter might have been the total of all the names which had appeared in the registers up to that date. Chaudenson offers a more probable explanation in *Genèse*: that the lower figure includes only those Europeans and slaves living on plantations, while the higher figure includes the entire population. If this is the correct explanation— and very strong support can be found in another census taken on January 1, 1735, which gives the total as "1 600 personnes de tout age, de tout sexe, de toutte condition, et de toutte couleur" (FOM G^1 505)—it remains of interest to note that in this particular "plantation society" less than half the population was apparently living or working on a plantation in mid-1735.

The second and third sections of *Genèse* Part Two deal with the numbers of Réunionnais and West Africans, respectively, who were present in Mauritius up to the end of 1735. Both sections contain important errors and misinterpretations of the facts, which will be discussed in B2.1, B2.2, and B2.3. There are also errors in Chaudenson's figures for Malagasy and Indian arrivals and, as these groups are important for establishing the proportion of slaves of West African origin, they will be examined in B2.4 below.

The fourth and final section of *Genèse* Part Two is essentially a summary of the previous three and a reaffirmation of Chaudenson's faith in the "Bourbonnais" theory of the origin of MC, which he presented in *Lexique*.

In what follows, I deal first with the peopling of Mauritius (B2). This chapter is restricted to those aspects of settlement that have been disputed and that are most relevant to the theories of Chaudenson and Goodman. I show that there were scarcely any Réunionnais who had settled in Mauritius by 1735 and that the numbers of potential first- or second-language speakers of "Bourbonnais" on the island after April 1723 were too small, absolutely and relatively, for them to have played a dominant role in the formation of MC. I also demonstrate that West Africans did indeed form a majority of the slave population for a few years, as claimed in *Towards*.

In Chapter B3, I look at a number of grammatical items occurring in MC and also in either RC or HC, drawing on early texts of these Creoles. I note that there appears to be only one grammatical item common to all the Indian Ocean Creoles (IOC) which is not found in any variety of ACF, and that the available evidence suggests that this may have been a Mauritian rather than a Réunionnais innovation. None of the other grammatical items discussed in B3 suggest a closer historical relationship between MC and RC than between MC and HC—quite the reverse, in fact.

Finally, in B4, I attempt to isolate the factors which may be responsible for certain differences between the geographically proximate MC and RC, as well as for certain similarities between the geographically distant MC and HC.

NOTES

1. I am grateful to all of those who were kind enough to comment on earlier drafts of this paper and/or to track down for me a number of important documents, including: John Beckett, Derek Bickerton, Annegret Bollée, Catherine Bozon-Verduraz, Anthony Cheke, Chris Corne, David Dalby, Morgan Dalphinis, Morris Goodman, Vinesh Hookoomsing, Alexander Hull, Shafeekh Jeeroburkhan, Robert Le Page, Ingrid Neumann, Hilary Perraton, Peter Stein, and Jeffrey Waite. It cannot be assumed, however, that any of these people share the views expressed in these pages.

I would also like to place on record my indebtedness to Christine Bouly and Aken Wong (Paris), Luc and Margaret Olivier and Palmesh Cuttaree (Mauritius), all of whom provided me with accommodation in 1978 when the bulk of the research for this paper was undertaken.

Finally, I would like to thank Michael Mann for valuable advice concerning the computer analysis of the population data.

2. Meyer based his opinion on a comparison of Chrestien (1831) and Thomas (1869) (Stein 1972:15).

3. As many thousands of Réunionnais spend their annual holidays in Mauritius, encounters between first-language speakers of RC and MC occur with some frequency. Normally effective communication is only achieved by one or both parties using the amount of French they command. The low level of interintelligibility between RC and MC is altogether inconsistent with Chaudenson's claim that MC in some sense derives from RC. To propose a common origin for these two Creoles demands both evidence of, and an explanation for, their subsequent sharp divergence. The *Lexique* explanation was decreolization in Reunion, but this was at odds with the evidence of the ca. 1722 text (cf. Hull [1975:9] 1979; and Corne in Part A of this volume).

Background 141

Chaudenson's recent claim (*Créoles,* p. 46) that "la parenté [between Indian Ocean Creoles] est évidente pour le témoin le moins averti" is quite simply false insofar as it is intended to apply to RC and any one of the other Indian Ocean Creoles.

4. The subject of the dissertation was proposed to me for the first time in July 1976, and the regulations required that the final text be submitted in October of the same year. It proved impossible to obtain copies of a number of works published in the Mascarenes within so short a period of time. In certain cases I was forced to rely on notes made on a visit to Mauritius fifteen months earlier. As will be apparent from the title, the peopling of Mauritius was not the principal concern of this dissertation.

5. Those who left Mauritius bound for Reunion before the end of 1735 include (with year of departure, or year that presence in Reunion was first attested, in parentheses): P. Bachelier (1725), L.-F. de Balmane (1725), J.-B. Bouchat de la Tour and his wife L. Bigot (1730), M. Bourigaut (1732), F. Butté (and his wife G.-J. Levesque and child?) (1731), J. Estève, his wife A. Benoist, and three children (1731), Desisles (1731), C. Didion, his wife and children (1735), A. Dubois (1735), A. Dupré and his wife J.-M. Leplanti (and child?) (1731), F. Dussart de la Salle (1730), F. Geoffroy (1735), N. Gouron, his wife D. Le Gouron, and one child (1730), A. Grimaud (1734), T. Infante, his wife M.-M. Boivin, and two children (1731), C. Lacan (1730), M. Colmok (1730), C. Le Heux and his wife J. Lorcy (1735), E. Luc (1731), J.-P. Macquaire and his wife (1735), L. Mascle and his wife A.-G. Gourrès (1731), N. Morel and his wife G. Lemeur (1732), P. Pluchon, his wife C. Gigot, and two children (1728), O. Rehel, his wife O. Le Houarno, and one child (1732), L.-F. Thonier de Nuizement, his wife M.-N. Goulet, and daughter (1735), A. Toucas and his wife M. Richart (and a child?) (1735), F. Vidal and his wife C. Briand (1735), J.-J. Zilvaiguer, his wife A.-M. Chotin, and two stepchildren (1725). The presence of most of these people in Reunion by 1735 at latest is attested in the census of that year. Those not found in the latter may perhaps have died before August 1735 or, in a few cases, may have merely visited Reunion en route for Europe. This list excludes all those definitely known to have returned to Europe (i.e., on vessels that called at Reunion before continuing their journey to France) such as Desfouilleuse (see B2.3.2), various employees of the Compagnie, and soldiers. Also excluded are two Lazarists, Borthon and Le Coq, who moved to Reunion after having spent several years in Mauritius. Note also that three of the people listed above, Levesque, Morel, and Lemeur, appear to have returned to Mauritius before 1740.

B2
The Contested Aspects of the Peopling of Mauritius to 1735

B2.1 Total Population During the First Four Years (1721-25)

Table 1 (pp. 143-48) sets out all the relevant information I have been able to obtain for the period from December 1721 to October 1725. Since the information in Table 1 is necessarily incomplete in certain respects, it cannot be claimed that the composition of the population which it suggests at any given time within this four-year period is entirely accurate. Nevertheless, the total population in October 1725 given at the foot of Table 1 (223 excluding maroons) is sufficiently close to that given in the census of October 18, 1725 (October 12, 1725 according to Chaudenson citing Lagesse)[1] to suggest that the two might be reconciled. The 1725 census figures are:

```
Q9 Officiers et employés..................................20
    Troupes ..............................................100
    Ouvriers .............................................28
    Domestiques...........................................5
    Femmes ...............................................13
    Enfants...............................................13
    Noirs de la Compagnie.................................24
    Noirs de divers particuliers..........................10
                                                         213
```
(Kaeppelin 1908:105)

The differences between the census figures above and those of Table 1 are of two kinds: 1) categorial differences; and 2) differences which reflect the incomplete nature of the data presented in Table 1.

The census makes no mention of Lazarists. It seems unlikely that they would have been thought of as "employés." It seems more probable that they were simply omitted from the document which Kaeppelin cites.

The census also fails to mention the free Réunionnais Creoles as such. As they were paid by the Compagnie—this is mentioned in the Lenoir report, parts of which are reproduced below—they might have been considered "employés" though, as will be seen, they were only temporarily such. As the last four Creoles (see Q32 below) were repatriated in 1726, there must have been at least four present in October 1725.

The Table 1 category of Swiss soldiers has no equivalent in the census. The two who remained were Ballard (died 1728) and Neizein (married 1729). It is far from clear where either might have appeared in the census table.

The remaining categories are substantially common to the census and Table 1. The latter notes 10 Compagnie employees. The presence of 8 of them is attested

The Contested Aspects of the Peopling of Mauritius   143

Table 1
Arrivals/Births and Departures/Deaths, December 1721 to October 1725

Note: The arrival of a person whose name is preceded by an asterisk is assumed to have been included in one of the groups of arrivals mentioned earlier, e.g., in the case of Meuron (see June 12, 1722), he is taken to be one of the Swiss soldiers who arrived two months earlier. *Quelques* has been consistently interpreted as 'five'. The order of categories (left to right) deliberately resembles that of the 1725 census with which it is compared in the text. All numbers of arrivals and departures followed by a superscript "e" are estimates.

			FREE POPULATION						UNFREE		
				Soldiers (incl. Officers)		Ouvriers, Domestiques,			Free Réunionnais	Slaves from		
Date	Ship and Passengers (or other particulars)	Lazarists	Compagnie Employees	Swiss	French	Others	Women	Children	Creoles	Reunion	Madagascar	Maroons
Dec 24, 1721	*Courrier de Bourbon*: Arrival of the acting governor Durongouet Le Toullec and 16 Réunionnais (ANM 4JJ 75 (5))		+1						+16 −10 6			
Mar 2, 1722	*Courrier de Bourbon*: Departure of 10 of the Réunionnais (Lougnon 1956:199; ANM 4JJ 75 (5))[a]											
Apr 4, 1722	*Atalante* and *Diane*: Arrival of at least the following:[b] 4 Lazarists (Adam, Borthon, Igou, Le Coq)	+4										
	8 Compagnie employees (De Comminge, Delesque, Duval de Hauville, Gast d'Hauterive, Guyenet, De Nyon, de Saint-Martin, Simon de Monsy)		+8 9									
	6 Swiss officers (Faillet, Faverger, Jacotet, Schmid-g, Wirtz, Zilvaiguer)			+6								
	84 Swiss soldiers (Ballard, Bienvenu, Freilik, Fribourg, Hayec, Misset, Neizein, Nicolle, Schmitt, Scriber, Vautrot . . .)			+84 90								
	2 Domestiques (valets of De Nyon and De Hauville)					+2						
	6 Married women (Mesdames Bienvenu, De Comminges, Faillet, Gast, Scriber, and Zilvaiguer)[c]						+6					
	4 Children: Mlle De Comminge, 2 children of Major Hubert, who died en route and whose widow married Zilvaiguer, and the survivor of the Gast twins born on the *Diane* (ANC C4 vl, ANM 4JJ 75 (14), ANM 4JJ 90 (7), Bechet, Chélin 1973:8, Lougnon 1956:20, RHL 1:483, RRM 4 7-15)							+4				
May 4, 1722	*Diane*: Departure of De Nyon and Durongouet for Reunion (De Rauville 1908:30-31)		−2 7									
( ), 1722	*Comte de Toulouse*: During De Nyon's absence, "un tres belhomme allemand" (Wilhem Leichnig?)[d] was put ashore by this vessel (ANC C4 vl)					+1 3						
Jun 12, 1722	*Diane*: De Nyon returned with 6 Creoles and about 30 slaves ("une trentaine" ANC C4 vl)		+1 8						+6 12		+30[e] 30	
	By this date, 23 of the Swiss arrivals had died, including Nicolle (accidentally shot by *Meuron) (Lougnon 1956: 201; ANC C4 vl)			−23 67								
Subtotal		4	8	67		3	6	4	12		30	

(continued)

(Table 1 continued):

Date	Ship and Passengers (or other particulars)	Lazarists	Compagnie Employees	Soldiers Swiss	Soldiers (incl. Officers) French	Ouvriers, Domestiques, Others	Women	Children	Free Réunionnais Creoles	Slaves from Reunion	Slaves from Madagascar	Maroons
(brought forward)		4	8	67		3	6	4	12		30	
Jun 13, 1722	De Nyon mentions the presence of the doctor François[e] and one Duquesnain, both Compagnie employees who may well have arrived the previous April (ANC C4 vi)		+2/10									
Jun 24, 1722	The Lazarist Frère Adam drowned (RHL 1:411-12)	−1/3										
Jul 12, 1722	Diane: De Nyon left for Reunion (ANC C4 vi)		−1/9									
( ), 1722	Vierge de Grace and/or Rubis: 5 soldiers (estimated)[f]				+5[e]/11							
Nov 29, 1722	Saint-Albin: De Nyon returned with Le Blanc, "un maître canonnier, six des ouvriers et cinq des soldats pris à Lorient en février précédent, ainsi que trois habitants de Bourbon: Auber, René Clain et Pierre Caron" (Lougnon 1956:213)		+2/11		+6/11	+6/9			+3/15			
Dec 8, 1722	Rubis: 65 slaves from Madagascar (ANC C4 vi)										+65	
Dec 12, 1722	De Hauville reported the presence of two deserters from an English ship: Provensal and Springal (ANC C4 vi)					+2/11						
Dec 18, 1722	De Nyon mentions presence of Denis Le Roux and notes that 19 of the Malagasies had become maroons (ANC C4 vi)										−19/46	+19
Dec 27, 1722	Lagesse (1972:21) claims that a few more soldiers arrived on a ship		+1/12		+5[e]/16							
Jan 2, 1723	(Ship not named, possibly the Rubis): Expulsion of Provensal and Springal; departure of the Creoles E. Robert and J. Fontaine for Reunion (ANC C4 vi); five of the maroons were recaptured (ANC C4 vi)					−2/9			−2/13		+5/51	−5/14
Feb 10, 1723	De Nyon notes that of a number of slaves (estimated at 12)[g] who ran away when surprised while trying to steal a pirogue a few days earlier, only 5 had so far been recaptured. Of those still at large was "un petit coquin quy apartien a un habittant de mascarin quy a esté lautheur de cet enlevement" (ANC C4 vi); De Nyon also notes that 4 more Creoles have arrived from Reunion and that one of them, later named as Jean Allaigre, can be moved to Port Louis (ANC C4 vi)								+4/17	−1/29	−11e/40 +5/45	+12[e]/26 −5/21
Mar 5, 1723	De Hauville mentions that a Malagasy slave has deserted (ANC C4 vi)										−1/44	+1/22
Mar 7, 1723	De Hauville reports having recaptured the deserter as well as two other Malagasies involved in the pirogue affair (ANC C4 vi)										+3/47	−3/19
Subtotal		3	12	67	16	9	6	4	17	29	47	19

(continued)

The Contested Aspects of the Peopling of Mauritius

(Table 1 continued):

Date	Ship and Passengers (or other particulars)	Lazarists	Compagnie Employees	Soldiers (incl. Officers) Swiss	Soldiers (incl. Officers) French	Ouvriers, Domestiques, Others	Women	Children	Free Réunionnais Creoles	Slaves from Reunion	Slaves from Madagascar	Maroons
(brought forward)		3	12	67	16	9	6	4	17	29	47	19
Apr 13, 1723	*Saint-Albin*: Departure of 30 Réunionnais (24 slaves and 6 Creoles); also left on this boat: Denis Le Roux, and a troublesome female Malagasy slave (Lougnon 956:230; ANC C4 vi)		$\frac{-1}{11}$						$\frac{-6}{11}$	$\frac{-24}{5}$	$\frac{-1}{46}$	
Apr 29, 1723	De Nyon mentions presence of Du Cotté (his gardener?)[h] (ANC C4 vi)											
May 17, 1723	*Rubis*: Le Coq, Du Cotté, Allaigre, and "le canonnier de M. Beauvolliers" left for Reunion (ANC C4 vi)	$\frac{-1}{2}$			$\frac{-1}{15}$	$\frac{+1}{10}$						
May 23, 1723	De Hauville reports that one of the Malagasy slaves has disappeared (ANC C4 vi)					$\frac{-1}{9}$						
May 28, 1723	De Nyon reports that the above-mentioned Malagasy has given himself up in Port Bourbon								$\frac{-1}{10}$		$\frac{-1}{45}$	$\frac{+1}{20}$
Jun 3, 1722	De Hauville's letter of this date—the last of the series—indicates that he is about to embark for France but does not name the vessel (ANC C4 vi)										$\frac{+1}{46}$	$\frac{-1}{19}$
( ), 1723	*Lys* and *Union*:[i] Brought one civilian with his wife and daughter, and 20 soldiers (*Genèse*, p. 44)				$\frac{+20}{35}$	$\frac{+1}{10}$	$\frac{+1}{7}$	$\frac{+1}{5}$				
Sep 20, 1723	*Triton*: Brought 8 officers, 7 cadets, and a proportion of the other passengers—crudely estimated as half—who included 94 soldiers, 43 workmen, 2 wives and 2 children of soldiers, 6 wives of soldiers, 3 children of workmen. Those definitely known to have disembarked at Mauritius include: the officers and soldiers, Baron, Balmane, Jean de Boulo,[j] Brousse, C. Dorlet de Bresson, Fantoux, Vachier . . . ; the workman Didion; the wives Mme de Boulo (M.-M. Aignan),[j] Mme Fantoux (F. Geoffroy), and Mme Didion; the twins born to Mme Didion on board the *Triton* (Lougnon 1956:227; ANM 4JJ 75 (13); *RHL* 1:.1; Bechet; Chelin 1973:12)			$\frac{+15}{}$ $\frac{+47^e}{97}$		$\frac{+21^e}{31}$	$\frac{+4^e}{11}$	$\frac{+3^e}{8}$				
ca. Dec 1723	*Argonaute*: Departure of De Comminge, his wife, and child (ANM B3 v298 f75)		$\frac{-1}{9}$				$\frac{-1}{10}$	$\frac{-1}{7}$				
Jan 22, 1724	Birth of Anne Marguerite Scriber (Bechet)							$\frac{+1}{8}$				
Feb 9, 1724	Request to De Nyon signed by (among others) Denis Le Roux, *Binial, *Ducuelle, *Saisse, and *Mandrou confirms return of first-named and presence of others (*RHL* 1:11)		$\frac{+1}{10}$									
Mar 13 1724	French soldier *Courtois killed by maroons (Bechet)				$\frac{-1}{96}$							
Apr 28, 1724	Swiss soldier Hayec killed by maroons (Bechet)			$\frac{-1}{66}$								
Subtotal		2	10	66	96	31	10	8	10	5	46	19

(continued)

146 BAKER

(Table 1 continued):

Date	Ship and Passengers (or other particulars)	Lazarists	Compagnie Employees	Soldiers (incl. Officers) Swiss	Soldiers (incl. Officers) French	Ouvriers, Domestiques, Others	Women	Children	Free Réunionnais Creoles	Slaves from Reunion	Madagascar	Maroons
(brought forward)		2	10	66	96 +3 99	31	10	8	10	5	46	19
ca. May 1724	*Neptune*: Brought at least the soldier Fornier de Changeac and the officers Gumont de la Tour and L. Mascle (Lougnon 1956:227)											
ca. Jun 1724	Death of the doctor François *(DBM)*		$\frac{-1}{9}$									
Jul 16, 1724	*Vierge de Grace*: Brought at least the officer Joseph de Bouloc and his wife A. de la Rivière, and the soldiers A. Clergeau, Curé (and his wife J. Helant), N. Girandin, L. Jacob, C. Le Heux, J. Launay, and C. Menot (ANC D2A; Lougnon 1956:253; ANM B3 v314)				$\frac{+8}{107}$		$\frac{+2}{12}$					
ca. Jul 1724	*Hercule*: Brought at least the soldiers J. Genu, A. Ledoux, P. Nicole, R. Robin, F. Sebelin; and Mlle Delvinquier (ANC D2A)				$\frac{+5}{112}$		$\frac{+1}{13}$					
Aug 21, 1724	*Duc de Chartres*: Brought at least the soldiers D. Brouillet, F. Landay, Ch. Milon, P. Pautre, F. Vidal, Th. Vigneux (ANC D2A)				$\frac{+6}{118}$							
Oct 30, 1724	Death of *P. Dubois recorded and presence of *D. Lalot attested (MA K A 1)				$\frac{-1}{117}$							
ca. Nov 1724	*Lys*: Brought at least the soldiers J. Cherel and L. Marchand (ANC D2A)				+2							
Nov 4, 1724	Marriage of Mandrou to M.-M. Crampon attests presence (or return)^k of the latter (Bechet)						$\frac{+1}{14}$					
Nov 21, 1724	Birth of Marie Gast (Bechet)							$\frac{+1}{9}$				
Nov 21, 1724	*Ressource*: According to Chélin, this ship brought a few more soldiers (estimated at 5)				$\frac{+5^e}{124}$							
ca. Nov 1724	*Royal-Philippe*: Took Schmidig back to Europe (Lougnon 1956:273)			$\frac{-1}{65}$								
ca. Nov 1724	*Union*: Brought at least Ch. Penisseau (ANC D2A)				$\frac{+1}{125}$							
ca. Nov 1724	*Lys*: Took 6 Swiss soldiers back to Europe (Lougnon 1956:273)			$\frac{-6}{59}$								
( ), 1724	Also known to have been present before the end of this year: *P. Pluchon and his wife *C. Gigot who gave birth to Madeleine Pluchon, *Descoublans (sous-lieutenant) and *G. H. B. de Bellecourt (enseigne) (Bechet; Lougnon 1956:253)						$\frac{+1}{15}$	$\frac{+1}{10}$				
	Having married D. de Saint-Martin in May 1724 (see note c), it seems certain that Michelle Duhamel was living in Mauritius prior to the end of 1724											
Subtotal		2	9	59	125	31	15	10	10	5	46	19

(continued)

(Table 1 continued):

Date	Ship and Passengers (or other particulars)	Lazarists	Compagnie Employees	Soldiers Swiss	Soldiers (incl. Officers) French	Ouvriers, Domestiques, Others	Women	Children	Free Réunionnais Creoles	Slaves from Réunion	Slaves from Madagascar	Maroons
(brought forward)		2	9	59	125	31	15	10	10	5	46	19
Feb 12, 1725	Birth of M.-C. Seriber (Bechet)											
Mar 11, 1725	Earliest known marriage between Malagasy slaves attests presence of godparents *A. Rivont (sergent, and his wife *M.-J. Delporte, and that the Lazarist Le Coq had returned (MA KA 1)	$\frac{+1}{3}$										
ca. Apr 1725	*Atalante*: Brought at least the soldier A. Touzas and his wife M. Richart (ANC D2A)				$\frac{+1}{126}$		$\frac{+1}{16}$	$\frac{+1}{11}$				
Apr 21, 1725	(Name of vessel to be established): A platoon drawn from soldiers in both Mauritius and Reunion was sent to Pondichery. I have estimated that approximately 60 men (including officers) were involved, and thus that about 30 left Mauritius (Bonnefoy 1853-454; RT 7:180)[1]				$\frac{-30^e}{96}$							
( ), 1725	According to Lougnon (1956:273), only 36 Swiss remained on the island at this time. Thus, 23 must have died or otherwise departed by this year. Most of the 36 returned to Europe on the *Duc de Chartres* and/or *Apollon* (presumably with their wives and children, where applicable). In addition, Zilvaiguer, his wife, and stepchildren moved to Reunion. Only Ballard and Neizein are known to have remained in Mauritius (Lougnon 1956:273; Ricquebourg; Bechet)			$\frac{-23}{36}$ $\frac{-34}{2}$			$\frac{-4}{12}$	$\frac{-4}{7}$				
( ), 1725	*Mme Brousse (ex-Mlle Delvinquier) gave birth to a daughter (Bechet)							$\frac{+1}{8}$				
( ), 1725	*Argonaute*: G. Prigent, a Compagnie employee bound for India, decided to stay in Mauritius where he subsequently became "greffier et secrétaire du conseil" (Olagnier 1936:136)		$\frac{+1}{10}$									
TOTAL		3	10	2	96	31	12	8	10	5	46	19

[a] Chaudenson casts some doubt on the departure of these Réunionnais by citing Lagesse who in turn quotes from notes made by another researcher who had consulted the log of the *Atalante*: "Nous avons trouvé sur ladite Isle M Durongouet, major de Mascarin avec quinze habitants" (*Genèse*, p. 56, note 2). Chaudenson does not quote the continuation of this sentence which Lagesse (1972:14) gives as: ". . . qui estoient venus pour arborer pavillon français auparavant." In the log itself the wording—in which "M¹" begins a new sentence—is as follows: "M¹ Derongouët major de mascarin avec quinze habitants qui estoient venu pour arbore pavillon françois au paravent que les holan⁵ en prisent possession, il est venu abord et a mis l'isle a la disposition de M¹ le Chev. de Nyon" (ANM 4J1 75 (14)). There is thus no suggestion that the writer of this log found fifteen inhabitants when the *Atalante* reached the island—he is merely referring to an earlier event. Further, Lagesse (1972:15) quotes from a letter written by De Nyon to the Compagnie immediately after his arrival in Mauritius in which he mentions the presence of Durongouet Le Toullec and "cinq ou six habitants" (I have not yet succeeded in finding the original of this letter). There is thus no reason to doubt that the other ten Réunionnais had left on the *Courrier de Bourbon* as recorded in that ship's log.

[b] I have ignored passengers who were bound for India and Reunion, and who are known to have subsequently continued their journey. There remains a curious discrepancy concerning the number of Swiss arrivals. The logs of both ships survive, and the daily entries appear to record all deaths of passengers and crew. The deaths of 34 soldiers are recorded in the *Diane*'s log, and of these, 11 occurred

(*continued*)

(Table 1 continued):

during the lengthy stopover in Brazil. The *Atalante*'s log records the deaths of 29 soldiers during the voyage proper and notes that 5 others deserted during the Brazil stopover. However, in contrast with the *Diane*, daily entries were suspended during the stay in Brazil in the *Atalante*'s log. Instead, a single entry covers this two-month period, and unfortunately there is a blank before the word "soldats" where it was clearly intended to insert the number who had died. As the *Atalante* was the larger of the two vessels, one would not expect the number of soldiers from this ship who died in Brazil to have been less than the 11 from the *Diane*. The evidence of these logs leads me to estimate that about 80 soldiers either died or deserted before reaching Mauritius, and thus to expect that there would have been around 130 arrivals out of the original 210. However, the figure given by Lougnon (1956:20) for early April 1722 is 90. The discrepancy of about 40 remains to be explained.

[c] This is five less than the total given by Lagesse (1972:57-58). She adds M.-A. George (Mme Bienvenu), C. Gigot (Mme Puchon), M. Graberin (Mme Malleser), M. Ogé (Mme Tauler), and Michelle Duhamel (Mme de Saint-Martin). Ogé and Graberin both married on board the *Atalante*. (The register used survives. It subsequently became the first parish register of Port Louis.) However, while neither of these two women nor their respective husbands are mentioned in the log as having died during the voyage, I have found no confirmation of their presence in Mauritius. George and Gigot were both present by 1725 (see other entries in Table 1), and it is entirely possible that either or both arrived in April 1722. Duhamel married the Mauritius-based Compagnie employee Didier de Saint-Martin in May 1724 (in Reunion?) according to Lougnon (1956:314, note 22). Her sister Madeleine traveled on the *Atalante* as the wife of Sicre de Fontbrune, and I have assumed that both continued their journey to Reunion in May 1722. (Michelle and Madeleine were sisters of the second wife of Deforges-Bouchet, at one time the governor of Reunion. It thus seems likely that Michelle accompanied here sister on the *Atalante* and lived in Reunion prior to her marriage to Saint-Martin.)

[d] De Hauville wrote to De Nyon that the *Comte de Toulouse* had left a German who was said to have been the instigator of an attempted mutiny. De Hauville wanted him to be allowed to stay in Mauritius: "Comme il est excellent chasseur et bon trompette, je l'ay mis au service de la Compagnie pour l'employer à la chasse." De Nyon approved of this decision (letters of June 12, 1722, et seq.; ANC C4 vi). Among the list of papers destroyed by the cyclone of February 2, 1731, there is "No. 23: Une dénonciation faite par les Officiers du Vaisseau le *Compte le Toulouse* contre le nommé Willem trompette, de la revolte qu'il tramoit dans le dit Vaisseau" (*RHL* 1:483). Among the otherwise exclusively Réunionnais signatures on a letter written in Mauritius dated October 16, 1730—the Réunionnais were *chasseurs de marrons*—that of Wilhem Leichnig is found (ANC C2 v23 f111). According to Ricquebourg (1976:519), a man of this name, born in Cologne "vers 1697," married in Reunion in 1732. The Mauritian administrative district name of Plaines Wilhems is attested as early as March 1735 as "Plaine de Villème" (*RT* 2:213). Thus, there is a strong possibility that the man who arrived on the *Comte de Toulouse* was the same as the man who married in Reunion ten years later and, further, that Plaines Wilhems is named after him. If so, it is still not entirely clear whether he remained in Mauritius from 1722 until at least 1730 when he worked with the Réunionnais *chasseurs* because of his knowledge of the island and then decided to travel with them to Reunion where he settled, or whether he left Mauritius for Reunion sometime between 1722 and 1730 and was recruited in the latter to accompany the Creoles because of his previous experience in Mauritius. Chélin's claim (1973:7) that Le Toullec discovered Wilhem Leichnig living in the center of Mauritius in February 1722 (mentioned in *Towards*, p. 2, note 1) appears to be without foundation. No such event is reported in the log of the *Courrier de Bourbon* which appears to be the only surviving document covering this period.

[e] Adrien Jean François was born in Paris (*DBM*) and was not, therefore, a "Créole de Bourbon," as claimed by Lagesse (1972:21).

[f] According to Kaeppelin (1908:103), "En août et septembre arrivèrent de France la *Vierge de Grâce*, le *Saint-Albin* et le *Rubis*, armés pour les Indes, qui devaient déposer dans les deux îles des approvisionnements et vingt soldats." This suggests that these three vessels brought about ten soldiers to Mauritius. As the *Saint-Albin* is known to have brought five in November 1722, I have assumed that a similar number arrived on the *Vierge de Grâce* and/or the *Rubis*.

[g] De Nyon wrote: "Nous n'avons attrappé que cinq des noirs quy avoient enlevé la Pirogue." This suggests to me that the five were probably a minority of those involved, whence the estimate of 12.

[h] De Nyon wrote that he was sending Du Cotté (described as "une bouche inutile" but status not indicated) to Port Louis to be sent on to Reunion. De Hauville replied that he had put "votre jardinier" (not named) on the *Rubis* as soon as he reached Port Louis in order to save rations. He subsequently listed Du Cotté among those who had left for Reunion (see May 17, 1723 in Table 1). (If Du Cotté had formed part of De Nyon's domestic staff, it seems certain that he would have arrived with De Nyon in 1722. This has been ignored above and below.)

[i] Chaudenson does not give the dates of arrival of these two ships but places them immediately before the *Triton*. I have done likewise.

[j] Of the brothers Jean Denis and Joseph de Bouloc, one arrived on the *Triton* and the other on the *Vierge de Grâce*. Each came with his wife. It is uncertain which couple arrived on which ship, but even if they are given in the wrong order here, the numbers present are in no way affected.

[k] Lagesse (1972:60) suggests that Crampon—from Rouen (MA KA 1): 1) arrived with her husband F. Le Thonnelier (in 1722?); 2) left for Reunion with her husband February 5, 1723; and 3) returned to Mauritius as soon as her husband died. I have no reason to doubt (1) although the date of arrival remains to be established. However, a list of the documents lost in the cyclone of February 4, 1731 includes "8. Un rapport au sujet au de la mort de François Tonnelier fondeur trouvé mort dans les bois" (*RHL* 1:482). This strongly suggests that he died in Mauritius rather than in Reunion.

[l] A Compagnie document dated November 9, 1723 (written in France) indicates that platoons *to be sent* to the Mascarenes should consist of 64 men including officers. However, the 100 troops and 10 or 12 officers present at the 1725 census in Mauritius formed two platoons, presumably of 55 or 56 men each. The estimated figure of 60 is thus the average of 64 and 56. (See also Kuczynski 2:751, and *RHL* 1:516.)

after December 18, 1725: Duquesnain, Gast, Guyenet, D. Le Roux, De Nyon (left December 1725), Prigent, Saint-Martin, Simon de Monsy. The exceptions are Delesque (wounded in February 1723 [Lougnon 1956:233]) and Le Blanc (no mention after March 1723 when he was *garde-magasin*). The total number of Compagnie employees present in October 1725 thus seems likely to have been in the range of 8 to 10.

Table 1 notes the arrival of 10 officers (8 on the *Triton*, 2 on the *Neptune*). However, Lougnon (1956:227) mentions the presence of 4 companies of soldiers in Mauritius from 1723; and if each had a captain, a lieutenant, and a second-lieutenant, there would have been 12 officers. Thus, it may be assumed that the number of officers in October 1725 was in the range of 10 to 12. Taken with the preceding paragraph, it is clear that the census figure of "20 officiers et employés" can be readily reconciled with Table 1, and further, that this census category definitely excludes any Lazarists, Réunionnais Creoles, and former Swiss soldiers.

The 10 to 12 officers must be deducted from the figure of 96 French soldiers in order for a comparison to be made with the census figure of 100. Thus, there is a shortfall of 14 to 16. The likeliest explanation is that the *Triton* may have left more than half of its soldiers in Mauritius in 1723. In support of this it may be noted that of the ten officers on this vessel eight disembarked at Mauritius and only two at Reunion (ANM 4JJ 75(13)). It would thus appear that Table 1 under-estimates the number of French soldiers on the island from at least 1723.

The Table 1 figure of "31 ouvriers, domestiques, and others" includes 28 work-men—the same number as the census—the valets of De Nyon and De Hauville, and the German Leichnig. It is probable that De Hauville's valet left with him in 1723, in which case there would be four domestics to account for. De Nyon refers to "mes domestiques" in a letter of April 25, 1723 (ANC C4 vl), and the sending of his gardener to Reunion was noted in Table 1. It seems likely that at least some of the "missing" four domestics formed part of De Nyon's household.

The 12 European women whose presence is noted in October 1725 by Table 1 are: Mesdames Jean and Joseph de Bouloc, Brousse, Curé, Didion, Fantoux, Gast, Mandrou, Pluchon, Rivont, Saint-Martin, and Toucas.[2] The thirteenth could well have been the first wife of R. Coupet, a former soldier in Mascle's company who was one of the first to turn settler (he obtained concession no. 3), whose wife is known to have died by 1728 (Bechet; *RHL* 1:474). The Table 1 figures are thus easily reconciled with those of the 1725 census.

The census notes 13 European children, whereas only 8 are mentioned as being present in October 1725 in Table 1. The latter include the children of Brousse (1), Didion (2), Gast (2), and Pluchon (1). The children not mentioned in Table 1 may have reached the island with their parents, or more probably, their births in Mauritius were recorded in the lost (first) parish register of Port Bourbon (= Grand Port). Of the European women present in October 1725, there are three who arrived well before that date and who are known to have given birth in 1727 or later:

Mme de Saint-Martin—arrived ca. 1724 (see above), gave birth to five children between 1729 and 1736.

Mme Jean de Bouloc—arrived 1723 (see Table 1, note j), gave birth to five children between 1727 and 1734.

Mme Joseph de Bouloc—arrived 1724 (see Table 1, note j), gave birth to a son in 1731, but the deaths of two other children are recorded in the parish registers without any indication of their ages.

It would be surprising if none of these three women had been the mother of children living at the time of the 1725 census.

Table 1 suggests that there might have been 5 Reunion slaves and 46 Malagasies in October 1725 rather than the 34 of the census. Evidence will be given below to show that De Nyon intended that all Reunion slaves (other than the one maroon) should return to their owners on that island as soon as they were able to travel. Assuming that they did so, the difference between Table 1 and the census is 12. It is conceivable that all of these became maroons between the departure of De Hauville in June 1723 and the census. This would suggest 31 maroons, or a higher figure if it is assumed that some of the 34 slaves in captivity in 1725 had been born on the island. (There is, however, no evidence of the latter. It is also likely that some slaves had died since becoming maroons.) Such a figure accords reasonably well with an estimate made by Dioré when visiting Mauritius a year later that there were then "trante a quarante noirs qui se sont randus dans les bois" (ANC C3 v5). (There are no known arrivals of slaves in 1725 or 1726, and the number of Compagnie-owned slaves in captivity declined from 24 in 1725 to 20 in mid-1726, as will be seen below.)

It will be apparent from the foregoing that Table 1 and the census of 1725 can be reconciled fairly easily. The major differences are that the table underestimates the number of French soldiers (i.e., probably more arrived on the *Triton* than the table suggests) while the census omits certain categories of people: the 3 Lazarists, the last 4 Reunion Creoles, and perhaps the German Leichnig (see also Table 1, note d). If these and the other points noted above are taken into account, it would appear that Table 1 might provide a reasonably accurate basis for calculating the composition of the population at any point within the period 1721-25.

B2.2 The Réunionnais Presence in Mauritius to 1735

The historical evidence concerning the policies adopted by the Compagnie's employees, in France and in the Indian Ocean, with regard to the peopling of Mauritius is set out in B2.2.1. In B2.2.2, I discuss Chaudenson's interpretation of the evidence he consulted, placing the main emphasis on the numbers of Réunionnais present in the period 1721-35. I list my conclusions in B2.2.3.

B2.2.1 The Policies of the Compagnie and Its Employees

On the day that De Nyon, the first French governor of Mauritius, set sail from Lorient (May 31, 1721) he signed a document entitled *Ordres et Instructions pour le sieur de Nyon*. The third paragraph of this begins:

Q10 Pendant le voyage de la *Diane* à l'Ile de France, le dit sieur de Nyon s'informera du dit Sr de Beauvoilier [*sic;* = De Beauvolliers, governor of Reunion] *s'il a pris des mesures conformément aux ordres* qui lui ont été ci-devant donnés par la Cie des Indes, pour engager quelques habitans de l'île de Bourbon à passer à celle de France pour s'y établir.

(*RRM* 4:7; italics added)

On the same day the Compagnie also wrote to De Beauvolliers:

Q11 La Compagnie ne doute pas que vous ne déterminiez quelques-uns des habitants de l'Isle de Bourbon à passer à celle de France pour s'y établir, *nonobstant ce que vous luy marquez par votre lettre du 10 octobre 1720; à présent qu'ils verront qu'on pense sérieusement à l'établissement de cette dernière, on doit présumer qu'ils s'y détermineront plus volontiers.* Le Sieur Denyon est chargé de l'exécution de cet article de concert avec vous; vous ferez choix de 4 ou 6 *familles* pour les faire passer auxquelles il sera accordé des concessions proportionnées à leurs forces.... Il est, comme vous le voyez d'une extrême importance que quelques familles y passent pour instruire les nouveaux colons dans la culture des caffés et des autres productions et pour prendre les saisons convenables pour semer et planter, vu que la situation des deux isles est presque la même. (Lagesse 1972:17; italics added)

These quotations indicate that the Compagnie wanted a few families to move from Reunion and settle in Mauritius. Such people, familiar with the agricultural calendar of comparatively neighboring Reunion, would have been able to pass on their local expertise to newly arriving settlers from Europe. This was to remain the policy of the Compagnie in France until Lenoir's 1726 report was received (in 1727). However, as will be seen below, what the Compagnie's officials living in France decided should happen in the Mascarenes, and what the representatives of the Compagnie based on those islands decided would or would not happen there, did not always coincide. It is clear from the italicized sections of Q10 and Q11 that an earlier proposal for sending Réunionnais to settle in Mauritius had not been received with enthusiasm or acted upon, and that the Compagnie was not entirely certain that De Beauvolliers would implement their new orders. All the available evidence indicates that he failed to send Réunionnais families to settle in Mauritius though he did send a number of men from Reunion to *visit* the new colony and the latter would have been competent to advise on, e.g., the best times for planting particular crops. However, before De Beauvolliers could have received the Compagnie's letter of May 31, 1721,[3] the Reunion Council had itself made an important decision with regard to Mauritius on October 10, 1721:

Q12 L'île de France, ci-devant île Maurice, étant de la dernière conséquence pour la conservation de cette île Bourbon, et ne voyant pas venir le bâtiment de la Compagnie qu'on attend depuis longtemps pour habiter ladite île de France, dans la crainte que quelque nation étrangère ne nous prenne [Azéma]/prévienne [Kaeppelin] et ne s'en empare, selon les derniers avis que nous en avons, en sorte qu'il ne fût plus possible de ravoir jamais cette île, le Conseil, assemblé à ce sujet, envisageant le préjudice extrême qu'en souffriraient la Compagnie et l'île Bourbon, a jugé absolument nécessaire de faire incessamment construire, aux frais de la Compagnie, une barque de 24 à 25 tonneaux pour porter sur ladite île de France douze ou quinze habitants, un aumonier et un chirurgien aux appointements de la Compagnie, et de nommer M. Durongouët [Le Toullec], major de l'île Bourbon, pour gouverneur de celle de France, avec des appointements convenables, *en attendant que la Compagnie y envoie une colonie.* (Azéma 1859:44; Kaeppelin 1908:98-99; italics added)

Following this decision, 16 Réunionnais and the acting governor Le Toullec reached Mauritius on December 24, 1721 (ANM 4JJ 75 (5)). After more than two months there, the log of the *Courrier de Bourbon* noted at the beginning of March 1722:

Q13a Mr Durongouet voyan que set isle etait inabitable et quil ne pouvais cultivé aucune chose nous a redonné 10 de ses abitan pour ramener a Mascarin, et quil aloit restoit jusqua quil auroit reçu des nouvel de La Compagnie. (ANM 4JJ 75 (5))

Thus, while Q12 suggests that the purpose of the Réunionnais presence in Mauritius was merely to discourage the Dutch or any other country from taking possession until such time as troops and settlers arrived from France, Q13a seems to indicate that some time was also to be devoted to assessing the island's agricultural potential.

Following the departure of the ten Réunionnais on the *Courrier de Bourbon* on March 2, 1722 (see Table 1, note a), Le Toullec and the six remaining Creoles were joined five weeks later by the survivors of the *Diane* and the *Atalante*. These two ships had taken more than ten months on the journey from Lorient (including a lengthy stopover in Brazil), and during that time a substantial proportion of the Swiss troops and other passengers had died. The exact number of those who arrived is not known, but it cannot be less than the 122 indicated in Table 1 and is unlikely to be as many as the much-quoted figure of 160 which, as Kuczynski has shown, is based on a misunderstanding of the 1726 census figure.[4] Neither ship called at Reunion before reaching Mauritius, contrary to the *Ordres* (Q10) which De Nyon had signed before leaving Lorient, but the new governor traveled there with his returning predecessor Le Toullec at the beginning of May 1722 (De Rauville 1908: 30-31). On May 16, 1722, the Conseil de l'Ile de Bourbon decided:

Q13b Qu'il convient dengager au moins six habitans creoles de cette Isle, et de tirer des autres habitants trante esclaves noirs pour passer tous a lisle de France. (*RHL* 1:508)

This same resolution makes it clear that the Réunionnais owners of these slaves were to be paid for every day their slaves were absent from Mauritius. Thus, there

The Contested Aspects of the Peopling of Mauritius 153

was no question of these slaves remaining permanently in Mauritius; they were being hired out.

De Nyon returned to Grand Port (Mauritius) with these six free Creoles and about 30 slaves on June 12, 1722. He wrote to his deputy, Duval De Hauville, based in Port Louis on the opposite of the island, the following day:

Q14   Je vous depesche Monsieur les deux noirs quy vous remettront la presente ... [several illegible words] j'en ay amene avec moy une trentaine de meme aux frais et risques de la Comp^e.... J'ay ici six creols de lisle bourbon quy ne sont venus qua condition qu'ils resteroient en ce port. Et ce meme à condition qu'ils commanderoient les noirs. (ANC C4 vl)

The identity of two of the Réunionnais Creoles in Mauritius in July 1722 is established by the *Procès-Verbal de la Levée de Cadavre du Frère Adam* dated July 9, 1722, in which both François Nativel and Jean Fontaine are separately described as "créole de l'Ile Bourbon" (*RHL* 1:411-12).

De Nyon set off for Reunion again on July 12, 1722 where he was to spend four months "pour y ordonner et tracer les fortiffications necessaires pour la deffence" (ANM B3 v294). While he was there, the Reunion Council made a resolution on October 2, 1722 which can scarcely have been to his liking:

Q15   Le Conseil Provincial de l'isle Bourbon assemblé au quartier de St. Paul, considérant l'extreme conséquence de fortifier incessamment les ports de l'Isle de France pour la garantir contre les tentatives des Hollandais du Cap, que l'on est informé avoir menacé d'armer pour venir s'en emparer, que le retardement du vaisseau le *St. Aubin* [sic], destiné à la traite des noirs nécessaires aux travaux de ses fortifications n'étant point arrivés pourrait donner le tems à ces Hollandais d'exécuter ce projet, et qu'enfin les habitants et noirs de cette Isle qui ont été envoyés à celle de France, causaient une dépense trop considérable à la Compagnie pour ne pas chercher tous les moyens de la faire cesser *en rappelant au plus tot ces habitants et noirs* dont le retour est d'autant plus nécessaire que la culture des caféiers souffre de leur absence, – a decidé d'expédier au plus tot le vaisseau le *Ruby* pour l'envoyer à la traite des noirs à Matatana et au fort Dauphin pour les porter en droiture à l'Isle de France, et les y ayant mis *repasser les habitants et les noirs qui y sont à celle-ci. (RHL* 5:336; italics added)

De Nyon returned to Mauritius in November 1722 on the *Saint-Albin:*

Q16   Qui avait mis à la voile de Bourbon le 12 novembre et y était arrivé le 29 avec Denyon, Leblanc ... un maître canonnier, six des ouvriers et cinq des soldats pris à Lorient en février précédent, ainsi que trois habitants de Bourbon: Auber, René Clain et Pierre Caron. (Lougnon 1956:213)

This brought the total number of free Réunionnais in Mauritius to 15 (according to the information currently available). The identities of two more free Réunionnais are established by a letter from De Nyon to De Hauville dated December 18, 1722:

Q17 Julien Lepinay Creol quy est dans ce port... Estienne Robert... aussy Creol. (ANC C4 vl)

De Nyon wrote to De Hauville again on December 27, 1722:

Q18 Je renvoye a l'Isle Bourbon par la Barque le nommé Jean Fontaine [a free Creole—see *Procès-Verbal* following Q14]. M^r le gouverneur m'ayant prié avec instance de luy envoyer avec estienne Robert que vous avez pres de vous et que vous feres s'il vous plaist embarquer sur Lad. Barque pour cette d^{te} Isle. (ANC C4 vl)

A letter from De Hauville to De Nyon dated January 6, 1723 mentions that "Robert Creol" was one of those who had left for Reunion on a boat (not named) four days earlier (ANC C4 vl). He did not mention Jean Fontaine by name, but it seems likely that he left at the same time since his death in Reunion in March 1723 is noted in Ricquebourg (1976:298-99). If the earlier total of 15 is correct, the departure of Robert and Fontaine would have reduced the total of free Creoles on the island to 13.

In his correspondence with De Hauville—or at least in the apparently near-complete series of letters, copies of which exist in Paris—there is no mention of the Reunion Council's decision of October 2, 1722 (see Q15). This may or may not have something to do with the tense relationship between the two men.[5] However, on March, 13, 1723, De Nyon wrote to his deputy:

Q19 N'ayant point de quoy les nourrir, je seray obligé de renvoyer par le *St Albin* tous les noirs de l'isle Bourbon avec les bouches inutiles. (ANC C4 vl)

Two weeks later (April 1, 1723), De Nyon wrote:

Q20 Jenvoyeray la semaine prochaine tous les noirs que j'ay icy de l'Isle Bourbon pour y passer par le *St Albin* avec tous les votres et les Creols. (ANC C4 vl)

On April 7, 1723 he wrote to De Hauville that:

Q21 J'ay fait partir ce matin, Monsieur, les noirs d l'Isle Bourbon [NB: they were to travel on foot from Grand Port to Port Louis where the *Saint-Albin* was moored, a distance of about 50 km]... affin que vous les fassiez embarquer... sur le *St Albin*, avec tous ceux de lad^e isle, quy sont pres de vous pour retourner a leur premiers maittres. J'en rends les noirs, et les Creols chez eux, vous m'envoyerez s'il vous plait, quatre des noirs malgastes de ceux que vous avez... quand le navire aura mis a la voille. (ANC C4 vl)

The *Saint-Albin* left Mauritius for Reunion on April 13, 1723 (De Hauville to De Nyon, same date, ANC C4 vl). Lougnon says that 24 slaves and 5 "habitants de Mascarin" (these figures are confirmed by De Hauville to De Nyon, April 13, 1723) left on the *Saint-Albin* and names the latter five as "Antoine Huet, François Nativel, Julien Lépinay, Antoine Dalleau et Jacques Milloe [?]" (Lougnon 1956:230; the [?] is Lougnon's).

The Contested Aspects of the Peopling of Mauritius 155

Given that "une trentaine" of slaves had arrived from Reunion in June 1722 (Q14) and that De Nyon had indicated clearly that all of them were to be sent back there (Q20, Q21), it may seem odd that only 24 left. However, De Nyon could send on the 50-km trek from Grand Port (the principal settlement at the time and the place where he was based) to Port Louis (where De Hauville was based and where the *Saint-Albin* was moored) only:

Q22 Tous ceux quy estoient en estat de marcher. (De Hauville to De Nyon, April 13, 1723, ANC C4 vl)

It remained De Nyon's intention that all other slaves from Reunion should return there as soon as possible:

Q23 J'ay plusieurs bouches inutiles qui nous affament en ce port que je voulois faire passer a Mascarin avec trois ou quatre noirs malades quy n'ont pu suivre les autres. (De Nyon to De Hauville, April 20, 1723, ANC C4 vl)

Nine days later (April 29, 1723) he wrote to his deputy:

Q24 J'ay encore icy dix à onze tant hommes que femmes et enfants inutiles avec 4 noirs de Bourbon et six négresses dont je souhaitterois pour estre débarassé attendu quils nous mangent.
Faittes embarquer sur le *Ruby* le frere Le Coq ... vous y ferez aussy embarquer le nommé Ducotté, quy est une bouche inutile. (ANC C4 vl)

In mid-May De Hauville wrote to De Nyon confirming that the following had left on the *Rubis:*

Q25 Denoisy, Le Coq, Du Cotté, alaigre, et le canonnier de M^r De Beauvolliers. Le pauvre M Grenier [captain of the *Rubis,* very ill at this time] est aussy embarqué. (dated May 17, 1723, ANC C4 vl)

Only Jean Allaigre is definitely Réunionnais, but the "canonnier de M^r De Beauvolliers" could well be the same person as the "maître canonnier" whose arrival the previous November was noted in Q16.

In what appears to be his last letter to De Hauville before the latter left Mauritius, De Nyon mentioned that there were:

Q26 Cinq Creols a la poursuitte de sept malagastes ... J'ay commandé aussy pour le meme sujet le Sr Wirtz avec Sept soldats et Coste.[6] (letter dated May 28, 1723, ANC C4 vl)

De Beauvolliers wrote to the Compagnie about Mauritius in September 1723:

Q27 A l'egard de l'isle de France, il me paroit, Messieurs, que les difficultez ne doivent point vous rebuter de cette isle si nécessaire pour la conservation de l'isle Bourbon; vous pourrez seulement en diminuer la garnison et n'y tenir qu'une trentaine de soldats dans chacun des deux ports avec les officiers, jusqu'a cequ'on ayt trouvé le moyen de detruire les rats, aprez quoy cette isle pourra s'entretenir d'elle mesme... on pourra toujours compter aprez la destruction des rats sur vingt deux habitations au flac, sur 4 ou 5 a la maison blanche... sur deux ou trois autres habitations a la riviere noire, selon l'avis de Mr Durongouët et des premiers habitants de l'isle Bourbon *que j'y avois envoyez pour la bien visiter et en prendre de sûres connoissances*. Dans tout le reste du terrain, ils avoient reconnu qu'on ne pourroit trouver que quelques jardins, quelques champs, quelques petites pieces propres a y mettre du ris. (ANC C3 v4; italics added)

The above quotation suggests three things (taken in reverse order):

1. That Durongouet [Le Toullec] and the 16 Réunionnais had gone to Mauritius in December 1721 to visit the island (but not to *settle* there) and to report on the agricultural potential of the land, thus confirming the impression gained from Q12 and Q13a above. There is nothing to suggest that any of the original 16 were still in Mauritius at the time this letter was written.
2. That there were no plantations ("habitations") operating in Mauritius at this time.
3. That the numbers of rats were so great that the island could not be colonized until after they had been brought under control and that, in the meantime, the French presence in Mauritius might be reduced to 60 soldiers and a few officers guarding the two ports.

Having come to the view expressed above, one would not expect the governor of Reunion to have taken steps to persuade Réunionnais families to settle in Mauritius. There is no evidence to suggest that he did.

That an enormous number of rats should apparently present a serious obstacle to would-be colonizers of the island may seem a somewhat doubtful proposition. Jonchée de la Goleterie, writing in 1729 when he owned land in Mauritius (even though he was one of the Compagnie's captains), implies that claims that the island could not be settled because of rats (and monkeys) were part of the Réunionnais' attempts to prevent the settling of Mauritius (see Q39 below). However, a letter written by De Nyon to the Compagnie the same month as De Beauvolliers' letter seems to confirm the extent of the problem:

Q28 Il n'est pas permis *Monsieur* d'estre aussy traversé par les contretems que je l'ay esté depuis mon arrivée dans l'Isle par des mauvaises testes.... Cette guerre domestique et intestine n'est rien en comparaison de celle que les rats, dont l'isle est si prodigieusement remplie que la multitude est au dela de toute expression. (letter dated September 3, 1723, ANM B3 v294)

The *Triton* brought soldiers from France in September 1723, and the following month she set sail for Reunion. The log of the *Triton* notes:

The Contested Aspects of the Peopling of Mauritius 157

Q29 Il s'est embarquez [at Port Louis] quelques ouvriers pour mascarin. (entry for October 31, 1723, ANM 4JJ 75 (13))

There is nothing to indicate just who these artisans might have been. They might perhaps have included some of the Frenchmen or Réunionnais who had arrived on the *Saint-Albin* in November 1722 (see Q16 above).

I have not found any document for 1724 or 1725 that mentions the presence of Réunionnais in Mauritius at that time, but as will be seen below (Q31, Q32), it seems likely that there were at least four.

In about September 1725 a priest on his way to India (from France) spent a few days in Mauritius and subsequently wrote a fairly long letter describing the island. His comments include:

Q30 Si l'on fortifie l'Isle de France, si de nouveaux Habitans y mettent quelque jour les terres en valeur; sa situation, & la commodité de ces Ports la rendront très-importante au Commerce. Mais il faut commencer par y exterminer les Esclaves fugitifs & les rats. (letter dated October 17, 1725, written in India soon after his arrival there; reproduced in *Lettres édifiantes* . . .)

This again suggests that there were no plantations at this time. There is nothing elsewhere in this letter to suggest that the population consisted of anyone other than soldiers, Compagnie employees, Lazarists, and slaves—many of the latter maroons. This is largely confirmed by the census of October 1725 as well as by Table 1.

In May and June 1726, Lenoir, the newly appointed chief of the Compagnie's operations in the Indian Ocean, called at Mauritius while on his way to take up his post in Pondichery. During his visit a number of *règlements* were enacted including one, dated June 3, 1726, which mentions the presence of:

Q31 Quatre des Creoles de l'Isle de Bourbon restez de ceux qui etoient venus icy pour donner chasse aux noirs marrons. (ANC C4 vl)

After his arrival in India, Lenoir wrote to the Compagnie at length about both Mauritius and Reunion. Four passages in this document dated July 28, 1726 are highly relevant to the peopling of Mauritius:

Q32 Les Creols qui avoient été envoyez de l'Isle de Bourbon pour les [= les nègres marrons] chasser ce qui ont beaucoup coûté à la Compagnie par leur nourriture et les journées qui leurs ont été payée, se font plaint que M de Nyon les avoit forcés a travailler et a porter les materiaux pour les fortifications, au lieu de laisser chasser les Negres; c'est ce qui les a empêchez de les detruire. *Les quatres derniers Creols* qui étoient encore dans l'Isle lorsque j'y suis arrivé [May 25, 1726] et *qui ont été retenus de force pendant longtems* m'ont assuré la même chose. Ils m'ont demandé à repasser à l'Isle de Bourbon. Je leur ay donné passage. (ANC C4 vl; italics added)

It seems likely that these Creoles left for Reunion on the boat which took Lenoir there: the *Jason,* which set sail for Reunion on June 6, 1726 (ANC C4 vl). So far, I have not found anything which proves that they left on the *Jason.* There is at least no doubt that they had left before De Beauvolliers visited Mauritius in November 1727 since he wrote on a copy of Lenoir's report of July 28, 1726 in the margin opposite the above-quoted paragraph (Q32):

Q33   Ils ont repassé a lisle Bourbon sans avoir fait grand chose. (ANC C4 vl)

Thus far, with only three exceptions, it has been shown that every Réunionnais whose name is known and who visited Mauritius in the two years following December 24, 1721 subsequently returned to Reunion. The three exceptions are those who arrived on the *Saint-Albin* in November 1722: Auber, René Clain, and Pierre Caron. The following information is derived from Ricquebourg.

René Clain was born at St. Paul (Reunion) in 1697 and married there in 1721. His wife gave birth to a child in Reunion in May 1723 (while her husband was apparently in Mauritius), but this child was not baptized until February 1725, whereas all Clain's other children were baptized soon after birth. The delay in baptizing this child might well be related to the father's absence. René Clain died at St. André (Reunion) in 1773 (Ricquebourg 1976:143-45).

Pierre Caron was born in Reunion in 1693 and married at St. Paul in 1717. His wife gave birth to a child in February 1720, but Ricquebourg (1976:121) notes no other births until November 1727 (after which time there were several). Caron might thus have been one of the "quatre derniers Creols" who spent longer than intended in Mauritius and who was repatriated by Lenoir.

It is fairly clear from Lougnon (1956:212) that Auber (not "Aubin" as Chaudenson states in *Genèse,* p. 44, while citing the same source) is referred to by surname only, because he is the same Jacques Auber whom this author mentions two pages earlier (Lougnon 1956:210). Jacques Auber was born in Reunion in 1694 and died there in 1782 (Ricquebourg 1976:7).

There is, in any case, nothing whatsoever to suggest that there were any free Réunionnais in Mauritius once the "quatre derniers Creols" had left.

Three more important passages from Lenoir's letter of July 28, 1726 remain to be quoted:

Q34   Les ouvriers et soldats se plaignent, ils demandent a repasser en France, aussitôt que leur engagement sera expiré. Il est difficile de les retenir de force. Ils deviennent alors mauvais ouvriers et mauvais soldats, leur laissant la *liberté* Il en restera volontiers la meilleur partie, surtout lorsque vos magasins seront pourvûs de boissons et qu'ils pourront avoir en payant les choses necessaires a leur entretien. Si vous pouviez y faire passez quelques filles ou femmes, les ouvriers et soldats resteroient, S'établiroient, l'Isle se peuplerois insensiblement; les soldats étoient nuds pieds, sans chapeaux, sont mal habillez et sans linge, c'est ce qui les degoûte, on leur aura distribué les chapeaux et les souliers que vous avez envoyez lorsque vous avez soin d'envoyer regulierement ce que vous leur devez

The Contested Aspects of the Peopling of Mauritius   159

fournir pour l'entretien et que cela leur sera exactement distribué, ils s'accoutumeront au pays et deviendront habitants. (ANC C4 vl)

Q35   Pour tirer de l'utilité de l'Isle il faut la peuple de monde. *Ne comptez pas qu'aucun des habitans de l'Isle de Bourbon y passent pour s'y établir.* Ils ont de la peine a se determiner a passer d'un quartier de leur isle a l'autre pour veiller a leurs habitations, joint a ce que *l'Isle de France est en mauvaise reputation chez eux par le moyen des Creols qui ont été envoyez et gardez de force beaucoup plus longtemps qu'ils n'auroient souhaité.* D'envoyer des familles de France, cela vous couteroit considerablement. Il en periroit une grande partie dans le voyage, l'autre mouroit de misere avant que d'être accoutumée a vivre a la maniere du païn et a cultiver. Je croy que le meilleur party seroit d'engager tous les ans des ouvriers, massons, faiseurs de briques et de chaux, quelques charpentiers et forgerons, qui fussent marié et, autant qu'il seroit possible, leur permettre d'embarquer leurs femmes, et les engager d'emmener avec eux de leurs parents, femmes ou filles et leur donner une ration pour vivre et des appointemens aux ouvriers. Il s'y accoutumeroient pendant les deux ou trois premieres années, personne ne penseroit a retourner en france, la colonie se peupleroit, les terres se defricheroient; elles produiroient comme celles de l'Isle Bourbon tous ce qu'on y semeroit. (ANC C4 vl; italics added)

Q36   J'ay remarqué, Messieurs, par les lettres que vous ecrivez a l'Isle de France que vous dites qu'il faut exciter les habitans a cultiver la terre pour avoir des vivres par eux memes .... Cela seroit juste, *s'il y avoit effectivement des habitans. Faites, s'il vous plait, reflexion qu'il n y a personne que vos employés ouvriers et soldats compris dans l'etat, que vous avez. On ne doit regarder aucun de ces gens la, tant qu'ils restent a votre service, comme habitans.* (ANC C4 v1; italics added)

In Q36, Lenoir makes it absolutely clear that there were simply no settlers in Mauritius at the time. In Q35, he suggests that the Compagnie could not rely on people moving from Reunion to settle Mauritius, not least because the free Réunionnais visitors had been forced to stay longer than they wanted, against their wishes. In Q34 and Q35, he suggests two different ways of peopling the island:

1. By improving the conditions of the soldiers, in particular by sending them women, and encouraging them to become settlers.
2. By recruiting married artisans each year in France and by allowing them to bring their relatives with them.

Both of these proposals were subsequently adopted. In a letter to Pondichery dated September 25, 1727, the Compagnie indicated that it had accepted Lenoir's recommendations:

Q37   Le compte que lui en a rendu M. Lenoir et la situation où il les a trouvées lorsqu'il est allé en dernier lieu aux Indes, et dont sans doute il vous aura informés, ont déterminé la Compagnie à faire les dépenses nécessaires pour mettre l'Ile de France en valeur. Pour cet effet elle y fait passer cette année des ouvriers de toutes les professions qu'elle a cru utiles; elle y envoie plusieurs familles qui ont demandé à s'y établir, elle y joint douze jeune filles qu'elle donnera ordre de marier à des soldats et des ouvriers, et pour mettre tous ces gens en état de travailler, elle donne ordre qu'on leur avance des esclaves, des outils pour la terre, des semences et graines et des vivres pendant un an ou deux, qu'ils s'obligeront de restituer en nature et du crû de leurs terres. (*CSP* 1:187-88)

The first consequence of this new policy was the arrival of the *Bourbon* in July 1728, which brought twelve young women who were to marry soldiers (as per Q34), as well as other settlers and soldiers.[7] At least six more ships brought settlers from France during the next two years, and three of these included young female passengers who were to marry soldiers. Thus the basic proposals of Lenoir were implemented. However, the prospect of remaining permanently in Mauritius seems to have held little appeal for some of the troops, at least initially, for a soldier found guilty of a serious offense in 1728 was actually sentenced to become a settler. The Compagnie was naturally displeased:

Q38 La Compagnie a reçeu la copie du jugement que le s^r de Brousse, en conseil de guerre, a prononcé contre le nommé Languedoc, soldat. Ce jugement est des plus irréguliers, car le Conseil s'arroge le droit qu'il n'a pas de faire grâce à un homme qu'il devoit condamner, et il luy impose la peine d'estre habitant, ce qui doit estre regardé comme une grace pour un honneste homme. (the Compagnie to Mauritius, September 24, 1729; *CBI* 1:93)

In November 1728, the *Mars* called at Mauritius and her captain subsequently prepared a proposal entitled *Projet donné à la Compagnie des Indes . . . pour L'Etablissement de l'Isle de France* which was handed to the Compagnie's officials on his arrival in Lorient the following year. Two passages in this document emphasized the need to find people from Europe and not from Reunion to settle the island:

Q39 Le bien de l'isle de France veut dont qu'elle soit independante de l'isle Bourbon, en voicy des raisons essentielles. Je commence par dire que la tranquilité n'y regnera jamais entre les officiers de plume et de guerre tandis que cette isle y sera subordonnée et que la desordre y sejournera.
 La longueur du tems qu'il faut pour avoir reponse des affaires criminelles fait que le crime reste impuny. Ce qui est trés contraire a la bonne police, et aux interêts de la Compagnie; Les autres inconvenients c'est l'idée generalle des Creolles de Bourbon qui craignent que cette isle ne leur porte prejudice a cause de ces ports et des caffés qui y viennent.
 L'extrême besoin qu'ils ont de noirs pour recueillir le caffé fairoit qu'ils n'en envoyeroient que peu a l'Isle de France. *Tout le monde sait que les Bourbonnais ont fait ce qu'ils ont peu pour empêcher cet établissement; si l'Isle n'a pas été abandonnée, il n'y a pas eu de leur faute* ayant toujours dit que le terrain n'etoit pas habitable raport aux Singes et aux rats . . . .
 La compagnie doit voir clairement de quelle utilité luy sera cette isle. Il est dont necessaire de n'épargner rien pour son etablissement, et d'y faire passer deux cens familles: qu'il y en ait cent de Laboureurs, vingt de massons [a long list follows]. *Une attention que l'on doit avoir c'est de ne pas permettre au Creoles de l'isle Bourbon d'y*

passer pour habitant, tant a cause de la lepre que sont gens parresseux et de mauvais exemple pour cette Colonie, il y a toutes sortes de raison pour ne leur permettre pas d'y habiter. (ANC C4 vl; italics added)

In spite of this and earlier remarks of Lenoir (Q33, Q36), a group of 35 Réunionnais Creoles *(chasseurs de marrons)* arrived in August 1730 and remained on the island for at least eight months. Other Reunion-born people known to have visited or settled in Mauritius before the end of 1735 comprise only a carpenter (perhaps one of the "quatre derniers Creols"—see below) and two sisters. Chaudenson mentions the carpenter and also a group of artisans who may have included some born in Reunion. All of these certain or possible visitors and immigrants will be discussed below.

B2.2.2 Chaudenson's Interpretation of the Numbers of Réunionnais and Their Roles

In section 2.2 of *Genèse,* Chaudenson is concerned both with the numbers of Réunionnais Creoles in Mauritius and their roles. In his first paragraph he writes:

Q40   Ph. Baker déclare: "I therefore assume that all the *habitants* and slaves from Reunion returned there at the end of 1722" [*Towards*], p. 12. Cette affirmation est aussi fausse qu'infondée. On peut constater que les Bourbonnais qui regagnèrent leur île natale ne le firent qu'en avril 1723 et que seulement vingt-neuf repartirent sur les quarante six dont la présence dans l'île était prouvée. (*Genèse,* p. 48)

The above passage calls for several remarks. First, my 1976 sentence is quoted without the slightest reference to the evidence which led to this assumption, namely, the resolution of the Reunion Council taken on October 2, 1722 to recall *all* slaves and free Creoles then in Mauritius just as soon as the *Rubis* could take a group of slaves from Madagascar to replace those from Reunion (see Q15 above). The *Rubis* did indeed arrive with Malagasy slaves just two months later. My assumption was thus entirely consistent with the evidence then available to me. Chaudenson has since shown that the majority (29) of those from Reunion did not leave until four months later, but I have shown above that at least two free Creoles had already left at the beginning of January 1723.

Second, Chaudenson's use of the phrase "leur île natale" implies that all who traveled from Reunion were also born there. There is every reason to suppose that all the free citizens—with the exception of the Compagnie employee Durongouet Le Toullec—were born there. However, I am not aware of any evidence suggesting that all or any of the Reunion-based slaves had been born on that island. The Reunion Council's resolution of May 16, 1722, part of which was quoted as Q13b, does not specify that the slaves to go to Mauritius were to be locally-born, and in that text, the word *Creole* is applied only to free citizens. Both De Nyon and De Hauville similarly apply the word *Creole* only to free Réunionnais, the Reunion slaves being invariably termed *noirs* (cf. Q14). It is clear both from the De Nyon and De Hauville correspondence and from Q15 that all these Reunion slaves were of working age. If, as Chaudenson claims, these slaves had been born in Reunion, then all those aged 18 or older in 1722—presumably the majority—would have been counted in the census of 1704, at which time there were 102 locally-born slaves out of a total slave population of 311 (*Lexique*, p. 456). Allowing that some of these would have already died, 30 would have formed a rather large proportion of locally-born slaves of working age in Reunion in 1722. Of approximately 1,100 slaves in Reunion in 1722 (*Lexique*, p. 458), there does not seem to be any a priori reason why only those born locally should have been selected to go to Mauritius. If the choice had been left to the slave owners—as it may well have been—one would expect them to have chosen those slaves they could most easily spare, i.e., their least useful slaves. Had the Reunion Council wanted to send only locally-born slaves, they would surely have stated this in their resolution. If Chaudenson has evidence that the slaves sent to Mauritius from Reunion had been born in Reunion, he should cite it; from the point of view of his own "Bourbonnais" theory, it is a matter of some importance to establish whether these slaves were likely to have been first- or second-language speakers of early RC. If Chaudenson does not have such evidence, he is not entitled to make such an assumption.

Third, Chaudenson's final sentence in Q40 leaves the impression that those who did not leave on the *Saint-Albin* remained in Mauritius permanently. (Indeed, there is an assumption running all the way through Chaudenson's article that all those from Reunion were settlers rather than visitors, apart from those who left in April 1723.) In fact, at least three of the people included in Chaudenson's "quarante six dont la présence dans l'île était prouvée" had already left long before April 1723—the non-Creole Le Toullec and the free Creoles Robert and Fontaine; while a fourth, a slave, had run off with the Malagasy maroons (for details, see Table 1). Lenoir indicates clearly that the last four free Creoles left in 1726 (Q32), while it was De Nyon's expressed intention to return to their owners the only four Reunion-based slaves whose presence he mentions after the departure of the *Saint-Albin* (Q23, Q24). Thus, there is nothing to indicate that any of the approximately 45 people from Reunion who were on Mauritius in November 1722 remained there permanently.

Chaudenson's next paragraph is as follows:

Q41 En décembre 1722, après l'arrivée du *Rubis,* il y avait à l'île de France:
—65 Malgaches (esclaves débarqués le 8 décembre 1722 dont une vingtaine s'enfuit immédiatement);
—46 Créoles de Bourbon (au moins) dont 30 esclaves;
—67 (?) soldats suisses (en mai, mais il y en avait 35 de malades);
—un nombre indéterminé d'officiers, d'employés et d'ouvriers (sans doute une trentaine).
(*Genèse*, p. 48)

These figures, which form the basis of Chaudenson's estimates of the Réunionnais proportion of the total population up to 1730, suggest a total of about 208 people (including maroons as well as anyone who might have died since May 1722). The most cursory comparison with Table 1 will reveal that he has overlooked four categories of people: Lazarists, French soldiers, European women and children. In order to assess the likely percentage of the total population which speakers of "Bourbonnais" formed, it is necessary to calculate the number of Swiss troops that might have been living in Mauritius from December 1722 on. All that is known is that there were 36 Swiss on the island in 1725 and that 7 others had left in November 1724. The maximum that might have died or otherwise departed between June 12, 1722 and 1725 is thus 24 (67 − 7 = 60 − 36 = 24). One way of estimating the numbers present from June 1722 would be to assume that they departed (by leaving or dying) at equal intervals from that date. Unfortunately, Lougnon does not tell us when in 1725 the majority of the remaining Swiss left. In the absence of precise information I will assume, for the purposes of this calculation only, that they left in the middle of 1725 and that the 24 "missing" Swiss were thus lost at intervals of 46 days. I apply this assumption to the figures in Table 2 (p. 164). All other figures are derived directly from Table 1. It should be borne in mind that the figures for Europeans take as their starting point the *minimum* possible number of arrivals on the *Atalante* and *Diane* (see, for example, note c to Table 1 or De Nyon's reference to "mes domestiques," p. 149) and that there were almost certainly more than the 114 suggested in Table 1 as having reached Mauritius in April 1722.

In Table 2, "Francophone" is applied to those whose first or second language is likely to have been (a variety of) French, and "Bourbonnophone" to first- or second-language speakers of "Bourbonnais." (I have assumed that the free Creoles would have belonged to both these categories.) It can be seen that the proportion of "Bourbonnophones" declined from 21 percent to 9 percent of the population between December 1722 and April 1723 as opposed to the "25 ou 30 percent" claimed by Chaudenson (*Genèse*, p. 48). Chaudenson continues:

Q42 Et même après avril 1722 [sic], il resta encore 17 Créoles de Bourbon (dont 6 esclaves) soit environ 10% de l'ensemble des habitants. Il ne fait pas de doute que ces esclaves durent servir à encadrer la population servile encore réduite en 1725 (34 esclaves à cette date).
Ce rôle d'encadrement dévolu aux Créoles de Bourbon n'est pas l'effet du hasard mais la volonté délibérée et souvent exprimé de la Compagnie des Indes. (*Genèse*, p. 48)

Again, there are several points raised here which require comment. First, "avril 1722" is clearly an error for "avril 1723" (cf. *Genèse*, p. 44). Second, his figure of "17 Créoles" corresponds to the 11 free Creoles, 5 Reunion slaves in captivity, and 1 Reunion maroon in Table 1. These are the Réunionnais whose arrival is established but whose departure by the end of April 1723 is not. The highest figures actually mentioned after the departure of the *Saint-Albin* are: 5 free Creoles

Table 2
Population of Mauritius, December 1722 to April 1723

Category	December 8, 1722		January 2, 1723		April 13, 1723	
Free population:						
Lazarists	3		3		3	
Compagnie employees	11		12		11	
Soldiers (incl. officers)						
— Swiss	64		63		61	
— French	11	56% Francophones	16	57% Francophones	16	64% Francophones
Ouvriers, etc.	9		6		6	
Women	6		4		4	
Children	4					
Reunion Creoles	15		13		11	
Slave population:						
From Reunion						
— captive	30	21% "Bourbonnophones"	30	19% "Bourbonnophones"	5	9% "Bourbonnophones"
— maroon	0		0		1	
From Madagascar						
— captive	65	30% Malagasy-speaking	51	29% Malagasy-speaking	46	33% Malagasy-speaking
— maroon	0		14		18	
Totals	218		221		192	

in Grand Port (Q26); 1 free Creole in Port Louis who left in May 1723—see Table 1; 4 Reunion slaves too ill to cross the island (Q23, Q24); and the "petit coquin" who had joined the maroons—a total of 11. "Bourbonnophones" would thus appear to have accounted for no more than between 6 percent (11) and 9 percent (17) of the total population at the end of April 1723. Third, the suggestion that the remaining Reunion slaves were used to *encadrer* the Malagasy slaves is without foundation. These Reunion slaves were left behind because they were too ill to travel, and it was De Nyon's intention to get rid of them as soon as possible because of the lack of food supplies (Q22, Q23, Q24). Finally, in the last sentence of Q42, Chaudenson apparently seeks to link his assumption that the Reunion slaves were to *encadrer* the Malagasies with the Compagnie's first policy on peopling Mauritius. This approach is somewhat devious since Chaudenson is using the term "Créole" to cover Reunion slaves who may or may not have been born there as well as free citizens of Reunion, whereas the Compagnie officials in France simply do not employ the term "Créole" at this time and refer only to the sending of free Réunionnais to Mauritius. In any case, it is essential to distinguish between policies recommended by the Compagnie in France and policies actually implemented by its officials *in situ*. It was the policy of the Compagnie in France for about six years that a few Réunionnais *families*—not unmarried men—should be sent to Mauritius to form the nucleus of a settlement there, as described earlier. This policy was expressed at various times from 1721 (Q11) until January 29, 1727:

Q43 L'Administration de Bourbon est autorisé à inviter quelques familles de cette Colonie à passer à l'Ile de France; elle usera, a cet effet, de toutes les voies de persuasion et de tous les ménagements convenables. (Bonnefoy 1853:5)

This was written shortly before the Compagnie had received the recommendations of Lenoir (Q32, Q34, Q35, Q36) *written* on July 28, 1726—recommendations which the Compagnie accepted and which caused it to abandon its earlier policy (Q11, Q43, etc.). (At this time, it took about five months for letters to travel between the Mascarenes and France, and probably about six months between India and France.) Thus, while it was the policy of the Compagnie in France that Mauritius should be peopled with at least some Réunionnais families, there is nothing to indicate that even one such family did so. Further, there is quite a lot of evidence that this policy was resisted in Reunion from the start (Q11, Q27, Q32); that it had not been implemented by mid-1726 and was not then expected to be implemented in the near future (Q35); and that it may well not have been a popular policy with French settlers in Mauritius (Q39).

After quoting the letter of May 31, 1721 from the Compagnie in France to Beauvolliers in Reunion (reproduced in part as Q11), Chaudenson writes:

Q44 Denyon se conforme point par point d'ailleurs à ces instructions et ramène de Bourbon six Créoles et trente exclaves, ces derniers constituant non seulement une masse de main-d'oeuvre mais surtout *l'encadrement futur* des esclaves malgaches qui arriveront quelques mois plus tard.

C'est donc un élément *permanent* de la politique de la Compagnie que de pousser des Créoles de Bourbon à s'installer à l'île de France; La Bourdonnais ne cache pas que ceux que l'on fait venir pour "chasser les marrons" seront fortement incitées à s'installer définitivement dans l'île comme "habitants" (Délibération du Conseil du 6 septembre 1736 in Mémoire de La Bourdonnais, p. 121). (*Genèse*, p. 49; italics added)

The six male Réunionnais Creoles that De Nyon brought to Mauritius were not the "4 ou 6 familles" (cf. Q11) that the Compagnie had wanted to form the nucleus of the settlement. Mention is made of the slaves' future *encadrement* of the Malagasies as if this formed part of a well-planned strategy. In fact, Q15 shows clearly that the Council's intention was that the Malagasies should provide an *alternative* "masse de main-d'oeuvre" so that *all* the free Creoles and slaves from Reunion could return there without delay. It is thus false to suggest that "en 1721 [*sic;* error for 1722], on envoie de Bourbon à l'île de France un contingent de 30 esclaves créoles chargé d'encadrer et de former les 65 Malgaches qui constituent le premier lot d'esclaves amenés dans l'île; ils accompliront en quatre mois cette tâche" (*Créoles*, p. 54). The De Nyon and De Hauville correspondence provides some evidence of free Creoles (not Reunion slaves) being used as NCOs over the Malagasies (cf. Q14). Q19 shows that lack of food—not the accomplishment of the task of rendering the Malagasies docile, as Chaudenson would have the reader believe—was the immediate reason for sending the Réunionnais away at that particular time. (Lack of food is a recurrent topic of this correspondence.)

Chaudenson claims in Q44 that it was a *permanent* feature of Compagnie policy to persuade Réunionnais to settle in Mauritius. As already noted, this is what the Compagnie in France would have liked to have happened in the period 1721-27, but there is nothing to suggest that such a policy was ever implemented by the Compagnie's officials in Reunion. The use of the word "permanent" is curious here since thus far in Chaudenson's section 2.2 no date later than 1725 has been mentioned and no evidence has been produced to suggest that the policy was of long duration. One can only assume that the author's intention is that the earlier dates should be linked in the reader's mind with the date of the 1736 *Délibération* mentioned at the end of the paragraph. He does not quote the actual text, which reads as follows:

Q45 Sur ce qui a esté représenté que, par l'augmentation considérable des familles dans cette isle [de Bourbon], plusieurs habitants se trouvoient dès à présent dans le cas de n'avoir à partager à ceux de leurs enfans qu'ils estoient sur le point d'établir, que très peu ou point de terre, et qu'*il seroit extrêmement avantageux à cette colonie de commencer de bonne heure à faire naistre aux jeunes créols l'idée de s'établir à l'isle de France, pour les tirer de la molle oisiveté dans laquelle plusieurs d'eux vivent*, en leur faisant envisager un avenir heureux dans la jouissance des concessions que le Conseil supérieur dud. lieu est en estat de leur donner avec les avances convenables tant en noirs qu'en effets des magasins pour travailler utillement à leur fortune; mais que, comme il ne seroit pas facile de les porter de gré à gré à cette transmigration, tant par les oppositions de leurs pères et mères fondées sur une tendresse mal entendue, que parce que ces jeunes gens dant la pluspart ne sont jamais sortis de cette isle, ont un préjugé mal fondé sur celle de France qu'il seroit à propos de détruire, il conviendroit de les accoutumer à y faire de temps en temps quelques voyages dans l'espérance que *voyant par eux mesmes avec combien de succez plusieurs Européens y travaillent à leur établissement,* et quelques uns d'eux venant à y demander de leur propre mouvement des concessions, les autres compatriottes pussent à leur exemple prendre le même party sans y paroistre aucunement forcez, il esté délibéré de commander un détachement de douze jeunes créols pour passer à l'isle de France sur l'*Atalante,* sous prétexte de les y faire rester trois à quatre mois pour y travailler utilement à la destruction des noirs marons, pour estre led. détachement, au bout dud. temps. relevé par un autre de même nombre, et ainsy continuer jusqu'à ce que plusieurs d'eux se soient déterminez à y faire leur établissement, ou que par leur reffus constant, l'inutilité de cette tentative soit bien avérée, lesd. créols à la ration ordinaire et à quinze livres par mois. Fait et délibéré à St Paul, en la chambre du Conseil, le 6 septembre mil sept cent trente six. Mahé de la Bourdonnay, Lemery-Dumont, Villarmoy, Dusart de la Salle, J. Brenier, d'Héguerty, L. Morel. Par le Conseil, G. Dejean. (Lougnon and Toussaint 1937:120-21; italics added)

The first italicized section indicates that these Creoles were to go to Mauritius for their own good and for the good of Reunion rather than because their presence was needed in Mauritius (a point which Lougnon and Toussaint themselves emphasize on p. 120). The second italicized section begs the obvious question: if there had already been Reunion people happily settled in Mauritius, successfully running their own plantations, would not the intention have been that the young Creoles should be inspired to do likewise by the obvious success of these Réunionnais rather than by observing the successful Europeans? This passage adds strong supporting evidence to that provided both above and below that there were few, if any, Réunionnais settlers in Mauritius at this time. Finally, it should be noted that this was a purely local decision and had nothing whatever to do with the Compagnie's officials in France. Chaudenson continues:

Q46 Comment peut-on d'ailleurs affirmer, comme le fait Ph. Baker: "I have not found any evidence to suggest that any other settlers or slaves [from Reunion] came to Mauritius until some time after 1735" (p. 14), alors que l'arrivée de trente-six Créoles de Bourbon en 1729 est un fait parfaitement connu et d'une importance considérable puisque la population européene totale de l'île ne comprend guère alors plus de deux cents personnes! (*Genèse,* p. 49)

The fact is less than perfectly known, for it was on August 14, *1730* that the *Méduse* brought *35* Réunionnais who were to hunt down maroons.[8,9] This was not an event of great linguistic significance because, by Chaudenson's own figures in *Genèse,* there could not have been less than 450 Europeans in Mauritius by August, 1730, and because it would be difficult to conceive of an occupation less likely to influence the speech habits of the rest of the population than that of searching for maroons in the less populated parts of the island.

Chaudenson omits the words "from Reunion" from the sentence he quotes from *Towards* in Q46 in which "other," in its context, clearly meant "other than those present in 1722." With this clarified, the sentence remains substantially valid, for there is nothing to show that any of these Creoles settled in Mauritius, and a great deal to suggest that they did not. Thirteen of these Réunionnais and the German Leichnig signed a statement dated October 16, 1730 in which it was noted that they had been "a la poursuitte des noirs marons pendant plus que quarante jours en deux differentes reprises" (ANC C2 v23 f111). *All* the signatories to this statement subsequently died in Reunion, and either 11 or 12 of them married there in the period 1731-39, as follows (all page numbers refer to Ricquebourg):

Pierre Mollet: born April 23, 1708, married in St.-Pierre July 7, 1733. (p. 596)
Jean-Baptiste Grondin: born March 29, 1711, married in Reunion July 29, 1732. (p. 350)
François Boyer: born March 18, 1707, married in Ste.-Suzanne September 29, 1733. (p. 85)
Thomas Elgar: born October 31, 1711, married in St.-Paul November 22, 1735. (p. 264)
Estienne Boyer: born May 26, 1709, married in Ste.-Suzanne November 13, 1731. (p. 72)
Jean-Baptiste Belon: born October 3, 1697, married in St.-Paul February 17, 1733. (pp. 42-43)
Jacques Pitou: born September 5, 1711, married in Ste.-Suzanne July 10, 1736. (p. 703)
Wilhem Leichnig: born in Cologne "vers 1697," married in St.-Paul January 30, 1732. (p. 519)
Joseph Grondin: born June 10, 1707, died in Ste.-Suzanne in 1778. (p. 350)
Pierre Folio: born September 12, 1711, date of first marriage unknown, remarried in St.-Pierre January 17, 1749.
[Pierre] De Guigné La Berangerie: born April 18, 1706, married in St.-Paul in 1723, died in St.-Denis in 1742; he fathered 8 children between 1724 and 1740, but none were born in the four years 1731-34 inclusive. (p. 380)
Jacques Fontaine: There were two people so named. One was born April 17, 1704, married in St.-Paul in 1725, died in St.-Denis in 1784 (p. 299); the other was born March 23, 1708, married in St.-Louis November 14, 1735, and died there in 1751. (p. 287)
[Louis] Joseph Gonneau: born August 25, 1709, married in St.-Paul November 9, 1734, and died there in 1772. (p. 332)
Georges Noel: born August 11, 1711, married in St.-Paul May 15, 1739, but acknowledged the father of a child born to an unnamed woman in Reunion October 21, 1736. (p. 635)

There is nothing whatsoever to indicate that any of the 35 *chasseurs* came to Mauritius with the intention of settling there, nor that any did in fact do so. Having arrived as a group, one would expect them to have left as a group. If so, their departure would have had to take place before any of the above were married in Reunion, i.e., before November 13, 1731. Details of their departure remain to be established. A letter from De Merville de Saint Remy (in Mauritius) to the Compagnie dated March 17, 1731 makes reference to the presence of "Les Creols de l'Isle Bourbon, au nombre de 35" (ANC C4 vl), but I have not found any later mention of these men in the Compagnie correspondence.

Most of the evidence cited by Chaudenson (*Genèse*, pp. 49-51) in support of his claim that Mauritius was peopled from Reunion concerns those who traveled from the latter to the former *after* 1735. Since Chaudenson, like myself, regards the period 1721-35 as "décisive pour l'étude des conditions de genèse du créole mauricien" (*Genèse*, p. 48), information relating to people who traveled from Reunion to Mauritius in the period 1736-68 seems largely irrelevant. In passing, it may be noted that the numbers he mentions are small, that making the journey from Reunion to Mauritius does not in itself prove that those concerned were fluent speakers of RC or that they traveled there to become settlers, and that none of those mentioned appear to have taken up economically or linguistically influential posts in Mauritius. Further, the arrival of small numbers of potential speakers of RC over a period of more than 30 years can scarcely be expected to have had much impact on the linguistic situation in Mauritius given that its total population increased overwhelmingly in that period as a result of immigration from Africa, Asia, and Europe: from 1,600 in January 1735, to 4,000 in 1738 (FOM G^1 505), to 18,777 in 1767 (Kuczynski 1948-49.2:758).

There remain three pieces of Chaudenson's evidence concerning the presence of Réunionnais people in Mauritius before the end of 1735:

1. Chaudenson (*Genèse*, p. 50) mentions Pierre Lorette, a carpenter and "Créole de Bourbon." It is clear from *RT* (17:70) that he had already left Mauritius prior to the date of the letter in which he is mentioned (February 22, 1731). He is probably the same person as Pierre Lauret born in St. Paul, Reunion, in 1696, who married there "vers 1730" and who fathered four children born in Reunion between January 1731 and 1740 (Ricquebourg 1976:470). While it is not clear precisely when he visited Mauritius he might conceivably have been one of the "quatre derniers Creols" repatriated by Lenoir in 1726— it is clear that his residence in Mauritius was a temporary one.
2. Referring to May 1734, Chaudenson (*Genèse*, p. 46) writes:

Q47 Cossigny remène de Bourbon des ouvriers et des matériaux. Lougnon [1958:74] mentionne le transport de matériaux mais non celui des travailleurs. Or, Cossigny débarque au Port Nord-Ouest [Port Louis] "tous les ouvriers, européens et indiens, qu'il a pu rassembler à Bourbon." [Toussaint 1936:17]

On April 4, 1731 the *Saint-Joseph* brought "50 coulis, 15 maçons, un charpentier et un forgeron malabares," of whom 5 *maçons* were sent on to Reunion the following month (*RT* 7:72). All these artisans were under the supervision of Gerbault, a Pondichery resident of French descent who traveled with them on the *Saint-Joseph*. On June 23, 1732, a letter from Reunion to Mauritius included the sentence: "Comme tous les Malabars doivent passer icy, vous nous enverrez aussi le sr. Gerbaut" (*RT* 7:135). One cannot be certain just who is meant by *tous*, but it seems quite likely that the reference is to the group that had arrived on the *Saint-Joseph* a year earlier. A letter from Reunion to the Compagnie of April 8, 1734 includes: ". . . á l'Isle de France. Nous allons envoyer par la *Diane*, qui doit y porter

M de Cossigny et tous ses ouvriers et attirail" (*CBI* 1933:196-97). The following month a letter from Reunion to Pondichery dated May 15, 1734 includes: "Cy joint l'état des Malabars qui restent actuellement en cette isle et celuy de ceux que nous venons d'envoyer à l'isle de France en conséquence des ordres de la Comp^{ie} reçus par *le Dauphin*" (*RT* 7:236). There is insufficient evidence here to draw firm conclusions, but it seems fairly clear that some or all of the artisans who reached Mauritius on the *Saint-Joseph* in 1731 traveled to Reunion the following year and returned to Mauritius on the same boat as Cossigny two years later. I have found nothing to indicate that there were also Europeans who came with him from Reunion and, as Toussaint does not state his source, it is not clear on what his information was based.

3. Chaudenson (*Genèse*, p. 50) writes:

Q52 A. D'Epinay (renseignements p. 87) cite un arrêté du Conseil provincial de l'île de France du 3 juin 1726 "relatif à des Créoles venus de l'île Bourbon pour être envoyés à la poursuite de noirs marrons." Or, d'après les documents dont nous disposons, la première arrivée de "chasseurs de marrons" est de 1729 [*sic*]; il n'est donc pas impossible qu'il y en ait eu d'autres avant.

In fact, June 3, 1726 is the date of Lenoir's *règlements*, and the document to which Chaudenson refers is without any doubt the one dealing with the repatriation of the "quatre derniers Creols" already mentioned in Q31 and Q32. Thus, this in no way implies the presence of any additional Réunionnais, or even a new occupation for the free Creoles, since De Nyon had written of sending "cinq Creols a la poursuitte de sept malagastes" (Q26) in May 1723.

Thus far I have set out the main facts concerning the Réunionnais presence in Mauritius in the period 1721-35, and I have also discussed such evidence as Chaudenson presents in *Genèse* and commented on his interpretation of the data. Wherever possible I have quoted from appropriate manuscripts of the period. I believe that it will already be apparent that there can have been very few Réunionnais who settled in Mauritius in this fourteen-year period. However, in an attempt to clear up any possible doubts, I have cross-checked all the names which occur in my data on the population of Mauritius in the period 1721-37, drawing on all the relevant sources listed in the bibliography and involving a total of about 3,500 names, with all the names in Ricquebourg's *Dictionnaire Généalogique des Familles de l'Ile Bourbon (1665-1767)*. This exercise has revealed a grand total of two people who were born in Reunion and who had settled in Mauritius by the end of 1735. These are two sisters, Françoise and Marie-Sébastienne Artur, who married the Mauritius-based Frenchmen François Mathieu de Saint-Remy and Jacques Romain Le François de Grainville, respectively, in Reunion on the same day, April 21, 1734, and who subsequently moved to Mauritius with their husbands. (Françoise gave birth to her first child in Mauritius in January 1735. The date of birth of Marie-Sébastienne's first child, who died in 1737, is uncertain, but her second child was born in Mauritius on January 1, 1736. Both sisters ultimately died in Mauritius.) As already noted above, all the free male Réunionnais who came to Mauritius at some point in the period 1721-35, and whose names are known, subsequently returned to Reunion and ultimately died there.

The Mauritian data also include information on slave ownership. Table 3 provides provisional findings for the period up to December 31, 1737.[10]

Table 3

Slave Owners and Slaves in Mauritius, January 1, 1727 to December 31, 1737

108[*]	Owners in Mauritius directly from France (or, rarely, another European country) who possessed at least:	887 slaves
1	Owner from Pondichery (Céré) who possessed at least:	23 slaves
27	Owners, place of origin undetermined, who possessed at least:	123 slaves
136	Total individual owners possessed at least:	1,033 slaves

In addition:
The Compagnie des Indes possessed at least:	204 slaves
The Congrégation de la Mission dite Lazariste possessed at least:	34 slaves
The slave owner remains unidentified in the case of:	61 slaves

Total number of slaves identified by name and/or owner in the parish registers and other documents consulted:	1,332 slaves

---

[*] Thus far I have been able to establish that at least 55 of these men had originally come to Mauritius as soldiers. This gives some indication of the extent to which Lenoir's policy of "military colonisation" (the phrase is Kuczynski's) was implemented.

This table is primarily concerned with ownership rather than actual numbers of slaves. The total number brought to the island or born there within this period is likely to be in excess of 2,000. Slaves who are mentioned in the parish registers (the principal source of these data) include those who were born or died in captivity, women who gave birth, and slaves of either sex who became Catholics. Other slaves are known from a variety of documents but generally because of their having been involved with legal proceedings. Thus, male slaves who did not become

Catholics and who did not get into conflict with the law were unlikely to be mentioned in the parish registers until they died. There is evidence in the registers (mass baptisms, multiple weddings) to suggest that the Lazarists were able to exert influence over privately-owned slaves to a considerably greater degree than over those owned by the Compagnie, and there is no doubt that the proportion of Compagnie-owned slaves was considerably greater than that suggested by Table 3.[11]

Of the 27 slave owners whose origin has yet to be established, there is not one whose name appears in Ricquebourg. There is thus nothing to indicate that any Reunion-born person owned a slave in Mauritius in this period.

In 1974, Chaudenson wrote:

Q53   Or, l'Ile de France est peoplée d'abord et surtout à partir de l'Ile Bourbon. Les esclaves introduits dans l'île, en plus grand nombre après 1730, se trouvent donc en présence d'une colonie homogène sur le plan linguistique, puisque maître et esclaves déjà installés y parlent une seule langue: le créole "bourbonnais." (*Lexique*, p. 446)

All the evidence presented above indicates that such a situation could never have obtained in Mauritius, there is not the slightest evidence that there existed even one plantation owned by a Réunionnais, by a speaker of "Bourbonnais." Chaudenson wisely refrains from reiterating this claim in *Genèse,* but nevertheless he concludes the section dealing with the Réunionnais presence in the early years in Mauritius as follows:

Q54   1. Il est faux de dire, comme le fait Ph. Baker, que tous les Créoles de Bourbon quittent l'île de France après décembre 1722. Ils jouent au contraire dès le début un rôle décisif; les esclaves créoles de Bourbon initient, quatre mois durant, les esclaves malgaches importés à leur vie nouvelle. Les Créoles de Bourbon jouent un rôle social important et constituent au moins:

– de juin 1722 à mi-avril 1723:   25% de la population totale de l'île
– de mai 1723 à aout 1729:   10% de la population européenne de l'île
– d'aout 1729 à mai 1730:   25% de la population européenne

2. Le bourbonnais est donc un élément important à prendre en compte dans l'étude de la genèse du créole mauricien puisque c'est sans doute, en particulier, la langue apprise par les premiers esclaves malgaches amenés dans l'île. (*Genèse,* p. 51)

For the reasons which led me, in 1976, to believe that all the Réunionnais who were in Mauritius in 1722 left at the end of that year, see Q15 and the paragraph following Q40 above. The unsubstantiated claim that all the slaves from Reunion were born there, which is repeated here, was also discussed following Q40. The remainder of Q54 (1) above consists of three claims about the percentage of the Mauritian population which the Reunion-based visitors formed. The available evidence suggests that all three claims are false. Table 2 indicates that speakers of "Bourbonnais" accounted for just about 20 percent of the total population between December 1722 and April 1723, rather than at least 25 percent, claimed by Chaudenson. Between May 1723 and August 1729 Chaudenson claims that "Créoles de Bourbon" formed at least 10 percent of the European population (or "population blanche," according to *Créoles*, p. 47). I assume that he refers to the proportion the free Reunion Creoles formed of the total free population excluding free Indian artisans. Tables 1 and 2 suggest that such people accounted for less than 10 percent of the free population at the beginning of May 1723, declining to less than 9 percent by the end of that month, and further declining from less than half that level to zero in 1726. It has yet to be shown that there were any free Creoles in Mauritius between mid-1726 and mid-1730. The second claim is thus false. The third claim—that free Réunionnais formed at least 25 percent of the European population from August 1729 to May 1730—is automatically invalidated by Chaudenson's having mistaken the date of arrival of the 35 *chausseurs de marrons* (in fact, it was August 14, 1730—Lougnon 1958:46). By the latter date, this group could not have formed more than 7 percent of the free non-Asian population.

Chaudenson's second conclusion is that "Bourbonnais" was the language learned by the first Malagasy slaves in Mauritius. In a similar passage in *Créoles* he writes:

Q55 On fait ainsi venir, dans les premiers mois de la colonie, un contingent d'esclaves *créoles de Bourbon chargé d'encadrer la première immigration servile malgache introduite dans l'île.* Si quatre mois plus tard, les esclaves bourbonnais repartent, *c'est parce qu'ils ont accompli ce qu'on attendait d'eux; il ne fait pas de doute qu'une des premières choses qu'ils ont dû enseigner à leurs nouveaux compagnons d'infortune est le créole* qu'ils parlaient eux-mêmes! (*Créoles*, p. 47; italics added)

In the above passage, I have italicized those sections which, to the best of my knowledge, are pure speculation on Chaudenson's part and for which he nowhere provides the necessary supporting evidence. I have already drawn attention to the following:

1. That Chaudenson has not shown that all or any of these slaves from Reunion were in fact born there (cf. section following Q40).
2. That the purpose of sending the first group of Malagasies to Mauritius was to make it possible for the Reunion slaves then present to return to their owners without delay, and thus that it was not any part of the Reunion authorities' intentions that "their" slaves be used to *encadrer* newly introduced slaves (Q15; see also discussion following Q44).[12]
3. That whatever De Nyon's motives for continuing to keep the Reunion slaves in Mauritius after, and in contravention of, the resolution of the Reunion Council of October 2, 1722 (Q15), the immediate reason for his decision to "repatriate" them was to reduce the number of people who had to be fed from the island's inadequate and rapidly diminishing stock of food (Q19). There is nothing to suggest that they had completed some vital, and hitherto unidentified, task.

It is necessary to repeat these things here because they are all relevant to the situation in which Chaudenson supposes that the Reunion slaves were engaged in teaching the Malagasies to speak "Bourbonnais"—a supposition which requires close examination.

It is clear from the De Nyon and De Hauville correspondence that the Reunion slaves disembarked at Grand Port. They appear to have remained there throughout the duration of their stay for it was from this port that those fit enough to do so walked across the island to Port Louis in order to board the *Saint-Albin* (letters of June 13, 1722, April 7, 1723, etc.; ANC C4 vl). A number of Malagasies worked for individual Compagnie employees and officers, presumably as *domestiques*. In letters dated January 6, 1723, January 18, 1723, and March 5, 1723, De Hauville refers to the following residents of Port Louis as owners of a total of seven slaves: himself (2), De Comminge (1), Sr Ballard (1), Mme d'Hautrive (1), Mme Faillet (1), and M^r Le Blanc (1) (ANC C4 vl). As Port Louis was the smaller of the two settlements during the first few years, it seems unlikely that there would have been fewer "privately-owned" slaves in Grand Port at that time. Thus, it seems reasonable to suppose that somewhere between a quarter and a third of the non-maroon Malagasies belonged to private individuals in the early part of 1723. (Note that the 1725 census indicates a similar proportion: 10 out of 34.) Some of the Compagnie-owned Malagasies worked in Port Louis where the only resident "Bourbonnais" speaker was Jean Allaigre (from mid-February to mid-May 1723 only, see Table 1). Thus, only the Compagnie-owned Malagasies based in Grand Port were likely to have been exposed to a good deal of "Bourbonnais" in the four months prior to mid-April 1723. Thereafter, there were very few first-language speakers of "Bourbonnais" on the island, and it has yet to be shown that there were any immediately after the departure of the last four Creoles in mid-1726.

To what extent might Europeans and/or Malagasies have acquired some knowledge of "Bourbonnais" in the period prior to 1726? From the point of view of the first Europeans, the free Creoles would surely have been people whose vocabulary included terms for the more important of the non-European flora and fauna of the island. Europeans might well have adopted a number of such terms from the free Creoles.[13] However, as the Europeans could have communicated adequately with each other, and no doubt with the free Creoles, in their own varieties of French, and as Europeans at all times greatly outnumbered the free Creoles, I find it inconceivable that any European would have sought to learn to speak "Bourbonnais."

If all the Reunion slaves had spoken nothing but "Bourbonnais," then those Malagasies who were both owned by the Compagnie and based in Grand Port (forming perhaps half of the total of non-maroon Malagasies) might well have been exposed to roughly equal amounts of regional varieties of metropolitan French and "Bourbonnais" during a period of four months. Whether such Malagasies would have recognized "Bourbonnais" as a quite separate entity from regional varieties of

French is a matter on which I prefer not to speculate. However, I would point out that from mid-April 1723 on there were at least seven times as many first-language speakers of (varieties of) French as speakers of "Bourbonnais" in Mauritius (cf. Table 2). To suppose that these Malagasies acquired "Bourbonnais" is therefore to suggest that they identified "Bourbonnais" rather than a (another?) variety of French as their target *and* had substantially achieved their target—all within the space of four months. I do not find that plausible. Further, I find it difficult to believe that any individual slave owner, soldier, or Compagnie employee from Europe—all of whom had contact with the Malagasies and, with few exceptions, remained in Mauritius over a much longer period than did the free Creoles or Reunion slaves—would have found it natural, convenient, or in any way desirable for slaves to acquire "Bourbonnais" rather than (an approximation of something they would more readily recognize as) French; because if slaves identified "Bourbonnais" rather than "European French" as their target language, slave owners, Compagnie employees, and soldiers would need to acquire "Bourbonnais" in order to communicate with the slaves. Finally, I would stress again that Chaudenson has not established that the slaves from Reunion had been born there. If these slaves had instead been representative of the slave population of Reunion at that time as a whole (without the slightest evidence to the contrary having been published, so far as I am aware, this seems a more reasonable working assumption than that they were all Reunion-born), then there would certainly have been some Madagascar-born slaves among them, and thus Malagasy would have been available as a medium of communication if not instruction between some Reunion slaves and the Malagasies. (In the censuses of 1704 and 1709, Malagasies formed 35 1/2 percent and 24 percent, respectively, of the slave population of Reunion; *Lexique*, p. 457.)

B2.2.3 Conclusions

1. There is nothing to suggest that the original policy of the Compagnie's officials in France of settling Mauritius with families from Reunion was ever implemented by the Compagnie's employees in the Mascarenes.
2. Of the free Réunionnais men who came to Mauritius in the period 1721-23, the evidence of Lenoir shows that only four remained there—were forced to remain there against their will—until 1726 when he visited the island and allowed them to return to their homes in Reunion.
3. Lenoir provided reasons for supposing that no Réunionnais *habitants* would want to settle in Mauritius. He proposed instead that Mauritius should be settled from France, a policy which was both accepted and implemented by the Compagnie's officials in France.
4. Jonchée de la Goleterie provided reasons for not allowing free Creoles from Reunion to settle in Mauritius. He, too, recommended that Mauritius be settled from France.

5. Two Réunionnais sisters are the only people born on that island who are definitely known to have settled in Mauritius by the end of 1735. In every other case where the full name of a visitor from Reunion is known, it can be proved that he subsequently returned home and ultimately died on the island where he was born.
6. There does not appear to be the slightest scrap of evidence to suggest that anyone living in Mauritius and owning land or slaves there up to the end of 1735 was born in Reunion.

It is thus entirely clear that the Réunionnais contribution to the peopling of Mauritius during the first fourteen years of French rule was absolutely minimal. I am not aware of any evidence to suggest that it was more than absolutely minimal in any later period of Mauritian history.

B2.3 The West African Presence in Mauritius to 1735

In order to save space in this section, it will be convenient to adopt the following abbreviations when referring to the sender or addressee of a letter:

Cie	The Compagnie des Indes in Paris or Lorient
Reu	The Compagnie's representatives in Reunion
Mau	The Compagnie's representatives in Mauritius
Pon	The Compagnie's representatives in Pondichery
Cha	The Compagnie's representatives in Chandernagor

B2.3.1 Policies

There had been Malagasy maroons in Mauritius since December 1722; by 1725, they had claimed the lives of a number of Europeans.[14] In that year, a visiting missionary noted:

Q56 Les Negres marons, ou fuyards, sont d'autres ennemis plus dangereux, mais dont il est plus aisé de se défaire. Ce sont des esclaves achetez à Madagascar, qui aprés avoir déserté les uns aprés les autres, se sont rassemblez dans les montagnes, & font de-là de trés-cruelles excursions sur leurs anciens maitres. (Du Cros 1728:17)

The Compagnie was certainly aware of the problem:

Q57 Cie to Reu, December 31, 1727:
Faittes attention cependant que si vous faittes quelque épreuve nouvelle et que vous y [= Mozambique] fassiez traitter quelques noirs, vous devez les destiner tous p^r l'Isle de France, ceux de Madagascar n'estant pas si dangereux à celle de Bourbon, parce qu'elle est beaucoup plus peuplée et que les habitations y sont plus rammassées.... Vous aurez attention à ne faire passer a l'Isle de France, du moins autant qu'il se pourra, que des noirs de Mozambique, ou des esclaves indiens, pour éviter de tomber dans les accidents qu'on y a essuyez des noirs de Madagascar, et dont on n'y est pas encore délivré. (CBI 1934:30, 63)

A few months later, the Compagnie mentioned, for the first time, the sending of West African slaves:

Q58 Cie to Reu, August 13, 1728:
La Compagnie fournissant des noirs de Guinée à l'isle de France, estime qu'il ne convient pas d'y en faire passer de Madagascar, du moins jusqu'à ce qu'il ait une assez bonne quantité des premiers pour n'avoir rien à craindre de l'introduction des autres. (*CBI* 1934:79)

Q57 and Q58 clearly indicate that the Compagnie favored introducing a substantial number of non-Malagasy slaves onto the island before obtaining any more slaves from Madagascar. Given the problems which Malagasy maroons posed for the French in Mauritius, this recommendation by the Compagnie was one with which its local representatives would surely have concurred. In any event, this policy was certainly implemented because, as will be shown below, there is nothing to indicate that any more Malagasies reached the island before November 1731, by which time more than 900 slaves had arrived from other sources, half of them from Senegal.

Given that Mauritius was four months' sailing time from West Africa, the latter might seem an inconvenient source of slaves for an island in the Indian Ocean. However, from the point of view of the Compagnie officials in France, there were at least three good reasons for supplying slaves from Senegal:

1. The Compagnie (and its immediate predecessor, the Compagnie du Sénégal) had been established at Gorée, an islet close to modern Dakar, for half a century. Since at least 1680, they had supplied slaves from Senegal to Haiti (Charlevoix 1730-31, 2:125), and to judge from a history of the latter published in 1731, slaves from Senegal enjoyed a particularly favorable reputation in Haiti at that time:

    Q59 Ces Sénégallois sont de tous les Negres les mieux faits, les plus aisés à discipliner, & les plus propres au service domestique. (Charlevoix 1730-31.2:498)

    In supplying slaves from Senegal to Mauritius, the Compagnie was thus dealing with a known quantity.
2. All the Compagnie's vessels bound for the Indian Ocean had to pass close to Cape Verde. Gorée was thus a convenient port of call. In article 4 of Jonchée de la Goleterie's proposals for the settlement of Mauritius (two earlier parts of which were quoted in Q39), this captain had quite independently proposed that whenever the Compagnie had reason to send a ship to the Indian Ocean without French settlers for Mauritius, this ship should call at Gorée and collect 50 or 60 slaves for the island (proposals dated April 20, 1729; ANC C4 vl).
3. Mozambique (mentioned in the December 31, 1727 letter, A57) was not yet a

viable alternative to Madagascar. Some degree of cooperation with the Portuguese was necessary before the French could obtain slaves for the Mascarenes on a large scale from Mozambique, and that seems not to have happened until 1733.[15]

Traveling by boat in the eighteenth century was a hazardous business due in particular to a lack of fresh food (rather than the danger of shipwreck). As West African slaves spent far longer on board ship than slaves from other sources, it is likely that a greater proportion of them died en route. However, Chaudenson would have the reader believe that they continued to die at a more rapid rate than other slaves even after disembarkation:

Q60a Il faut ajouter que les survivants [from West Africa] arrivaient très affaiblis et que beaucoup d'entre eux périssaient rapidement des suites des fatigues et des maladies de la traversée. Sans rappeler la lettre écrite à propos de l'arrivée de la *Badine,* on peut citer, la même année, une autre lettre à propos des esclaves ouest-africains amenés à Bourbon sur le *Duc de Noailles:* "Ils arrivèrent exténués et hors d'état de rendre lontems aucun service" [*CBI* 1934:14]; les "habitants" peu soucieux de les acquérir au comptant, même à bas prix, ne les achetaient que "payables en café"! (*Genèse,* p. 53)

This requires several comments. To begin with the least important, the wording of the final part suggests that it was extraordinary for slaves to be sold against coffee. It was not, and in this case, it is what the Compagnie had proposed:

Q60b Cie to Reu, August 13, 1728:
L'intention de la Compagnie est que la moitié des noirs [from West Africa] estimée pour l'Isle de Bourbon y soit vendue sur le pied de deux cent piastres la pièce d'Inde, au comptant ou en caffé. (*CBI* 1934:77)

Second, Chaudenson implies that these slaves were sold for less than plantation owners were normally willing to pay. In fact, they were sold for *more*. At that time, 200 piastres was the equivalent of 720 livres (*CBI* 1934:127). The 188 West Africans who arrived on the *Duc de Noailles* were sold for a total of 71 870 livres, or an average of 383 livres per slave. This was not much more than half of what the Compagnie had hoped to obtain, but it was appreciably more than the price paid for Malagasies at that time. The same ship brought 361 slaves from Madagascar a few months later, and they were sold for 103 205 livres, an average of 286 livres per slave (Lougnon 1958:59). What the Compagnie had proposed was that West Africans should be sold at double the normal price paid for "pièce d' Inde"[16] Malagasy slaves. In this particular case, the West Africans were in poor condition but still raised more than the price then paid for the very best slaves from Madagascar. During the period 1729-65 as a whole, West African slaves were normally sold at about twice the price of those from Madagascar:

The Contested Aspects of the Peopling of Mauritius 179

Selling Price of "pièce d'Inde" Slaves in the Mascarenes
1729-1765

Origin of Slaves	Price Range	Mean
West Africa	600-720 livres	660 livres
South East Africa	400-540 livres	470 livres
Madagascar	300-400 livres	350 livres
India	200-300 livres	250 livres

(derived from Filliot 1974:218)

West African slaves could not have consistently commanded a considerably higher price than other slaves if there had not been buyers who considered them worth the extra cost.

Last, and most important, Chaudenson claims that many of the West Africans died soon after arrival. Apart from the extreme case of the *Badine*—163 deaths among 200 slaves during the voyage and a further eight deaths within twelve days of the ship's arrival—Chaudenson cites no evidence in support of this. I have checked all the entries in the parish registers for the period August 18, 1728 to January 1, 1738—the registers are complete for this period—and have found nothing to suggest that mortality was higher among West Africans than among Malagasies or Indians. It is surely obvious that if West Africans had had a higher rate of mortality, or had been physically or otherwise less competent than Indian, Malagasy, or Mozambique slaves, the Compagnie would not have continued to supply them to Mauritius until 1767.[17]

The senior employees of the Compagnie based in Mauritius were in a position to choose from the newly arrived slaves those they judged to be best suited for work on the Compagnie's projects. All the West Africans who arrived during the three years 1736-38 were retained by the Compagnie (FOM G^1 505). La Bourdonnais indicated that he wanted the supply of slaves from Senegal to continue:

Q61   Mau to Cie, March 5, 1737:
      Mais plus que tout cela il nous faut des noirs. N'oubliez pas Messieurs de fair passer vos navires a Goret pour en prendre. (ANC C4 v2)

La Bourdonnais received more than 200 West African slaves on the *Griffon* in 1739 and was delighted:

Q62   Mau to Cie, January 19, 1740:
      La traitte du *Griphon* à esté d'une grande ressource pour recruter les noirs ouvriers, et en augmenter le nombre. *Les noirs yolofs, Bambaras, et Guinés sont infiniment plus robuste et d'un bien plus grand travail que touttes les autres castres de Madagascar, de Mozambiques et de l'Inde.* Si vous pouviés vous determiner, Messieurs, à envoÿer encor icy une traitte semblable, on auroit de beaux et forts noirs pour remplacer dans les atteliers principaux les noirs faibles, infirmes, ou paresseux qu'on est obligé de garder

faute d'autres et pour completter la marine de ce port, au moyen de quoy on renverroit tous les Lascards. (letter signed by La Bourdonnais; italics added; ANC C4 v4)

Two decades later, West Africans probably formed only a comparatively small minority of the total slave population. Nevertheless, they appear to have been particularly favored by the Compagnie's employees in Mauritius for, as the following extract from the *Recensement générale des Noirs, Negresses et Enfants appartenants à la Compagnie, existant au vingt Avril 1761 non compris ceux du Port Sud-Est* [= Grand Port] clearly shows, they were still very much the numerically dominant group among the Compagnie-owned slaves:

Q63		*hommes*	*femmes*
	Guinée[18]	138	234
	Mozambique	89	42
	Malgaches	98	112
	Americain	1	0
	Macaos[19]	1	1
	Creols	17	45
	Indiens	73	26
	Mamille[20]	1	0
	Total	418	460

(Note: The terms *hommes* and *femmes* were applied to slaves aged 14 years or older.)
(FOM G^1 505)

La Bourdonnais and his successors were able to draw on first-hand experience in choosing which slaves were to work for the Compagnie.[21] It is clear that the preference was for West Africans.

B2.3.2 Numbers

Table 4 (p. 181) sets out Chaudenson's *Genèse* figures for West African arrivals side by side with the best information currently available to this author. Conflicting information is discussed in the following.

According to Chaudenson, a total of 481 West African slaves came to Mauritius (and did not die within a few days), almost two-thirds of whom came from Juda, whereas my figures show a total of 695, more than two-thirds of whom came from Gorée. Such major differences require a detailed explanation:

The Méduse
Q64) Cie to Reu, August 13, 1728:
Celle-cy [= cette lettre] vous parviendra par le vaisseau la *Méduse*, que la Compagnie, sur vos demandes réitérées, a jugé à propos d'expédier pour aller à son comptoir de Juda traitter et charger quatre cent noirs et les remettre ensuite par égal moitié, aux Isles de Bourbon et de France. (*CBI* 1934:76)

Table 4
West African Arrivals in Mauritius, June 22, 1729 to August 31, 1734

Date	Ship	From Gorée C	From Gorée B	From Juda C	From Juda B
Jun 22, 1729	*Méduse:* from Juda				
	C: 237 − 25% ÷ 2 arrivals			89	
	B: at least 178 arrivals				178
May 9, 1730	*Diane:* from Gorée				
	C: 248 arrivals; of these, half of 172 in good health were for Reunion and half of those in poor health are taken to have died soon after arrival in Mauritius	124			
	B: 248 arrivals		248		
Jul 12, 1730	*Vierge de Grâce:*				
	C: 260 arrivals from Juda			260	
	B: 260 arrivals from Gorée		260		
Oct ( ), 1730	*Indien:* to Reunion				
	C: 33 Juda slaves			-33	
	B: 32 Gorée slaves		-32		
Jun 5, 1731	*Badine:* from Gorée				
	C&B: 37 arrivals, 8 of whom died within a few days	29	29		
Aug 31, 1734	*Charolais:* from Gorée				
	C&B: 12 Bambaras	12	12		
Totals		165	517	316	178

C = Chaudenson; Total 481
B = Baker; Total 695

Q65 Cie to Mau, September 30, 1728:
Elle vous prévient qu'elle fera encore embarquer plusieurs passagers sur le *Duc de Chartres,* afin que vous preniez vos mesures pour leur fournir également la subsistance, et que vous réserviez des noirs que la *Méduze* doit vous porter, pour leur en fournir. (*CBI* 1934:80)

Q66 Juda *(Méduse)* to Cie, February 12, 1729:
J'ai chargé à votre adresse sur le navire la *Méduze,* de la Compagnie, cap^{ne} Dhermitte, la quantité de deux cent trente sept captifs, sçavoir: cent un homme, cinquante huit femmes, quarante un négrillons et trente sept négrittes, suivant le connoissement cy joint. (*RT* 23:141)

Q67 Mau to Reu, ca. August 1729:
J'ay très examiné les ordres de la Compagnie au sujet des noirs que le vaisseau "la *Méduse*" m'a remis; je n'ay peu m'y conformer entièrement.... Cependant, quoyque par ma dernière [lettre] j'aye eu l'honneur de vous ecrire que je les distribuerois à tous les habitants qui cryoient fortement pour en avoir, et que j'en garderois un sixième en consequence desd. ordres, pour les passagers du *Duc de Chartres* je n'en ay délivré que la moitié et ay gardé l'autre moittié pour en disposer suivant vos ordres, laquelle d. moittié ... j'ay remis à Monsr. Maupin. (*RT* 7:60)

Q68 Extract from *Memoire pour le Sr Desfoüilleuse Ecuyer cy devant habitant de l'isle de France Contenant les motifs qui l'ont determiné a repasser en France,* dated August 1, 1731;
Sur la fin du mois de juin de lad. année [1729], arriva le V^{au} la *Méduse,* chargé d'une carguaison de Noirs et de Negresses de Guinée, Et le 2 juillet suivant, on fit la distribution de la moitié de lad. carguaison, aux habitants, dans laquelle ledit Sr Desfoüilleuse fut comprit pour un noir et une negresse, comme simple habitant, sans avoir egard a son credit, ny a sa société, aux [illegible word] de laquelle il etoit obligé de former deux habitations; Et il fut réservé, suivant les ordres de la Compagnie, l'autre moitié de lad. Carguaison, pour la distribution apres l'arrivée du vaisseau le *Duc de Chartres* [whose passengers included the new governor Maupin] ... et le 1er Octobre de lad. année, il [= Maupin] se contenta, dans la distribution qu'il fit, de la moitié des Noirs de lad. carguaison du V^{au} la *Méduse* [NB: reference is to second half of these slaves, cf. Q65], de donner seulement une negritte aud. Sr Defoüilleuse, tandis qu'il donna 4: 5: et 6: Noirs ou Negresses aux passagers arrivez avec luy. (ANC C4, carton 86, liasse 1731)

While Q64, addressed to Reunion, states that the slaves were to be divided equally between the two islands, the Compagnie's letter to Mauritius written six weeks later makes no mention of any of these slaves having to go to Reunion. (Because of the wind patterns in the Indian Ocean, ships normally called at Mauritius before Reunion.) Q67 and Q68 indicate between them that half of these slaves were distributed soon after the *Méduse* arrived and that the other half were distributed six weeks after Maupin had arrived on the *Duc-de-Chartres* with an important group of settlers.

According to Chélin, a census was taken in November 1729:

Q69   Entry for November 24, 1729:
       Recensement de la colonie: 486 noirs, y compris 178 de Guinée; 89 soldats. (Chélin 1973:14)

This census, which was reported in *Towards,* is simply ignored by Chaudenson. While the ultimate source of Chélin's figures remains to be established, it cannot be seriously supposed that he invented them. In fact, Chélin's figures agree not approximately but *exactly* with the figures presented later in Table 7 (pp. 195-96). The relevant facts at this stage are as follows.

There were 20 Compagnie-owned slaves in June 1726. There were 10 privately-owned slaves in October 1725. An additional 20 Malagasy slaves were brought to Mauritius in January 1727 on the *Alcyon,* but there is no evidence of additional Malagasy arrivals before 1731. (References for these, and for the statements about slave arrivals elsewhere in this paragraph, will be given below.) Therefore, one would not expect the total number of Malagasies to have been greater than 50 in 1729. In 1728 and 1729, 258 Indian slaves and artisans reached Mauritius (*Genèse,* p. 53; my own information substantially concurs with this). The likely total of Malagasies and Indians is thus about 308. If one adds Chélin's 178 Guinea slaves, one arrives at precisely his total of 486 *noirs* (the *Méduse* is the only ship to have brought slaves from West Africa to Mauritius by the date of the census).

One additional piece of evidence may be cited. In this early period the word "Guinée" is applied only to those territories bordering what in French is termed the *Golfe de Guinée* (see note 18). As the *Méduse* was the only ship to bring slaves from Juda by 1735—this claim will be substantiated below—it is a near certainty that any slave described in the parish registers as "de Juda" or "de Guinée" by December 31, 1735 was among those who arrived on the *Méduse.* The following numbers of women were described by either or both of these terms and had married and/or given birth by the end of 1735:

       22 "de Guinée"
       19 "de Juda"
       _2_ on one occasion "de Guinée" and on another "de Juda"
       43 Total

Q66 mentioned 58 women who boarded the *Méduse* at Juda. If, as Chaudenson suggests, about 25 percent of them would have probably died during the voyage, one would expect 43 or 44 of them to have reached Mauritius. However, of the above-mentioned 43 ("de Guinée" and/or "de Juda"), four would have been aged 16 years or younger at the time of boarding the *Méduse* and thus might have been termed *negrittes* rather than *femmes.* Nevertheless, this still suggests that the great majority of women on the *Méduse* disembarked at Mauritius. If one similarly applies the 25 percent mortality rate to the total of 237 slaves (Q66), one would expect about 178 arrivals—precisely the figure noted by Chélin for the November

1729 census. All the evidence presented above strongly suggests that most if not all the *Méduse* slaves disembarked at Mauritius and that few if any went on to Reunion.

Chaudenson claims that Lougnon confirms that the *Méduse* received all these slaves at "Corresp. XXXVI" (*Genèse*, p. 45). I take him to mean *CBI* 1934:xxxvi, where Lougnon discusses the taking of West African slaves to the Mascarenes and mentions the *Méduse* but says nothing about where these slaves disembarked. Filliot (1974:184) claims that the *Méduse* disembarked "environ 200 esclaves" at Reunion in July 1729 but cites no source, while his other mentions of this vessel (1974:183-84) refer to sources already discussed above; it thus appears that his figure of 200 was obtained by halving the one mentioned in Q64. There appears to be no solid evidence to show that the *Méduse* took any West Africans to Reunion.

The Diane, the Vierge de Grâce, and the Indien

Q70 Cie to Reu, September 5, 1729:
La Compagnie expédie les vaisseaux la *Vierge de Grace* et la *Diane*, le premier pour aller charger des noirs à Juda, et le second pour en aller prendre au Sénégal, l'un et l'autre pour les transporter aux Isles de Bourbon et de France.
Les capitaines ont ordre d'en laisser la moitié à l'Isle de France et de vous remettre l'autre moitié. (*CBI* 1934:84)

Q71 Journal a Robert Pilote (log of the *Vierge de Grâce*):
Le mercredy 14.12.29 nous avons eu ordre de maitre nos marchandises de traite que nous avions pour judas a terre pour aler au Senegal prendre nos negre pour mascarin. (ANM 4JJ 112)

Q72 Mau to Reu, May (or June) 12, 1730:
J'ay chargé sur le vaisseau la *Diane*... une bonne partie des effets que le vau. le *Mars* avoit laissé icy.... J'ay fait embarquer 86 testes de Noirs, que nous avons réparties moitié par moitié avec Mr Tortel sur la totalité qu'il a amené, à la reserve des malades qui n'avroient pas été possibles d'embarquer, *lesquels j'ay vendu à l'encan.* (*RT* 7: 61-62)

Q73 Reu to Cie, December 20, 1730:
Que le vaisseau la *Dianne*... venant du Sénégal, mouilla à St-Paul, Isle de Bourbon, le 26 juin 1730, chargé de 304 tetes de noirs, en ayant debarqué 248 à l'Isle de France, et apporté 76 à celle de Bourbon.... Que le vaisseau la *Vierge de Grace*... venant de Gorée, mouilla à l'Isle de France le 12 juillet 1730 avec 291 tetes de noirs, de 304 chargé à Gorée, qu'il en a été retenu 260 à l'Isle de France et envoyé 31 à l'Isle Bourbon, qui ont été aussi vendus. (*CBI* 1934:132)

Q74 Reu to Mau, November 23, 1732:
Par le connoissement du 23 aoust 1730 des noirs embarqués sur la *Méduse*, il paroit qu'il a été chargé 24 noirs, 6 négresses et une négritte.... Par le connoissement et facture signé... de l'*Indien*, il paroit qu'il a été embarqué 24 noirs pièce d'Inde du Sénégal, cinq négresses dont deux ont chacune un enfant à la mamelle, deux négrillons et une négritte du Sénégal, un noir indien, faisant en tout le nombre de 33 sans prise. Cela

The Contested Aspects of the Peopling of Mauritius 185

fait donc la quantité de 64 noirs embarqué sur les deux vau. Il en est mort un à bord; reste 63. Et nous avons trouvé 69! (*RT* 7:149)

Q75   Mau to Reu, June 17, 1732:
La Compagnie nous écrit que vous luy avés porté des plaintes de ce que nous ne vous avions pas envoyé la moitié des noirs que la *Diane* et la *Vierge de Grace* nous ont apportés en 1730 de leur traite à Gorée, et que nous vous en avons fait passer étoit le rebut des deux traites. Ces plaintes ne nous parroissent pas bien fondées à l'égard de la qualité, puisque votre portion avoit été séparée au Port Bourbon [= Grand Port] avec égalité, ni à l'égard de la quantité, *puisque toutes les traites de Madagascar ont été pour vous et vous ont bien dû dédommager du petit nombre que nous avions retenu.* (*RT* 7:131-32; italics added)

Q76   La *Diane* commandé par Tortel avait ramené le 28 juin 1730, 304 nègres du Sénégal, dont 298 furent débarqués à l'Ile de France et 6 à Bourbon. (Olagnier 1936:76)

Q77   La *Diane* remit à l'Ile de France 248 Sénégalais, et à Bourbon 76. (*CBI* 1934:xxxvi)

Q78   La *Diane*... 9 mai 1730 Arrivée à l'Ile de France. Y remet 248 esclaves tirés du Sénégal.... 28 juin Arrivée à Bourbon. Y remet 76 esclaves embarqués à Gorée. (Lougnon 1958:52)

Q79   Le 28 juin de la même année [1730], la *Diane* arrive du Sénégal avec 304 têtes de noirs dont 76 pour Bourbon et 248 pour l'Ile de France [ANC C3 v5]. (Verguin 1956:51)

Q80   En juin (ou juillet) 1730, la *Diane* débarquait 248 esclaves à l'île de France et 76 à Bourbon (de Gorée). (Filliot 1974:184)

Q70 shows that the original intention was that the *Vierge de Grâce* should go to Juda (as both *Genèse*, p. 46 and Filliot 1974:184 suggest actually took place). However, Q71 indicates that the orders were changed and that this vessel went to Senegal instead, as is separately confirmed by Q73 and Q75. Q73 also indicates that there was very little mortality on this vessel (a mere 4 percent) and that 260 of the 291 who reached Mauritius disembarked there, the other 31 being taken on to Reunion on the *Méduse* (cf. Q74).

The figures for the *Diane* are less clear. Chaudenson assumes that 248 is the total number of slaves who reached the Mascarenes and that the 76 (or 86) who arrived in Reunion must be deducted from that figure. Neither Lougnon, Verguin, nor Filliot—all of whom had the opportunity of inspecting the documents personally—interprets the wording in that way. All three suggest that the total number of slaves brought by the *Diane* was 324 (248 + 76), which in turn implies that the first occurrence of 304 in Q73 is a scribe's error for 324.[22] In the figures which follow, I take the majority's interpretation to be the correct one.

The second problem concerns the number of slaves—76 or 86—who reached Reunion in June 1730. Mauritius claims to have put 86 on board, but Reunion acknowledges having received only 76. Following Lougnon and other writers, the number landed in Reunion is unrelated to the 248 who disembarked at Mauritius and is thus of no immediate interest.

The third problem is the number of Senegalese taken on to Reunion on the *Indien*. As the figure of 33 (not including two babies) includes one Indian, the number to be deducted is 32 (not 33 as per Chaudenson in *Genèse*, pp. 46, 53). As these were slaves from Senegal, they might have first traveled to Mauritius on either the *Vierge de Grâce* or the *Diane*.

Finally, Chaudenson takes Q72 at its face value and therefore assumes that only 172 (86 X 2) arrived in good health, and that the other 76 were ill. Further, he arbitrarily suggests that half the latter would probably have died more or less immediately and so should not be counted among the arrivals (*Genèse*, p. 53). The pretense that many of those arriving on the *Diane* were ill is not maintained in Q75 where it is admitted that Mauritius kept more than its fair share, and where it is further suggested that the Reunion authorities had no cause for complaint since they had had all the slaves brought to the Mascarenes from Madagascar [since 1728].[23] It may also be added that the parish registers record the death of only one person brought from Senegal in the 12 months following the *Diane*'s arrival, that of a Bambara slave who died on September 30, 1730. Chaudenson's estimate of 38 deaths does not appear to merit serious attention.

My interpretation of the facts concerning those who arrived on the *Diane* and the *Vierge de Grâce* are summarized below (with Chaudenson's interpretation in parentheses, excluding one error and the seemingly altogether unjustified assumption concerning mortalities).

	Mauritius	Reunion
Diane: brought to the Mascarenes	248 (162)	76 (86)
Vierge de Grâce: disembarked at Mauritius	291 (291)	
	539 (453)	
Méduse (ex-*Vierge de Grâce*): taken from Mauritius to Reunion	-31 (-31)	+31 (+31)
	508 (422)	107 (117)
Indien (ex-*Diane* or *Vierge de Grâce*): taken from Mauritius to Reunion	-32 (-32)	+32 (+32)
Final Position	476 (390)	139 (149)

B2.4 The Proportion of West Africans among the Non-French in Mauritius, 1727-35

As it is not merely the number of West Africans that is disputed but also their number in proportion to the total non-French population, it is necessary to examine Chaudenson's figures for other slave arrivals before the former can be calculated. The information which Chaudenson gives conflicts with that currently

The Contested Aspects of the Peopling of Mauritius 187

available to this author with regard to arrivals and, occasionally, departures of both Malagasies and Indians. These are dealt with separately below.

In a few cases it is the numbers who left Madagascar or India rather than the numbers who reached the Mascarenes that are known. In others, the precise division between Mauritius and Reunion is not known. In such cases I have adopted the following conventions, which are broadly in line with those proposed by Chaudenson (*Genèse,* p. 57, note 15):

1. Where only the number put on board is known, 12 percent is deducted for mortalities during the voyage.
2. Where the division between Mauritius and Reunion is not known, where there are no special reasons for supposing that slaves disembarked at one island rather than the other, and where the vessel concerned is known to have visited both islands consecutively, it has been assumed that slaves were distributed equally between the two. (In contrast to Chaudenson, I do this because it seems the fairest way of dealing with such cases. I do not pretend that the Compagnie's orders to this effect were actually carried out since the available evidence leaves little doubt that such was rarely the case.)
3. All estimated figures are followed by a superscript "e."

B2.4.1 Arrivals from Madagascar

Reasons for supposing that none of the 34 slaves—24 belonging to the Compagnie and 10 to private individuals—present at the time of the 1725 census were from Reunion were given in section 2.2 above. All the available evidence suggests that these were Malagasies who had arrived in December 1722 (and, possibly, a few children born to them since). By June 1726, the number of slaves belonging to the Compagnie was only 20 (Lenoir's report; ANC C4 vl). If the number of privately-owned slaves had remained the same, then the total number of slaves on the island in June 1726 would have been 30. No additional slaves are reported to have arrived before January 1727. The various figures, according to Chaudenson and this author, are set out in Table 5 (p. 188).

The total of 429 under Chaudenson in Table 5 differs from his total of 474 (*Genèse,* p. 54) for two reasons. The *Genèse* figure includes the 65 Malagasies who arrived in 1722, but excludes the 20 he notes as having arrived on the *Astrée* in 1735 (*Genèse,* p. 46). Thus, 474 - 65 + 20 = 429. The figure of 119 for the number of Malagasies who arrived in 1735 (*Genèse,* p. 54) appears to be an error for 139.

While the difference between the two totals is small, there is disagreement or doubt concerning the number who disembarked in the cases of 11 of the 14 vessels. Each case is discussed separately below, in chronological order following Table 5.

Table 5

Malagasy Arrivals in Mauritius, 1727-35

Date	Ship	Chaudenson	Baker
Jan 3, 1727	*Alcyon*	20	20
Aug 15, 1729	*Sirène*	77[e]	0
Nov ( ), 1731	*Légère*	24	18
Sep 16, 1732	*Subtile*	0	72
Apr 21, 1733	*Saint-Jean l'Evangéliste (Saint-Paul)*	57	0
Oct ( ), 1733	*Diane*	112	112
Dec 8 1733	*Saint-Jean l'Evangéliste (Saint-Paul)*	0	0
Dec 15 1733	*Méduse*	0	39
Jan 1, 1735	*Diane*	54	54?
Jan 13, 1735	*Astrée*	20	18[e]
Jun 27, 1735	*Diane*	65	65
Aug 5, 1735	*Reine*	0	24
Sep 21, 1735	*Atalante*	0	24
Dec 29, 1735	*Jupiter*	0	10
Total (in part, estimated)		429	456

Sirène, August 15, 1729:

Chaudenson cites Lougnon (1958) in support of his assumption that half of the slaves on the *Sirène* were taken to Mauritius. Lougnon (1958:45) writes only: "Départ de Madagascar où on a traité 175 esclaves." He says nothing about where they disembarked. There are strong reasons for supposing that none of them were landed at Mauritius. First, there is the evidence of Q57 and Q58 (2.3.1) that it was Compagnie policy at this time not to introduce any Malagasy slave into Mauritius until there were a good many slaves from other sources. While the Mauritian authorities were not too particular about observing the Compagnie's instructions when it did not suit them, there is every reason to suppose that they were more concerned with the presence of Malagasy maroons on the island than were the Compagnie's officials in France. Evidence for the latter is also provided by the case of the next ship bearing Malagasies which called at the island. This was the *Légère* in 1731 (see below under *Légère*), from which the Mauritians took less than one-sixth of the slaves on board—in marked contrast to their behavior when the arrivals were West Africans.

Second, the Desfouilleuse document, parts of which were quoted in Q68, is wholly concerned with explaining why this former settler abandoned his concession as a result of the failure of the Compagnie's officials in Mauritius and, in particular, the then governor Maupin, to provide him with the slaves he felt he deserved. The Desfouilleuse document mentions all the vessels which are definitely known to have brought slaves to Mauritius between June 1729 and February 1730,[24] and the author complains of his treatment on each occasion:

> *Méduse* (first distribution: "un noir et une negresse"; second distribution: "seulement une negritte"); *Indien* (∅ slaves); *Royal-Philippe* (∅ slaves); and finally the *Saint-Pierre* ("un moyen noir galeux"). (ANC C4, carton 86, liasse 1731)

It is most improbable that the author of this detailed document could or would have omitted mention of the *Sirène* if it had indeed disembarked any slaves at Mauritius. A further piece of evidence is Q75, which noted in June 1732 that "toutes les traites de Madagascar ont été pour vous [= Reunion]."[25]

Légère, November ( ), 1731:

Chaudenson cites Lougnon (1958:61) whose information coincides with Reu to Cie, December 20, 1731 (*CBI* 1933:161). However, the information from Mauritius is that 18, not 24, disembarked:

Q81 Mau to Reu, November 15, 1731:
> Mr. Morphy [captain of the *Légère*] a mouillé en ce port le neuf du présent; nous ne retenons de sa carguaison en esclaves que six noirs pour les travaux, six négresses et six négrillons. (*RT* 7:78)

Support for the figure of 18 rather than 24 can also be found in *RT* (7:131). As there were 150 slaves on board the *Légère* when she left Antongil (*CBI* 1933: 161), and as 126 were landed in Reunion (Lougnon 1958:61), it would appear that 24 was the number *not* disembarked at Reunion rather than the number who left the ship at Mauritius, i.e., six mortalities out of 150 would be well below the average.

Subtile, September 16, 1732:

The *Subtile* obtained 90 slaves in Madagascar in the early part of 1732 but visited Mahé (India) before reaching Mauritius in mid-September where 72 Malagasies disembarked (*CBI* 1933:20). Chaudenson does not mention their arrival.

Saint-Jean l'Evangéliste (Saint-Paul), April 21, 1733:

Chaudenson cites Lougnon (1958:111; in fact, p. 114), but the latter indicates only that the *Saint-Jean l'Evangéliste* collected 57 slaves at Fort Dauphin before visiting both islands. Chaudenson provides no evidence that any of these slaves disembarked at Mauritius. This was originally a Portuguese vessel which the Reunion authorities had confiscated in May 1732. They appointed a Frenchman as the ship's captain and used her for two trips to Madagascar before she was condemned as unseaworthy. Thus, this ship took her orders from the Reunion authorities rather than from the Compagnie. Given that Reunion was attempting to increase the numbers of slaves there as fast as possible at this time, it is hardly to be supposed that the one vessel over whose movements they had complete control would be used to supply their rivals in Mauritius with slaves (*CBI* 1933:41, 145-46).

Saint-Jean l'Evangéliste (Saint-Paul), December 8, 1733:

This vessel left Madagascar with 104 Africans from Mozambique transferred from the *Vierge de Grâce,* and with 27 Malagasies. It called at Mauritius on December 8, 1733 and left for Reunion the following day. It reached Reunion with 108 slaves on December 19, 1733 (Lougnon 1958:114). Chaudenson (*Genèse,* p. 46) writes that this vessel "laisee à l'île de France 23 esclaves sur les 131 qu'il transportait" and cites Lougnon (1958:114), who makes no mention of any of these slaves having disembarked at Mauritius, nor have I found any support for this in any other document. For the reasons set out in the preceding paragraph (see entry dated April 21, 1733), it is particularly unlikely that the *Saint-Jean l'Evangéliste* would have allowed any slaves to disembark at Mauritius unless the Reunion authorities had expressly instructed the captain to do so. In addition, it may be noted that the *Vierge de Grâce* originally had 368 Mozambique slaves on board. Of the 264 who remained after the transfer of 104 to the *Saint-Jean l'Evangéliste,* 117 had died before the vessel reached Reunion (Lougnon 1958:83-84). It would not be surprising, therefore, if it should turn out that the difference between the 131 slaves on the *Saint-Jean l'Evangéliste* at Madagascar (of whom 104 were Africans transferred from the *Vierge de Grâce*) and the 108 who subsequently reached Reunion was attributable to mortality on the journey rather than to any having left the ship at Mauritius.

In addition, it must be noted that the figure of zero appears in Table 5 under Chaudenson for this vessel only because Chaudenson has taken the 23 slaves he assumes to have been landed from this ship to have come from Mozambique rather than Madagascar (in line with the mathematical probabilities). Finally, it may be noted that I have not found the term "Mozambique" applied to any slave in Mauritius, in the parish registers or in any other documents, prior to a January 1737 reference to a number of slaves who died soon after arriving from Mozambique earlier the same month on the *Jupiter* (MA KA3; *RT* 7:274).

Méduse, December 15, 1733:

The *Méduse*, transporting slaves and cattle from Madagascar, was wrecked off the north coast of Mauritius in December 1733. Thirty-nine slaves were saved from the wreckage (Lougnon 1958:87). Chaudenson does not mention this in *Genèse*.

Diane, January 1, 1735:

Chaudenson cites Lougnon (1958:74), but Lougnon does not say how many slaves were on board the *Diane* or were landed in Mauritius, and Chaudenson gives no other source for the figure of 54. It is certain, however, that as many slaves as were on the *Diane* disembarked at Mauritius, because the Reunion authorities complained to the Compagnie about this (*CBI* 1933:271).

Astrée, January 13, 1735:

Chaudenson cites Lougnon (1958:81) where Lougnon indicates only that "une vingtaine" (about 20) slaves were on the *Astrée* when she left Madagascar. Thus, procedure (1) (B2.4, p. 187) applies. Lougnon (*CBI* 1933:lviii) indicates elsewhere that none of these slaves went to Reunion.

Reine, August 5, 1735:

According to Lougnon (1958:99), the *Reine* reached Mauritius on August 5, 1735 and 24 slaves disembarked. This vessel is not mentioned in *Genèse*.

Atalante, September 21, 1735:

From the *Atalante*, "16 noirs, 1 femme, 5 negrillons, 2 negrittes" disembarked on September 21, 1735 (MA OA 100F). According to Lougnon (1958:98), this vessel had spent the preceding months at Madagascar. This shipment is not mentioned in *Genèse*.

192 BAKER

Jupiter, December 29, 1735:
The date and details are contained in Lougnon and Toussaint (1937:155). This shipment is not mentioned in *Genèse.*

One additional doubt remains. According to Lougnon:

Q82 La *Diane* et la *Méduse* ... ramenèrent de Madagascar, de 1732 à 1735, en une quinzaine de voyages, plus de 1,300 esclaves, *desquels moins de 200 furent déposés à l'Ile de France,* et plus de 1,100 à Bourbon. (*CBI* 1933:xxi; italics added)

According to the figures in Table 5, these two vessels brought 270 slaves to Mauritius within that period.

B2.4.2 Arrivals from India

So far as is known, there were no Indians in Mauritius before 1728. Arrivals for the period 1728-35 are set out in Table 6 (p. 193). I have separated slaves from paid artisans throughout since there is nothing to suggest that the two groups formed a single community. However, the majority of both the slaves and the artisans would almost certainly have been speakers of Dravidian languages though there were at least a few from Bengali-speaking areas of India (see note 25).

Chaudenson (*Genèse,* p. 53) gives a total of 485 *Esclaves (ou travailleurs) indiens.* In this, his arithmetic appears to be at fault, since the correct total, according to the information he gives in *Genèse,* pp. 44-47, should be 481, as in Table 6.

Indian arrivals in 1730 are given by Chaudenson (*Genèse,* p. 53) as 132 (rather than the 45 shown under Chaudenson in Table 6), and in 1731 he notes 73 (as opposed to 156 = 83 + 73 in Table 6).[26] Differences in Table 6 are detailed in the following, again in chronological order:

Sirène, March 24, 1729:
I am satisfied that the total of 208 given as having arrived on the *Mars* and on the *Sirène* is a reasonable estimate in light of the evidence currently available to this author, but I have reservations as to the details.[27]

Indien, October ( ), 1730:
This is the Indian whose departure is mentioned in Q74 above.

Saint-Joseph, April 4, 1731:

Q83 Mau to Reu, May 12, 1731:
Nous avons reçu 50 coulis, 15 maçons, un charpentier et un forgeron malabares. Nous vous envoyons cinq maçons: cy-joint copie collationnée de leur engagement. (*RT* 7:72)

Royal-Philippe, November 24, 1731:
These four Indian slaves were sent to Reunion by Maupin on the *Royal-Philippe*

The Contested Aspects of the Peopling of Mauritius 193

Table 6
Indian Arrivals and Departures, Mauritius, 1728-35

Date	Ship*	Chaudenson Slaves and Non-Slaves	Baker Slaves	Baker Non-Slaves
Nov 11, 1728	*Mars*	28	28†	
Mar 24, 1729	*Sirène*	180	90	90
Nov ( ), 1729	*Indien*	10	10	
Nov 12, 1729	*Royal-Philippe*	40	40	
Mar ( ), 1730	*Saint-Pierre* (see note 24)	45	45	
Oct ( ), 1730	*Indien*:			
	B: 1 Indian slave taken to Reunion		-1	
Apr 4, 1731	*Saint-Joseph*:			
	C: 50 coolies, 15 maçons, 40 esclaves dont 18 seulement restent	83		
	B: as above but with the addition of a carpenter and a blacksmith; and minus 5 of the masons who went to Reunion			
Nov 19, 1731	*Royal-Philippe*	73	18	62
Nov 24, 1731	*Royal-Philippe*:		38	35
	B: took 4 Indian slaves belonging to Maupin to Reunion		-4	
Apr 30, 1732	*Saint-Pierre*:			
	B: took 9 *lascars* back to Pondichery	12	-9	
Mar ( ), 1733	*Saint-Joseph*			12
Mar ( ), 1735	*Saint-Pierre*:			
	C: 10 esclaves indiens	10	5e	
	Total (in part, estimated)	481	269	190
			459	

* Where figures are disputed, details are provided.
† ANC C2 v9 f180 gives this figure as 27.
e Figure is an estimate.

in November 1731 (*RT* 7:117).

Saint-Pierre, April 30, 1732:
At least some of the Indian artisans returned to India when their contracts had expired, as the following quotation indicates:

Q84 Mau to Reu, April 30, 1732:
Nous renvoyons à Pondichery le tendel et les neuf lascars qui servoient dans cette isle et dont le tems est expiré. (*RT* 7:125)

Saint-Pierre, March ( ), 1735:
Chaudenson cites Lougnon (1958:111), but the latter writes only: "Armé pour les îles. Y porte des tissus et une dizaine d'esclaves." As Lougnon does not indicate how many of these slaves went to which island, one can only follow procedure (2) as per B2.4 (p. 187).

B2.4.3 Tables 7, 8, and 9 (pp. 195-98)
It would be well to begin by stressing what these tables do *not* show. First, various "minor slave movements" are omitted because my information on them is incomplete. These are of several kinds:

1. Some slaves became maroons. There is reason to suppose that Malagasies were more disposed to become maroons than other slaves because for them there existed the possibility of constructing or appropriating a boat and sailing back to Madagascar. However, there were also West African and Indian maroons before 1735.[28]
2. Slaves (and non-slaves) involved in criminal proceedings were frequently required to appear in court in Reunion. In a few cases, documents merely mention, without specifying the reason, that a particular slave left for Reunion. In cases where the reason is not found in some other document, there is no way of determining whether this was a temporary absence (for a court appearance, as above) or a permanent departure such as (3), (4), or (5) below.
3. Of the fairly substantial number of settlers who abandoned their concessions in Mauritius and moved to Reunion before the end of 1735, some were allowed to take their slaves with them. A letter from Mauritius to the Compagnie in France dated March 17, 1731 indicates that more than 40 privately-owned slaves had left the island for Reunion in this way during the previous eight months (ANC C4 vl).
4. There are a few examples of slaves being sent to Reunion as "gifts"—in double quotation marks, as it is not always possible to distinguish them from category (5).
5. There was a certain amount of illegal slave dealing from Mauritius to Reunion. Lougnon and Toussaint (1937:185, note 116) note that La Bourdonnais was

The Contested Aspects of the Peopling of Mauritius   195

Table 7
Summary of Non-French Arrivals less Departures, Mauritius, 1727-35

Date	SLAVES					TOTAL SLAVES	Total West Africans	Indian Non-Slaves	Total Indians	TOTAL NON-FRENCH
	Madagascar	Gorée	Juda	India						
Present on: Jan 1, 1727	30	0	0	0		30	0	0	0	30
Arrived in:										
1727	20	0	0	0		20	0	0	0	20
	50	0	0	0		50	0	0	0	50
1728			0	28		28	0	0	28	28
	50	0	0	28		28				
1729		0	178	28			178	0	28	78
				90		268		90	180	358
				40		40			40	40
				10		10			10	10
	50		178	168		396	178	90	258	486
1730		248		45		293	248		45	293
		260				260	260			260
		-32		-1		-33	-32		-1	-33
		476	178	212		916	654	90	302	1,006
1731	50	29		18		65	29	62	80	127
	18			38		38		35	73	73
				-4		-4			-4	-4
	68	505	178	264		1,015	683	187	451	1,202
1732	72					72		-9	-9	63
	140	505	178	264		1,087	683	178	442	1,265

(continued)

(Table 7 continued):

Date (brought forward):	Madagascar	SLAVES Gorée	Juda	India	TOTAL SLAVES	Total West Africans	Indian Non-Slaves	Total Indians	TOTAL NON-FRENCH
1733	140	505	178	264	1,087	683	178	442	1,265
	112				112				112
	39				39				39
		12			12	12	12	12	12
	291	505	178	264	1,238	683	190	454	1,428
		12			12	12			12
1734	291	517	178	264	1,250	695	190	454	1,440
Arrived by: Jun 4, 1735	54				54				54
	18			5	23			5	23
	363	517	178	269	1,327	695	190	459	1,517
Arrived between: Jun 5, 1735 and Dec 31, 1735	65				65				65
	24				24				24
	24				24				24
	10				10				10
	486	517	178	269	1,450	695	190	459	1,640

The Contested Aspects of the Peopling of Mauritius 197

Table 8
Approximate Composition of the Slave Population and the Total Non-French Population
at the End of Each Year 1727-35 (based on Table 7)

| Date | SLAVES | | | | All Slaves | Total W. Africans | Indian Non-Slaves | Total Indians | Total Non-French |
	Madagascar	Gorée	Juda	India					
Present on Jan 1, 1727	100% 100%	0% 0%	0% 0%	0% 0%	(100% = 30) (100%)	0% (0%)	0%	(0%)	(100% = 30)
Dec 31, 1727	100% 100%	0% 0%	0% 0%	0% 0%	(100% = 50) (100%)	0% (0%)	0%	(0%)	(100% = 50)
Dec 31, 1728	64% 64%	0% 0%	0% 0%	36% 36%	(100% = 78) (100%)	0% (0%)	0%	(36%)	(100% = 78)
Dec 31, 1729	13% 10%	0% 0%	45% 37%	42% 35%	(100% = 396) (81%)	45% (37%)	18%	(53%)	(100% = 486)
Dec 31, 1730	6% 5%	52% 47%	19% 18%	23% 21%	(100% = 916) (91%)	71% (65%)	9%	(30%)	(100% = 1,006)
Dec 31, 1731	7% 6%	50% 42%	17% 15%	26% 22%	(100% = 1,015) (84%)	67% (57%)	16%	(38%)	(100% = 1,202)
Dec 31, 1732	13% 11%	47% 40%	16% 14%	24% 21%	(100% = 1,087) (86%)	63% (54%)	14%	(35%)	(100% = 1,265)
Dec 31, 1733	24% 20%	41% 35%	14% 13%	21% 19%	(100% = 1,238) (87%)	55% (48%)	13%	(32%)	(100% = 1,428)
Dec 31, 1734	23% 20%	42% 36%	14% 13%	21% 18%	(100% = 1,250) (87%)	56% (48%)	13%	(31%)	(100% = 1,440)
Jun 4, 1735	27% 24%	39% 34%	14% 11%	20% 18%	(100% = 1,327) (87%)	53% (45%)	13%	(31%)	(100% = 1,517)
Dec 31, 1735	33% 30%	36% 31%	12% 11%	19% 16%	(100% = 1,450) (88%)	48% (42%)	12%	(28%)	(100% = 1,640)

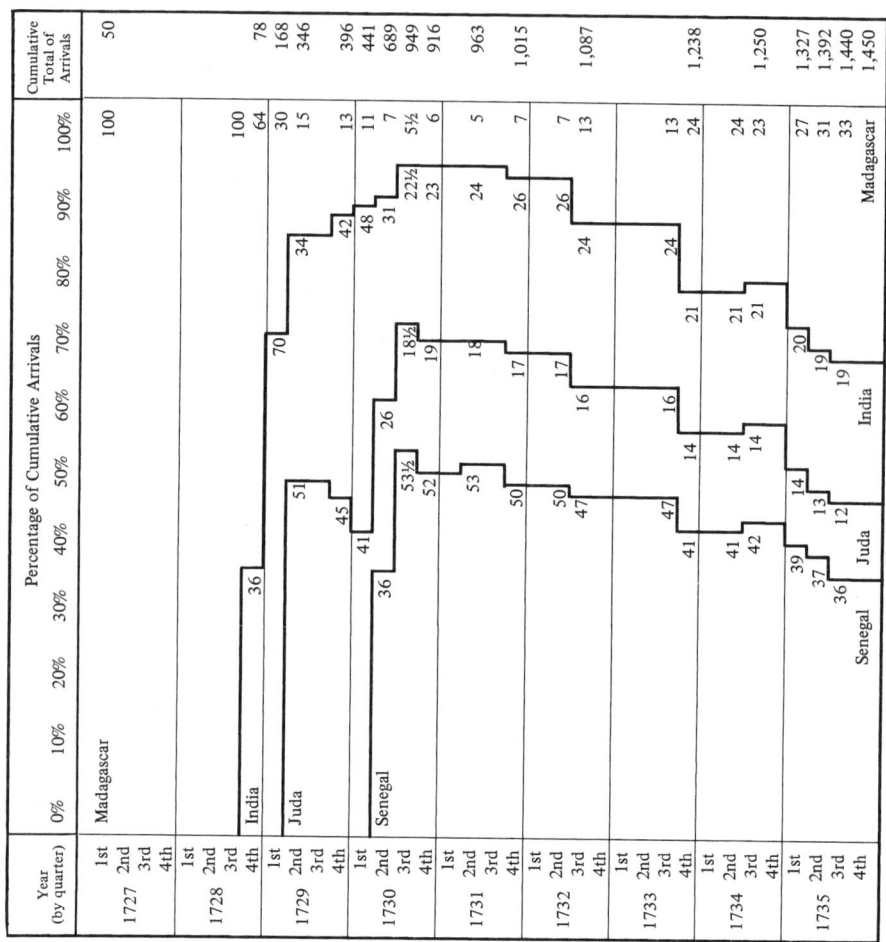

Table 9
Approximate Composition by Place of Origin of Slave Population of Mauritius, 1727-35

personally involved in this trade. Earlier, one of the many complaints made against Maupin was:

Q85   No. 7 Que led. Sr Maupin a encore fait passer a l'Isle de Bourbon une quantité de noirs sans aucune facture ny connoissement par les vaisseaux *Le Duc de Chartres*, *La Diane* et *l'Indien*.... C'est le commerce clandestin de noirs. (document dated March 5, 1731; ANC C4, carton 86, liasse 1731)

Second, the information relating to free Indian artisans is far from complete. Table 7 shows only one case where a group of such Indians returned to India on the expiration of their contracts. There may well have been others who did not choose to remain in Mauritius permanently. In addition, there is evidence of Indian artisans moving between Mauritius and Reunion (and vice versa) (cf. the section following Q47 in B2.2), but lack of precise details forces me to omit this.

Third, Table 7 ignores births and deaths altogether. An excess of deaths over births appears to have been usual in slave communities generally (Curtin 1969: 28ff.).

Fourth, a group of 87 slaves owned by the Compagnie in Mauritius *returned* from Reunion to Mauritius on the *Jupiter* in October 1735 (Lougnon and Toussaint 1937:155; FOM G^1 505). I have yet to determine when they traveled to Reunion.

While the figures given for the end of 1729 in Table 7 agree with those of the census taken in November of that year, it will be clear that, because of all the above-listed factors, the further one moves from 1729, the greater will be the tendency for Table 7 to overstate the numbers of slaves actually present in captivity. The chief value of Table 7 is, thus, not so much the figures themselves but what the comparison of the figures in the different columns tells us about the likely composition of the non-French population during this period. For this reason, the same information is presented in percentage form in Tables 8 and 9.

Tables 8 and 9 suggest that:

Malagasies formed an absolute majority of slaves, and of the total non-French population, up to the beginning of 1729.

Senegalese slaves (from Gorée) formed half or a little over half of the total slave population for two years from mid-1730, and were numerically the largest group from a single territory, of both the slaves and the total non-French population, from mid-1730 to the end of 1735.

Benin slaves (from Juda) formed an absolute majority of slaves for a few months in 1729 and remained the largest group of slaves from a single territory until the end of that year.

West African slaves (from Gorée and Juda together) formed an absolute majority of the slave population from mid-1730 to mid-1735, and an absolute majority of the total non-French population from mid-1730 to the last quarter of 1733.

Indians briefly formed an absolute majority of the slaves at the beginning of 1729, and Indian artisans and slaves together formed an absolute majority of the total non-French population from early 1729 to mid-1730.

Chaudenson (*Genèse*, p. 54) gives a total of 1,463 non-French arrivals for the period 1721-35, comprising 481 West Africans, 485 Indians (including artisans), 474 Malagasies, and 23 from Mozambique. However, as noted above, the figures for Malagasies (should be 494) and Indians (should be 481) are not consistent with the information given elsewhere in *Genèse*. Even with these adjustments, Chaudenson's figures are not strictly comparable with those in Table 7 in that he covers the period from 1721 and thus includes all 65 Malagasies who arrived in 1722, whereas Table 7 begins with the 30 of these who had survived in captivity to January 1727. If the difference of 35 is deducted from the amended version of Chaudenson's figures, a fair comparison can be made, as in Table 10 (p. 201).

As can be seen, the net effect of all the errors and omissions noted earlier is small as far as Indians and Malagasies are concerned. However, in the case of West Africans, the difference is very substantial. This results from the following:

1. Contrary to the evidence of the 1729 census, Chaudenson assumes that half of the 178 (his estimate) slaves from Juda disembarked at Reunion.

    Difference: 89

2. Chaudenson interprets the evidence concerning the numbers who arrived on the *Diane* in a manner different from those who have personally examined the relevant documents.

    Difference: 86

3. Chaudenson arbitrarily assumes that 38 of those who arrived on the *Diane* died soon afterward. This figure is not supported by documentary evidence.

    Difference: 38

4. The number of adult Senegalese who left on the *Indien* was shown above to be one less than the figure given by Chaudenson.

    Difference: 1

    Total: 214

By failing to include these slaves, Chaudenson's "pourcentages réels" (*Genèse*, p. 54) suggest that West Africans formed about 9 percent less of the total non-French population at the end of 1735 than do the more soundly-based percentages in Table 8. Chaudenson concludes his section on West African immigration with the words:

Q86   Les esclaves de l'Afrique de l'Ouest ne représentèrent donc en fait qu'à peine un tiers de ceux qui arrivèrent à l'île de France et non 60% [29]; si l'on ajoute qu'ils venaient de régions très différentes (Guinée et Sénégal), on ne voit pas pourquoi ils auraient dû

Table 10

Slaves and Non-French Artisans in Mauritius, 1727-35*

Origin	Numbers			B – C	Percentages		
	B	C	G		B	C	G
West Africa	695	481	(481)	+214	42.38	33.31	(32.87)
India (slaves)	269	459 481	(485)	-22	16.40 27.99	33.31	(33.15)
India (artisans)	190				11.59		
Madagascar	486	459	(474)	+27	29.63	31.79	(32.39)
Mozambique	0	23	(23)	-23	0.00	1.59	(1.59)
Totals	1,640	1,444	(1,463)	+196	100.00	100.00	(100.00)

B = Baker; C = Chaudenson; G = *Genèse*, p. 54)

---

* These dates include those present *on* January 1, 1727, as well as all those who arrived during the years 1727-35.

jouer dans la genèse du parler local un rôle plus important que les Malgaches ou les Indiens. (*Genèse*, p. 54)

What matters is not the proportion of West Africans at one particular moment (e.g., June 4, 1735 in *Towards* or December 31, 1735 in *Genèse*), but the percentage they formed over a period of years. Tables 8 and 9 show clearly that West Africans formed a significantly greater proportion of both the slave population and the total non-French population than Chaudenson's "à peine un tiers" would have the reader believe, from mid-1729 until some time after the end of 1735,[30] and that for almost all of this period they formed an absolute majority of the slaves. As for their having come from "régions très différentes," it should be noted, in the context of Goodman's (1964) theory *only,* that slaves from two different French trading posts on the West African coast might have been exposed to essentially the same "West African Pidgin French."

There can be no doubt that, for a few years, a majority of the slaves in Mauritius were from West Africa. This is one aspect in which the peopling of this island differs from that of Reunion and resembles, during an early period of the settlement of the colony only, that of the French Antilles. The possible linguistic significance of this will be discussed in the next section.

NOTES

1. Here and wherever there is conflicting information, if one source indicates having consulted primary sources while another does not, I will assume that the former is more likely to be correct (i.e., in this case, Kaeppelin).

2. There is ample proof in parish registers and other documents that all but Mme Didion and Mme Rivont were present after this date. The Didion family was living in Reunion at the time of the 1735 census (*RT* 3:101). However, the only evidence of Mme Rivont's presence in Mauritius is that noted in Table 1 (see under March 11, 1725).

3. It took about five months on the average for a letter to reach the Mascarenes from France. Several copies were made of each letter, and these were dispatched by different ships to avoid the problems which would otherwise result if a ship were to be delayed or to change its destination.

4. According to an *arrêté du Conseil Provincial* of June 5, 1726 (during Lenoir's visit), the population then included:

38	people *"au service de la Comp^{ie}"* (including the governor, officers, and *"divers ateliers"*)	
20	slaves *("tant hommes que femmes et enfants")*	
106	soldiers (2 companies of 53 men)	
164	Total	(*RHL* 1:516-17)

This is the ultimate source of the suggestion that 160 people arrived on the *Atalante* and *Diane* in 1722 which appears in Chaudenson (*Genèse*, p. 44) as: *"Selon certaines sources* [Chaudenson cites none], *il y aurait eu 160 survivants."* As Kuczynski (1948-49.2:750) puts it, rather succinctly: "160 is Pitot's figure. He gives E Piston as his source. Piston in fact refers to 160 people including the Governor, 30 men, 20 slaves and two platoons of 53 men. Piston refers to 1726."

5. De Hauville dismissed Wirtz, the senior Swiss officer based in Port Louis, during De Nyon's absence in Reunion. On his return, De Nyon immediately reinstated Wirtz. De Hauville never forgave De Nyon for this act.

6. Jean Coste acted as courier between De Nyon and De Hauville on several occasions, a role otherwise performed by: soldiers; Reunion (free) Creoles; or the Malagasy slave belonging to the Lazarist Borthon. It is fairly clear from Q26, as well as from references to Coste elsewhere in this correspondence, that he did not belong to any of these three categories. It is conceivable that he was a European *domestique*.

7. Chaudenson (*Genèse*, p. 42) misinterprets Lougnon in suggesting that all the passengers on the *Bourbon* disembarked at Mauritius. In fact, Lougnon (1958:42) wrote: "Le *Bourbon* ... Amène aux îles une trentaine de soldats." I am not aware of anything to suggest that any members of three of the families mentioned by Lougnon—Gaucher, Jupin, and Verdière—disembarked at Mauritius. (People with these surnames were living in Reunion in 1735.)

8. On p. 45 of *Genèse* against the same wrong date (August 14, 1729) marked with a symbol to indicate that these Réunionnais were not mentioned in *Towards*, Chaudenson sees fit to write under "arrivants": "36 Créoles de Bourbon. On espère que cette omission n'est pas volontaire!" Taken together with "un fait parfaitement connu" in Q46, the impression is created that this is one of the better-known facts of Mauritian history. It is not. Nor is there any reason why it should be.

9. Lougnon (1958:46) writes: "Emmène à Maurice le directeur générale Pierre Benoît, le sieur de Belcourt [*sic*], et 35 créoles qui vont donner la chasse aux marrons." As Chaudenson gives the same page reference, it would appear that he has assumed Bellecourt to be a man born in Reunion. In fact, Bellecourt was one of the most notorious residents of Mauritius at this time who was obliged to travel to Reunion on several occasions in connection with criminal proceedings brought against him. He came to Mauritius directly from France as an army officer in ca. 1724 (Lougnon 1956:253).

10. I have not pursued the analysis of the parish registers beyond this date because the frequency with which ethnic adjectives are applied to slaves declines substantially thereafter.

11. Table 3 implies that Compagnie slaves accounted for little more than 15 percent of the total. The censuses of 1735 and 1738, while not quite as complete as one might wish, give grounds for supposing that the proportion of slaves belonging to the Compagnie increased from about 22 percent in 1735 to nearly 39 percent in 1738 (FOM G^1 505).

12. The text of Q15 was reproduced in *Towards*. Chaudenson must be aware, therefore, that this conflicts somewhat with his claim that the Reunion slaves were "chargé d'encadrer la première immigration servile malgache introduite dans l'île" (extract from Q54(1)). Chaudenson makes no mention of the Reunion Council's decision of October 2, 1722 (Q15) in either *Genèse* or *Créoles*.

13. Quite a number of the RC terms for non-European flora and fauna are of Malagasy origin (cf. *Lexique*, pp. 495-535) and some of these are attested in local (Réunionnais) usage by Du Bois (1672). Thus, it is likely that certain plants, fish, etc., would have been known both to Malagasy slaves and to speakers of "Bourbonnais" by essentially the same names.

14. While only two such deaths—those of Courtois and Hayec—are noted in Table 1, Du Cros (1728:18) suggests that ten Frenchmen had been killed in a single encounter. Du Cros learned of this from a soldier. While the account was probably based on some actual event, the details and, in particular, the number of mortalities could well be an exaggeration. For this reason I have excluded it from Table 1.

15. The first major shipment of slaves from Mozambique to the Mascarenes appears to have taken place in 1733 when the *Vierge de Grâce* obtained 368, more than 100 of whom had died

before the vessel reached Reunion (Lougnon 1958:83-84). There does not seem to have been any substantial landing of Mozambique slaves in Mauritius until January 2, 1737 when the *Jupiter* brought 102 (Lougnon and Toussaint 1937:155). The earliest use of "Mozambique" as an ethnic adjective in the parish registers also dates from January 1737.

16. This term is defined by Labat (1728.4:233) in the following passage: "Lorsqu'ils sont piece d'Inde, c'est-à-dire qui ne sont pas au dessus de trente ans, ni au dessous de dix, à qui il ne manque ni doigts, ni yeux, ni oreilles, ni dents, & qui ne sont ni bossus ni boiteux."

17. Filliot (1974:187); Chaudenson (*Créoles*, p. 45, note 3) writes erroneously that "les dernières immigrations de Noirs de l'Afrique de l'Ouest remontent aux années 1730."

18. During the first half of the eighteenth century, the term "Guinée" was applied in Mauritius to what is known in English as the Slave Coast, excluding Sénégambia. A writer on Compagnie affairs in 1746 applies this term more widely: "On comprend sous le nom de Guinée cette étenduë de Côtes en Afrique situées depuis la Riviere de Sierralionne jusqu'as Cap de Bonne-Espérance" (Du Fresne de Francheville 1746:125). In the second half of the eighteenth century the term in Mauritius appears to have been applied to the whole of West Africa (including Senegambia) as in Q65.

19. An apparent reference to the Portuguese enclave of Macao. (In modern MC /makaw/ is a pejorative term for a person of Chinese descent.)

20. I have not found this term used in any other document nor have I been able to establish to what territory or ethnic group it refers. (Perhaps an error for Ma*n*ille in the Philippines?)

21. La Bourdonnais' immediate successor P. F. B. David (governor from 1746 to 1753) had spent almost all his adult life (from ca. 1728) working for the Compagnie in Senegal before taking up his appointment in Mauritius. (See also Filliot 1974:186.)

22. Several copies were normally made of letters exchanged between the Compagnie's representatives in France and the Mascarenes, each copy being sent on a different ship. In making several copies by hand of the same letter, it seems likely that errors were occasionally made.

23. The only exception would appear to be the 18 Malagasies retained from the *Légère* in November 1731.

24. In the Desfouilleuse document, February 1730 is given as the month during which the *Saint-Pierre* arrived. Lougnon (1958:108) gives the date as "Mars (?)." I have followed Lougnon in Table 6.

25. For example, 13 of the Indian slaves sent from Pondichery on the *Sirène* in 1729 had been sent there earlier from Chandernagor (near Calcutta) (Pon to Cha, February 28, 1729; *CPC* 1:10).

26. Chaudenson appears to have included the 1731 *Saint-Joseph* arrivals in his 1730 figure, but instead of adding 18 slaves to the 50 coolies and 15 maçons (= 83, which if added to the 45 who arrived on the *Saint-Pierre* would give 128), he appears to have deducted the 18 who remained from the total of 40 who arrived (= 22, which if added to the 50 coolies, 15 maçons, and the 45 on the *Saint-Pierre* would give 132, the figure Chaudenson gives for 1730).

27. These reservations are: (1) see Table 6, note †; (2) I am doubtful of the justification for assuming the same mortality rate for paid artisans as for slaves; (3) my reading of the available evidence is that the approximately "400 Indiens" to whom Chaudenson (*Genèse*, p. 45) refers include the 27 or 28 (Table 6, note †) for Lenoir's plantation in Mauritius sent earlier on the *Mars* but may perhaps exclude the 13 from Bengal mentioned in note 25, 173 slaves for individual plantation owners in Reunion, 100 slaves 8 to 18 years old from the Pondichery area specifically for Mauritius, and either 95 (*CSP* 1:238) or 99 (*RT* 7:187) artisans identified as destined for Mauritius (*CSP* 1:238). The numbers bound for Mauritius thus range from 195 (100 + 95) to 212 (13 + 100 + 99). If 12 percent is deducted for mortalities during the journey, the respective figures are 173 and 187, and the average of these—180—equals the figure proposed by Chaudenson (*Genèse*, p. 53).

28. Trials of recaptured maroons to 1735 show that these included slaves of all the main ethnic groups (MA JB1-3).

29. The 60 percent refers to the early pages of *Towards* in which I attempted to estimate the likely composition of the slave population *to* (rather than *on*) June 4, 1735 (the date La Bourdonnais arrived in Mauritius to take up his position as governor of the Mascarenes). The figures in *Towards* are not comparable with those in *Genèse* for two reasons, neither of which Chaudenson mentions. First, the period of time under consideration differs by seven months (ending June 4, 1735 in *Towards* compared with December 31, 1735 in *Genèse;* all known arrivals during those seven months were Malagasies). Second, Chaudenson is basically concerned with arrivals, whereas *Towards* was concerned with survivals. In 1976 I did assume what now appears to be an unreasonably high rate of mortality, but the purpose of this— reconciliation with La Bourdonnais' mid-1735 figures—was made clear. Chaudenson's figures are not strictly those of arrivals. Apart from various errors to which attention is drawn in the text, Chaudenson excludes from his figures West Africans he knows or assumes to have died after arrival, yet he includes Malagasies known to have died, become maroons, or otherwise disappeared by 1725 or 1726.

30. Whereas Filliot (1974:187) has shown that West Africans continued to arrive until 1767, and whereas Toussaint (1967) has established that the great majority of slaves introduced into Mauritius in the period 1773-94 were from Mozambique (cf. Baker 1972:36, note 6), the relative numerical strength of the different ethnic groups among the slave population from 1735 on has yet to be determined. The information on slave arrivals given by La Bourdonnais in 1740 (Lougnon and Toussaint 1937:155-56), taken together with such details of the movements of the vessels involved as I have been able to assemble, suggest that, of the cumulative total of slave arrivals to the beginning of 1740, about 42 percent were Malagasies, 25 percent were West Africans, 18 percent were from Mozambique, and 12 percent were Indians; I have not been able to find any clear indication of the origin of a further 3 percent. These figures should be regarded as provisional.

B3
Links between MC and Other French Creoles: Some Evidence from Early Texts

B3.1 The "Bourbonnais" Contribution to Other Indian Ocean Creoles

In 1974, Chaudenson claimed that non-Creolophone slaves introduced into Mauritius in the early years of settlement would have found themselves in an exclusively "Bourbonnais"-speaking society. The relevant passage was quoted earlier and is repeated here for convenience:

Q87 Or, l'Ile de France est peuplée d'abord et surtout à partir de l'Ile Bourbon. Les esclaves introduits dans l'île, en plus grand nombre après 1730, se trouvent donc en présence d'une colonie homogène sur le plan linguistique, puisque maître et esclaves déjà installés y parlent une seule langue: le créole "bourbonnais." (*Lexique*, p. 446)

If this had not been the case, MC could only have been, initially at least, a direct continuation of "Bourbonnais." Indeed, Chaudenson appeared to take the view that it was RC which had diverged most from "Bourbonnais," due to the strong influence of (varieties of) French in Reunion, and that it was Rodrigues Creole (RoC) which, of all the Indian Ocean Creoles, had probably remained closest to "Bourbonnais" (*Lexique*, pp. 1117-18). This position was at odds with the fact that the text of ca. 1722 includes features of modern RC which have never been attested in MC, thus suggesting that RC has changed little during two and a half centuries—an anomaly to which attention was first drawn by Hull (1975:9 [1979]). This now being generally recognized, there is no reason to use two names where one would suffice, and I will thus refer hereafter only to "RC," prefacing this with an adjective or date where appropriate.

While seeming to indicate that he had not modified his earlier position in any significant way—"Nous n'avons donc pas lieu de revenir sur l'hypothèse présentée en 1972 concernant le rôle du bourbonnais dans la genèse du créole de l'île de France" (*Genèse*, p. 55)—in another 1979 publication Chaudenson revealed that his view of the nature of the contribution of early RC to MC had in fact changed considerably:

Q88 L'étude du peuplement conduit en effet à penser que la langue parlée à Bourbon avant 1721 ... a joué un rôle important dans la genèse du parler mauricien en raison du nombre et du rôle social des colons et des esclaves venus de l'île voisine et qui utilisaient ce "bourbonnais." Le créole mauricien peut à cet égard être considéré comme un parler de "deuxième génération" [1] (c'est-à-dire lui-même issu d'un créole), ce qui conduit à limiter le rôle et l'importance du groupe des Africains de l'Ouest arrivés certes quelques années seulement après le début de la colonisation de l'île, mais dans une situation linguistique déjà stabilisée par l'utilisation du bourbonnais qui a sans doute servi de "lingua franca" et donné un caractère particulier à la phrase première, généralement dite de pidginisation. (*Créoles*, p. 46)

Q89 Le créole de première génération [see note 1] serait dans cette hypothèse le "bourbonnais" ... le mauricien serait un créole de "seconde génération" puisqu'il se développe à partir d'une situation linguistique qui ne comporte pas que le français et des langues serviles mais, outre ces langues, un créole "importé," le bourbonnais qui sert dès le début de langue de relation et est *probablement* appris aux premiers esclaves introduits dans le pays. Nous verrons que cette hypothèse fondée sur l'approche sociohistorique se trouve vérifiée et confirmée par l'analyse linguistique comparée des documents anciens en créole et par la comparaison structurelle des parlers en cause. Les créoles des Seychelles et de Rodrigues seraient des parlers de troisième génération dans la mesure à la fois où ils apparaissent ultérieurement (un demi-siècle et plus après le mauricien) et où ils empruntent à la fois aux deux autres créoles dans le cadre d'un processus *identique* à celui du parler de deuxième génération (la relation avec le créole mauricien est certes dominante mais cependant les créoles seychellois (surtout) et rodrigais présentent avec le réunionnais des traits communs (que ne connaît parfois pas, ou plus, le mauricien) et qui ne permettent pas de mettre sérieusement en doute la relation entre les créoles français de l'océan Indien. (*Créoles*, p. 51; italics added)

It is clear from both Q88 and Q89 that now Chaudenson does not view MC as a mere continuation of early RC but rather as what emerged from a multilingual situation in which RC, French, and the languages brought by slaves were all represented. Nevertheless, the use of the verb *issu* in both Q88 and the first sentence of Q89 indicates that he regards RC as the major input to MC. This could only have been the case, however, if there had been a substantial number and/or proportion of first- and/or second-language speakers of RC in Mauritius in the period (from 1728) when the island was transformed into a multilingual society by the arrival of substantial groups of slaves of diverse origins. The evidence of Chapter B2 indicates a lack of RC speakers at the crucial time. The sociohistorical part of Chaudenson's thesis seems to be ill-founded so far as the peopling of Mauritius is concerned. Support for this, alleged to be found in the comparison of early texts of MC and RC, will be examined below.

The suggestion (in Q89) that the Creole languages of the Seychelles (SC) and Rodrigues (RoC) evolved initially in circumstances identical to those in which MC had arisen half a century earlier requires comment. Even if, as will be discussed in Chapter B4, some of the slaves who reached Mauritius from West Africa, Madagascar, and India in the period 1722-35 had had some exposure to a hypothetical "West African Pidgin French" or a specialized form of French in use on the ships which had brought them to the island, few if any could properly be described as Creolophone on arrival. By contrast, Rodrigues appears to have been peopled *exclusively* by those who were already Creolophone.

According to North-Coombes (1971:54ff.), the continuous habitation of Rodrigues dates from the arrival of Mauritian settlers in 1792. Ten years later a number of would-be settlers arrived from Reunion to where most of them quickly returned.

The only exceptions were Rochetaing and his 12 dependents who spent three years in Rodrigues before returning to Reunion in 1805 (1971:58-59). Later, following the political division of the two principal Mascarene islands and the abolition of slavery in Mauritius, some former slaves are known to have emigrated from the latter to Rodrigues.[2] Unless it were the case that the 15 slaves belonging to Rochetaing in 1804 (1971:61) were taken to Rodrigues from Reunion and remained in Rodrigues when their owner returned to Reunion—and there is nothing to suggest that such was the case[3]—it would appear that nearly everyone who settled permanently in Rodrigues was already a speaker of MC. RoC did not, then, "borrow" from MC and RC since, from 1792, it quite simply was MC. It has yet to be demonstrated that RoC possesses anything that can be traced reliably to RC—and thus to Rochetaing and his dependents—rather than to early MC.

The situation in the Seychelles was different again in that the first permanent inhabitants included free citizens and slaves from both Reunion and Mauritius (Bollée 1977a:4-5). Their descendents might, therefore, have been in a position to acquire features of both RC and MC, to evolve a "composite" Creole, before substantial numbers of non-Créolophone slaves arrived. However, whereas a small number of grammatical items which suggest RC influence on SC have been identified (cf. section A6.4), it is universally acknowledged that modern SC is far closer to MC than to any other variety of Creole French. This cannot be satisfactorily explained by the Seychelles having been administered until the early part of the present century as a dependency of Mauritius situated 1,000 miles away (see *Lexique*, p. 448). It could well be that MC speakers greatly outnumbered RC speakers fairly soon after the continuous habitation of the Seychelles began, but a detailed survey of the peopling of the archipelago is needed in order to establish whether this was in fact the case.

B3.2 Attestations of Grammatical Items Shared by MC and Other Indian Ocean Creoles or Varieties of American Creole French

The greater part of Goodman's (1964:21-95) work is devoted to "Comparative Etymologies" in which 40 items occurring in most or all of the Creoles on which he had sufficient data are discussed in detail. These include 18 verbs, nouns, or adjectives ("lexical items") and 22 "function words" and "grammatical particles" ("grammatical items"; 1964:17-18). Goodman draws attention to some seemingly remarkable similarities among the different French Creoles. However, Chaudenson has suggested with good reason that some similarities among the different French Creoles ought to be expected:

Q90 Or il est clair que, dans une étude de ce genre, les divergences entre les parlers ont au moins autant d'importance que les ressemblances; en effet, pour nous limiter aux Antilles et aux Mascareignes, ces îles furent colonisées à peu près à la même époque, par des colons français généralement originaires des mêmes provinces et qui devaient parler les mêmes dialectes; il n'y a donc pas lieu de s'étonner de constater d'évidents rapports entre ces créoles; en revanche, quand sur des points grammaticaux ou lexicaux importants ils divergent, on peut à juste titre s'interroger sur les causes de ces différences. (*Lexique,* p. 592)

Given (1) the above view; (2) the fact that there are major grammatical differences between MC and RC (see Part A and B3.2.1-B3.2.5); (3) that Chaudenson regards MC as, in some sense, a derivative of RC (cf. Q88); and (4) that Goodman's work is well known and has generally been highly regarded, it is a matter for considerable regret that Chaudenson has not yet provided an explanation of why MC and Haitian Creole (HC) happen to share a number of striking innovations (discussed below) not attested in RC. There may well be some unsatisfactory aspects to Goodman's theory—as I will suggest in Chapter B4—but neither Chaudenson nor anyone else has yet *disproved* it.

If it had been the case that MC was initially a mere continuation of early RC (cf. Q87) or that RC was the major input to MC (cf. Q88, Q89), it might reasonably be expected that there would be at least some grammatical items common to all Indian Ocean Creoles and yet absent from all varieties of American Creole French. A preliminary search suggests that the only such item may be /ban/, the marker or emphasizer of plurality (cf. Baker 1972:78).

In sections B3.2.1-B3.2.5 below, data drawn from early texts concerning /ban/ and other grammatical items will be presented. All of these items have been seen at some time, by one or more authors, as evidence of a close historical relationship either between HC and MC or between RC and other Creoles of the Indian Ocean. The items discussed are:

3.2.1 The Emphasizer of Plurality: /ban/
3.2.2 Third Person Reprise (SC, MC, HC) and the RC "Predicate Precursors"
3.2.3 The Personal Pronouns (HC, MC, RC)
3.2.4 The Negators /napa/ and /pa/ (RC, MC, HC)
3.2.5 "Predicate" Markers (RC, MC, HC)

In restricting attention almost exclusively to the HC variety of American Creole French, I wish to make it clear that I do so primarily because of the importance attached to the similarities between HC and MC by Faine and Goodman. I do not doubt, however, that there are remarkable similarities shared by other varieties of American Creole French—notably that of Louisiana—and MC. There is also a second reason for restricting attention to HC, namely, because a more varied selection of early texts is available for this than any other Creole of the region. Early texts are the only available evidence of the nature of particular French Creoles in former times. Writers of popular travel books might conceivably have been more concerned to convey something of the "quaintness" of the speech of a colony, perhaps "corrected" a little to make it more intelligible to prospective readers, than they were to provide linguists of later times with as faithful a representation of the language as they could manage.[4] Texts typeset by non-Creolophones abroad might be particularly liable to contain printing errors.[5] It is even possible that a traveler who had failed to collect suitable samples during his voyage might subsequently plagiarize other published works after his return.[6] Such dangers can, I think, be minimized by studying texts in chronological order since such irregularities will then tend to be self-evident. In spite of these reservations, I am satisfied that the great majority of the texts consulted are genuine attempts to represent accurately, within the limitation imposed by French orthographic tradition, the speech of the inhabitants of the territories concerned—except in the few cases I have drawn attention to in the notes.

The chronology of attestations is obviously a matter of importance, and I have dated texts according to when they were (probably) written rather than by their year of publication. The conventions adopted are, e.g., "1803" (thought to have been written in that year), "-1803" (written in 1803 or earlier), "1803-" (written in 1803 or later), and "-1803-" (written ca. 1803). Where, in a given territory, two or more texts bear the same year in their reference (ignoring hyphens), they are arbitrarily distinguished as, e.g., 1802a, -1802b, 1802c-, -1802d-, etc. (to identify the source of a text, see the chronological list following the bibliography).

Finally, it should be made clear that I am not claiming that there existed at one time only a single uniform variety of a particular French Creole. Several regional varieties of a French Creole may formerly have existed or may still exist in territories as large as Haiti or as mountainous as Reunion.

B3.2.1 The Emphasizer of Plurality: /ban/

Chaudenson, noting that /ban/ functions both as a plural marker and a count noun, remarks:

Q91   Ces emplois sont caractéristiques de cette zone [Indian Ocean] et les parlers de la Caraïbe ne semblent pas les connaître; *ils sont, en tout cas, anciens puisqu'on les retrouve dans les quatre parlers.* (Lexique, p. 956; italics added)

The count noun is attested in MC from the middle of the nineteenth century:

MC1 (1855) *ein band' p'tits miletons*
        'a shoal of baby mullet' (Lolliot 1855:67)

As a plural marker, i.e., without a preceding determiner, /ban/ is not attested in MC until 30 years later (consistently written *band* by Anderson):

MC2 (1885) *é li rapport trant piéce l'arzan là, av band cef prétr é zanciein*
        'And [he] brought again the 30 pieces of silver to the chief priests and elders'[7] (Anderson 1885:84)

MC3 (1885) *Lherla band soldat gouverner, condir Jésu dan palé*
'Then the soldiers of the governor took Jesus into the common hall'
(Anderson 1885:86)
MC4 (1885) *band cef prétr avec scrib é zanciein, zot mok li*
'The chief priests mocking him with the scribes and elders'
(Anderson 1885:87)

In Baissac's 1880 grammar, /ban/ is found only with a preceding indefinite article: "Une quantité, *éne bande,* qu'on prononce aussi *éne banne.* Il a répandu une quantité d'eau par terre. *Li fine fane éne bande dileau partére"* (1880: 66). (Such use of /ban/ is entirely obsolete today since this may only occur with count nouns.) The same is true of Baissac's folktales apart from *tout ça bande lamisère* 'quelles épreuves cruelles' (1888:176-77) in which it is not entirely clear whether *bande* functions as an emphasizer of plurality or should instead be glossed as 'large amount of'. In any event, there is no example of /ban/ *alone* preceding a noun as a marker of plurality in either Baissac 1880 or 1888. It thus appears that this was lacking in the speech of the *antiques nénènes* 'very old nursemaids' whom Baissac regarded as the last surviving people who still recalled the tales told before the abolition of slavery and from whom he collected his stories (1888:iii), but was present in the speech of those such as Anderson who had been born on the island two decades after the emancipation of the slaves.[8] In short, /ban/ clearly acquired its function as the marker or emphasizer of plurality during the course of the nineteenth century.

The earliest examples of /ban/ as a plural marker I have yet found in RC are in Fourcade (1930). In that text, /ban/ occurs with some frequency and thus can scarcely then have been a new feature of RC.

It seems clear from the above that /ban/ alone did not function as the plural marker at the beginning of the nineteenth century in any Indian Ocean Creole but had acquired this status in MC by 1885 at the latest. Whether this was a Mauritian innovation—a distinct possibility on the available evidence—or not, remains to be determined. However, one can at least conclude—in contrast to Chaudenson (cf. Q91)—that the presence of a grammatical (or lexical) item in all the Indian Ocean Creoles does *not* prove that this was a feature of eighteenth-century RC; and that the political separation of these territories into two (later, three) units did not prevent an innovation of the Creole of one island from being adopted into the Creole of another.

B3.2.2 Third Person Reprise (SC, MC, HC) and the RC "Predicate Precursors"
In popular French the third person masculine pronoun is frequently heard following any third person subject other than a pronoun:

F1   *Le charretier il bat ses bourrins* (Bauche 1920:156)

F2 *nos poules ils pondent bien* (Cohen 1967:392)
F3 *Ma soeur il chante* (Bollée 1977a:61, footnote)

Note that phonetically *il* is [i] preconsonantally and [il] prevocalically, while *ils* is also [i] preconsonantally but [iz] prevocalically. This pleonastic use of a third person pronoun is a long-standing feature of popular French. Something superficially similar is to be found in a number of Creoles:

In SC, the reflex is /i/ regardless of whether a consonant or a vowel follows. In most SC sentences having a third person subject (for the exceptions, see Corne 1974-75), the presence of an immediately following /i/ is obligatory, as in:

SC1 (1974) *ban solda i larg sô lake*
       'the soldiers let go his tail' (Corne 1974-75:68)
SC2 (1977) *dimiel i bô*
       'the honey is good' (Corne 1977a:35)

As the /i/ is phonetically identical to the third person singular pronoun *i* (preposed form), it can be seen as a repetition or "reprise" of the subject (Corne 1977a; but see also note 3 in Chapter A5). Note that this may follow a plural subject (SC1) and that, while this resembles popular French usage, the third person plural pronoun in SC (and in both MC and RC) is *zot*.[9]

In MC the third person singular pronoun *li* is similarly repeated after third person subjects, singular or plural (other than *li* itself), in early texts:

MC5 (1749) *ça blanc là li beaucoup malin; li couri beaucoup dans la mer là haut; mais Madagascar li là* (Grant 1886:166)[10]
MC6 (-1805) *mon paye li bon aussi*
       'my country [is] also good' (Pitot 1805:373)
MC7 (-1822) *Comper' Zaco li ramassé*
       'Brother Monkey picks [it] up' (Chrestien 1831:8)
MC8 (-1831) *Ça z'enfants là li zolis*
       'those children [are] cute' (Chrestien 1831:51)

There is thus a very close parallel between *li* reprise in early MC and *i* reprise in modern SC. However, *li* reprise appears to have been optional rather than obligatory in MC, to judge from texts from 1822 on, and it occurs with decreasing frequency in later texts. In modern MC it still occurs sporadically as in:

MC9 (1970) *Kohper Renar li fin dir: nu pu sorti dipi sizer bomateh*
       'Brother Fox had said: "We'll set off at six o'clock in the morning" '
       (Baker 1972:208)

Third person reprise is also found in early HC texts:

HC1 (1776a) *corde la li pas bon*
'the rope is not good' (Nicolson 1776:57)
HC2 (1790) *Pays moi li là*
'Mine [*sic*] country there' (Wimpffen 1817:186)

In RC, what I take to be a reflex of popular French pleonastic *il, ils* is found in early texts as *l (l')* or occasionally *il (y l')* before a vowel, and *y* before a consonant:

RC1 (1799) *nous autres y les plus que les blancs*
'We are more numerous than the whites' (*Lexique*, p. 966)
RC2 (1829) *ça les bien vrai*
'That's very true' (*Lexique*, p. 972)
RC3 (1829) *moi l'a oublié dire à vous*
'I forgot to tell you' (*Lexique*, p. 969)
RC4 (1856) *Z'ouvrier z'aut' l'appell' Dédale*
'the artisan they called Dédale' (Héry 1883:32)
RC5 (1884) *malhère l'arrive la case ton tantine'*
'a calamity has occurred at your auntie's house' (Focard 1884:183)
RC6 (1884) *vou l'arpousse à moi*
'you repulsed me' (Focard 1884:237)
RC7 (1930) *Mi l'aime à vous*
'I love you' (Fourcade 1976:4)
RC8 (1799) *nous y tuent tous les blancs*
'We ['ll] kill all the whites' (*Lexique*, p. 1148)
RC9 (1799) *si toi y veut quitter ton maitre'*
'If you want to leave your master' (*Lexique*, p. 1148)

In examples RC4, RC5, and RC6, *l'appell', l'arrive,* and *l'arpousse* appear to be derived from **l'a appell', *l'a arrive,* and **l'a arpousse,* respectively—i.e., two successive occurrences of [a] having coalesced (for *l'a*, see B3.2.5 below).

Examples RC1-RC9 show that the RC reflexes of popular French pleonastic *il* and *ils* differ from the *i* or *li* reprise of SC, MC, and HC on three main counts:

1. The RC forms occur following first, second, and third person subjects, both singular and plural, and not merely following third person subjects (apparently in common with other French Creoles, *i* alone is not attested following the pronoun *li*).
2. While the reprise item is phonetically identical to the third person singular pronoun (preposed form) in SC *i* and HC, MC *li*, none of the RC forms /l/, /il/, and /i/ are identical with the RC third person singular pronoun (preposed form) /li/.[11]

214 BAKER

3. SC, MC, and HC have and had only a single reprise item, whereas RC has two such items and appears to have previously had three (cf. RC1 and RC7, and see also below regarding the second of these).

In view of these differences, the designation "third person reprise" is obviously inappropriate for the RC forms. I will term them "predicate precursors."

In modern RC there are two predicate precursors: /l/ and /i/. The /l/ form is found, apparently exclusively, with derivatives of the French auxiliaries *être* and *avoir*, e.g., [l e], [l ete], [l a], etc. (It may well be that first-language speakers of RC identify the /l/ as an integral part of these "markers," but this is not relevant to what follows.) The /i/ form precedes true verbs (in the French sense), i.e., not *être* or *avoir*. Example RC7, *Mi l'aime à vous,* might well have been a grammatically unacceptable sentence in 1930 since the same text also contains:

RC10 (1930)*Mi aime pas danse la Polka*
          'I don't like to dance the polka'   (Fourcade 1976:100)

There is no trace of the RC predicate precursor in any known genuine MC text. However, as *Lexique* includes six examples which might be interpreted as such, it is necessary to clear up any possible misunderstandings which may have resulted. The chief source of the problem is Vinson (1882) in which what can only be described as "partially Reunionized" versions of certain Chrestien (1822) 1831 lyrics are presented as if they were the MC originals. All the examples of Chrestien's work which appear in *Lexique* are taken from secondary sources (Vinson 1882 and Freycinet 1827). The six lines attributed to Chrestien by Chaudenson (*Lexique,* pp. 967-68, 972) are reproduced below, numbered X10-X15, with each line followed by the corresponding line which appears in Chrestien (1831),[12] these being numbered MC10-M15:

X10 *zipon y amar' dans lé rein*
MC10 *Zipon amar' dans lé-rein*   (1831:18)

X11 *Quand zaut' y appelle moi zane*
MC11 *Quand zaut' appell' moi Zanot*   (1831:18)

X12 *vous y en a trop l'argent*[13]
MC12 *vous y en a trop l'arzant*   (1831:25)

X13 *çà qui son bouch' li trop doux*
MC13 *Ça qui son la-bouss' li trop doux*   (1831:8)

X14 *moi choisir ça qu'lé plis zoli*
MC14 *Moi soizir ça qui plis zoli*   (1831:5)

X15 *son nation li trop tourdi*
MC15 *son nation là trop tourdi* (1831:26)

Examples X10 and X11 are from Vinson (1882) and include the predicate precursor *y* where there are none in the originals. Example X14 includes the RC sequence *qu'lé* which is not found in any known MC text. Example X13 resembles the original except that the first syllable of MC /labus/ is omitted, no doubt to conform with RC usage, and the *ss'* (/s/) of the original is replaced by *ch'* /ʃ/. The *li* in this example is a third person reprise such as is found frequently in Chrestien's work, as was noted earlier. Examples X12 and X15 come from a translation of a Lafontaine item which Chrestien gave to Freycinet in 1818. Apart from a possible misprint,[14] this differs only marginally from the version subsequently published in Mauritius. However, the *y* of *y en a* appears to be an integral part of this verb at this time and is found as *yenna, iéna* (later, *éna*) in other MC texts. Finally, there is the *li* reprise of X15 which corresponds to *là* in MC15. While there are many examples of *li* reprise in Chrestien's work, it does not appear to have been an obligatory item. It is entirely absent from MC16, for example:

MC16 (-1822) *Mon li-lit ein' p'tit natt' malgace*
Mon l'oreiller, morceau bois-blanc;
Mon gargoulett', ein' vié calbasse
'My bed [is] a little Malagasy sleeping mat. My pillow [is a] piece [of] "white-wood." My water-pot [is] an old calabash'
(Chrestien 1831:16)

This, and many other examples which could be quoted from Chrestien, suggests that **son nation trop tourdi* would have been an acceptable sentence at that time. The *là* of MC15 is what Valdman has recently termed the "particulariser" (1978b: 72), which aptly describes its principal function. However, in this example, the noun *nation* is already adequately particularized by *son* 'his/her/its'. The use of *là* here thus appears redundant. This line is the penultimate of a fable, the last three lines of which are (differences between the 1818 and 1831 versions are noted):

Li voulé galoppé bien vite,
X15 (1818)
MC15 (-1822) *Mais son nation $_{là}^{li}$ trop tourdi,*

Et li té $_{perdi}^{perdé}$ son pari
(Freycinet 1827:412; Chrestien 1831:26)

Each of these lines contains precisely eight syllables. In view of the remarks above, it might perhaps be deduced that the author's principal need was to find an eighth syllable, and that the change from *li* to *là* was of no greater semantic significance then than it would be today.

On the slim evidence of X13-X15 (ill-founded in the case of X14), Chaudenson interpreted MC *li* reprise and the non-MC **lé* as the equivalent of the present tense form of the RC copula (including the predicate precursor) [l e] and wrote:

Q92   L'auteur paraît user indifféremment de "lé" ou "li"...
        Si l'on songe que pour le morphème de passé les parlers des Mascareignes présentent le même alternance vocalique (réun. [té]; maur., rod. [ti]), on peut essayer de reconstituer l'évolution d'ensemble des systèmes:

	Réun. (ancien)	(mod.)	Maur. (anc.)	(mod.)	Seych.
Prés.	"l'est," "les"	[lé]	"lé," "li"	∅	[i], ∅
Passé		[lété], [té]		[ti]	[i ti], [ti]

(*Lexique*, pp. 972-73)

Though not clearly stated, the RC "prés." and "passé" forms are those found in equational sentences and differ somewhat from "markers" attested with true verbs (see B3.2.5). In view of the remarks above concerning third person reprise in MC and SC, and the non-attestation of **lé* as a copula in MC, a more accurate comparison between old RC and MC, and modern RC, MC, and SC, would surely be as follows:

	RC		MC		SC
	-1880	modern	-1880	modern	modern
"present"	*l'est, les*	[l e]	∅	∅	∅
"past"	*l'était*	[l ete], [te]	*été, té, ti*	[ti]	[ti]

Chaudenson assumes that SC reprise *i* is derived from RC predicate precursor *i* (*Lexique*, p. 966). Corne draws attention to the fact that, in occurring only after third person subjects, SC reprise *i* more closely replaces the reprise of popular French than RC *i* (1977a:39; cf. also Bollée 1977a:61). But it is clear from his discussion of the phenomenon that he is inclined to derive SC *i* from both popular French reprise and RC *i*. However, if as was suggested earlier (B3.1) the first permanent inhabitants of the Seychelles had included speakers of MC, RC, and popular French, then the first people born there would have had varying degrees of exposure to MC (optional) *li* reprise, to popular French third person /i/ (variants /il/, /iz/) reprise, and to the RC predicate precursors *i* and *l*. Thus, SC *i* reprise may derive, to a greater or lesser extent, from all three of these languages spoken by early inhabitants, rather than from only one (Chaudenson) or two (Corne) of them (for Corne's view, see note 2 in Chapter A5).

B3.2.3 Personal Pronouns

Goodman (1964) notes a total of seven personal pronouns in the various French Creoles. He derives six of these from the French disjunctives *moi, toi, lui, nous, vous,* and *eux,* and the seventh from *vous/eux autres*. No French Creole appears to have or to have had pronouns derived from more than six or fewer than five of these: the distinction between less formal *toi* and more formal *vous* is not attested, or has not survived, in several French Creoles,[15] while few have pronouns derived from both *eux* alone and *vous/eux autres*.

The earliest attestations of personal pronouns in HC, MC, and RC are set out in Table 11 (pp. 218-20). While forms of all seven are found in Haiti before 1800, it is far from certain that all of these occurred in a single variety of HC at that time since the texts concerned come from three or more widely separated points within that territory. Vowelless variants of the preposed forms are attested in HC from 1797 on, and somewhat later in RC, but these are omitted from Table 11.

All the postposed pronouns of RC have an initial *a*-. Chaudenson has demonstrated that this vowel must be considered an integral part of the postposed pronouns (since nouns in this position do not similarly follow *a*-), and he attributes this to Malagasy influence with secondary support from French *à moi, à toi,* etc. (*Lexique,* pp. 952-55). Because an example of such a postposed pronoun is found in the ca. 1722 text, this was apparently a feature of RC, i.e., of Chaudenson's "Bourbonnais," before the colonization of Mauritius began. However, no such postposed pronouns are found in any MC text at any time. In ca. 1800, both HC and MC had preposed first and second person singular pronouns which contrasted phonetically with their postposed forms. In both these Creoles, it is the postposed pronouns which correspond to the French disjunctives, and thus it is preposed [mo] ([mõ]) and [to] which *appear* to be innovations. Goodman (personal communication) believes that the alternation between [o] and [we] ([wẽ], [wa]) stems from a different phonological treatment of French orthographic *oi* in prefinal (unstressed) and final (stressed) position (cf. also Goodman 1964:25-26, 36-38). Goodman may well be right, but some early HC and MC texts have only *moi* and *toi* as the preposed forms. It is at least possible, therefore, that in both these French Creoles there was formerly only a single pronunciation for both the first and second person pronouns whether pre- or postposed, and that [mo] ([mõ]) and [to] were later developments resulting from the loss of the final vowel and the syllabification of the semivowel. Other changes in the form of the preposed HC pronouns can be readily attributed to the influence of the following grammatical item. For example, the vowelless forms of preposed HC pronouns are first attested before *a,* the reduced form of the future marker *va* (in the 1797 text), while the syllabic [m] variant of the first person singular pronoun is attested first before the negator (written *m'pas*) and before the anterior marker (written *m'té*) (both in the 1824 text). If HC [mo] ([mõ]) and [to] were local innovations, the anterior marker [te], which clearly derives from Fr. *était, été,* etc., might

Table 11
Early Attestations of Personal Pronouns (excluding vowelless variants)*

Etymon	Creole	Preposed Only	Pre- & Postposed	Postposed Only
moi	HC	moi 1776a	moi 1785	
	MC	mo -1792- mon 1797 mo, mon, moué, moi mô, mo		moué, moi -1802a† moi -1805
	RC	moin	moi 1818b§	à moin -1722-
toi	HC	toi 1776a		toué 1797
	MC	to		toi 1818a
	RC	to toi 1799		à toi 1849
lui	HC	li 1749	li 1776a	
	MC	lui li	li -1805	
	RC			aly, à lui 1799 à li 1828

(continued)

(Table 11 continued):

Etymon	Creole	Preposed Only	Pre- & Postposed	Postposed Only
	HC	nous 1790b	nous -1792-	
nous	MC	nous 1769	nous 1816	
	RC	nous 1799		à nous 1849
		nous		
	HC		vous -1792-	
vous	MC		vous -1805	
	RC	vous		à vous 1799
	HC	vous autres 1790b		z'autres 1791
				vous-autes 1796
nous autres	MC	zotte -1805	zote 1802c	
vous autres			sautres 1816	
eux autres			zaut' 1818a	
	RC	nous autres 1799	eux autres 1799	
		z'aut'		à z'aut' 1828

(continued)

(*Table 11 continued*):

Etymon	Creole	Preposed Only	Pre- & Postposed	Postposed Only
eux	HC	*yo* 1796	*yo* 1797	

* Vowelless variants are known from 1797 in HC, as is mentioned briefly in the text, and somewhat later in several other Creoles.
† The author of this text, the naturalist Descourtilz, traveled widely and spent a total of four years in Haiti. It is clear from Vol. 3 of his work that he acquired fluency in HC during his stay (in part in detention). The apparent variation between preposed /mo/ and /mwe/ is not a feature of any one of the many samples of HC in this work; rather, some samples have only preposed /mo/ while others have only preposed /mwe/. It could well be that these forms reflect the different social and geographical varieties of HC which the author encountered. A Haitian assessment of the Creole in this work could be valuable.
§ The use of *moi* alone in all positions is a particular feature of Chrestien's works and of a few other pre-1840 texts, on which I have commented in *Towards*, pp. 47-49. All texts purporting to represent the speech of slaves, and all texts without exception from 1840 on, have consistently preposed *mo* in contrast with postposed *moi*. The only text in which mixed conventions are found is a catechism of 1828 which has three times as many occurrences of preposed *mo* as of preposed *moi*. The choice of graphic *moi* rather than *mo* in preposed position in this text appears to be entirely unrelated to any syntactic or phonological rule.

have been involved in that process. The sequence of mid-vowels in *[mwe ete] (*[mwẽ ete]) and *[twe ete] could well have coalesced to *[mwete] (*[mwẽte]) and *[twete], respectively. If so, such forms might perhaps have been reanalyzed as either [mw]/[tw] + [ete] (in which case the [w] might have been syllabified wherever there was a following consonant, perhaps on the analogy of the HC pronoun *yo*), or as [mwe] ([mwẽ])/[twe] + [te] (in which case the abbreviated form of the anterior marker would have been potentially available following other items). If this suggested origin of HC *mo* and *to* is correct—and all that can be claimed is that it is not contradicted by the available textual evidence—then the implication would seem to be that MC *mo* and *to* were separate but parallel innovations. However, it is far from certain that French orthographic *oi* was ever pronounced *[we] in either *moi* or *toi* in MC. The only alternatives to the latter spellings found in nineteenth-century texts are *moa* and *toa* (Anderson 1885), and Focard makes the point that the final [a] of these pronouns is a feature which distinguishes MC from RC (1884:219). Thus, it seems less likely that the first two vowels of MC [mwa ete] would have coalesced to give *[mwate] or *[mwete]. While some support for the latter is to be found in Chrestien's 1822 text, in which there is fairly consistent use of *té* following a vowel and *été* following a consonant, both *mo* (-1805) and *té* (1816) are attested earlier in texts which provide no evidence of such a distribution. The markers *a* (reduced form of *va*) and *après* might seem obvious alternatives to *été* as grammatical items which could have been involved in the emergence of MC *mo* and *to,* but I have been unable to find any textual evidence in support of this. Given the importance which Goodman (1964: 129-31) and others have attached to the shared *mo* and *to* forms of MC and HC, it is to be regretted that early texts do not settle the question of whether the Mauritian forms were an independent development or not.

Apart from the absence of *yo* in the Mascarene Creoles, there is nothing in Table 11 to suggest that MC derives its pronoun system from RC rather than directly from French, from HC, or from a hypothetical "West African Pidgin French." A theory which seeks to ascribe to RC a major influence in the evolution of MC must be able to account for two things:

1. The absence of the RC postposed forms with an initial *a-* from all known MC texts.
2. The presence of preposed *mo* and *to* in both MC and HC (and other varieties of American Creole French, formerly if not currently) and the absence of these from all known RC texts.

Chaudenson's "Bourbonnais" theory of the origin of MC fails to provide an explanation for either of these. The facts of the early peopling of Mauritius set out in Chapter B2 suggest that (1) is to be expected. The precise significance of (2) remains to be established, however.

222 BAKER

B3.2.4 The Negators /napa/ and /pa/ (RC, MC, HC)

Goodman notes that /pa/ is the negator in all the French Creoles on which he had data, and that this almost invariably occurs predicate-initially. Apart from obsolete usage in the Creole of French Guiana and some apparently conflicting information concerning Louisiana Creole,[16] the only exception he mentions is *ve pa* (< *vouloir* + *pas*), a kind of negative verb attested in HC and in the French Creoles of the Lesser Antilles and Louisiana (1964:92). In fact, this is found in several nineteenth-century MC texts, including those of Chrestien, and though now obsolete in MC, this also occurs in modern SC and, marginally, in RoC (Corne 1977a:172; Corne and Stein 1979:76). In RC, however, the negator *pa* invariably follows the first verb encountered (cf. A1.8, this volume) and is attested only in this position from the earliest texts:

RC11 (1799)*moin n'a pas aucune imagination avec personne*[17]
    'I don't have any intrigue with anyone'   (*Lexique*, p. 1148)
RC12 (1848)*li tire pas son casquette*
    'He doesn't take his cap off'   (*Lexique*, p. 1152)
RC13 (1884)*Plère pas mon enfant*
    'Ne pleure pas mon enfant'   (Focard 1884:193)
RC14 (1930)*mon livre l'est pas trop gros*
    'my book is not too big'   (Fourcade 1976:3)

While preposed /pa/ is the most frequently encountered form of the negator in MC today, from 1769 to 1888 the only form attested is /napa/ (written *n'a pas, na pas*, etc.):

MC17 (1769) *ça n'a pas bon*
    'that's not good'   (Bernardin de St.-Pierre 1773.1:257)
MC18 (-1805) *mo n'a pas conné bon Dié pour blanc*
    'I don't know the white man's God'   (Pitot 1805:373)
MC19 (1818a)*N'a pas nous zence-ça*
    'Ce ne sont pas de nos gens cela'   (Freycinet 1827:407)
MC20 (-1831) *nà pas dir' li marcé*
    'Don't say he walked'   (Chrestien 1831:50)

In some of the early MC texts, in addition to its role as negator /napa/ functions as a negative verb (corresponding to French *il n'y a pas*):

MC21 (-1805) *n'a pas l'optal, n'a pas sourzin?*
    'isn't there a hospital, isn't there a doctor?'   (Pitot 1805:373)

Links between MC and Other French Creoles   223

That /napa/ formerly had two distinct functions is illustrated by MC22 and MC23 which occur in the same text:

MC22 (-1822) *bon-tems fini, Vivres n'a pas . . . n'a pas maïs*
'the good times are over. There are no supplies . . . there's no maize'
(Chrestien 1831:11)

MC23 (-1822) *fair' trois morceaux, N'a pas piti, n'a pas gros, Tout gal'*
'make three portions, not small, not big, all the same size'
(Chrestien 1831:15-16)

In both the -1805 and the -1822 texts, the positive verb 'have' is attested as *y en a* (cf. B3.2.2). The earliest known combined attestation of the negator and this verb is found in the first MC catechism:

MC24 (1828) *li na pas y-en à commencement, li na pas y-en à la fin*
'He (God) has no beginning, He has no end'   (Lambert 1888-92:73)

The negator is also attested with the positive verb 'have' in items which Chrestien added for the second (1831) edition of his work:

MC25 (-1831) *Quand moi zène moi té-bête, N'a pas y-en-a la raison'*
'When I was young I was stupid, [I] didn't have any sense'
(Chrestien 1831:51)

While sporadic examples of the negative verb *n'a pas* are found in a few later texts (1855, -1860-), this is entirely obsolete today, though still current in SC (Corne 1977b:173).

The fact that the negator in nineteenth-century MC texts is /napa/ rather than /pa/ as in other French Creoles seems to have been viewed as a problem by Goodman and caused him to devote a separate paragraph to the origin of the MC form. Had he had access to a wider range of early HC texts, he would have found examples of both /napa/ and /pa/ in that Creole too (cf. also HC1, p. 213):

HC3 (1802b) *Mangé n'a pas dou dan bouche*[18]
             'Nul mets ne plait à ma bouche'   (Ducoeurjoly 1802.2:393)
HC4 (1811)   *Mangé pa dou dan bouche à moi* [see note 18]
             'Nul mets ne plait à ma bouche'   (Anon. 1811:71)
HC5 (-1802a) *oiseau ci làlà n'a pas gagné malice pièce*
             'Cet oiseau n'est pas méchant'   (Descourtilz 1809.3:226-27)
HC6 (1802b) *ly pas tendé*
             'Il n'a pas entendu'   (Ducoeurjoly 1802.2:314)

HC7 (1802b) *vous pas coné métié a vou*
          'vous ne savez pas votre métier'   (Ducoeurjoly 1802.2:350)
HC8 (-1802a) *Na pas français . . . na pas tiré*
          'Ce ne sont pas les Français, ne tirez pas'
                        (Descourtilz 1809.3:369; ellipsis as per original)
HC9 (1802b) *N'a pas tardé davantage*
          'ne tarde pas davantage'   (Ducoeurjoly 1802.2:393)

Where the negator follows an overt subject, the form /pa/ is found more frequently than /napa/ in the 1776-1802 texts, and after 1802, only /pa/ appears to be attested in this position. However, where the negator occurs clause-initially, *only* /napa/ is found in all texts consulted from 1776 to 1854 (cf. Bigelow 1877: 56). Clearly, the negative imperatives *na pas tiré* (HC8) and *n'a pas tardé* (HC9) cannot derive directly from French *ne tirez pas* and *ne tarde pas*, respectively. In order to account for /napa/ in negative imperatives, it seems necessary to suppose that this rather than /pa/ had earlier been the unique form of the negator; in other words, that HC3 and HC5 are isolated survivals from what had earlier been the norm (interestingly enough, in this context HC3 is from the lyric of a song originally composed in the middle of the eighteenth century; see note 18). Far from being a feature of MC that sets it off from HC and varieties of American Creole French, as Goodman (1964:93) implies, /napa/ appears to be another grammatical item formerly common to both MC and HC.

If Chaudenson's "Bourbonnais" theory were correct, it would be necessary to explain why the negators attested in MC (from 1769) and RC (from 1799) should differ both in form (MC /napa/, RC /pa/) and, more crucially, in the positions in which they occur (only predicate-initially in MC, never predicate-initially in RC). Neither problem arises if, as the study of the peopling of Mauritius to 1735 in Chapter B2 suggests, there were too few RC speakers in Mauritius for them to have played a significant role in the early development of MC.

B3.2.5 "Predicate Markers" (RC, MC, HC)

In this section I use "predicate markers" (or simply "markers") as a cover term for the "tense and aspect markers" of MC (Baker 1972:106ff.), as well as for those items in RC and HC which most closely resemble them in form and/or function.[19] (For the very different status of these items in RC, compared with MC and IdeFC generally, see Chapters A1, A2, and A6.) A thorough survey of the "markers" of all the principal varieties of Creole French has yet to be undertaken. All that is attempted here, however, is a comparison between the *graphic forms* of these attested in HC, MC, and RC in documents written before 1900. Thus, the semantic values of the "markers" are not specified[20] (access to speakers of eighteenth- and nineteenth-century varieties of these Creoles being impossible, this could not in any event be done with much precision).

Links between MC and Other French Creoles 225

In order to facilitate comparison of the graphic forms attested in HC, MC, and RC *only,* the etymon of each "marker" is assigned a code, as set out in Table 12:

Table 12

French Etyma of "Predicate Markers" in RC, MC, HC

Code	Etymon	Attested in	Code	Etymon	Attested in
$\emptyset$		RC MC HC	3^a	aller	HC
1^a	être	RC	3^b	va	RC MC HC
1^b	est	RC	3^c	s'en va	RC
1^c	était, été	RC MC HC	4	pour	RC MC HC
1^d	sera	RC	5	après	RC MC HC
1^e	serait	RC HC	6	fini	RC MC HC
2^a	a	RC	7	fait que	MC HC
2^b	avait	RC	8	sorti	RC HC
2^c	aura	RC	9	vient de	RC
2^d	aurait	RC			

In MC and HC and most other French Creoles, the set of "markers" which can occur in stative predicates is a subset of those found in nonstative or "dynamic" (Baker 1972:99ff.) predicates. Thus, the "markers" of MC and HC can each be presented in a single table (Tables 15 and 16, pp. 230-33). In RC, however, the "markers" that are found in stative predicates are not a subset of those that can occur in dynamic predicates. (For additional information see Chapter A1.) Thus, two tables are needed for RC (Tables 13 and 14, pp. 226-229). In order to compare the MC or HC system with that of RC, it is thus necessary to compare Tables 15 or 16 with both 13 *and* 14.

It is not yet clear precisely what value first-language speakers of RC attach to the predicate precursors (B3.2.2). It remains to be determined whether the past form of the RC copula is perceived as a single morpheme /lete/ or whether this phonetic sequence is felt to consist of two morphemes, /l/ and /ete/, of which only the latter is considered to be the past form of the copula. In view of this, and as there are examples in which the precursor is not separated by either a space or an apostrophe from what follows, I have in every case reproduced in Tables 13 and 14 any trace of a precursor which precedes or forms part of a "marker."

If the problem of the status of the precursor in RC is temporarily overlooked, Tables 14, 15, and 16 may be compared in terms of etyma. This reveals that:

5 are common to RC, MC, and HC *(était/été, va, pour, après, fini)*

Table 13

"Markers" Attested in Stative Predicates in RC, 1722-1892 and 1930

Text	∅	1^{b*} est	1^d sera	$3^b + 1^a$ va être	$1^c/(2^a + 1^c)$ était/(a été)	Others
-1722-1793						
1799		l'est	sera	va etre		
		y l'est	y sera			
		y les				
		n'a pas				
1820						
1828†	∅	l'est			l'était	
		n'est pas			n'a pas 'tait	
		n'a pas			n'a pas tè	
1829		les				
1848		il est				
1849†	∅	l'est	s'ra		l'était	
		n'a pas			n'a pas 'tait	
		n'a plis			n'a pas té	
1856†	∅	l'est	y s'ra		l'était	
		n'a pas			n'a pas 'tait	
		n'a plis			lété	
		n'a point				
1863	∅					
1882		lé	sera		l'était	
			s'ra		l'até	
					l'a té	
1883	∅					
1884a§	∅	lé			étai	
		l'é			l'a té	
		l'est			l'a te	
1884b§	∅	lé				
1884c§	∅	li				
		lé				
1887		l'é				
		lé				
-1892		l'è				

(continued)

(Table 13 continued):

		1^{b*}	1^d	Code and Etymon $3^b + 1^a$	$1^c/(2^a + 1^c)$	
Text	∅	est	sera	va être	était/(a été)	Others
1930	∅	l'é	sera		l'était	l'avait été
		l'est	y s'ra		l'étaient	lavait été
		y lé	y sera		l'a été	n'aura
		l'a	s'ra		l'été	
		n'a pas			lété	
		i'est				
		l'es				
		la				
		lé				
		y l'est				

---

* Two-way variation is attested between /l e/ (usually precursor + present copula) and /l a/ (usually precursor + completive "marker") in RC (Corne A1.1, 1.2 above). Variation between /l/ and /n/ is found in a number of terms in IdeFC, RC, and other Creoles. In RC the conditional and the conditional perfect "markers" show both /l/ ~ /n/ and /a/ ~ /e/ variation: /l ora/, /n ora/, /l ore/, /n ore/ (Corne, A1.2 above). However, whether the apparent forms of the present copula *l'est, n'est, n'a,* and the past copula *l'était, l'a té, n'a* (pas) *té* noted in Héry's works can legitimately be regarded as a related set of variants cannot readily be determined unless additional pre-1880 RC texts come to light.

† The Héry 1883 text has been subdivided into 1828, 1849, and 1856 on the basis of the information provided by Sauzier (1904:255-57). (According to Sauzier, Héry died in Reunion in 1856 and therefore could not have revised anything republished after that date.)

§ As Focard distinguishes between three varieties of RC, so I have divided the examples he gives into the same categories: 1884a (RC of the "noirs indigènes"), 1884b (RC of the "créoles des bois," that is, Whites), and 1884c (RC of the "caffres"). The *li* of the 1884c text in Table 13 is discussed in note 11.

Table 14
"Markers" Attested in Dynamic Predicates in RC, 1722-1892, 1930

Text	∅	(2ᵇ)	1ᶜ était (qui) (a) été	2ᵇ*	3ᵇ	3ᶜ	CODE AND ETYMON 4	5	6	8	9	2ᵇ⁺⁶	Others
-1722-1793	–		l'était qui	a	va	s'en va	pour	après	fini	sorti	vient de	a fini	
1799	∅		été	la	va								
	–			là	y va	s'en va							
1820	∅		l'était qui	la	va	s'en va		après	fini			l'a fini	voudra
1828†	∅		l'était	l'a		s'a va		l'après					n'manz'ra pas
				n'a									pendiait, babiait
				l'a									
1829	–												
1832	∅				va								
1848	∅												
1849†	∅		l'était	la	va								paira, don'ra pas, n'gagn'ra pas
			tait	l'a									çantait, trouvait
				l'									la vient
1856†	∅		l'était	la	va			après			vient d'		épous'ra, f'ra, n'acout'ra plis,
				l'a									donn'ra pas, etc.
				l'									donn'rait pas
				l'a									louait, grattait
				la									l'était pour
1863	–		l'a été		va								
1882	–		l'a té		va	s'en va					y vient d'	la fini	
			l'a té		a						i viens		
			t'é										
1883	∅		la té		a	sava	pou	apiré	fini				
1884a§	∅		la té qui	la	ava			y apiré					
			l'a té	l'a	va								
				là	a								
				n'a									

(continued)

Table 14 (continued):

CODE AND ETYMON

Text	∅	(2^b)	1^c était (qui) (a) été	2^{b*}	3^b	3^c	4	5	6	8	9	2^{b+6}	Others
1884b§	–			a	va	s'en va	pour	après	fini	sorti	vient de	a fini	
1884c§	∅			la	va								
-1887	–			la	a						y viens d'		
				l'a	a v'								
					va								
-1892	∅		l'était qui	l'à	va	i ça va		l'après	fini		y vient de	la fini	l'était qui çava
1930	∅		l'était y	l'a	a	y ça va						la fini	l'étaient en train de
			l'été qui	la	va	y çava						l'a fini	y venait de
			l'été y	n'a		sava							tombera pas, punira pas, etc.
			l'était			çava							dirait, disait, etc.
			la été										l'était après, l'été après
			laté qui										lé après
			l'étais qui										l'était fini, l'été fini
			l'étaient qui										l'avait
													n'aura
													n'aurait
													n'aurait été
													lé en train de
													en train de

*, †, §: See corresponding notes to Table 13, p. 227.

Table 15
"Predicate Markers" Attested in MC, 1749-1885

CODE AND ETYMON

Text	∅	1ᶜ était, été	3ᵇ va	4 pour	5 après	6 fini	7 fait que	1ᶜ+3ᵇ était va	1ᶜ+4 était pour	1ᶜ+5 était après	1ᶜ+6 était fini	1ᶜ+7 était fait que
1749	∅											
1769	∅											
-1805	∅											
1816	∅	été té te	va		après	fini fini						
1818a	∅	té été	va va	pour		fini fini						
1818b	∅	té été	va	pour	après	fini	fait que					
-1822	∅	été été té	va									
1828	∅	été té	vat va va* a		après	finie fini						
1830	∅											
-1831	∅	été été té	va			fini						
1832-	∅	été été té	va		après	fini						
1835	∅	été té	va			fini						
-1837	∅	été té	va va			fin† fin,'						
1840	∅	ti té	va va		après	fin,' fini	fêq'					
1855	∅	ti				fine						
-1860	∅	ti	va a									
1867	∅	té ti	va à	pour		fini† fine fin, fin†	fêque	ti va tia	ti pour		te fin'	
1870	∅	té ti								ti après	ti fine	

(continued)

Table 15 (continued):

CODE AND ETYMON

Text	∅ ∅	1ᶜ être, été	3ᵇ va	4 pour	5 après	6 fini	7 fait que	1ᶜ+3ᵇ était va	1ᶜ+4 était pour	1ᶜ+5 était après	1ᶜ+6 était fini	1ᶜ+7 était fait que
1878	∅	té ti				fini fin'	féque				ti fin'	té faique
1880	∅	té ti	va	pour	après	fine	féque	té va	té pour	té après ti après	té fine ti fine	
Others (1880): *va fine* 1ᶜ+3ᵇ+6; *té va féque* 1ᶜ+3ᵇ+7; *va pour* 3ᵇ+4.												
1885	∅	té ti	va	pour	apré	fine	fec	ti va	ti pour	té apré ti apré	té fine ti fine	
Others (1885): *va fine* 1ᶜ+3ᵇ+6; *ti va fine* 1ᶜ+3ᵇ+6; *va apré* 3ᵇ+5.												

* This text contains seven examples of *va* and only one of *a*. There is one obvious misprint in this text (mentioned in note 5) and, as no other example of *a* has yet been noted before ca. 1860, it could well be that the 1830 *a* is a printing error for *va* (the text was typeset in London, i.e., by a non-Créolophone).

† The 1840 and 1870 texts were both written by Anglophones for whom *fin* might seem a natural way of representing /fin/. The single occurrence of *fin* in the Descroizilles 1867 text, in contrast to the large number of occurrences of *fine* in the same text, may perhaps be a printing error.

Table 16
"Predicate Markers" Attested in HC, 1776-1886, 1936

CODE AND ETYMON

Text	∅ ∅	1^c était, été	3^a aller	3^b va	4 pour	5 après	6 fini	7 fait que	8 sorti	1^c+3^b était va	1^c+4 était pour	1^c+5 était après	1^c+6 était fini	1^c+7 était fait que
1776a	∅													
1776b	∅	té												
1785	∅	étois	alé											
1790a	∅											étois après		
1790b	∅													
1791 -1792-	∅	té				après								
		te												
1796	∅			va					sorti					
1797	∅			a		après								
-1802a	∅	té		va		après								
1802b	∅	té *	alé	va		après †	fini		sorti			té après	té fini	
		été	allé	a		l'après								
Others (1802b): té seré 1^c+1^e; valé 3^b+3^a; seré té 1^e+1^c.
1802c	∅	té		va										
		te		a										
		té		va										
1802d	∅	té	alé	va		après								
1811	∅	t'		a		apré								
Others (1811): v'apré 3^b+5.
1824	∅	té	allé	a						t'a		t'apré		
-1830-	∅		allé	a		après				tà				
1854	∅	té		va						ta		t'a près	té fini	
				a										

(continued)

Table 16 (continued):

CODE AND ETYMON

Text	∅ ∅	1^c était, été	3^a aller	3^b va	4 pour	5 après	6 fini	7 fait que	8 sorti	1^c+3^b était va	1^c+4 était pour	1^c+5 était après	1^c+6 était fini	1^c+7 était fait que
1877	∅	té		va		a pé apé pé	fini			ta ta va				
1886	∅	té	va a		pu	pé				ta		ta pr ta pé t'apé t'ap		
1936	∅	té	va a ava		pu	apé ap apr pé apo	fin	fèk	sòt	té va t'a t'ava	té pu		té fin	té fèk

Others (1936): *av'ap* 3^b+5; *a pu* 3^b+4; *a fin* 3+6; *t'a fin* 1^c+3^b+6.

* While *té* and *été* (particularly the former) occur with some frequency in this text, there is also one example of *ti* which I have assumed to be a printing error and therefore have omitted from this table.

† There is only one example of *l'après* in this text but several of *après*. However, it seems unlikely that the former could result from a printing error. The HC equivalents of a number of French verbs listed in the glossary of this work have initial *l'*, e.g., HC *l'ouvri* (Fr. *ouvrir*).

1 is exclusively shared by RC and HC *(sorti)*
1 is exclusively shared by MC and HC *(fait que)*
3 are found only in RC *(a, s'en va, vient de)*
1 is found only in HC *(aller)*

It may be observed that there is no "marker" shared exclusively by MC and RC and that every "marker" attested in MC has an etymon for which there is a corresponding "marker" in HC, without exception. The similarity between MC and HC extends, more significantly, to the combinations in which they are attested. Apart from three apparently aberrant examples in the 1802b HC text, the set of possible combinations of "markers" in HC (at any time) and in MC (in the nineteenth century) appears to be essentially the same, as follows:

1. Two-part "markers" consisting of 1^c *(était/été)* followed by any one of the "markers" derived from 3^b, 4, 5, 6, or 7.
2. Two-part "markers" consisting of 3^b *(va)* followed by any one of the "markers" derived from 4, 5, 6, or 7.
3. Three-part "markers" consisting of 1^c and any of the two-part "markers" listed under (2).

That essentially the same combinations should be found in HC and nineteenth-century MC texts is the more remarkable in that several of these are either very rare or obsolete in MC today.[21]

While only one two-part "marker" is found in nineteenth-century RC texts *(l'était pour)*, four others ($1^c + 3^c$, $1^c + 5$, $1^c + 6$, $1^c + 8$) are found in the 1930 text and/or in modern RC. Provided one simply overlooks the precursor, these can be seen as two-part "markers" of type (1). I have not found any RC examples of the combinations $1^c + 2^b$ or $1^c + 3^b$, nor any of types (2) and (3) in any text. Two other combinations found in RC are *l'était qui* (modern /l ete i/, /te i/) (A1.6), and *la fin(i)*, which will be discussed briefly below. Three of the "markers" common to RC and MC require comment:

Pou(r)

Attested in nineteenth-century RC only in the 1883 Trouette translation of a Baissac 1880 MC text (corresponding to *pour* in the original). In modern RC it normally (*Lexique*, p. 340) or very rarely (Corne) follows the copula, and with or without the copula, it can only be negated by a preceding *pa* (cf. A1.7, A1.8).

Après

Attested in nineteenth-century RC only in Héry and as *apiré* or *y apiré*[22] in Trouette's translation of the Baissac folktale. Every Trouette *(y) apiré* corresponds to a Baissac *après*. The 1828 Héry text also includes an example of *l'après*, one of two forms found in Fourcade (1930), the other being *lé après*. Thus, it seems that /l apre/ is probably a reduction of /l e apre/ (precursor + copula + *après*). In modern RC, Chaudenson (*Lexique*, p. 339) notes three present tense possibilities: *mwa apré (graté), mi apré (tir...), nu l apré (rod...)*. Note that in *mwa apré (graté)* the pronoun does not have its usual form /mwẽ/, while in *mi apré (tir...)*, /mi/ results from the contraction of /mwẽ/ and the precursor /i/. Like *pou(r)*, the negator must precede, not follow, *après*. It thus seems clear that the status of these two "markers" differs from all others in RC (note that other RC "markers" are all derived from French verbs, in contrast to both *pou(r)* and *après*).

Fini

Attested by itself as a "marker" in nineteenth-century RC only in Héry (1828) and Trouette (1883). There are three occurrences in the latter text. Two correspond to *fine* in Baissac's MC original while the third "translates" MC *faique*, which may indicate not only that /fek/ did not then (as it apparently does not now) exist in RC, but also that Trouette did not know of any obvious way of expressing the immediate past in RC at that time. *Fini* is also attested in the combination *la fini* or *l'a fini* (followed by a verb) in Héry (1828) and Vinson (1882). As both elements can today separately express the completive aspect, this is indeed a curiosity. Corne and Moorghen (1978) note four (or six) ways in which a verb can be marked for the completive aspect in modern RC: *mwẽ la mãze, mwẽ la fin(i) mãze, m i fin(i) mãze, mwa fin mãze* (and Corne adds a seventh in A3.2 in this volume). Note the unusual form of the pronoun in *mwa fin mãze–mwa* rather than *mwẽ*–which is apparently found in this form only where either /fin/ or /apre/ immediately follows. Chaudenson suggests that /fin/ appears not to occur in negative constructions (*Lexique*, p. 344). I take that to mean that *mwẽ la mãze* and *mwẽ la fin(i) mãze* might be negated by placing /pa/ immediately after /la/, and that if **m i fini pa mãze* is probably an acceptable negated form of *m i fin(i) mãze*, then **m i fin pa mãze* is probably equally not acceptable (Corne, personal communication). If, as Moorghen (1975:9) convincingly suggests, *mwa fin mãze* derives from *mwẽ la fin mãze* (i.e., one form of *mwẽ la fin(i) mãze*), then it could well be that the as yet unconfirmed **mwa pa fin mãze* is acceptable to at least some first-language speakers of RC (cf. also A3.2).

From the above it will be clear that *pour, après,* and *fini*–three "markers" which help to confer a certain degree of "family resemblance" on RC and MC– are found in the works of only two authors of nineteenth-century RC texts. Of these, Héry was not a native speaker of RC, and his work is severely criticized by Focard (1884). However, while Focard (1884:217) complains of Héry's use of an MC form on one occasion (*vini* instead of RC *veni*), he does not comment on Héry's use of markers, and I am not aware of any reason for supposing that Héry had any firsthand experience of spoken MC.[23] As for Trouette, while his translation was bound to be closely modeled on the MC original, it can hardly be supposed that he selected "markers" which were not then current in RC. Thus, while it is to be hoped that additional nineteenth-century RC texts will come to light which will make it easier to assess the significance of the Trouette and Héry texts, one cannot, in the meantime, attach a great deal of importance to the absence of the markers *pour, après,* and *fini* in other known pre-1900 texts.

Corne and Moorghen (1978:64) note that modern RC appears to have, in effect, two "marker" systems—one "French" (employing forms of *avoir*) and one resembling that of MC—and that in the "double" form of the completive, /la fin/, the two systems are combined. From the preceding paragraphs it can be seen that /pu/, /apre/, and /fin/ differ from the other "markers" in Table 14 in a number of respects (cf. also sections A1.4 and A1.7 in this volume). This suggests that they may be, and may have been, less fully integrated into RC than are, and were, the corresponding "markers" in MC. Note also that the abbreviated form /fin/ is found in MC as early as 1840 yet appears not to occur in any RC text up to 1930. Similarly, no abbreviated form of /apre/ has yet been attested in RC so far as I am aware, but the full form appears to have been long obsolete in MC, having given way entirely to /pe/ and its somewhat infrequent variant /ape/. In RoC, however, /apre/ is still marginally extant (Corne and Stein 1979:74). Chaudenson's "Bourbonnais" theory implies that anything shared by RC and MC was established first in RC. If so, it is curious that *pour, après,* and *fini*—especially the abbreviated forms of the two latter—should be attested far earlier in MC than in RC.

Even if it were supposed, despite the lack of evidence, that the RC of ca. 1722 had possessed all or most of the "markers" attested subsequently in RC and/or MC, it would still be necessary to account for the remarkable fact that speakers of MC had adopted only those "markers" from them which are also attested in HC. It is surely obvious that an adequate explanation of this is unlikely to be found in a theory which insists that early RC was *the* major input to MC.

B3.3 Summary and Conclusion

Only one grammatical item, /ban/, was noted which currently occurs in all the Indian Ocean Creoles and which has not been reported as such in any variety of American Creole French. The available textual evidence suggests that this may well have been a nineteenth-century Mauritian innovation which subsequently passed into other Indian Ocean Creoles.

Most of the other grammatical items examined fall into one of two main categories. First, there are those RC items, all attested before 1800 as well as in modern RC, of which there is no trace in any known MC text. These include:

1. The precursors [l] and [i].
2. The set of initial *a-* postposed pronouns.
3. The postposed negator [pa].

4. The "markers" *l'était qui* (modern [te i]), *s'en va* (modern [sava]), and *l'a* (modern [l a]).

Second, there are those items which MC currently and/or formerly shares or shared with HC which are not attested in RC. These include:

5. *Li* reprise.
6. The preposed pronouns *mo* and *to*.
7. The preposed negator *n'a pas*.
8. The immediate past "marker" /fek/.
9. The majority of the two- and three-part "marker" combinations.

In addition, while the individual MC "markers" might be derived as easily from popular French as from some external source, the fact that MC quite simply lacks any "marker" which is not also attested in HC is, at the very least, remarkable.

It will be apparent from the above that the comparison of the available early texts of RC, MC, and HC fails to show that RC and MC formerly had more in common, so far as grammatical items are concerned, than they have today. Taken together with the detailed account of the peopling of Mauritius to 1735 and the minimal contribution of speakers of RC to that process set out in Chapter B2, this leaves, I believe, little possible doubt that Chaudenson's theory of a "Bourbonnais" origin for MC—in either his "strong" (1974) or "weak" (1979) version—is incorrect.

NOTES

1. In Q88 and throughout Q89, the gratuitous analogy is to "generations" of computers. (Computers built with thermionic valves, transistors, and integrated circuits are known, for good chronological reasons, as first, second, and third generation computers, respectively.) Given the importance most Creolists attach to the first generation of people born into a pidgin-speaking situation, and given also the widespread if often inappropriate use of the word "genetic" to describe relationships between particular Creole languages, Chaudenson's adoption of computer terminology would seem unwelcome even if the parallel were less obscure.

2. An unpublished, undated report by Lloyd to the British Colonial Office (received by the latter on April 8, 1840) concerning the situation on the island following the emancipation of the slaves divides the slaves into four categories of which the fourth consists of those emigrating to Rodrigues and Diego Garcia. (CO 167-227; eleventh, unnumbered page.)

3. Of the 82 slaves living in Rodrigues on December 3, 1804, 15 belonged to Rochetaing and the remaining 67 to four Mauritians, most of them to Marragon. All 24 Rodrigues-born slaves—not 22 as erroneously stated by Chaudenson (*Créoles*, p. 51)—belonged to the Mauritians who had settled on the island up to ten years before Rochetaing's arrival (North-Coombes 1971:61). When the British occupied Rodrigues in August 1809, there were said to be "about 41 slaves in all, Marragon possessing more than half that number" (North-Coombes 1971:72). It seems unlikely that half the slaves would have died within a span of four and a half years, and rather more probable that the 15 belonging to Rochetaing in December 1804 had left with their owner in March 1805.

4. The 1785 HC sample quoted by Valdman (1978a:98) might well be an example of this.
5. A hymn in MC published in London in 1830 contains the word *casab'* 'breakable' where *capab'* 'able' was clearly intended (Anon. 1830:61). A conversation in MC in a book written by a former French settler but published in La Rochelle in 1840 includes the word *dimande* 'request' where the context requires *dimonde* 'person' (Maure 1840:353). In this particular case, the conversation did in fact concern a request for money, and it is thus easy to see how a typesetter partially able to understand the MC dialogue might have deduced logically but wrongly that handwritten *dimonde* ought to have been *dimande*.
6. A book published in Paris in 1810 and entitled *Cri des colons contre un ouvrage de M. l'eveque et senateur Grégoire, ayant pour titre de la littérature des nègres...* contains the following: "Mais pourquoi, les nègres qui sont si savans dans l'art de la parole, n'ont-ils pas montré à parler aux singes, qui, selon eux, sont des petits hommes fort adroit, mais fort paresseux, qui ne veulent pas apprendre à parler, pour qu'on ne les fasse pas travailler? Les nègres de Saint-Domingue, qui ont oublié leur langue primitive, disent, dans leur idiome d'aujourd'hui,: *singes, ça ptit monde, qui malouc trop, to pas vle palé, pou que to pa fair travail*" (Anon. 1810: 38-39). About ten years after his visit to Mauritius and two years after the publication of *Cri des colons...*, Milbert published an account of his journey which included the following: "Les singes se rapprochent tellement de l'homme par leur organisation et leur intelligence, que les nègres les appellent des hommes paresseux. Ils disent dans leur jargon: *ça petit di monde là n'a pas voulé palé pour na pas travail.* 'Ce petit monde-là ne veut point parler pour ne pas être obligé de travailler'" (1812.1:240-41). The similarity between these two is striking. Note also:

1. I have found nothing else to indicate that monkeys were regarded as or termed *petit di monde* in Mauritius, this animal being known as /zako/ or (now obsolete) /mak/.
2. There is no graphic tradition of omitting French-derived post-vocalic *r* in MC. By contrast, the tradition is of long standing in HC, cf. *jou* 'jour' and *pou* 'pour' in a 1776 text (Nicolson 1776:56; the omission of post-vocalic *r* is not systematic, however, throughout this text).
3. Elsewhere Milbert (1812.1:271) offers *femme à moi* as the "MC" for 'my wife'. No such construction is found in any other text purporting to be MC. This structure is found in one RC text dating from 1820 (*Lexique*, p. 1149) and is attested in (some varieties of) HC from 1776 (Hilliard d'Auberteuil 1776-77.2:68).
4. With the exception of the shortest four-word sentence, all examples of "MC" given by Milbert are aberrant in one or more respects.

While the above does not prove that Milbert's "MC" is totally bogus, his examples clearly need to be regarded with extreme caution. I make no further reference to them in Chapter B3.
7. MC2, MC3, and MC4 are from Anderson's translation of the *Gospel according to Saint Matthew*. Rather than translate a translation, I have given the corresponding excerpts from the King James version of the English Bible. (I do not wish to imply by this that Anderson necessarily worked from this original. He would also have been familiar with the French version.)
8. Anderson was born in Mauritius in about 1852.
9. In SC preposed *i* contrasts with postposed *li* (Bollée 1977a:48, Corne 1977a:34). Examples in which *zot* is itself the reprised item are noted in both MC (see example MC4) and in modern SC (Bollée 1977a:62).
10. The verb *couri* has long been obsolete in MC. In some early texts, 'wander about' would appear to be a suitable gloss. In this particular case it refers to a ship changing direction. It is not entirely clear whether vessels bringing slaves from Madagascar deliberately changed course often, with the express intention of confusing the slaves' sense of direction before arrival, or whether the somewhat complicated maneuvers which were necessary in order to enter Port Louis harbor were interpreted as the former. In giving this example, Grant was making the

point that Malagasy slaves were aware of the direction in which Madagascar lay and hoped someday to be able to sail back there. This explained, MC5 may be glossed: 'Those whites are cunning; they change course a lot up there [pointing] but Madagascar is over there [pointing in a different direction]'.

11. However, Focard gives two examples of RC sentences first in the "créole des indigènes" (RC^i) and then in the "créole des Cafres" (RC^c) in which the (precursor plus) copula *lé* of RC^i is replaced by *li* in RC^c. This *looks* like *li* reprise, but as this appears to be found only in equational and locative sentences, corresponding to the distribution of the copula in modern RC, and never before a verb, it seems that this was a variant pronunciation of *lé* associated with Mozambique slaves rather than genuine third person reprise.

12. It is clear from Chrestien (1831) which items had originally appeared in the 1822 edition and which were added for the enlarged 1831 edition. All the examples MC10-MC15 given here were first published in 1822. However, as what may well be the only surviving copy of the 1822 edition (in the Carnegie Library, Curepipe) has partially disintegrated due to severe insect damage, all page references are to the more widely available 1831 edition.

13. In fact written *l'arzent* in Freycinet (1827:411).

14. The last line contains *perdé* 'lose'. This could well be a misprint for *perdi*, the form found in most if not all other texts.

15. Chaudenson's publications suggest that such a distinction is becoming obsolete in MC. In 1974 he notes only *to* in one table and comments below: "le mauricien aussi connaît [u], mais n'en use guère" (*Lexique*, p. 975). In 1979 he omits to mention the /u/ form altogether (*Créoles*, p. 90). In fact, the distinction between respectful /u/ and familiar /to/ is of considerable social significance in Mauritius and shows not the slightest sign of falling into disuse. The existence of /titwaye/ 'tutoyer' in even the most basilectal varieties of MC is evidence of the importance of the /u/ versus /to/ distinction.

16. According to Lane (1935:15), "A general rule is that it [= *pa*] immediately follows the auxiliary particles derived from *être* (i.e. *te, sa se*), but precedes the others *((a)pe, (a)le)*. In the habitual present it follows the main verb, i.e. 1. [habitual present] *mo kup pa*, 2. [present prog.] *mo pa 'pe kupe*, 3. [preterite] *mo pa kupe*, 4. [habitual past] *mo te pa kupe*, 5. [past prog.] *mo te pa 'pe kupe*, 6. [future] *mo pa 'le kupe*, 7. [future perfect] *mo sa pa kupe*, 8. [future prog.] *mo sa pa 'pe kupe*, 9. [conditional] *mo se pa kupe* [printed *sa* in apparent error], 10. [prog. conditional] *mo se pa 'pe kupe*. Ingrid Neumann (personal communication) broadly confirms Lane's statement which, as she points out, is confusingly misquoted in Goodman (1964:92) where Lane's key word "precedes" is replaced by "follows." However, Neumann finds, in contrast to Lane, that *pa* invariably *follows* imperatives today. Neumann has kindly provided me with a good deal of additional information concerning negation in this Creole, parts of which I have attempted to summarize as follows (any errors therein are therefore my responsibility):

pa always precedes *gẽ* 'have', *ye pa gẽ ẽ ʃaʳ* 'they don't have a car'
pa follows "presentatives," *(e)na pa* . . . 'there isn't/aren't . . .'; *se pa* . . . 'it's not . . .'
pa follows finite modals, *li te pɸ pa kuri la* 'he couldn't go there', but precedes nonfinite modals, *no p ole ye konɛ* 'we don't want them to know'; note that this accounts for one of the two apparently conflicting examples which Goodman (1964:92) quoted from Fortier.

Neumann (forthcoming) will include a detailed statement on negation in Louisiana Creole French.

17. It is important to note that *n'a pas* in this example is a verb *na* 'have' (cf. Corne in A1.2) followed by the negator. This is not an equational sentence, and thus the resemblance to MC17 is merely superficial.

18. HC3 and HC4 are the corresponding lines from two of the three known HC versions of the lyric of a song of which Moreau de Saint-Méry (1797.1:65) wrote: "Elle a été composeé, il y a environ quarante ans, par M. Duvivier de la Mahautière."

19. It cannot be assumed that a graphically identical item attested in two or more of these French Creoles has or had the same status in each of them. For example, it is clear from Valdman (1978a:218) that the status of /fin/ in modern HC differs from its status in modern MC. Nor can it be assumed that an item attested both in the nineteenth century and today in the same French Creole has had the same status throughout that period. For example, encountering /((f)i)n fek/ more frequently than /fek/ alone in MC in the period 1965-70 and finding greater support for the former rather than the latter among informants as the "correct" form, I was inclined to regard /fek/ as an item then in the process of acquiring "aspect marker" status whereas the evidence of old texts (see Table 15 below) shows that it could occur without a preceding /((f)i)n/ 150 years ago.

20. One clear case of a phonetically identical "marker" having distinct semantic values in different French Creoles is /fin/. This marks the completive in modern MC, but in modern HC it marks the "immediate past," rather like /fek/ (Valdman 1978a:218).

21. Modern equivalents of the two- and three-part markers listed under "others" in Table 15 have been reported as judged acceptable by certain MC informants (cf. Corne 1970:14-15; Papen 1978b:334-50). However, in a total of five years of living in Mauritius, I have failed to encounter any of these in spontaneous speech.

22. Trouette appears to have attempted to reflect the pronunciation of a person whose mother tongue had CVCV structure only.

23. On the same page Focard complains of Héry's *gros la pluie* which he corrects as *beaucoup la plie*. However, /gro lapli/ is good MC for 'heavy rain', 'heavy downpour'.

B4
Identifying the Origins of MC

In the period 1727-30, the non-French population of Mauritius increased from about 30, all apparently Malagasies,[1] to perhaps 1,000, mainly first-language speakers of one of the following (in approximate order of decreasing magnitude; cf. B2.4 above): Wolof,[2] Tamil (and perhaps other Dravidian languages), Fon,[3] Malagasy, Bambara,[4] and Bengali.[5] In the same period there was also a substantial net increase in the number of Europeans on the island. Just how many is difficult to determine because: details of troop arrivals and departures are incomplete; some soldiers were able to change to settler status by marrying; and nonsoldiers who did not find local conditions to their liking were free to move to Reunion or to return to France (and quite a number did so, as was noted in B2.2). However, the available evidence suggests that, including the 35 *chasseurs de marrons* from Reunion who spent several months in Mauritius from August 1730, the total number of first-language speakers of a variety or derivative of French[6] on the island at the end of 1730 is likely to have been 400-600.[7] In this multilingual environment, the free and non-free needed to be able to communicate with each other, especially in work-oriented situations, while slaves also needed to be able to communicate with other slaves whose first language was not the same as their own. What I will term "a vehicle suitable for inter-ethnic communication" was clearly needed. Thus, a key question is: was there a preexisting vehicle *readily available* to fulfill this role or not? The theories of Chaudenson, Faine, and Goodman all assume, to a greater or lesser extent, that the answer to this question is in the affirmative.

Chaudenson's view is that the vehicle was early RC (the 1974 "strong" version of his theory) or that early RC was the major input to a new vehicle (the 1979 "weak" version). That early RC already existed in Reunion is implied by the ca. 1722 text. That this was *readily available* in Mauritius in the period 1727-30 has not been established. It was shown earlier (Chapter B2) that for four months following the arrival of the first slaves direct from Madagascar at the end of 1722 people able to speak RC as a first or second language accounted for about one-fifth of the total population of Mauritius, and that this proportion appears to have declined from less than 10 percent in April 1723 to nil by mid-1726. For Chaudenson's theory to remain valid, it would seem necessary to suppose that these first Malagasies identified RC, the language of the disappearing minority, as their target, rather than the (varieties of) metropolitan French of the majority (until 1728 at least); that they continued to practice this (with whom?) even after the departure of the last four *Créoles de Bourbon* in mid-1726; and that they either passed this on to the approximately 1,000 non-Francophones who arrived in the period 1727-30 (and also, presumably, to the European arrivals) (Chaudenson's "strong" version), or "their" RC was somehow *the* major influence on the way all newcomers coped in the multilingual situation (Chaudenson's "weak" version). Even the arrival of 35 *chasseurs de marrons* from Reunion in August 1730 could have provided little assistance for the task of propagating RC since these men were principally engaged in tracking down former slaves in otherwise uninhabited parts of the island. Neither the "strong" nor the "weak" version of this scenario is plausible.

Compared with conditions in 1730, the Malagasies who arrived in 1722 were, for several years, in a fairly simple linguistic situation in that everyone who could not speak some form of Malagasy could speak a variety or derivative of French. Those Malagasies who were not assigned to senior Compagnie employees or army officers as *domestiques* might have been exposed to more RC than French in the four months to April 1723, but this can scarcely have been the case for anyone thereafter. To what extent these Malagasies would have recognized RC as anything other than just one of the varieties of French spoken by all non-Malagasies then on the island is uncertain; it is at least clear that, insofar as any slaves ever identified a particular language as their target in the years before there were any locally-born MC-speaking slaves (see below), they were most unlikely to have selected RC as such at any time from April 1723 on. Of those living in Mauritius in 1727-30 who intended or were destined to remain there permanently, it has yet to be demonstrated that there was a single first- or second-language speaker of RC among them.[8] RC was thus neither readily available for adoption as the vehicle of interethnic communication, nor is it apparent that there were speakers of it in a position to exercise an important degree of influence over those who participated in the multilingual situation of 1727-30 or thereafter. Furthermore, nothing was found in Chapter B3 to suggest that any grammatical item of MC could more convincingly be derived from RC rather than from French or another source. That early Réunionnais visitors to Mauritius were well placed to pass on their names for varieties of flora and fauna hitherto unfamiliar to those arriving from Europe, and that some grammatical and, in particular, lexical items would have been carried from Reunion to Mauritius *and vice versa* during the course of two and a half centuries is not to be doubted. However, in the search for the origins of MC as a grammatical system—rather than as a collection of thousands of lexical items—the "Bourbonnais" theory is essentially a red herring: there do not appear to be any grounds for supposing that speakers of RC played a major role in the emergence of MC.

For Faine, the preexisting vehicle would have been a "composite patois" developed by sailors from various parts of France over the centuries (1939:18). Faine had earlier sought to derive HC—of which he was a native speaker—mainly from Norman French dialects. On discovering the extent of the similarities between HC and MC through Baissac's publications, he abandoned his earlier ideas in favor of a nautical patois which could have been transported to both territories. In his view, both HC and MC were, initially, "simplifications" of this same patois (1939: 18).

The former existence of a patois such as Faine envisaged appears to be less than an established fact, but it would be unreasonable not to allow both that sailing, as an occupation, must have required its own rather specialized terminology, and that the conditions of living in the restricted environment of a ship must have been particularly favorable to dialect leveling. If something not totally different from Faine's "composite patois" had indeed existed, it would have been readily available to the extent that there would have been speakers of this on board every French ship which visited the various French trading posts and colonies overseas. But wherever settlers from different parts of France were brought together, one would expect a certain amount of dialect leveling to result. If two or more colonial territories received their white settlers from a broadly similar range of speakers of French dialects, the "composite patois" of each might well have resembled one another quite closely (cf. also *Lexique,* p. 592, quoted as Q90 above). Thus, common elements in geographically distant French Creoles are not necessarily attributable to a specifically *nautical* "composite patois." However, it might be unwise to dismiss Faine's theory without first attempting to assess just how much influence the professionally seaborne French might have been able to exert on the speech habits of an island colony in the early days of its settlement.

Everyone who traveled to one of the (future) Créolophone territories must have had at least some verbal contact with French sailors. The extent to which slaves might have acquired something from the speech of sailors would depend on their age and sex—women and children generally spent far less time than men under hatches—and on the duration of the journey: 106 days on average from Gorée to Mauritius (range: 92-120 days), 43 days from Pondichery (33-55 days), and 24 days from Madagascar (9-38 days).[9] However, while most passengers were to make only one journey, the typical sailor must have made several. Visiting places that were already Créolophone—most of the French-owned islands in the Caribbean must have been Créolophone prior to the French occupation of Mauritius—sailors would have had direct contact with locally established slaves, e.g., in the handling of cargo, and they would also have had opportunities to witness and participate in conversations among a relatively wide range of the people living there. Thus, sailors were in a position to acquire a substantial amount of expertise in communicating with people whose first language was not French and who were living in, or destined to live in, a society controlled by French speakers. They were thus potentially able to make use of such skills.

Lougnon (1958) provides information from which indications of the amount of time spent by sailors in Mauritius in the period 1727-35 can be calculated. For this nine-year period, he notes a total of 156 visits made by ships and, of these, there were 105 by ships based at a French port for which he is able to provide precise dates of both arrival and departure.[10] The aggregate number of days which these 105 ships spent in Mauritius is 2,537, an average of 24 days per visit (range: 2-134 days). If it can reasonably be assumed that the additional 34 visits made by other ships based at French ports for which Lougnon lacks a precise date of arrival and/or departure were of similar average duration, then there was the equivalent of one French ship at the island throughout this nine-year period. Such limited data as I have available on crewing suggest that about one hundred men were normally employed on each vessel.[11] Numerically speaking, sailors are clearly a statistically significant factor. However, there is nothing to indicate that just one "nautical patois" existed, or that the collective expertise of sailors in communicating with non-Francophones would have equipped them all with a single uniform "pidgin" or even "Creole" which they propagated everywhere. Thus, I think it unlikely that the sailors on the various ships which took slaves to Mauritius or visited the island for other reasons in the period 1728-30 were in a position to offer, collectively, a *single* preexisting vehicle suitable for inter-ethnic communication in Mauritius. It remains the case, nevertheless, that every slave and European settler had the opportunity of learning at least something from the speech of sailors on their journey to Mauritius. For those who knew no French on embarkation, the process of acquiring French lexical items must have begun on board ship.

Since at least 1968, Hull has sought "to reconstruct a hypothetical 'Maritime French' . . . a form of the language which might have been used on French ships engaged in the slave trade and in commerce with American ports" (1968:255). While stressing that this would differ from Faine's "composite patois" in that the latter "had creolized grammar" (1968:267, note 43), it is not apparent that the forms of speech which Faine and Hull, respectively, envisaged as having been in use on French ships would have differed in terms of their availability to people bound for or already living in Mauritius in the eighteenth century, and so additional comment on Hull (1968) is not required. However, Hull ([1975] 1979) seeks to marry "Maritime French" with Goodman's (1964) theory, and I will return to this below.

For Goodman, the preexisting vehicle would have been in use in one or more of the depots from which the French obtained slaves in West Africa, such as Gorée or Juda. The problem is not so much to prove that such a form of speech did exist at the right time and in the right place(s)—though this has not been adequately demonstrated so far—as to show that a significant proportion of slaves could have acquired a fluent knowledge of it before embarkation. Slaves taken from West Africa were not generally former free citizens of areas adjacent to depots but were more often effectively prisoners of war as a result of upheavals in places such as the kingdoms of Jolof (see note 2) and Dahomey, inland from the depots of Gorée and Juda, respectively. If any slaves acquired something which might loosely be termed "pidgin French" (or a subsequent development of such a form of speech) *before* leaving Africa, they could have done so only while en route for and/or in a slave depot. While there may have been occasions in the comparatively early days of the transatlantic slave trade when captives spent several weeks or even months in a depot while awaiting the arrival of a ship, this can scarcely have been the case once the trade became well organized—as it most certainly had long before the French acquired Mauritius. It was simply not in anyone's interest to keep slaves in depots longer than was absolutely necessary, and thus it seems unlikely that most West African slaves bound for the Indian Ocean spent anywhere near as much time in a depot as on board ship.

In the case of Mauritius it was shown in Table 7 (B2.4.3) that following the arrival of more than 600 slaves from West Africa in 1729-30 there were few others from there until after 1735. Thus, if a form of speech from West Africa with a mainly French-derived lexicon were to have provided Mauritius with a vehicle suitable for inter-ethnic communication, as Goodman's theory predicts, then given the multilingual situation in Mauritius from 1728 on, it would need to have been brought by (a proportion of) the West Africans who arrived by 1730. I have not so far found any documentary evidence to support this. The records that survive of court cases involving slaves for the period 1729-35 do not show that West Africans were able to give evidence without an interpreter any more frequently than other slaves.[12] The lack of probability that any of these slaves had spent enough time in a depot to acquire a form of speech the existence of which has not been proved, and the lack of evidence that any African reached Mauritius with a fluent knowledge of it, lead me to conclude that while not impossible, it is unlikely that "West African Pidgin French" was readily available for adoption as the vehicle of interethnic communication on the island in 1728-30.

Hull ([1975] 1979:208) seeks to go beyond Goodman (1964) by naming a place (Juda) and a time (from 1671) at which "Pidgin French" arose "as a deliberate *calque* of Gulf of Guinea Port[uguese] Cr[eole], using mainly Mar[itime] Fr[ench] material." He shows that *if* "Pidgin French" resulted from the relexification of a preexisting Portuguese-based Creole, Juda might well have been the location where that process began. However, his supporting evidence consists essentially of a quotation from Barbot[13] and the claim that the predicate markers /ka/ and /ke/ of the French Creoles of the Lesser Antilles and French Guiana are derived from the phonetically and functionally very similar markers of Gulf of Guinea Creole Portuguese. He may well be right about the latter (though see Valdman 1978b:91-92), but his theory as a whole lacks sufficient historical and linguistic evidence. In particular, it would seem necessary to establish during what period and to what extent Benin was the principal source of slaves for the French, and by this I mean the principal source of *all* slaves reaching French territories in the Caribbean area—not merely those transported by French vessels; as Curtin (1969: 121) has shown, a very substantial proportion of the slaves who passed into French ownership during the seventeenth century crossed the Atlantic in non-French vessels. So far as the origins of MC are concerned, Hull's theory does not provide a more readily available vehicle suitable for inter-ethnic communication in the Mauritius of 1728-30 than do the theories of Faine and Goodman except to the extent that in assuming that this development of [West African] "Pidgin French" would have been known both to slaves from Benin (and Gorée?) *and* to sailors, the numbers of potential speakers reaching the island would have been greater.

The strongest linguistic evidence favoring the theories of Faine, Goodman, and Hull is provided by certain features shared by MC and HC, such as those noted in B3.2. If none of these theories have been found to be altogether satisfactory, the need to find an adequate explanation for these shared features is in no way diminished, and I will return to this question below.

From the foregoing it will be apparent that there is a lack of strong evidence to support theories that a preexisting vehicle suitable for inter-ethnic communication was *readily* available when Mauritius became a multilingual society (after 1728). If no such vehicle had been available, the probable immediate consequence would surely have been pidginization *in situ*. Bickerton has sketched such a process as follows:

Q93 That pidginization is a process that begins by the speaker using his native tongue and relexifying first only a few key words . . . ; that, in the earliest stages, even the few superstrate words will be thoroughly rephonologized to accord with substrate sound system and phonotactics; that, subsequently, more superstrate lexicon will be acquired, but may still be rephonologized to varying degrees and will be, for the most part, slotted into syntactic surface structures drawn from the substrate; . . . that, even when relexification is complete down to grammatical items, substrate syntax will be partially retained, and will alternate, apparently unpredictably, with structures imported from the superstrate. (1977:54)

Bickerton realizes this point of view on the basis of data relating to immigrant laborers in Hawaii in the present century. I am sure this is an accurate summary of what happens wherever people select an established language of their new environment as their target but receive no formal help with its acquisition. However, I am far from sure that the involuntary immigrants who reached Mauritius in the period 1728-30 would have had an inclination to select French, or any other preexisting language, as their target. In the absence of any obvious "vehicle suitable for inter-ethnic communication," settlers and Compagnie employees would have addressed the slaves who worked under them in French. Slaves were thus bound to acquire French lexical items during the course of their work. Whenever slaves wanted to speak to others who did not share their own ancestral language, they would need to draw on the vocabulary of the situations of which both parties had experience, namely, the workplace and, to a lesser extent, the (earlier) routine of life on board ship. Communication among slaves of differing ethno-linguistic groups must have been quite as important to them as—and certainly no less frequent than—communication between slaves and non-slaves. Since the language of those who imposed slavery was the only one to which all immigrants were obligatorily exposed, the lexical content of the pidgin which slaves began to speak was inevitably largely French. However, if they did not aim to acquire the French language as such, they would not be motivated to abandon the grammatical structures of their mother tongues except where these proved a barrier to communication. In such cases they would need to select structures employed by other pidgin speakers, structures which might be drawn from the ancestral languages of other slaves or from French. If, as I believe, the principal aim of slaves was inter-communication, then to the extent that pidgin enabled them to achieve this, they might be said to have been engaged in constructing their own target language.

Children born to slaves in Mauritius from 1727 (see below) seem certain to have been exposed to pidgin from an early age, even if their parents consistently addressed them in an ancestral language. As no single ancestral language could have provided a means of communication with the majority of other children, but all would have had some exposure to pidgin, it would surely have been pidgin that children would have been likely to use initially among themselves, regardless of the relative extent to which they might have employed pidgin or an ancestral language with their parents. As adult slaves were required to work from daybreak until nightfall six days a week (D'Unienville 1838.1:286-87), children would have spent somewhat less time with their parents and somewhat more time in the company of other children than is usual in most societies. From the wide range of differing pronunciations of individual lexical items and grammatical constructions encountered in the pidgin of adults (heavily influenced by their own ancestral language), it seems likely that children would tend to adopt the more frequently heard pronunciations and the more recurrent grammatical structures. This might go some way toward stabilizing pidgin, but it would do little to make it a more flexible medium. If adult pidgin speakers had little difficulty in finding people with whom they could converse in their own ancestral language in their free time, the limitations of pidgin would be less problematic for them, as Bickerton remarks (1977:64). But children would certainly want to be able to converse with each other without any kind of restrictions. If pidgin were inadequate for expressing certain things or permitted their expression only in a clumsy manner, children would have had a vested interest in overcoming such limitations. They might theoretically have achieved the latter by adopting rules from any of the ancestral languages spoken by foreign-born slaves. However, insofar as they had occasion to witness Francophones talking among themselves, children would have been aware that many of the lexical items heard in pidgin also formed part of the Europeans' vocabulary. The language of the Europeans was, in some sense, one which included more of the lexicon of pidgin than any of the ancestral languages; and unlike pidgin, the Europeans' language did have adequate grammatical rules. Therefore, French presented *one* obvious source of the additional elements that might be required for the "expansion" of pidgin. I will revert to this below.

A letter written in Mauritius in June 1749 contains the following:

Q94 They will direct their hand to the point where it lies and exclaim, in their corrupted French, "Ça blanc la li beaucoup malin; li couri beaucoup dans la mer là haut; mais Madagascar li là." (Grant 1886:166)

The author of this passage was a French-born plantation owner of Scottish descent who comments on the fact that his Malagasy-born slaves entertain the hope that they will one day be able to sail back to their island, and that they know in which direction it lies. This short sample of "their corrupted French" does not differ in any respect from the MC found in a range of texts dating from the early part of the nineteenth century.[14] If this is MC—I do not claim that such a short text *proves* that MC existed by 1749 beyond all possible doubt—then the generally accepted view of how creole languages develop from pidgins would lead one to expect that there was already a locally-born MC-speaking population living in Mauritius in 1749. The earliest surviving record of the birth of a child to slave parents is dated 1727. Between 1727 and January 1, 1738 the baptisms of 465 children born to slave mothers are recorded in the parish registers (MA KA and KH). Even allowing for a high rate of infant mortality, there can be little doubt that the majority of them would have been alive in 1749 when they would have been between 11 and 22 years of age. I am satisfied that it was these children, or at least a proportion of them, who were responsible for transforming pidgin into something better suited to their needs, and thus for determining some of the more basic characteristics of MC.

The 1749 text is, however, attributed to a Malagasy. Even if it is accepted that from the moment there was a sufficiently large number of locally-born children for them to be in frequent verbal contact with one another they began to move pidgin in the direction of MC, it may still be wondered if foreign-born slaves would have sought to acquire the form of speech of these children rather than that of pidgin-speaking (or even French-speaking) adults. Obviously much would depend on the individual, his age, and his circumstances. Many of those brought to Mauritius as slaves were children, and this was particularly the case with Malagasies in the early years—for example, the ages of the Malagasies who arrived on the *Astrée* (see B2.4.1 above) in 1735 ranged from 2 to 13 years only. (They were baptized soon after arrival, and their ages are given in the parish registers.) Most of these children would surely have grown up having considerable exposure to the speech of locally-born children of roughly their own age. It is thus not merely possible but also, I believe, fairly probable that there were some Malagasies in Mauritius in 1749 with a command of the form of speech used by locally-born slaves.

MC is identified as a language for the first time in 1773, in an advertisement in issue number 5 of the first newspaper to begin publication on the island:

Q95 Un jeune Négrillon Mozambique, nommé Favori, âgé de 13 ans, appartenant au Sr. Pierre Maheas, habitant à la Montagne Longue, a disparu depuis le 31 Janvier. Comme ce jeune noir s'est probablement égaré & qu'il n'entend pas la langue créole, il n'aura pu dire le nom de son maître ni retrouver sa maison. On prie ceux qui en auront connoissance d'en donner avis audit Sr. Maheas. (*Annonces, affiches et avis divers pour les colonies des isles de France et de Bourbon,* issue of February 10, 1773, p. 20; italics removed)

Identifying the Origins of MC 249

This clearly indicates that it was MC rather than French or any other language which the newly introduced, foreign-born slave needed and was expected to acquire. In other words, MC was the target by 1773. I do not believe that MC deposed any other language in order to achieve this position. Rather, I think that the aim "to acquire the ability to communicate with those who did not share their mother tongue," which I attributed above to slaves arriving in the early years, was initially partly satisfied by pidgin which the locally born gradually developed into MC. The aim remained essentially the same, but the target evolved. The motivation for foreign-born slaves to learn the languages of those born locally has been suggested by Le Page:

Q96 Newly arrived slaves were referred to scathingly by the established creole African society, and many must have sought to identify as quickly as possible with this society, to become initiates. (Le Page 1972:80)

If the African, Malagasy, or Indian transported to a life of slavery in Mauritius had wanted to identify with the locally-born slaves, the people who knew most about how to cope with the situation in which he found himself, there could surely have been no more effective way for him to do so than by acquiring the ability to talk like they do.

I suggested earlier that French would have been *one* obvious source of elements (rules, grammatical and lexical items) which the first generation of locally-born slaves might have sought to adopt in order to transform pidgin into a language adequate for their needs. The extent to which this particular potential might have been realized would have been clearly related in part to the nature and degree of access these slaves had to the French-speaking population at the time they were growing up in Mauritius, the years when many of the more basic characteristics of MC must have been determined. Individual circumstances would no doubt have varied a great deal. The child whose mother worked as a domestic slave for a French family might well have been in a position to acquire French with little more effort than that family's own offspring. By contrast, the child raised in Camp Yolof (see note 2), the compound for Compagnie slaves close to Port Louis harbor,[15] probably had very little opportunity of hearing native-speaker French at least until old enough (10 years?) to be required to work. The extent to which MC in the second half of the eighteenth century included features of French not present in pidgin in the first half might nevertheless be related to the *average* degree of access this generation had to the French-speaking population. If so, and if it can be further assumed that the locally born in other French colonies employing slave labor developed their own characteristic and comparatively stable forms of speech on the same kind of time scale as Mauritius, then comparison of the early peopling of Reunion, Mauritius, and Haiti might be expected to shed some light on differences and similarities among their respective French Creoles.

Reunion has been continuously inhabited since 1663 (*Lexique*, p. xi). From the details Chaudenson provides of a census taken in 1686 (*Lexique,* pp. 455-56), it appears that the population in that year was as set out in Table 17:

Table 17
The Population of Reunion in 1686

European Men and Their Families	Adults Male	Adults Female	Children Male & Female
14 Frenchmen, 14 Malagasy women and their 50 children	14	14	50
12 Frenchmen, 12 "Portugaises des Indes," and their 42 children	12	12	42
10 French couples and their 33 children	10	10	33
2 Dutchmen and their wives (one French; one born in Reunion)	2	2	
Non-European Men and Their Families (if any)			
8 Malagasy couples and their 24 children	8	8	24
16 single Malagasy males	16		
12 single Indian males	12		
	74	76	149

TOTAL: 269

While it is apparent that the free population outnumbered the slaves, it is not entirely clear just how many of the above belonged to the latter category.[16] In three later censuses the proportion of the free population to slaves was as follows:

Year	Free Population	Slave Population	Total
1704	423 (58%)	311 (42%)	734
1709	507 (57%)	387 (43%)	894
1713	633 (54%)	538 (46%)	1,171

(Figures derived from *Lexique,* p. 458)

Thus, the population increased very slowly in Reunion in the fifty years to 1713, averaging a net gain of only 23 persons a year.

As indicated earlier, Mauritius has been continuously inhabited since the end of 1721. By 1730 the population totaled about 1,500, one third of whom were Europeans, while the remainder, apart from fewer than one hundred free Indian artisans, were slaves. By 1767, forty-six years after the founding of the settlement, the population had grown to 18,777 and was comprised of 80 percent slaves, 17 percent whites, and 3 percent free non-whites (Kuczynski 1948-49.2:758). The average net gain in population was 408 persons a year from 1721 to 1767.

Louis XIV laid claim to the coastal areas of western Hispaniola in 1664, and the first permanent settlements there date from not later than 1667 (Perusse 1977:xi; Charlevoix 1730-31.2:125).[17] The earliest census of Haiti I have been able to find is for the year 1715, at which time the total population numbered 38,723 and was made up of 79 percent slaves, 17 percent Whites, and 4 percent free non-Whites (FOM G^1 509). The average net gain in population was 807 persons a year from 1667 to 1715.

It is clear from the above that free citizens in Reunion accounted for more than 50 percent of the total population throughout the first half-century of settlement of that island. By contrast, the free population of both Mauritius and Haiti accounted for barely one fifth of the total after a similar period of French rule. In the case of Mauritius, it was shown earlier that slaves outnumbered the free population before the end of the first decade of settlement, but I have not been able to determine whether that was also the situation in Haiti. In absolute terms, Mauritius and Haiti were both populated at a much faster rate than Reunion—in fact, 18 and 35 times as rapidly, respectively. Thus, whereas the majority of the population of Reunion in 1686 was locally born, such was never the case in Mauritius during the period of French rule, and given the even faster rate of settlement in Haiti, this was almost certainly true there too. As a result of these differences, if the first generation of locally-born slaves in all three territories had been inclined to look to the speech of the free population for elements with which to "expand" the pidgin they heard from their parents and other foreign-born slaves, they would certainly have had the opportunity of doing so far more effectively in Reunion than in either Mauritius or Haiti.[18] (The extent to which the RC verbal system, in particular, is significantly closer to French than is that of MC is discussed by Corne in Part A.)

If major differences between the French Creoles spoken on the geographically proximate islands of Reunion and Mauritius can be related to the dissimilar ways in which they were populated, it certainly does not immediately follow that the striking similarities between MC and HC (cf. B3.2) might in like fashion be attributed to the relative lack of access to native speakers of French available to the first generation of slaves born in both the geographically distant territories of Mauritius and Haiti. Some similarities might be expected to result from this, certainly. For example, Heine (1979) provides a list of thirty-four features which are characteristic of African pidgins, and Bollée (1977b:105-10)[19] shows that a number of these are also found in SC (all of which also occur in MC) and HC. Of all the features Heine lists, the two which strike me as being of particular importance are:

1. "The pidginisation process seems to be marked by a drift towards bisyllabic word structure" (Heine 1979:90). Heine cites evidence showing that this holds true both where the lexical source language has a significantly higher syllable-to-word ratio and where the lexical source language has an average of less than two syllables a word.
2. "The object pronoun follows the verb. In most Bantu languages, for example, the object pronoun precedes the verb whereas all Bantu pidgins known have the opposite order" (Heine 1979:94).

It would appear that both these features cannot readily be explained either in terms of the lexical source languages of the pidgins concerned, or in terms of the mother tongues of those who participated in the development of these pidgins. This seems to suggest that such characteristics were determined, in ways not yet understood, by the human brain. This in turn suggests that if both MC and HC developed initially from quite separate pidgins and if French were the principal source of elements which were used to expand both these pidgins, but the degree of access to first-language speakers of French was relatively low in both countries, then MC and HC might be expected to include certain features of the kind Heine lists which were common to the pidgins from which each separately developed (and which are common to all known African pidgins). However, Heine does not list any features that are as specific as the preposed pronouns *mo* and *to* (B3.2.3) or the essentials of the predicate marker system (B3.2.5) which were shared by MC and HC in the nineteenth century. With reference to precisely this marker system, Bickerton offers the following explanation:

Q97 But the [first generation] child creole speaker will be driven to "expand" the pidgin. Practically every account of the relationship between pidgins and creoles has suggested that some such "expansion" must take place, but no account has previously suggested how this might be done. It is obvious that the process must consist of internalising linguistic rules for which there is no evidence in terms of linguistic outputs. If such rules are not induced from primary data, they must be derived directly from the human *faculté de langage*, which must in consequence contain some kind of analog for the instructions, "If your input language has no nonpunctual aspect marker, employ a locative expression preverbally." (Bickerton 1977:64)

In a more recent article, Bickerton goes on to suggest:

Q98 That possibly the kind of blueprint of language that we have wired into our heads is not a blueprint which defines language negatively in terms of formal universals, but rather one that defines language positively in terms of at least certain core structures, certain basic semantic or syntactic structures which are already there. (1979:15)

Q99 As a child grows up in a normal language-speaking community, he starts to change from these innate rules, to adapt these rules in the direction of the language that he is doomed to learn.
But in a pidgin-speaking community where he can have no correction, overt or covert, he cannot be corrected and therefore does not change these rules. (1979:16)

According to this view, the predicate marker system of HC and nineteenth-century MC—and creoles in general regardless of the languages from which the bulk of their lexicon is drawn (Bickerton 1977, 1979)—would have its source in innate rules common to all children. Taken together with the earlier suggestion that the degree of access to native speakers of the principal language of the free population may have been a key factor in determining certain basic characteristics of the creole language of the first generation of locally-born slaves, this seems to offer the prospect of finding an adequate explanation for both striking similarities between MC and HC, and major differences between MC and RC. However, even if this hypothesis were to be proved correct—not a simple matter as Bickerton (1979:17) acknowledges—anyone wishing to account for all the grammatical features shared by MC and HC would still want to know which of these have their source in neither French nor innate rules.

In Chapter B2 I showed that West Africans formed a majority of the slave population of Mauritius in the period 1730-35, but in Chapter B4 I gave my reasons for thinking it improbable that these people brought with them the kind of "West African Pidgin French" that Goodman (1964) had envisaged. I have not yet discussed the possibility that some of the grammatical features shared by MC and HC might have their source in those West African languages which were taken separately to both Mauritius and Haiti by people from Senegal and Benin. To take one example, Bentolila is reported to have shown that the predicate marker system of Fon closely resembles that of HC (Valdman 1977:180), and thus that of nineteenth-century MC (B3.2.5). As Fon is the principal language of southern Benin and as Africans from Benin briefly formed a majority of the slave population of Mauritius in 1729 (B2.4.3), it is possible that the Fon marker system might have served as a model for those who began to develop MC (and, separately, HC). However, as the essentials of this marker system are also shared by creole languages spoken in places where there were never any Fon speakers such as Hawaii and Sudan (Bickerton 1979:3), Bickerton's hypothesis offers a more satisfying explanation in this case. But quite a number of other grammatical features, not obviously derivable from varieties of French, are shared by MC and HC. It remains to check whether each of these exists in other creole languages (including some in whose evolution West Africans played no part) as well as in appropriate African languages in order to assess whether Bickerton's hypothesis offers a more probable explanation than that of the influence of a particular African language (or group of languages) in these cases too.

A somewhat related matter is whether anything of grammatical significance might have passed from HC or another variety of American Creole French into MC as the result of people with some knowledge of the former visiting or settling in Mauritius. The two Haitian slaves, indigo cultivators, who were sent to Mauritius in 1738 (*Lexique,* p. 1093) are unlikely to have had a major influence on MC even if the first generation of MC speakers was then quite literally in its infancy. While sailors were numerically of greater importance, I suggested earlier that insofar as they were able to speak "Creole" or "pidgin" they would not have been in a position to offer, collectively, a uniform variety of this. It also has to be mentioned that many of the 1,673 European settlers who reached Mauritius in the period 1787-97 (and who formed a quarter of the European population in 1797) are believed to have come from the Antilles (Prentout 1901:649). Given these dates, some of them are likely to have come from Haiti. The three above-mentioned groups of people no doubt introduced a number of lexical items into MC[20] (cf. *Lexique,* pp. 594-632), but their contribution to its grammar could well have been negligible.

In attempting to find an explanation both for differences between MC and RC and for similarities between MC and HC, a number of possible contributory factors have been mentioned; these may be summarized as follows:

1. The relatively low degree of access to the Francophone population available to the first locally-born slaves in Mauritius and Haiti, in contrast to those in Reunion. (That the structure of the population in Mauritius and Haiti was nearly identical, in terms of Whites, slaves, and free non-Whites, after a half century of French rule, was shown above, but it has yet to be established how far back this close parallel extends.)
2. Features common to all known African pidgins and which are not attributable either to the mother tongue of the pidgin speaker or to the language from which most of the lexicon of the pidgin is drawn seem likely to have also been features of pidgins formerly spoken in Mauritius and Haiti from which MC and HC separately developed. Some of these features may have survived in both these French Creoles.
3. Innate rules as envisaged by Bickerton could be the source of identical grammatical structures in any number of creole languages which developed independently of one another.
4. The influence of African languages carried to both Mauritius and Haiti in the early years of the peopling of these two territories. There are three principal languages or language groups concerned:[21] Fon (and other "Kwa" languages spoken in a continuous belt from eastern Ivory Coast to western Nigeria), Wolof (and possibly other "West Atlantic" languages of the Senegambia such

as Seereer, Pulaar-Fulfulde, Jola, etc.), and the Mande group of which "Bambara" (Bamana) is one variety.
5. The impact of settlers and visitors already familiar with, and perhaps speakers of, HC or another variety of American Creole French on the speech of the slave population of Mauritius.

Of these factors, I regard (5) as the least likely to have influenced the grammar of MC, and such influence, if any, would seem altogether impossible to prove. It should be possible, however, to begin to assess the relative importance of the other four factors when:

a. A thorough search has been made for additional early texts in MC, HC, and RC, and their contents carefully examined.
b. The facts concerning the early peopling of Haiti have been established.
c. The full list of non-French-derivable grammatical items and rules common to MC and HC is known, and when the presence or absence of these both in other creole languages (including those in whose evolution West Africans played no part) and the relevant languages of Africa has been checked.

This would prepare the ground for a theory able to account for differences between MC and RC as well as for similarities between MC and HC, in detailed rather than general terms.

NOTES

1. As was shown in B2.2, at least four of the slaves who had been too ill to walk across the island to board a ship bound for Reunion with their compatriots remained in Mauritius at the end of April 1723. If they subsequently regained their health, it seems likely that they would have been returned to their owners in Reunion. However, until their departure has been definitely confirmed, the possibility that one or more of them remained in Mauritius permanently cannot be ruled out.
2. Wolof is the language of the *Yolof* people whose *Djolof* or *Jolof* kingdom formerly occupied a large area of western Senegal still known by the latter name today.
3. The first language of the overwhelming majority of people living in the southern third of Benin, and of 63 percent of the total population of that country, is today Fon or another closely related "Kwa" language (Yai 1977:243).
4. The slaves who arrived on the *Charolais* in 1734 (see Table 4 in B2.3.2) were not the first Bambaras to reach Mauritius. A slave named Apollon was identified as a *negre bambara* at a court hearing on March 5, 1731 at which it was stated that there were others belonging to this ethnic group on the island (MA JB 1; see also note 12 below and the penultimate paragraph of B2.3.2 above).
5. That teen-age slaves were sent to Mauritius from Chandernagor (near Calcutta) in Bengal is known (*CSP* 1:238). That they were speakers of Bengali is not certain, but there can be little doubt that their mother tongue would have been an Indo-Aryan language.

6. By "variety or derivative of French" I refer to "Bourbonnais" and to French as spoken in, for example, Pondichery, as well as to metropolitan varieties of French.

7. In addition to my research on the slave population of Mauritius, I have also been studying the free population and hope to publish the details in due course. With regard to the figures for Europeans given in *Genèse,* it should be noted that these fail to take account of departures, particularly troop departures.

8. I do not rule out the possibility that the need for people with specific skills may have led to the recruitment of a very few individual Réunionnais to work in Mauritius on a short-term basis at this or any other time.

9. Derived from Lougnon (1958). Figures are based exclusively on journeys made without any intervening port-of-call (all ships from Juda to Mauritius in the period 1727-35 called at Príncipe or another port en route). I have excluded from the figures for Madagascar one 67-day journey which must have resulted from quite exceptional circumstances.

10. A number of vessels made more than one visit. Eleven visits were made by French ships based in India and six by non-French ships.

11. Lougnon (1958:11, note 8) gives the tonnage of these ships as ranging from 90 to 850 tonneaux (tx), with an average of not less than 500 tx. I have details of both the crew and the tonnage of just three of the vessels which visited Mauritius in the period to 1735, as follows: *Atalante,* 500 tx, crew of 100 (ANM B3 v294 f426); *Diane,* 330 tx, crew of 80 (ANM 4JJ90 (7)); *Triton,* 500 tx, crew of 134 (ANM 4JJ75 (13)).

12. The records which survive in MA JB 1/2 suggest that wherever a slave was unable to express him- or herself in a language understood by the court, another slave of the same ethnic group would act as an interpreter. The one exception noted concerns the Bambara slave mentioned in note 4: "trouvant qu'il ne nous entendoit point et qu'il ne pouvoit repondre à Notre interrogat, et qu'il n'etoit trouvé aucun noir de la castre qu'y entende le françois nous l'avons remis entre les mains de la garde pour le conduire au corp de garde" (MA JA 1).

13. Hull quotes from the 1732 edition of Barbot's text which is an English translation of the unpublished French original. Hull does not indicate when Barbot made his journey. The year is given as 1682 by Le Page (1960:32; for a detailed commentary on Barbot's journey, see also Debien, Delafosse and Thilmans 1978). Thus, the passage which Hull quotes refers to the situation at Juda ten rather than sixty years after the founding of the French trading post. This might seem to add further weight to Hull's theory but, against that, one must note the evidence of Labat (1730) relating to 1725-27. Vintilă-Rădulescu (1976:155) mentions that this work includes words and phrases in "arada" (Fon or a related language) intended for doctors responsible for the health of slaves during the sea journey. However, the phrases include *Diguè meraquebo* 'Mais je ne veux que de bons Negres' and *Memiton vè* 'Ce Negre est trop cher', as well as cardinal numbers and terms relating to physical condition and health. In my opinion, this vocabulary was intended for Europeans engaged in purchasing slaves in good physical condition in Benin, and in selling them to ships calling at Juda, rather than for European doctors looking after the health of slaves on board ship. If so, the implication is that it was the dominant African language of the area, rather than "broken Portuguese" or some other pidgin or Creole, which the European slave trader at Benin found useful to acquire.

14. There are three differences between the 1749 text and modern MC:

   i. The verb *couri* is now obsolete.
   ii. *Beaucoup* no longer functions as an adjectival intensifier (as in *beaucoup malin*) although it continues to function as a quantitative adverb (as in *couri beaucoup*).
   iii. *Li* is rarely found following a third person subject today (but see B3.2.2 above).

As stated in the text, all these features of the 1749 sample occur in a number of nineteenth-century publications in MC.

15. The area of Port Louis which continues to be known as Camp Yoloff today corresponds to the location of the living quarters of slaves belonging to the Compagnie (or, from 1767, to "le Roi"), marked on several eighteenth-century maps (e.g., Thoreau de la Martinière 1781, Vuillemin ca. 1795). However, the name *Camp Yoloff* does not itself appear on these maps. While the earliest attestation of the name I have yet found comes from the 1830s (Diary of Jean Lebrun, LMS papers), I am inclined to think that the name probably dates from the period 1730-35 when Yolofs were the most numerous ethnic group among the slave population.

16. One might suppose that all the children of mixed descent would have remained in the free population. Chaudenson (*Lexique*, p. 459) writes of these children: "Ces métis sont en majorité des enfants, la première génération née à Bourbon. Ils seront ensuite sans doute classés suivant leur condition soit comme blancs, soit comme noirs." In the censuses of 1704 and subsequent years, the term "noirs" is synonymous with "esclaves" (*Lexique*, p. 458).

17. A complicating factor which I have not yet been able to unravel satisfactorily is the extent to which those who settled in Haiti from 1667 might have included people previously living on Ile de la Tortue, a former haven for filibusters off the northern coast of Hispaniola.

18. There appears to be an interesting parallel between Barbados, of the territories where Creole English is spoken, and Reunion, among the Créolophone territories. Barbados had a much higher proportion of Europeans than did Jamaica in 1667, and this proportion declined much more slowly in Barbados than in Jamaica where people of African descent outnumbered Europeans by about 10 to 1 in the mid-eighteenth century (Le Page 1960:15-18). However, while it is generally recognized that "Bajan" is significantly closer to "standard" English than is Jamaican Creole (cf. Reinecke et al. 1975:376), a detailed comparison has yet to be undertaken.

19. Bollée (1977b) in fact refers to a paper which Heine presented at the International Conference on Pidgins and Creoles held at the University of Hawaii in January 1975 (which I have not had the opportunity of reading): "Some Generalizations on African-based Pidgins." It is apparent—both from the similarity of this title to that of Heine (1979) and from the fact that the numbers allotted to Heine's features to which Bollée refers correspond to those in Heine (1979)—that the latter is a revised version of the former.

20. I accept without reservation that every immigrant was potentially able to introduce lexical items into MC. Ross and Moverley (1964:244) in their study of Pitcairnese, provide an interesting example of a lexical item which can be reliably attributed to just one immigrant. The word [mɔ:gə] 'thin', of apparent ultimate Spanish or Portuguese origin, occurs with precisely this sense and pronunciation in the Creole English of St. Kitts, the island on which Midshipman Edward Young, one of the original *Bounty* mutineers, was born. (I am grateful to Robert Le Page for drawing this example to my attention.)

21. The Bantu languages potentially constitute a fourth.

B5
Summary and Conclusions

In Chapter B1, I drew attention to two matters:

1. That Chaudenson's (1974) claim that MC is derived from RC is closely related to his belief that Mauritius was settled, initially, mainly from Reunion.
2. That Chaudenson's (1974) rejection, with respect to MC, RC, RoC, and SC, of Goodman's (1964) hypothesis of a West African origin for all French Creoles starts from the assumption that all the French Creoles of the Indian Ocean stem from a single "Bourbonnais" origin.

In Chapter B2, the peopling of Mauritius up to the end of 1735 was examined in detail, and it was shown:

1. That the Réunionnais contribution to the permanent settlement of Mauritius was virtually nonexistent in that period.
2. That West Africans accounted for a majority of the slave population of Mauritius for approximately five years at a crucial early stage of the settlement of the colony (1730-35).

In Chapter B3, a number of grammatical items currently or formerly found in MC and in one or more other French Creoles were examined, drawing on early texts from Mauritius, Haiti, and Reunion (Haiti was chosen from among the varieties of American Creole French both because of the importance Faine and Goodman have separately attached to similarities between HC and MC, and because a wider range of early texts is available for this French Creole than for any other of the region.) Nothing was found to suggest that MC and RC formerly shared more grammatical items than they do today, while a number of such items were discussed which are or were common to both MC and HC and which have not been attested in RC.

Chapters B2 and B3, taken together with the evidence presented by Corne in Part A of this volume, lead me to conclude that neither the facts of the peopling of Mauritius nor the comparison of grammatical features of the French Creoles of that island and Reunion provides grounds for supposing that MC derives from RC or was heavily influenced by RC in the early stages of its development. Insofar as MC and RC share features not found in any variety of American Creole French and not obviously derivable from a variety of French, some probably result from the influence of languages which slaves and/or indentured laborers took to both islands (Tamil, Malagasy, Macua and other Bantu languages of southeast Africa) which were totally absent from the French-owned American territories in the seventeenth and early eighteenth centuries. Other shared features may be attributed to one island's innovation subsequently being adopted by others in the region (for example, the plural marker *ban*). The problem of accounting for features common to MC and HC, yet absent from RC, is more complicated.

In the beginning of Chapter B4, I examined a number of theories specifically concerned with the relationship of MC to one or more other French Creoles and found all of them to be unsatisfactory in one respect or another. I then compared the peopling of Reunion, Mauritius, and Haiti during the first half century of French rule in each territory. I found that Reunion differed from the others in two significant respects: the proportion of first-language speakers of French was considerably higher in Reunion than in Mauritius or Haiti, while the latter two were populated at a much faster rate than Reunion. This explains, I believe, why MC and HC have verbal systems that are much further removed from French than is that of RC. However, this does not in itself account for all the features shared by MC and HC but not found in RC. Three other potentially important factors were identified: (1) features common to all known African pidgins (Heine 1979) are retained in both MC and HC; (2) innate rules common to all children on which those brought up in a largely pidgin-speaking community draw in order to "expand" that pidgin if they are not obliged, or do not have the opportunity, to acquire a nonpidgin language (Bickerton 1977, 1979); (3) the influence of African languages taken to both Mauritius and Haiti (Fon, Wolof, and those of the Mande group, etc.). I do not claim that this list is complete. Nor do I rule out the possibility that a *small* number of identical innovations might have occurred altogether independently of one another in both Mauritius and Haiti (the preposed pronouns *mo* and *to* might be just such innovations).

In this study I do not provide a simple solution to the problem of accounting for striking similarities between MC and HC because I do not believe there is just *one*. My hope is that I have nevertheless succeeded in identifying at least some of the factors involved. If so, the task ahead is to determine their relative importance.

BIBLIOGRAPHY

Alleyne, Mervyn C. 1971. Acculturation and the Cultural Matrix of Creolization. In Hymes 1971:169-86.
———. 1979. On the Genesis of Languages. In Hill 1979:89-107.
———. 1980a. *Comparative Afro-American.* Ann Arbor: Karoma.
———. 1980b. Introduction. In *Theoretical Orientations in Creole Studies,* ed. by A. Valdman and A. Highfield, pp. 1-12. New York: Academic Press.
ANC, see Archives Nationales, Archives des Colonies.
Anderson, Samuel. 1885. *L'Evangil sélon S. Matthié (dan langaz créol Maurice).* London: British and Foreign Bible Society.
ANM, see Archives Nationales, Archives de la Marine.
Anon. ca. 1792. *Grand débat entre Duffay et consorts, Polverel et Sonthonax les égorgeurs et les brûleurs de Saint-Domingue,* n.p.
Anon. 1796. Proclamation de Sonthonax. In Valdman 1978a:101.
Anon. 1802. Proclamation de Bonaparte. In Valdman 1978a:101.
Anon. 1802. Proclamation de Leclerc. In Valdman 1978a:101-2.
Anon. 1810. *Cri des colons contre un ouvrage de M. l'evêque et senateur Grégoire, ayant pour titre de la littérature des nègres . . .* Paris.
Anon. (1811) 1821. *Idylles, ou essais de poësie creole, par un colon de St.-Domingue.* Cahors.
Anon. (1824) 1831. Parabole de l'Enfant Prodigue en créole de Saint-Domingue, Port-au-Prince. In Anon. 1831:93.
Anon. 1830. *Representation of the state of government slaves and apprentices in the Mauritius; with observations, by A Resident who has never possessed either land or slaves in the colony.* London.
Anon. 1831. *Mélanges sur les langues, dialectes et patois . . .* Paris.
Anon. ca. 1860. *Catéchisme Créole.* Mauritius.
Archives Nationales, Archives des Colonies. Série C2: Correspondence générale. Inde (C2 v9, v23); Série C3: Correspondence générale. Bourbon (C3 v4, v5); Série C4: Correspondence générale. Ile de France (C4 v1, v2, v4, carton 86); Série D2A: Recrues pour les troupes des colonies.
Archives Nationales, Archives de la Marine. Série B3: Correspondence reçue (B3 v294); Série 4JJ: Journaux de bord, XVIIe-XIXe siècles (4JJ 75, 4JJ 90, 4JJ 112).
Asgarally, Renée. 1977. *Quand montagne prend difé.* Mauritius: Mascarena University Publications.
Audain, M. J. J. 1877. *Recueil de proverbes créoles.* Port-au-Prince.
Azéma, Georges. 1859. *Histoire de l'Ile Bourbon depuis 1643 jusqu'au 20 décembre 1848.* Paris: Plon.

Bailey, Beryl Loftman. 1966. *Jamaican Creole Syntax.* Cambridge: Cambridge University Press.
Bailey, Charles-James N. 1973. *Variation and Linguistic Theory.* Arlington, VA: Center for Applied Linguistics.
Baissac, Charles, 1880. *Etude sur le patois créole mauricien.* Nancy: Imprimerie Berger-Levrault.
———. 1888. *Le folklore de l'île Maurice.* Reprinted 1967. Paris: Maisonneuve et Larose.
Baker, Philip. 1972. *Kreol. A Description of Mauritian Creole.* London: Hurst.
———. 1976. *Towards a Social History of Mauritian Creole.* Unpublished B Phil dissertation. University of York.
Barassin, Jean. 1957. Compte-rendu de Octave Bechet: Inventaire des registres paroissiaux de l'île de France.... *RT,* nouv. sér. 2:235-36.
Barat, Christian, Michel Carayol, and Claude Vogel. 1977. *Kriké kraké.* Saint-Denis, Reunion: Centre universitaire.
Barbot, John. 1732. *A Description of the Coasts of North and South-Guinea....* London: Churchill.
Bauche, Henri. 1920. *Le langage populaire.* Paris.
Bechet, Octave. 1951-56. *Inventaire des registres paroissiaux de l'île de France, 1722-1767.* Port Louis.
Bentolila, Alain. 1971. *Les systèmes verbaux créoles: comparaisons avec les langues africaines.* Thèse de 3e cycle, Université de Paris V-René Descartes. Cited in Valdman 1977:180.
———. 1978. Créole d'Haïti—nature et fonction—fonction naturelle. *Etudes créoles* 1:65-75.
Bernardin de Saint-Pierre, Jacques-Henri. 1773. *Voyage à l'Isle de France....* Paris: Merlin.
Besant, Walter. 1870. The Mauritius Patois. *The Athenaeum* no. 2253:889-90.
Bickerton, Derek. 1975. *Dynamics of a Creole System.* London: Cambridge University Press.
———. 1977. Pidginization and Creolization: Language Acquisition and Language Universals. In Valdman 1977:49-69.
———. 1979. Beginnings. In Hill 1979:1-22.
———. 1981. *Roots of Language.* Ann Arbor: Karoma.
Bigelow, John. 1877. *The Wit and Wisdom of the Haytians.* New York.
Bollée, Annegret. 1977a. *Le créole français des Seychelles. Esquisse d'une grammaire—textes—vocabulaire.* Tübingen: Niemeyer.
———. 1977b. *Zur Entstehung der französischen Kreolendialekte im Indischen Ozean.* Geneva: Droz.
———. 1977c. Remarques sur la genèse des parlers créoles de l'Océan Indien. In *Langues en contact—Pidgins—Creoles—Languages in contact,* ed. by Jürgen M. Meisel, pp. 137-49. Tübingen: Narr.

———. 1978. Reduplikation und Iteration in den romanischen Sprachen. *Archiv für das Stadium der neuren Sprachen und Literaturen,* 215.2:318-36.
———. 1981. *Le vocabulaire du créole haïtien et du créole seychellois: une comparaison.* Paper presented to the IIIe Colloque international des études créoles, St. Lucia, May 1981.
Bonneau, Alexandre. 1856. Les Noirs, les Jaunes et la littérature française en Haïti. *Revue contemporaine* 5.29:107-55.
Bonnefoy, Théophile. 1853. *Table générale alphabétique et analytique pour servir aux recherches à fiare au Greffe de la Cour Suprême de l'Ile Maurice concernant les lois et autres dispositions réglementaires et administratives de cette colonie . . . .* Port Louis.
Broadbridge, Claire. 1980. *Some Devices for Focus in Trinidadian.* Society for Caribbean Linguistics, Occasional Paper No. 14.
Calvet, Louis-Jean. 1974. *Linguistique et colonialisme: petit traité de glottophagie.* Paris: Payot.
Carayol, Michel and Robert Chaudenson. 1973. Aperçu sur la situation linguistique à la Réunion. *Cahiers du Centre universitaire de la Réunion,* 3:1-44.
———. 1977. A Study in the Implicational Analysis of a Linguistic Continuum: French–Creole. *Journal of Creole Studies,* 1.2:179-218.
———. 1978a. *Les aventures de Petit Jean.* Paris: Edicef.
———. 1978b. *Lièvre, Grand diable et autres.* Paris: Edicef.
CBI, see Lougnon, ed., 1933, 1934, 1935.
Cellier, Pierre, ed. 1979. *Pédagogie du français. Cahiers du Centre universitaire de la Réunion,* 10.
Cellier, Pierre and Pierre-Marie Moorghen. 1979. La compréhension du français dans les manuels de lecture à la Réunion. In Cellier 1979:63-131.
Chafe, Wallace L. 1970. *Meaning and the Structure of Language.* Chicago and London: University of Chicago Press.
Charlevoix, P. F. X. 1730-31. *Histoire de l'isle espagnole ou de S. Domingue.* Paris.
Chaudenson, Robert. 1974. *Le lexique du parler créole de la Réunion.* Paris: Champion.
———. 1979a. A propos de la genèse du créole mauricien: le peuplement de l'Ile de France de 1721 à 1735. *Etudes créoles,* 2:43-57.
———. 1979b. *Les créoles français.* Paris: Nathan.
———. 1979c. Le français dans les îles de l'Océan Indien (Mascareignes et Seychelles). In *Le français hors de France,* ed. by Albert Valdman, pp. 543-617. Paris: Champion.
Chélin, Antoine. 1973. *Une île et son passé: Ile Maurice (1507-1947).* Port Louis.
Chrestien, François. (1822) 1831. *Les essais d'un bobre africain.* Port Louis.
———. 1838. *Album tropical, ou Recueil de pièces inédites et autres du portefeuille de François Chrestien, et faisant suite au Bobre Africain.* Port Louis.
Christie, Pauline. 1976. *A Re-examination of Predicate Marking in Dominican*

Creole. Paper presented to the conference on "New Directions in Creole Studies," University of Guyana, August 1976.

Clark, Ross. 1979. In Search of Beach-la-Mar: Towards a History of Pacific Pidgin English. *Te Reo*, 22:3-64.

Cohen, Marcel. 1967. *Histoire d'une langue: le français*. Paris: Editions Sociales.

Comhaire-Sylvain, Suzanne. 1936. *Le créole haïtien. Morphologie et syntaxe.* Wetteren, De Meester, and Port-au-Prince: by the author.

Corne, Chris. 1970. *Essai de grammaire du créole mauricien.* Auckland: Linguistic Society of New Zealand.

———. 1973. Tense and Aspect in Mauritian Creole. *Te Reo*, 16:45-59.

———. 1974-75. Tense, Aspect, and the Mysterious *i* in Seychelles and Reunion Creole. *Te Reo*, 17-18:53-93.

———. 1977a. *Seychelles Creole Grammar. Elements for Indian Ocean Proto-Creole Reconstruction.* Tübingen: Narr.

———. 1977b. Notes on Seychelles Creole Phonology. *Te Reo*, 20:95-110.

———. 1977c. Get "V-ed" in Indian Ocean Creole. *Journal of Creole Studies*, 1.2:219-35.

———. 1977d. A Note on "Passives" in Indian Ocean Creole Dialects. *Journal of Creole Studies*, 1.1:33-57.

———. 1978. Ile de France, Bourbon et la syntaxe des langues créoles. *Etudes créoles*, 1:77-89.

———. 1980. A Re-evaluation of the Predicate in Ile-de-France Creole. In Muysken, ed., 1980:103-24.

———. 1981. Analyse contrastive du prédicat en réunionnais et en créole de l'Isle de France. *Bulletin de l'Observatoire du français contemporain en Afrique Noire*, 2:46-78.

Corne, Chris and P.-M. J. Moorghen. 1978. Proto-créole et liens génétiques dans l'Océan Indien. *Langue française*, 37:60-75.

Corne, Chris and Peter Stein. 1979. Pour une étude du créole rodriguais. *Etudes créoles*, 2:58-84.

Créoles, see Chaudenson 1979b.

Cri des colons, see Anon. 1810.

CSP, see Martineau 1920.

d'Ans, André-Marcel. 1968. *Le créole français d'Haïti. Etude des unités d'articulation, d'expansion et de communication.* The Hague and Paris: Mouton.

DBM, see *Dictionnaire de biographie mauricienne*.

Debien, Gabriel. 1962. *Plantations et Esclaves à Saint-Domingue*. Dakar.

Debien, Gabriel, Marcel Delafosse, and Guy Thilmans. 1978. Journal d'un voyage de traite en Guinée, à Cayenne et aux Antilles fait par Jean Barbot en 1678-79. *Bulletin de l'Institut Fondamental de l'Afrique Noire*, série B, 40.2:235-395.

Defos du Rau, Jean. 1960. *L'île de la Réunion. Etude de géographie humaine.* Bordeaux: Institut de Géographie.

De Rauville, Hervé. 1908. *L'Île de France contemporaine*. Paris: Dubuisson.
Descourtilz, M. E. 1809. *Voyages d'un naturaliste* . . . . 3 volumes. Paris.
Descroizilles, Henri Charles. 1867. *Navire fine engazé or the Mauritius in danger*. Port Louis.
Dictionnaire de Biographie Mauricienne/Dictionary of Mauritian Biography. 1941-. Port Louis.
Du Bois, ( ). 1674. *Les voyages faits par le sieur Dubois aux isles Dauphine ou Madagascar et Bourbon ou Mascarenne ès années 1669-1672*. Paris.
Dubois, Jean and Françoise Dubois-Charlier. 1970. *Eléments de linguistique française: syntaxe*. Paris: Larousse.
Ducoeurjoly, S. J. 1802. *Manuel des habitans de Saint-Domingue*. Paris: Lenoir.
Du Cros, ( ). 1728. Author of a letter written in 1725, published in *Lettres édifiantes et curieuses, écrites des missions étrangères par quelques missionnaires de la Compagnie de Jésus*, 18:9-23. Paris: Leclerc.
Du Fresne de Francheville, Joseph. 1746. *Histoire de la Compagnie des Indes avec les titres de ses concessions & priviléges* . . . . Paris.
d'Unienville, M. C. A. Marrier. 1838. *Statistique d l'Île Maurice et ses dépendances* . . . . Paris: G. Barba.
F( ). 1863. *Notice historique, géographique et religieuse sur l'île Bourbon ou de la Réunion*. Versailles.
Faine, Jules. 1937. *Philologie créole. Etudes historiques et étymologiques sur la langue créole d'Haïti*. 2nd ed. Port-au-Prince: Impr. de l'Etat.
–––. 1939. *Le créole dans l'univers. Etudes comparatives des parlers français-créoles. Tome I. Le Mauricien*. Port-au-Prince: Impr. de l'Etat.
Filliot, J.-M. 1974. *La traite des esclaves vers les Mascareignes au XVIIIe siècle*. Paris: Office de la recherche scientifique et technique outre-mer.
Focard, Volcy. 1884. Du patois créole de l'île Bourbon. *Bulletin de la Société des Sciences et Arts de la Réunion*, ( ):179-239.
FOM, see Ministère de la France d'Outre-mer.
Fontaney, Louise. 1980. Le verbe. In *Eléments de description de Punu*. Ed. by F. Nsuka-Nkutsi, pp. 51-114. Lyon: C.R.L.S.
Forman, Michael L. 1972. *Zamboangueño Texts with Grammatical Analysis: A Study of Philippine Creole Spanish*. Ph.D. dissertation, Cornell University.
Fourcade, Georges. (1930) 1976. *Z'histoires la caze*. Marseilles: Jeanne Laffitte.
Freycinet, Louis Claude Desaulces de. 1827. *Voyage autour du monde exécuté sur les corvettes de S. M. l'Uranie et la Physicienne pendant les années 1817, 1818, 1819 et 1820*. . . . Vol. 2.2. Paris.
Gee, J. P. 1974. *"Get Passive": On Some Constructions with "Get."* Bloomington: Indiana University Linguistics Club.
Genèse, see Chaudenson 1979a.
Gilman, Charles. 1979. Cameroonian Pidgin English, a Neo-African Language. In Hancock et al., 1979:269-80.

Givón, Talmy. 1979. Prolegomena to Any Sane Creology. In Hancock et al. 1979: 3-35.
Goodman, Morris F. 1964. *A Comparative Study of Creole French Dialects.* London, The Hague, and Paris: Mouton.
Grant, Louis Charles. 1886. *Letters from Mauritius in the Eighteenth Century* . . . . Mauritius.
Gros, ( ). 1791. *Isle St.-Domingue, Province du Nord. Récit historique sur les évènements qui se sont succédés . . . depuis le 26 octobre 1791, jusqu'au 24 décembre de la même année,* n.p.
Gross, Maurice. 1979. On the Failure of Generative Grammar. *Language,* 55: 859-85.
Gueunier, Nicole. 1980. Problèmes d'édition et d'analyse de textes oraux produits dans une communauté rurale réunionnaise. *Etudes créoles,* 3.1:42-53.
Hall, Robert A., Jr. 1953. *Haitian Creole. Grammar–Texts–Vocabulary.* Philadelphia: American Folklore Society.
Hancock, Ian F. 1973. Malacca Creole Portuguese: A Brief Transformational Outline. *Te Reo,* 16:23-44.
–––. 1976. *Krio.* Austin, University of Texas, Department of English. Mimeo, 30 pp.
–––. ca. 1977-78. *Grammatical Sketch of Louisiana Creole French.* Mimeo, 5 pp.
Hancock, Ian F., Edgar Polomé, Morris Goodman, and Bernd Heine. 1979. *Readings in Creole Studies.* Ghent: Story-Scientia.
Harrison, S. 1972. *The Language of Norfolk Island.* M.A. thesis, Macquarie University.
Héry, M. L. (1828, 1849, 1856) 1883. *Esquisses africaines. Fables créoles et Explorations dans l'intérieur de l'île Bourbon.* Paris: J. Rigal.
Highfield, Arnold R. 1979. *The French Dialect of St. Thomas, U.S. Virgin Islands: A Descriptive Grammar with Texts and Glossary.* Ann Arbor: Karoma.
Hill, Kenneth C., ed. 1979. *The Genesis of Language: The First Michigan Colloquium, 1979.* Ann Arbor: Karoma.
Hilliard d'Auberteuil, ( ). 1776-77. *Considérations sur l'état présent de la colonie française de saint-domingue.* Paris.
Holm, John. 1980. The Creole "Copula" that Highlighted the World. In *Perspectives in American English,* ed. by J. L. Dillard, pp. 367-75. The Hague: Mouton.
Hull, Alexander. 1968. The Origins of New World French Phonology. *Word,* 24: 255-69.
–––. (1975) 1979. On the Origin and Chronology of the French-based Creole. In Hancock et al. 1979:201-15.
Huttar, George L. 1975. *Some Kwa-like Features of Djuka Syntax.* Paper presented to the International Conference on Pidgins and Creoles, Hawaii, January 1975.
Hymes, Dell, ed. 1971. *Pidginization and Creolization of Languages.* London: Cambridge University Press.

Jansen, Bert, Hilda Koopman, and Pieter Muysken. 1978. Serial Verbs in the Creole Languages. *Amsterdam Creole Studies,* 2:125-59.
Janvier, Louis Joseph. 1886. Berceuse haïtienne, Zangui (L'Anguille). *Revue des Traditions Populaires,* 1:21-23, 107.
Jones, Steve. 1980. Social Change and Language Change: The Development of an Urban Variety of St. Lucian Creole. Honors thesis, Cornell University.
Jourdain, Elodie. 1956. *Du français aux parlers créoles.* Paris: Klincksieck.
Kaeppelin, Paul. 1908. *Les escales françaises sur la route de l'Inde, 1638-1731.* Paris: Challamel.
Koutsoudas, Andreas. 1978. *The Question of Rule Ordering: Some Common Fallacies.* Bloomington: Indiana University Linguistics Club.
Koutsoudas, Andreas, Gerald Sanders, and Craig Noll. 1974. The Application of Phonological Rules. *Language,* 50.1:1-28.
Kuczynski, Robert René. 1948-49. *A Demographic Survey of the British Colonial Empire.* London: Oxford University Press.
Labat, Jean-Baptiste. 1728. *Nouvelle relation de l'Afrique occidentale....* Paris.
———. 1730. *Voyage du Chevalier des Marchais en Guinée, isles voisines, et à cayenne fait en 1725, 1726 & 1727.* Paris.
Lagane, R. 1967. Les verbes symétriques: économie morphosyntaxique et différenciation sémantique. *Cahiers de lexicologie,* 10:21-30.
Lagesse, Marcelle. 1972. *L'Ile de France avant La Bourdonnais.* Port Louis: Mauritius Archives Publications.
[Lambert, Richard.] (1828) 1888-92. Catéchisme en créole de l'Ile Maurice en 1828. *Bulletin de la Société de Linguistique de Paris,* 7:122-32.
Lane, George S. 1935. Notes on Louisiana French. II. The Negro-French Dialect. *Language,* 11:5-16.
Laray, H. 1888-92a. Catéchisme en créole de l'Ile Maurice en 1828. *Bulletin de la Société de Linguistique de Paris,* 7:122-32.
———. 1888-92b. Chansons créoles de la Réunion. *Bulletin de la Société de Linguistique de Paris,* 7:146-52.
Laurent, Joëlle and Ina Césaire. 1976. *Contes de mort et de vie aux Antilles.* Paris: Nubia.
Le Brun, Jean. 1816. *Journal.* Unpublished ms. London Missionary Society Collection, School of Oriental and African Studies, University of London.
Lefebvre, Gilles R. 1976. Français régional et créole à Saint-Barthélemy (Guadeloupe). In Snyder and Valdman 1976:122-46.
———. 1979. *Langue et société à Saint-Barth (Antilles françaises): parlers populaires et traditions ethnographiques.* Paper presented to the colloquium "Etudes créoles et développement," Seychelles, May 1979.
Le Page, Robert B. 1960. An Historical Introduction to Jamaican Creole. In *Jamaican Creole,* ed. by Robert B. Le Page, pp. 1-124. (Creole Language Studies, no. 1.) London: Macmillan; New York: St. Martin's Press.

———. 1972. *Processes of Creolisation*. York: University of York, Department of Language.
———. 1977. Processes of Pidginization and Creolization. In Valdman, ed., 1977: 222-55.
Lettres édifiantes..., see Du Cros 1728.
Lexique, see Chaudenson 1974.
Lloyd, J. A. 1840. [Letter concerning the emancipated slaves in Mauritius, addressed to John Irving of the Colonial Office, London.] Unpublished ms., PRO CO 167/226.
LMS, see London Missionary Society.
Lolliot, Pierre. 1855. *Poésies Créoles*. Port Louis.
Lombard, Alf. 1938. *L'infinitif de narration dans les langues romanes: études de syntaxe historique*. Uppsala: Almqvist & Wiksell; Leipzig: Harrassowitz.
London Missionary Society: Archives of the Council for World Mission. Mauritius: incoming letters, boxes 1-5; Madagascar/Mauritius: journals, boxes 1 and 2.
Lougnon, Albert, ed. 1933. *Correspondence du conseil supérieur de Bourbon et de la Compagnie des Indes. 10 mars 1732-23 janvier 1736*. Saint-Denis, Reunion.
———, ed. 1934. *Correspondence du conseil supérieur de Bourbon et de la Compagnie des Indes. 22 janvier 1724-30 décembre 1731. Ensemble quatres lettres de la Compagnie au conseil provincial de l'île de France. 31 décembre 1727-24 septembre 1729*. Saint-Denis, Reunion.
———, ed. 1935. *Correspondence du conseil supérieur de Bourbon et de la Compagnie des Indes. 23 janvier 1736-9 mai 1741. Ensemble trois lettres de la Compagnie au conseil supérieur de l'île de France. 17 février-29 décembre 1738*. Saint-Denis, Reunion.
———. 1956. *L'île de Bourbon pendant la Régence*. Paris.
———. 1958. *Le mouvement maritime aux îles de Bourbon et de France pendant les premières années du règne personnel de Louis XV (1727-1735)*. Nérac, France.
Lougnon, Albert and Auguste Toussaint, eds. 1937. [Mahé de La Bourdonnais' 1740] *Mémoire des isles de France et de Bourbon, adressé au Controleur général Orry de Fulvy*. Paris.
MA, see Mauritius Archives.
Markey, T. L. and Peter Fodale. 1980. *Lexical Diathesis, Focal Shifts, and Passivization: The Creole Voice*. Paper presented to the Society for Caribbean Linguistics Third Biennial Conference, Aruba, September 1980.
Martineau, Alfred, ed. 1920. *Correspondence du Conseil supérieur de Pondichéry et de la Compagnie des Indes*. Volume I. Pondichéry.
Maure, André. 1840. *Souvenirs d'un vieux colon de l'Ile Maurice....* La Rochelle: Frédéric Boutet.
Mauritius Archives. Series OA: French East India Company — Divers (OA96-OA100); Series JB: Procédure criminelle (JB1-JB3); Series KA and KH: Reg-

isters of births, marriages and deaths in the parishes of Port Louis and Grand Port (to 1738).

McKibbin, Juliette and Chris Corne. 1980. La morphologie verbale dans le mauricien du XIXe: implications pour la nature du prédicat? *Etudes créoles*, 3:24-40.

Meyer, Paul. 1872. Compte-rendu de J. J. Thomas, "Theory and Practice of Creole Grammar." *Revue critique d'histoire et de littérature*, 6:156-57.

Meyer, Truus. 1980. *Quelques idées sur la troncation de la voyelle finale dans le mauricien du XIXe siècle*. Ms., 11 pp.

Milbert, Jacques Gérard. 1812. *Voyage pittoresque à l'Ile de France, au Cap de Bonne Espérance et à l'Ile de Ténériffe*. Paris.

Ministère de la France d'outre-mer. Série G^1: Recensements, Etat-Civil (G^1 505, 509).

Moorghen, Pierre-Marie J. 1975. *Analyse des marqueurs pré-verbaux des créoles de l'Océan Indien*. Paper presented to the International Conference on Pidgins and Creoles, Hawaii, January 1975.

Moreau de Saint-Méry, L. E. 1797. *Description topographique, physique, civile, politique et historique de la partie française de l'isle Saint-Domingue*. Philadelphia.

Morgan, Raleigh, Jr. 1959. Structural Sketch of Saint Martin Creole. *Anthropological Linguistics*, 1.8:20-24f.

———. 1976. The Saint Martin Creole Copula in Relation to Verbal Categories. In Snyder and Valdman 1976:147-65.

Mourelatos, Alexander P. D. 1978. Events, Processes, and States. *Linguistics and Philosophy*, 2:415-34.

Muysken, Pieter, ed. 1980. *Generative Studies on Creole Languages*. Dordrecht and Cinnaminson: Foris Publications.

Neumann, Ingrid. 1978. *Die orale Tradition der Seychellen und ihre Quellen*. Staatsarbeit, Universität Köln.

Nicolay, W. 1835. Proclamation. Pour noirs esclaves dans Maurice. *Recueil des lois, ordonnances, proclamations, notes et avis du gouvernement publiés à l'Ile Maurice pendant l'année 1835*. Port Louis.

Nicolson, ( ). 1776. *Essai sur l'histoire naturelle de St. Domingue*. Paris.

North-Coombes, Alfred. 1971. *The Island of Rodrigues*. Port Louis.

Olagnier, Paul. 1936. *Un grand colonial inconnu: le gouverneur Benoist Dumas*. Paris.

Papen, Robert A. 1975. *Nana k nana, nana k napa, or, the strange case of "e-deletion" verbs in Indian Ocean Creole*. Paper presented to the International Conference on Pidgins and Creoles, Hawaii, January 1975.

———. 1978a. Etat présent des études en phonologie des créoles de l'Océan Indien. *Etudes créoles*, 1:35-63.

———. 1978b. *The French-based Creoles of the Indian Ocean: An Analysis and Comparison*. Ph.D. dissertation, University of California, San Diego.

Perusse, Roland I. 1977. *Historical Dictionary of Haïti.* New Jersey.
Piston, Eugène. 1847. *Chronique de l'Ile de France: La Bourdonnais.* Port Louis.
Pitot, Henri. 1878. *Soirées d'abat-vent.* Port Louis.
Pitot, Thomy. An XIII [ca. 1805]. Quelques observations sur l'ouvrage intitulé Voyage à l'Ile de France . . . . *RHLM,* 2:372-74.
Prentout, Henri. 1901. *L'Ile de France sous Decaen.* Paris: Hatchette.
Recueil trimestriel de documents et travaux inédits pour servir à l'histoire des Mascareignes françaises. 1932-1949; nouvelle série, 1953-. Saint-Denis, Reunion.
Reinecke, John E. et al. 1975. *A Bibliography of Pidgin and Creole Languages.* Honolulu: The University Press of Hawaii.
Rens, L. L. E. 1953. *The Historical and Social Background of Surinam's Negro-English.* Amsterdam: North-Holland.
Revue historique et littéraire de l'Ile Maurice. 1887-94. Port Louis.
Revue retrospective de l'île Maurice. 1949-55. Port Louis.
RHL, see *Revue historique . . .*
Ricquebourg, L. J. Camille. 1976. *Dictionnaire généalogique des familles de l'Ile Bourbon (1665-1767).* Aix-en-Provence.
Roberts, Peter A. 1977. *Duont:* A case for Spontaneous Development. *Journal of Creole Studies,* 1.1:101-8.
Ross, Alan S. C. and A. W. Moverley. 1964. *The Pitcairnese Language.* London: Andre Deutsch.
Rosset, Alfred. 1967. *Les premiers colons de l'île Bourbon.* Paris: Editions du cerf-volant.
RRM, see *Revue retrospective . . .*
RT, see *Recueil trimestriel . . .*
Saint Jacques Fauquenoy, Marguerite. 1971. Le verbe "être" dans les créoles français. In *Langues et techniques, nature et société,* Vol. 1, *Approche linguistique,* ed. by Jacqueline M. C. Thomas and Lucien Bernot, pp. 225-31. Paris: Klincksieck.
–––. 1972. *Analyse structurale du créole guyanais.* Paris: Klincksieck.
Saint-Quentin, M.-F.-J. Auguste de. 1872. Notice grammaticale & philologique sur le créole de Cayenne. In *Introduction à l'histoire de Cayenne, suivie d'un recueil de contes, fables et chansons en créole,* ed. by Alfred de Saint-Quentin. Antibes: J. Marchand.
Sauzier, Théodore. 1904. Bibliographie des patois créoles des Mascareignes. *Revue de Linguistique et de Philologie Comparée,* 37:251-66.
Snyder, Emile and Albert Valdman, eds. 1976. *Identité culturelle et Francophonie dans les Amériques (I).* Québec: Presses de l'Université Laval.
Stein, Peter. 1972. *Les études sur le parler créole de l'Ile Maurice. Compte-rendu de cent ans de recherches (1870-1970).* Unpublished Staatsexames-Hausarbeit, University of Marburg.
Taylor, Douglas. 1971. Grammatical and Lexical Affinities of Creoles. In Hymes 1971:293-96.

———. 1977. *Languages of the West Indies.* Baltimore and London: Johns Hopkins University Press.
Tesnière, Lucien. 1951. Le duel sylleptique en français et en slave. *Bulletin de la Société de Linguistique de Paris,* 47:57-63.
Thomas, John Jacob. (1869) 1969. *The Theory and Practice of Creole Grammar.* London and Port of Spain: New Beacon Books.
Thoreau de la Martinière, René. ca. 1780. *Plan du Port Louis de l'Isle de France.* Ms.
Todd, Loreto. 1979a. Review of Corne 1977a. *Language,* 55:916-19.
———. 1979b. Cameroonian: A Consideration of "What's in a Name?" In Hancock et al. 1979:281-94.
Toussaint, Auguste. 1936. *Port-Louis, deux siècles d'histoire (1735-1935).* Port Louis: La Typographie Moderne.
———. 1967. *La route des îles.* Paris.
Towards, see Baker 1976.
Trouette, Emile. 1883. Le conte du chat botté en patois créole de l'île de la Réunion. *Revue de Linguistique et de Philologie Comparée,* 16:64-71.
Valdman, Albert. 1970. *Basic Course in Haitian Creole.* Bloomington: Indiana University; The Hague: Mouton.
———. 1973. La copule dans les parlers français créoles. *Canadian Journal of Romance Linguistics,* 1:93-111.
———, ed. 1977. *Pidgin and Creole Linguistics.* Bloomington and London: Indiana University Press.
———. 1978a. *Le créole: structure, statut et origine.* Paris: Klincksieck.
———. 1978b. On the Structure and Origin of Indian Ocean Creole [Review article of Baker 1972 and Chaudenson 1974], *Romance Philology,* 32:65-93.
Verguin, J. 1956. La politique de la Compagnie des Indes dans la traite des noirs à l'île Bourbon (1662-1762). *Revue Historique,* 216:45-58.
Vinson, Auguste. 1882. Les origines du Patois de l'île Bourbon. *Bulletin de la Société des Sciences et Arts de la Réunion,* ( ):88-129.
Vintilă-Rădulescu, Ioana. 1976. *Le Créole Français.* The Hague and Paris: Mouton.
Voorhoeve, Jan. 1980. Multifunctionality as a Derivational Problem. In Muysken, ed., 1980:25-34.
[Vuillemin, F.] ca. 1795. [Map of] *Le Port Nord-Ouest.* Ms.
Waite, Jeffrey. 1981. Predicate Marker Combinations in Isle de France Creole. *Te Reo,* 24:13-26.
———. Forthcoming. *The Realis System in Isle de France Creole.*
Washabaugh, William. 1979. On the Sociality of Creole Languages. In Hill 1979: 89-107.
———. 1980. Pursuing Creole Roots. In Muysken, ed., 1980:85-102.
Werner, Alice. 1919. *Introductory Sketch of the Bantu Languages.* London: Kegan Paul, Trench, Trubner.

Wimpffen, Francis Alexander Stanislaus, Baron de. 1817. *A voyage to Saint Domingo in the years 1788, 1789 and 1790.* London.

Yai, O.-B. 1977. Dahomey. In *Langues et politiques de langues en Afrique noire. L'expérience de l'UNESCO,* ed. by A. I. Sow, pp. 241-50. Paris: Nubia.

Chronological List of Creole Texts Cited in Chapter B3

Year	Creole	Source
-1722-	RC	Chaudenson 1974:1147
1749	MC	Grant 1886:166
1769	MC	Bernardin de Saint-Pierre 1773.1:257
1776a	HC	Nicolson 1776:56-57
1776b	HC	Hilliard d'Auberteuil 1776-77.2:68
1785	HC	Valdman 1978a
1790a	HC	Wimpffen 1817:186
1790b	HC	De Bien 1962:138
1791	HC	Gros 1791:7
-1792-	HC	Anon. ca. 1792:6-15
1793	RC	Chaudenson 1974
1796	HC	Anon. 1796
-1797	HC	Moreau de Saint-Méry 1797.1:37, 65
1799	RC	Chaudenson 1974
-1802a	HC	Descourtilz 1809.2:129, 303, 352; 3:113-353
1802b	HC	Ducoeurjoly 1802.2:283-393
1802c	HC	Anon. 1802 (Bonaparte)
1802d	HC	Anon. 1802 (Leclerc)
-1805	MC	*RHLM*, 2:372-74
1810	HC	Anon. 1810:39, 185
1811	HC	Anon. 1821
1816	MC	Le Brun 1816 (entry dated July 9)
1818a	MC	Freycinet 1827:407-11
1818b	MC	Freycinet 1827:411-12
1820	RC	Chaudenson 1974
-1822	MC	Chrestien 1831:6-26
1824	HC	Anon. 1831:93
1828a	MC	Lambert 1828
1828b	RC	Héry 1883:27-33, 36-40
1829	RC	Chaudenson 1974
1830a	MC	Anon. 1830
-1830b-	HC	Bonneau 1856
-1831	MC	Chrestien 1831:39-55
1832a	RC	Chaudenson 1974
1832b-	MC	Chrestien 1838
1835	MC	Nicolay 1835
-1837	MC	Maure 1840:70, 352-53

Year	Creole	Source
1840	MC	Lloyd 1840
1849	RC	Héry 1883:17-26, 34-35, 41-42
1854	HC	Bigelow 1877
1855	MC	Lolliot 1855
1856	RC	Héry 1883:43-61
-1860	MC	Anon. ca. 1860
1863	RC	F( ) 1863:236
1867	MC	Descroizilles 1867
1870	MC	Besant 1870
-1877	HC	Audain 1877
1878	MC	Pitot 1878
1880	MC	Baissac 1880
1882	RC	Vinson 1882
1883	RC	Trouette 1883
1884a	RC	Focard 1884
1884b	RC	Focard 1884
1884c	RC	Focard 1884
1885	MC	Anderson 1885
1886	HC	Janvier 1886
-1887	RC	*RHLM*, 2:145-46
-1892	RC	Laray 1888-92
1930	RC	Fourcade 1976
1936	HC	Comhaire-Sylvain 1936

NAME INDEX

Adam, 143, 144, 153
Aignan, 145
Allaigre, 144, 145, 155
Alleyne, M. C., 6, 86, 88, 119, 121, 125, 261
Amastae, J., 10
Anderson, S., 70, 210, 211, 221, 238, 261, 274
Anonymous ca. 1792, 261, 273
Anonymous 1796, 261, 273
Anonymous 1802, 261, 273
Anonymous 1810, 238, 261, 273
Anonymous 1811, 223, 261, 273
Anonymous 1830, 238, 261, 273
Anonymous 1831, 261, 273
Anonymous ca. 1860, 69, 261, 274
Apollon, 255
Artur, 170
Asgarally, R., 85, 261
Auber, 144, 153, 158
Audin, M. J. J., 261, 274
Azéma, G., 152, 261

Bachelier, 141
Bailey, B. L., 87, 262
Bailey, Ch.-J., 106, 262
Baissac, C., 2, 47, 49, 52, 69, 70, 72, 73, 82, 86, 88, 96, 97, 127, 134, 211, 234, 235, 242, 262, 274
Baker, P., 4, 10, 31, 38, 42, 43, 45, 49, 67, 82, 84, 85, 86, 88, 89, 92, 101, 112, 113, 115, 118, 120, 121, 125, 127, 128, 129, 132, 136, 137, 161, 167, 172, 188, 193, 205, 209, 212, 224, 225, 262, 271 (see also *Towards* in Subject Index)
Ballard, 142, 143, 147, 174
Balmane, 141, 145

Barassin, J., 138, 262
Barat, C., et al., 12, 13, 24, 56, 57, 66, 98, 262
Barbot, J., 245, 256, 262
Baron, 145
Bauche, H., 211, 262
Bechet, O., 138, 143, 145, 146, 147, 149, 262
Beckett, J., 140
Bellecourt, 146, 203
Belon, 168
Benoist, A., 141
Benoît, P., 203
Bentolila, A., 48, 122, 253, 262
Bernardin de Saint-Pierre, J.-H., 222, 262, 273
Besant, W., 262, 274
Bickerton, D., 10, 22, 42, 46, 66, 89, 99, 108, 109, 121, 122-23, 124, 125, 128, 140, 246, 247, 252, 253, 254, 259, 262
Bienvenu, 143, 148
Bigelow, J., 224, 262, 274
Biggs, B., 10
Bigot, 141
Binial, 145
Boivin, 141
Bollée, A., 4, 10, 31, 34, 42, 44, 45, 49, 85, 88, 89, 92, 93, 100, 114, 117, 118, 124, 127, 129, 140, 208, 216, 238, 252, 257, 262
Bonneau, A., 263, 273
Bonnefoy, T., 147, 165, 263
Borthon, 141, 143, 203
Bouchat de la Tour, 141
Bouet-Willaumez, ( )., 132
Bouloc, 145, 146, 148, 149, 150
Bouly, C., 140

Bourigaut, 141
Boyer, E., 168
Boyer, F., 168
Bozon-Verduraz, C., 140
Brenier, 167
Briand, 141
Broadbridge, C., 84, 263
Brouillet, 146
Brousse, 145, 147, 149, 160
Butté, 141

Calvet, L. J., 10, 263
Carayol, M., 10, 11, 12, 13, 30, 56, 58, 61, 109, 262, 263
Cellier, P., 127, 263
Céré, 171
Césaire, I., 76, 267
Chafe, W., 47, 263
Charlevoix, P. F. X., 177, 251, 263
Chaudenson, R., 3, 4, 5, 6, 10, 11, 12, 13, 17, 21, 22, 24, 30, 35, 49, 54, 58, 61, 64, 66, 81, 83, 94, 105, 106, 108, 109, 110-14, 115, 117, 118, 120, 121, 124, 129, 132, 135-40, 141, 142, 147, 158, 161-74, 178, 179, 180, 183, 185, 186, 187, 188, 189, 190, 191, 192, 193, 194, 200, 202, 203, 204, 205, 206, 208, 209, 210, 211, 214, 216, 217, 221, 224, 235, 236, 237, 239, 241, 242, 250, 257, 258, 263, 271, 273 (see also *Créoles, Genèse,* and *Lexique* in Subject Index)
Cheke, A., 140
Chélin, A., 143, 145, 146, 148, 182, 183, 263
Cherel, 146
Chotin, 141
Chrestien, F., 67, 82, 101, 140, 212, 214, 215, 220, 221, 222, 223, 263, 273
Christie, P., 48, 101, 104, 263

Clain, 144, 153, 158
Clark, R., 10, 124, 264
Clarke-Smith, A., 69
Clergeac, 146
Cohen, M., 212, 264
Colmok, 141
Comhaire-Sylvain, S., 75, 76, 115, 264, 274
Corne, C., 4, 11, 12, 13, 18, 23, 27, 31, 34, 35, 36, 37, 39, 42, 43, 44, 45, 48, 49, 50, 52, 53, 63, 67, 68, 69, 70, 72, 75, 78, 79, 81, 84, 85, 90, 92, 95, 97, 100, 101, 110, 127, 129, 140, 212, 216, 222, 223, 227, 234, 235, 238, 239, 240, 258, 264
Cossigny, 169, 170
Coste, 155, 203
Coupet, 149
Courtois, 145, 203
Crampon, 146, 148
Curé, 146, 149
Curtin, P., 245
Cuttaree, P., 140

Dalby, D., 140
Dalleau, 154
Dalphinis, M., 140
d'Ans, A. M., 75, 264
David, 204
De Beauvolliers, 151, 155, 156, 158, 165
Debien, G., 256, 264, 273
De Comminge, 143, 145, 174
Deforges-Bouchet, 148
Defos du Rau, J., 58, 105, 108, 264
De Guigné La Bérangerie, 168
De Hauville, 132, 143, 144, 145, 148, 149, 150, 153, 154, 155, 161, 162, 166, 174, 203
Dejean, 167
Delafosse, M., 256, 264
Delesque, 143, 149

NAME INDEX 277

Delporte, 147
Delvinquier, 146, 147
De Merville de Saint-Remy, see:
    Mathieu de Merville de Saint-Remy
De Noisy, 155
De Nyon, 132, 143, 144, 145, 147, 148, 149, 150, 152, 153, 154, 155, 156, 157, 161, 162, 163, 164, 165, 166, 173, 174, 203
D'Epinay, A., 170
De Rauville, H., 132, 143, 265
Descoublans, 146
Descourtilz, M. E., 220, 223, 224, 265, 273
Descroizilles, H. C., 68, 69, 70, 72, 73, 82, 231, 265, 274
Desfouilleuse, 141, 182, 189, 204
Desisles, 141
d'Hautrive, see: *Gast d'Hauterive*
Dhermitte, 182
Didion, 141, 145, 149, 150
Dioré, 150
Dorlet de Bresson, 145
Du Bois, ( )., 203, 265
Dubois, A., 141
Dubois, P., 146
Dubois, J., 35, 265
Dubois-Charlier, F., 35, 265
Ducoeurjoly, S. J., 76, 223, 224, 265, 273
Du Cotté, 145, 148, 155
Du Cros, ( )., 132, 203, 265
Ducuelle, 145
Du Fresne de Francheville, J., 204, 265
Duhamel, 146, 148
D'Unienville, M. C. A. M., 247, 265
Dupré, 141
Duquesnain, 144, 149
Duronguet Le Toullec, 143, 147, 148, 152, 156, 161, 162
Dussart de la Salle, 141, 167

Duval de Hauville, see: *De Hauville*
Duvivier de la Mahautière, 240

Elgar, 168
Estève, 141

F( ), 265, 274
Faillet, 143, 174
Faine, J., 75, 84, 98, 106, 126, 134, 209, 241, 242, 243, 244, 246, 258, 265
Fantoux, 145, 149
Faverger, 143
Favori, 248
Ferrère, 4, 6
Filliot, J.-M., 179, 184, 185, 204, 205, 265
Focard, V., 13, 30, 64, 65, 66, 72, 78, 112, 213, 221, 222, 227, 235, 239, 240, 265, 274
Fodale, P., 84, 85, 99, 114, 268
Folio, 168
Fontaine, Jacques, 168
Fontaine, Jean, 144, 153, 154, 162
Fontaney, L., 100, 265
Forman, M., 100, 265
Fortier, A., 239
Fourcade, G., 12, 13, 22, 30, 64, 114, 213, 214, 222, 235, 265, 274
François, 144, 146, 148
Freilik, 143
Freycinet, L., 67, 72, 78, 214, 215, 222, 239, 265, 273
Fribourg, 143

Gast d'Hauterive, 143, 146, 149, 174
Gaucher, 203
Gee, J., 79, 265
Genu, 146
Geoffroy, 141, 145
George, 148
Gerbault, 169

278 NAME INDEX

Gigot, 141, 146, 148
Gilman, C., 101, 265
Giraudin, 146
Givón, T., 122, 266
Gonneau, 168
Goodman, M., 2, 3, 5, 73, 76, 77, 78, 115, 126, 134-36, 137, 140, 202, 208, 209, 217, 221, 222, 223, 224, 239, 241, 244-46, 253, 258, 266
Goulet, 141
Gouron, 141
Gourrès, 141
Graberin, 148
Grant, C., 212, 238, 247, 266, 273
Grenier, 155
Grimaud, 141
Grondin, J.-B., 168
Grondin, Joseph, 168
Gros, ( )., 266, 273
Gros, M., 47, 266
Gueunier, N., 109, 266
Gument de la Tour, 146
Guyenet, 143, 149

Hall, R. A., 75, 266
Hancock, I., 10, 84, 104, 119, 266
Harrison, S., 123, 266
Hayec, 143, 203
Heine, B., 252, 257, 259, 266
Hélant, 146
Héry, L., 64, 66, 72, 213, 227, 234, 235, 236, 240, 266
Highfield, A., 20, 29, 94, 261, 266
Hill, K. C., 262, 266
Hilliard d'Auberteuil, ( )., 238, 266, 273
Hoareau, F., 10
Hojird, E., 10
Hollyman, J., 10
Holm, J., 10, 88, 266
Hookoomsing, V., 140
Hubert, 143

Huet, 154
Hull, A., 10, 23, 74, 104, 106, 116, 140, 206, 244-46, 256, 266
Huttar, G., 10, 87, 88, 266
Hymes, D., 261, 266, 270

Igou, 143
Infante, 141

Jacob, 146
Jacotet, 143
Jansen, B., et al., 104, 119, 267
Janvier, L. J., 267, 274
Jean, G., 10
Jeeroburkhan, S., 140
Jonchée de la Goleterie, 156, 175, 177
Jones, S., 84, 267
Jourdain, E., 115, 267
Jupin, 203

Kaeppelin, P., 142, 148, 152, 202, 267
Katupha, M., 101
Koutsoudas, A., 50, 267
Kuczynski, R. R., 138, 148, 152, 169, 171, 202, 251, 267

Labat, J.-B., 204, 256, 267
La Bourdonnais, 137, 139, 166, 167, 179, 180, 194, 204, 205
Lacan, 141
La Fontaine, 67, 215, 267
Lagane, R., 99, 267
Lagesse, M., 137, 142, 144, 147, 148, 151, 267
Lalot, 146
Lambert, R., 67, 223, 267, 273
Landay, 146
Lane, G. S., 73, 104, 239, 267
Languedoc, 160
Laray, H., 67, 78, 267, 274
Launay, 146
Laurent, J., 76, 267

NAME INDEX 279

Lauret, 169
Le Blanc, 144, 149, 174
Le Brun, J., 257, 267, 273
Le Coq, 141, 143, 145, 147, 155
Ledoux, 146
Lefebvre, G., 20, 115, 267
Le Gouron, 141
Le Heux, 141, 146
Le Houarno, 141
Leichnig, 143, 148, 149, 150, 168
Lemery-Dumont, 167
Lemeur, 141
Lenoir, 142, 151, 157, 158-59, 160, 161, 162, 165, 169, 170, 171, 175, 187, 202, 204
Le Page, R. B., 117, 140, 256, 257, 267
Lepinay, 154
Leplanti, 141
Le Roux, 144, 145, 149
Le Thonnelier, 148
Le Toullec, see: *Duronguet le Toullec*
Levesque, 141
Lincoln, P., 10
Lloyd, J. A., 237, 268, 274
Lolliot, P., 68, 86, 210, 268, 274
Lombard, A., 88, 99, 268
Lorcy, 141
Lorette, see: *Lauret*
Lougnon, A., 138, 139, 143, 144, 145, 146, 147, 148, 149, 153, 154, 167, 169, 173, 178, 184, 185, 189, 190, 191, 192, 194, 199, 203, 204, 205, 243, 244, 256, 263, 268
Louis XIV, 251
Luc, 141

Macquaire, 141
Maheas, 248
Malleser, 148
Mandrou, 145, 146, 149
Mann, M., 140

Marchand, 146
Marie, 4, 6
Markey, T., 10, 84, 85, 99, 114, 268
Marragon, 237
Martineau, A., 264, 268
Mascle, 141, 146, 149
Mathieu De Mervilles de Saint-Remy, 168, 170
Maupin, 182, 189, 192, 193, 199
Maure, A., 238, 268, 273
McKay, B., 10
McKibbin, J., 10, 48, 49, 51, 52, 70, 269
Meisel, J., 262
Menot, 146
Meuron, 143
Meyer, P., 134, 140, 269
Meyer, T., 10, 70, 269
Milbert, J. G., 238, 269
Milloe, 154
Milon, 146
Misset, 143
Mollet, 168
Mondon, F., 10
Mondon, R., 10
Moorghen, P.-M., 10, 12, 23, 27, 31, 37, 56, 63, 78, 79, 92, 110, 127, 235, 236, 263, 264, 269
Mooten, D., 10
Moreau de Saint-Méry, L. E., 240, 269, 273
Morel, L., 167
Morel, N., 141
Morgan, R., 10, 104, 269
Morphy, 189
Mourelatos, A., 47, 269
Moverley, A. W., 123, 257, 270
Muysken, P. 269

Nativel, 153, 154
Neizein, 142, 143, 147

Neumann, I., 10, 34, 48, 74, 98, 104, 140, 239, 269
Nicolay, W., 67, 269, 273
Nicole, 143
Nicolle, 146
Nicolson, ( )., 213, 238, 269, 273
Noel, 168
Noll, C., 50, 267
North-Coombes, A., 207, 237, 269
Nsuka-Nkutsi, F., 265

Ogé, 148
Olagnier, P., 147, 185, 269
Olivier, L., 140
Olivier, M., 140

Papen, R. A., 2, 6, 8, 10, 12, 13, 17, 22, 24, 27, 28, 31, 34, 35, 38, 49, 50, 52, 54, 79, 92, 100, 112, 127, 129, 240, 269
Pautre, 146
Penisseau, 146
Perraton, H., 140
Perusse, R. I., 251, 270
Piston, E., 202, 270
Pitot, H., 69-70, 270, 274
Pitot, T., 67, 212, 222, 270
Pitou, 168
Pluchon, 141, 146, 148, 149
Polomé, E., 266
Prentout, H., 254, 270
Prigent, 147, 149
Provensal, 144

Rehel, 141
Reinecke, J. E., 257, 270
Rens, L. L. E., 125, 270
Richart, 141, 147
Ricquebourg, L. J. C., 4, 6, 147, 148, 154, 158, 168, 169, 170, 172, 270
Rivière, 146
Rivont, 147, 149, 202

Robert, E., 144, 154, 162
Robert (pilot), 184
Roberts, P., 95, 96, 270
Robin, 146
Rochetaing, 208, 237
Romain Le François de Grainville, 170
Ross, A. S. C., 123, 257, 270
Rosset, A., 105, 270

Saint Jacques Fauquenoy, M., 48, 76, 103, 270
Saint-Martin, 143, 146, 148, 149, 150
Saint Matthew, 70, 261
Saint-Quentin, A., 76, 267
Saisse, 145
Sanders, G., 50, 267
Sauzier, T., 30, 227, 270
Savy, G., 10
Savy, M.-T., 10
Schmidig, 143, 146
Schmitt, 143
Sebelin, 146
Seriber, 143, 145, 147
Sicre de Fontbrune, 148
Simon de Monsy, 143, 149
Snyder, E., 270
Sow, A. I., 272
Springal, 144
Stein, P., 10, 31, 43, 72, 79, 85, 90, 95, 140, 222, 236, 264, 270

Taulet, 148
Taylor, D., 76, 79, 85, 87, 99, 104, 122, 270
Tesnière, L., 97, 271
Thilmans, G., 256, 264
Thomas, J. J., 140, 269, 271
Thonier de Nuizement, 141, 271
Thoreau de la Martinière, R., 257, 271
Todd, L., 10, 35, 48, 87, 95, 101, 103, 119, 271
Tonnelier, 148

Tortel, 184, 185
Toucas, 141, 147, 149
Toussaint, A., 135, 139, 167, 169, 170, 192, 194, 199, 204, 205, 268, 271
Trouette, E., 234, 235, 236, 240, 271, 274

Vachier, 145
Valdman, A., 11, 16, 23, 34, 35, 48, 75, 76, 101, 103, 120, 121, 122, 215, 238, 240, 245, 253, 261, 263, 270, 271, 273
Vautrot, 143
Vencatachellum, V., 10
Verdière, 203
Verguin, J., 185, 271
Vidal, 141, 146
Vigneux, 146
Villarmoy, 167
Vinson, A., 214, 215, 235, 271, 274
Vintilă-Rădulescu, I., 30, 256, 271
Vogel, C., 262
Voorhoeve, J., 47, 271
Vuillemin, F., 257, 271

Waite, J., 10, 42, 44, 125, 140, 270
Washabaugh, W., 95, 96, 271
Werner, A., 100, 271
Wimpffen, F. A. S., 213, 272, 273
Wirtz, 143, 155, 203
Wong, A., 140
Wong Too, D., 10

Yai, O.-B., 255, 272
Young, E., 257

Zilvaiguer, J.-J., 141, 143, 147

SUBJECT INDEX

a, 115-16, 228-33
Africa, 169, 255
Africans, see: East Africans; West Africans
"Afro-French," 119, 127
American Creole French, 2-6, 134, 135, 137, 209-10, 236, 254, 258
    combinations of particles, 104
    comparison with IdeFC and RC, 103-4
    copula, 35, 48, 103
    final vowel truncation, 73-75
    predicate system, 103-4
    se, 35, 48
    ye, 35, 48
Angotil, 190
Asia, 169
Atlantic Creoles, 86-88, 104

Bambara (language), 241, 255
Bambaras, 179, 181, 186, 255-56
ban, 116, 209-10, 236, 259
Bantu, 100-101, 116, 124, 257-58
Barbadian Creole English, 84, 257
Bengal, 204, 255
Bengali, 192, 241, 255
Benin, 199, 244-46, 253, 255, 256
Bourbon, 3, 106, 132, 135, 137-38, 151-58, 160, 165-70, 173, 178, 180, 184-85, 192, 199, 206
"Bourbonnais" (language), 3-6, 110-14, 128-29, 132, 135, 137, 140, 162-65, 172-75, 203, 206-8, 217, 221, 224, 236-37, 241-42, 256, 258
Bourbonnais (people), see: Réunionnais
Brazil, 148, 152

Calcutta, 204, 255
Cameroonian, 87, 95, 101, 119
Camp Yolof, 249, 257
Canadian French, 116
Cape Verde, 177
Caribbean Creole French, 6, 243
Catholics, 171-72

284 SUBJECT INDEX

causement cafre, 12
Census
  Haiti 1715, 251
  Mauritius October 1725, 142-43, 149-50, 157, 174
  Mauritius November 1729, 182-83, 199
  Mauritius January 1735, 139, 203
  Mauritius March 1735, 139
  Mauritius June 1735, 139
  Mauritius 1738, 203
  Mauritius 1767, 251
  Reunion 1686, 250
  Reunion 1704, 105, 107, 175, 250, 257
  Reunion 1709, 105, 175, 250
  Reunion 1713, 250
  Reunion August 1735, 141
  Reunion 1788, 107
Chagos Creole, 31
Chandernagor, 176, 204, 255
chasseurs de marrons, 148, 161, 168, 170, 173, 203, 241-42
Chinese, 204
Cilaos, 108
"classic" Creole tense/aspect system, 46
Cologne, 148, 168
Compagnie des Indes, 141, 150-53, 155-57, 163, 165-71, 175-80, 182, 187, 189-90, 194, 204
Compagnie employees, 142-49, 159-61, 164, 174-75, 179-81, 242, 246
complementizer 'say', 119
copula
  American Creole French, 35, 48, 103
  Isle de France Creole French, 33-35, 40, 46, 48, 103
  Reunion Creole French, 13-14, 25-27, 103
créole des Bas, 12, 65, 107, 109-10
créole des Hauts, 12, 65, 109-10
Créoles, 136-38, 141, 173, 203-4, 207, 237, 239, 264
Créoles de Bourbon, see: Réunionnais
Curepipe, 239

dâ-"gerundive," 97-98, 100
Dahomey, see: Benin
Dakar, 177
Diego Garcia, 237
Djuka, 87

SUBJECT INDEX 285

Dominican Creole French, 48, 76
Dos-d'Ane, 58, 59, 60, 61-62, 66, 127
double predication, 85-89, 99, 128
   Bickerton, 89
Dravidian, 192, 241
dual
   body parts, 115
   sylleptic, 96-97, 100
Dutch *(hollandais)*, 132, 147, 152, 153, 250

East Africans, 105, 107-8, 117, 124-25, 176, 179-80, 190-91, 201, 204-5, 239, 248-49
East African substrate, 100-101, 122
Etang Salé, 58, 59, 60, 61
Europe, 139, 141, 146, 147, 160, 169, 175
Europeans, 105, 107, 117, 138, 139, 142-50, 159, 160, 174, 176, 203, 241, 247, 250, 251, 254, 256
"expansion" of pidgin, 247, 252, 259

final vowel truncation
   American Creole French, 73-78
      Goodman, 73
   applicability in RC, 55-62
   emphasis, 51, 68
   gaŷ construction, 80-81, 91
   Haitian Creole French, 74-76
   indefinite subject deletion, 89-92
   Indian Ocean, 64-73
   Isle de France Creole French, 32, 36, 46, 47, 49-54, 62-63, 64, 67-73, 118
   Lesser Antillean and French Guiana Creole French, 76-77
   Louisiana Creole French, 73-74
   Mauritian Creole French, early, 67-73
   origins, 64-78
   Reunion Creole French, 14, 15, 49, 54-66, 72, 109, 118
      defining continuum, 57-62, 109
   Rules
      1: 50, 54
      2: 50-51, 55
      2': 54-55, 62
      2'': 75-76
      3, 4: 51, 54
      5: 52, 54, 55, 70, 74, 76

286 SUBJECT INDEX

Seychelles Creole French, 72
Flacq, 156
focusing
   without deletion, 85-89
   predicate-fronting, 89-92
Fon, 241, 253, 254, 255, 256, 259
Fort Dauphin, 105, 153, 190
français créolisé, 12
France, 105, 107, 145, 151, 152, 156, 157, 158, 159, 165, 166, 167, 171, 175, 177, 182, 189, 202, 204, 241, 242
French
   acquisition of French lexical items by slaves, 244, 246
   as formerly spoken on ships, 106, 207, 242-44
   popular French, 211-12, 216, 237
   French superstrate, 121
French Antilles, 202, 208, 245, 254
French Guiana Creole French, 76-77, 222, 245

gaŷ construction, 79-85, 91, 99, 100, 128
Genèse, 136, 137, 139, 145, 147, 158, 160, 163, 167, 168, 169, 170, 172, 178, 180, 183, 184, 185, 186, 187, 190, 191, 192, 200, 202, 203, 205, 206, 256, 265
get passives, 79-85
Gorée, 177, 179, 180, 181, 184, 185, 195, 196, 197, 199, 243, 244, 246
Grand Coude, 58, 59, 60
Grand-Ilet, 58, 59, 60, 61, 62, 127
   French forms, 61
   "decreolization," 62
Grand Port (Port Bourbon), 145, 149, 153, 154, 155, 165, 174, 180, 185
Guadeloupean Creole French, 76
Guinée, 177, 179, 180, 182, 183, 200
   meaning of this term in the 18th century, 204
Gulf of Guinea Creole Portuguese, 245
Gullah, 119
Guyana, 109

Haiti (St. Domingue), 177, 210, 220, 238, 254, 261
   early settlement of, 126, 249, 251, 255, 257, 259
Haitian Creole French, 134, 242, 251, 252, 254
   aspectual particles, 104
   double predication, 87
   fek, 113, 225, 232-33

SUBJECT INDEX 287

final vowel truncation, 74-76
grammatical features shared with Isle de France Creole, 209, 213, 218-25, 230-34, 246, 253, 254, 255, 258, 259
lâ-"gerundive," 98
negator *(na)pa,* 222-24
personal pronouns, 217-21, 252
predicate markers, 224-37, 240, 252, 253
rete/truve construction, 83-84
third person reprise, 213-14
Hawaii, 123, 246, 253, 257
Hispaniola, 251, 257
hollandais, see: Dutch

Ile de la Tortue, 257
indefinite subject deletion, 89-92, 99-100
India, 147, 157, 159, 165, 179, 187, 190, 192-95, 196, 197, 198, 256
Indian languages, 4; see also: Dravidian, Tamil
Indians, 105, 107, 108, 117, 124, 125, 139, 169, 170, 179, 185, 187, 192, 193, 197, 200, 201, 202, 205, 241, 250, 251
  free artisans, 173, 183, 194, 195, 196, 197, 199, 200, 201, 204
  slaves, 176, 180, 183, 184, 193-97, 200-201, 204, 249
Indo-Portuguese, 105, 107
innate rules, 253, 254, 259
interintelligibility of Indian Ocean Creole French dialects, 115, 135, 140, 141
Isle de France Creole French
  a, 31, 36, 42-43, 230-31
  a n, 44
  action, active, 32, 36-40, 46-47, 49-54, 55, 68, 69, 70, 80-81, 89-92
  adverbial preposed morphemes, 32, 45
  akot, 39
  anterior, 31, 42, 54, 124-25
  anu, 45
  ape, 31, 37-38, 43, 72, 236
  apre, 43, 72, 117, 230-31
  auxiliary adverbs, 32, 45
  ava, 31, 42-43
  ban, 116, 209-10, 236, 259
  bat(e), 47
  classes of lexemes, 47
  combinations of preposed particles, 44, 125, 230-31, 240
  comparative sentences, 33
  completive, 31, 36-37, 43

copula, 33-35, 40, 46, 48, 103
definite future, 42-43
definition, 2, 6, 8
ete, 33-35, 38-40, 48, 230-31
fek, 31, 43-44, 113-14, 230-31
fin, 31, 36-37, 38, 43, 45, 75, 101, 230-31
    Bantu substrate, 101
(fi)n fek, 44
final vowel truncation marking action, 32, 36, 46, 47, 49-54, 62-63
fini, 43, 230-31
focusing, 40-41
future, 31, 42-43, 45-46
gard(e), 47
gardiê, 47
gaŷe, 47
gaŷ construction, 79-83
"gerundive," 63
habitual/universal present, 42
immediate completion, 31, 43-44
in, 31, 36-37, 38, 43
indefinite future, 42-43
interrogative sentences, 33
irrealis, 31, 42-43, 45-46
kot, 39
lager, 31
lapes, 46
lexical multifunctionality, 31, 46-47, 82
locative sentences, 33
mo versus *ma,* 116
n, 31, 36-37, 38, 43
ni, 94
negator *pa,* 31, 44-45, 222-24, 239
origins, 117-18, 241-55
pa gaŷ kôprâ, 83
particles of tense/aspect, 31, 41-44, 224-25, 230-31, 234
past, 31, 42
pe, 31, 37-38, 43, 72
peser, 46
predicate heads, 31-32
predicate system, 31-48, 230-31
process, processive, 32, 36-40, 46-47, 49-54, 80-81
progressive, 31, 37-38, 43

PS rules, 35
pu, 31, 42-43, 230-31
re-, 38
sagrê, 46
se, 40-41, 48
semantic categories, 32
shared features with RC, 115-16, 209-11, 234-36
state, stative, 32, 36-40, 46-47, 49-54, 80-81, 89-92
statives
   durative, 37
   nondurative, 36
subjects of sentences, types of, 32
summary of predicate system, 46-47
sylleptic dual, 96-97, 100
tense/aspect, 41-46
third person reprise, 212-16, 237
ti, 31, 39-42, 230-31
ti a(va), 43, 44, 230-31
ti a n, 44
ti fek, 44
ti n, 44
ti pe, 44
ti pu, 43, 44, 230-31
va, 31, 42-43, 230-31
variation, 45, 125, 126
Ivory Coast, 254

Jamaica, 257
Jamaican Creole English
   aspectual particles, 104
   complementizer 'say', 119
   double predication, 87
   duont, 95
   get construction, 84
Jola, 255
Jolof, 244, 255
Juda, 180, 181, 182, 183, 184, 185, 195, 196, 197, 198, 199, 244, 245, 256

Kikongo, 100
Krio, 119, 122
Kwa language group, 88-89, 254, 255; see also: Fon

La Digue, 119
lascars, 180, 193, 194
Lazarists, 141, 142, 143-47, 149, 150, 157, 163, 164, 171, 172, 203
Lesser Antillean Creole French
   aspectual particles, 104
   double predication, 87
   final vowel truncation, 76-77
   ve pa, 222
lete ki, 18-23, 94-95, 106, 120
lexical multifunctionality
   American Creole French, 103-4, 120
   Isle de France Creole French, 31, 46-47, 120
Lexique, 135, 136, 139, 140, 162, 172, 175, 203, 206, 208, 209, 210, 213, 214, 216, 217, 222, 234, 235, 238, 239, 243, 249, 250, 254, 257, 268
Lorient, 144, 151, 152, 153, 160, 176
Louisiana Creole French, 3, 209
   dô-"gerundive," 98
   final vowel truncation, 73-74
   negator *pa,* 104, 222, 239
   particles, 104

ma, mâ, 115-16
Macao, 180, 204
Macua, 101, 122, 258
Madagascar, 3, 135, 143-47, 161, 175, 176, 177, 178, 179, 185, 186, 187-92, 194, 195, 196, 197, 198, 238, 239, 241, 243, 247, 256
Mafate, 108
Mahé, 190
Maison Blanche, 156
"Malabar," 108, 169, 170, 192
Malacca Creole Portuguese, 84
Malagasies, 105, 107, 117, 125, 132, 139, 150, 154, 155, 161, 162, 164, 165, 166, 172, 173, 174, 175, 176, 177, 178, 179, 180, 183, 187-92, 194, 199, 200, 201, 202, 203, 204, 205, 239, 241, 242, 248, 249, 250
Malagasy, 3, 4, 105, 107, 120, 217, 241, 258
Mamille, 180, 204
Mande, 255, 259
Maritime French, 106, 207, 242-44
Maroons, 132, 143-47, 150, 157, 162, 163, 164, 165, 167, 170, 176, 177, 189, 194, 205, 241, 242
Martinique Creole French, 115
Mascarenes *(Mascareignes),* 135, 138, 141, 148, 165, 175, 178, 179, 184, 185,

186, 187, 202, 203, 204, 205, 208, 216, 221
Mascarin, 132, 144, 147, 152, 154, 155, 157
Matatana, 153
Maurice, 132, 152, 203
Mauritian Creole French
   ban, 209-11, 236
   dâ-"gerundive," 97, 101
   double predication, 85-86
   fek, 75, 230-31
   fek fin, 44
   final vowel truncation in early MC, 67-73
   first speakers, 248
   gaŷ construction, 82-83, 100
   indefinite subject deletion, 89-92
   koze sif, 82
   kut ke kut, 88
   migration of speakers of MC to Rodrigues and the Seychelles, 207, 208
   negator *(na)pa,* 222-24, 237
   numerical slang, 82
   origins of, 3, 135, 136, 172, 206, 207, 209, 241-55, 258
   personal pronouns, 217-21, 237, 239, 252
   predicate system, 31-48, 224-37, 240, 252, 253
   role of Réunionnais in its beginnings, 137, 140, 161, 206-7
   shared features with American Creole French, particularly that of Haiti, 134, 137, 209, 213, 218-25, 230-34, 246, 253, 254, 255, 258
   shared features with Reunion Creole, 209-11, 234-36
   sylleptic dual, 96-97
   third person reprise, 212-16, 237
   "truculent" questions, 34, 39-40
Mauritius
   Dutch occupation, 132
   early settlement of, 6, 117, 135-39, 142-205, 249, 251, 258, 259
   former names of, 132
   sailing time from various places to, 243
   sociohistorical conditions in the formative period of MC, 120
monkeys *(singes),* 156, 160
Montagne Longue, 248
Mozambique, 108, 176, 177, 178, 180, 190, 191, 200, 203, 204, 205
   slaves from Mozambique, see: East Africans

natural semantax, 108, 122-25
negative emphatic (rhetorical) questions, 92-95

Nigeria, 254

pa, sentence initially, 95-96, 100
Pacific Pidgin English, 124
pa i construction, 92-95, 100
Papia Kristang, 84
Paris, 148, 154, 176
parler des Isles, 121
parler malbar, 12
parler ti-cafre, 12
Petits Blancs, 108, 109
Philippine Creole Spanish, 100
Philippines, 204
pidgin, "expansion" of, 247, 249, 252, 259
pidginization, 207, 246-48
pièce d'Inde, definition of, 204
Pitcairn, 123, 257
Plaine des Cafres, 108
Plaine des Palmistes, 108
Plaines Wilhems, 148
predicate fronting, 89-92, 99-100
predicate system
    American Creole French, 103
    early attestations of markers in RC, MC, and HC, 224-37
    Isle de France Creole French, 31-48
    Reunion Creole French, 13-27
Pondichery, 147, 157, 159, 169, 170, 171, 176, 193, 194, 204, 243, 256
Port Louis, 144, 148, 153, 154, 155, 157, 165, 169, 174, 203, 238, 249, 257
Portugaises des Indes, 105, 107, 250
Portuguese
    cooperation with, 178
    language, 256, 257
    vessel confiscated, 190
Principe, 256
proto-Indian Ocean Creole, 11
Providence Island Creole English, 95-96
Pulaar-Fulfulde, 255
Punu, 100

rats, 156, 157, 160
reduplication of adjectives, 115

SUBJECT INDEX 293

Reunion
    Départementalisation, 105, 108
    early settlement of, 94, 104-8, 249, 250, 251, 259
    history, 104-8
    indentured labor, 108
    locally-born children, 107
    other names of, 132
    regional French, 12, 109
    sociohistorical conditions in the 17th century, 120
    travelers between Mauritius and Reunion (in both directions), 138, 139, 141, 143, 144-47, 148, 154, 155, 156, 157, 158, 169, 170, 184, 208, 241, 255
Reunion Council, 151, 152, 153, 154, 161, 162, 166, 167, 173, 203
Reunion Creole French
    a, 16, 29, 56, 108, 123, 228-29
    -a/-e contrast, 13-15, 18
    a- (initial element in postposed pronouns), 218-19, 221, 236
    affixes, 17-18
    alô, 48
    ana, 14
    anô, 48
    apre, 24, 29, 228-29, 234
    aspects, 23-25
    auxiliary *a(v)uar,* 14-15
    ava, 16, 29, 56, 228-29
    âtren, 24, 229
    ban, 211
    Bickerton's theory of creolization, 123
    conjunctions, 27
    continuum, 5, 12, 15, 18, 22, 27, 56, 57-62, 66, 108-11, 127
    copula, 13-14, 25-27
    "core system," 11, 16, 30
    "Creole" features in verbal system, 29-30
    data base, 12
    data base for definition of continuum, 57-58
    dâ-"gerundive," 98
    definite future, 16, 23-24
    definition, 12
    double predication, lack of, 88
    et, etr, 13, 226-27
    ete, te (past participle), 13, 228-29
    fek, lack of, 113-14
    final vowel truncation, 14, 15, 49, 54-63, 64-66, 72

294 SUBJECT INDEX

fin(i), 16-17, 29, 56-57, 75, 108, 123, 124, 228-29, 235-36
fini + adjective, 17, 29, 112, 116
focusing, 28
future negative
    va, 18
    -ra, 17-18, 228-29
gaŷ construction, lack of, 113-14
gaŷe, 14, 83
habitual/universal, 23
i, 18-23, 25, 213-14
immediate past, 24
immediate future, 24
indefinite future, 16
infinitival suffixes, 18
infinitives, 15, 16, 18, 27, 54-57
    final vowel truncation, 54-57
influence on SC, 114-15, 129
invariable bases, 15-16, 29, 116, 123
Kriké kraké, 57-58
la, le as auxiliary, 14
late, lete as perfect, 15, 228-29
lave, 14
le, la, (le)te
    as copula, 13-14, 216, 226-27
    as "presentatives," 28
/le ki/, 18-23, 92-93
lete ki, 18-23, 94-95, 106, 120, 228-29, 237
lora/e, 14
mua, 56
muê, 56
nana, 14
nave, 14
ne, *nete, 28
negator *pa*, 25, 222-24, 236, 239
nora/e, 14, 229
omission of subject *(l)i*, 22-23
origins, 104-11, 135
orthography, 13, 57
particles, 16-17, 27, 29
past, 18-23
past suffix *-e*, 18, 21-23, 62-63
past participles, 13, 15-16, 54-57

final vowel truncation, 54-57
perfect, 15, 16-17, 56
personal pronouns, early attestations of, compared with those of Mauritian and Haitian Creole French, 217-21
pluperfect, 15, 16-17
po, apo, 24
"predicate markers," early attestations of, compared with those of Mauritius and Haitian Creole French, 224-37
"predicate precursors," 211-16, 225, 236, 239
predicate system, 13-27
present, 18-23
present participles, 15
"presentative" copula, 27-29
progressive, 23, 24, 25, 29
pur, bô pur, 24, 25, 29, 228, 234
relative clauses, 22
sa((v)a), 16, 23-24, 56, 228-29, 237
se, sete, 27-29
semantics of verbal system, 29
shared features with IdeFC, 115-16, 206-7, 211, 234-36, 258
s(o)ra/e, 13-14, 93
    early attestations, 226-27
sort, 24
speakers of RC in Mauritius in the first years of settlement, 161-76, 241, 242
speakers of RC in Rodrigues and the Seychelles in the first years of settlement, 206-8
specific subject deletion, 91-92
sylleptic dual, 96-97
te, past participle, 13, 228
te fin(i), 16-17, 56
te i, 14, 17, 21-22, 25
tense/aspect marking, 13-30
text of ca. 1722, 3, 4, 6, 64, 78, 106, 111, 112, 123
ti, 14, 22
va, 16, 18, 56, 228-29
variation, 8, 12, 30, 45, 55-62, 64-66, 108-11, 116, 123-24, 126, 127-29
verbal system, 11-30
vien, 24, 228-29
West African influence, 3
zero copula, 30
Réunionnais (people born in Reunion), 105, 107, 108, 109, 135, 137, 138, 139, 140, 142-76, 203, 241, 242, 256, 257, 258

Rivière, Noire, 156
Rodrigues
    early settlement of, 118, 207-8, 237
Rodrigues Creole French
    apre, 43
    dâ-"gerundive," 97
    double predication, 85-86
    gaŷ construction, 81-82
    indefinite subject deletion, 90-91
    ni, 94
    origins, 3, 135, 207-8
    predicate system, 31-48
    sylleptic dual, 96-97
    ve pa, 222
Romance verb + *que* + verb, 88, 100
româs, 129
Rouen, 148

sailors
    their possible influence on Creole French, 121, 134, 243-46, 254
Saint-André, 158
Saint Barts and Saint Thomas, 20-21, 23, 29, 94, 115
Saint Denis, 168
Saint Kitts, 257
Saint-Louis, 168
Saint Lucian Creole French
    final vowel truncation, 76
    twape construction, 84
Saint-Paul, 153, 158, 167, 168, 169, 184
Saint-Pierre, 168
Sainte-Suzanne, 58, 59, 60, 61, 66, 127, 168
Salazie, 108
Seereer, 255
Senegal, 177, 179, 184, 185, 186, 198, 200, 204, 253, 255
Senegambia, 204, 254
sentence initial *pa*, 95-96, 100
serial verbs, 104, 119
Seychelles
    early settlement of, 117, 208, 216
    liberation of Africans, 100
    settlers from Reunion, 93, 117, 208

Seychelles Creole French
  dâ-"gerundive," 97-98
  double predication, 85-86
  fek, 75
  gaŷ construction, 55, 79-81, 91
    indefinite subject deletion, 91
  gaŷe, 53
  i reprise, 31, 33-34, 39, 41, 100-101, 211-16, 238
  "impersonal" sentences, 41
  indefinite subject deletion, 90-92
  mâz ki mâz, 88
  negative emphatic questions, 92-95
  negative emphatic statements, 92
  ni, 94
  oli, 39
  origins, 3, 135, 207, 208
  orthography, 13
  pa i construction, 27, 92-95, 100
  pa + sentence, 95-96, 100
  predicate system, 31-48
  pur-dir, 119
  RC influence, 114-15, 129, 207-8
  sylleptic dual, 96-97
  to/tua/tô, 127, 129
  ve pa, 222
shared syntactic features of IdeFC and RC, 96-98
ships
  Alcyon, 183, 188; *Apollon*, 147; *Argonaute*, 145, 147; *Astrée*, 187, 188, 191, 248; *Atalante*, 143, 147, 148, 152, 163, 167, 188, 191, 202, 256; *Badine*, 178, 179, 181; *Bounty*, 257; *Bourbon*, 160, 203; *Charolais*, 181, 255; *Comte de Toulouse*, 143, 148; *Courrier de Bourbon*, 143, 147, 148, 152; *Dauphin*, 170; *Diane*, 143, 144, 147, 148, 149, 152, 163, 169, 181, 184, 185, 186, 188, 191, 192, 199, 202, 256; *Duc de Chartres*, 146, 147, 181, 199; *Duc de Noailles*, 178; *Griffon*, 179; *Hercule*, 146; *Indien*, 181, 184, 186, 189, 192, 193, 199; *Jason*, 158; *Jupiter*, 188, 191, 192, 199, 204; *Légère*, 188, 189, 190, 204; *Lys*, 145, 146; *Mars*, 160, 184, 192, 193, 204; *Méduse*, 167, 180-83, 184, 185, 188, 189, 191, 192; *Neptune*, 146, 149; *Reine*, 188; *Ressource*, 146; *Royal-Philippe*, 146, 189, 192, 193; *Rubis (Ruby)*, 144, 148, 153, 155, 161, 162; *Saint-Albin*, 144, 145, 148, 153, 154, 155, 157, 158, 162, 163, 174; *Saint Jean l'Evangéliste (Saint-Paul)*, 188, 190, 191; *Saint-Joseph*, 169, 170, 192, 193, 204; *Saint-Pierre*, 189, 193, 194, 204; *Sirène*, 188, 189, 192, 204; *Subtile*, 188, 190; *Triton*, 145, 148, 149, 150, 156, 256; *Union*, 145, 146; *Vierge de*

SUBJECT INDEX

Grâce, 144, 146, 148, 181, 184, 185, 186, 190, 191, 203
slavery, abolition of, 208, 211
slaves
  Americain, 180
  Creole (Mauritian born), 180, 242, 249, 253
  emigration of former slaves from Mauritius to Rodrigues and Diego Garcia, 237
  from East Africa, see: East Africans
  from India, see: Indians
  from Madagascar, see: Malagasies
  from Reunion, 143-47, 150, 152, 153, 154, 160, 161, 162, 163, 164, 165, 166, 172, 173, 174, 175, 255
  from West Africa, see: West Africans
  lack of slaves owned by Réunionnais, 172
  Mamille, 180
  owned by the Compagnie, 142, 150, 171, 172, 174, 183, 187, 199, 202, 203, 249, 257
  price of, 179
  "privately-owned," 142, 171, 172, 174, 183, 187, 194
Slave Coast, 204
soldiers, 139, 141, 142, 143-47, 148, 149, 150, 155, 156, 157, 158, 159, 160, 163, 164, 171, 175, 183, 202, 203, 241, 256
South East Africa, 179
Spanish, 257
specific subject deletion in RC, 91-92
Sudan, 253
surface convergence in IdeFC and RC, 63
Swahili, 101, 122
Swiss troops, 139, 142, 143-47, 148, 149, 152, 162, 163, 164, 203
sylleptic dual, 96-97, 100

Tamil, 241, 258
target language, 107, 120, 175, 241, 242, 246, 247, 249
Towards, 136, 137, 138, 139, 140, 168, 183, 202, 203, 205, 220, 271
Trinidadian Creole English, 84
Trinidadian Creole French, 134

universal substratum, 122-23

verb + *que* + verb, 88
verb serialization, 104, 119

West Africa
  languages, 120, 241, 253, 254, 255, 256, 259
  Pidgin French, 3, 77, 121, 134, 135, 137, 202, 207, 244, 245, 253, 258
  substrate, 88-89, 96, 122, 125, 134, 249
West Africans, 107, 117, 121, 122, 125, 126, 134, 135, 136, 137, 139, 140, 176-86, 189, 194, 195, 196, 197, 199, 200, 201, 202, 204, 206, 221, 241, 244, 245, 253, 255, 258
"West Atlantic" language group, 254
Wolof, 241, 254, 255, 259

Yolof, 179, 249, 255, 257

Zamboangueño, 100
zot, 115, 212